# PROPHET of COMMUNITY

## The Romantic Socialism of Gustav Landauer

## EUGENE LUNN

Gustav Landauer—literary critic, mystical philosopher, and left-wing activist—was Germany's major anarchist thinker at the beginning of the twentieth century. In this full-scale intellectual biography, Mr. Lunn depicts the evolution of Landauer's social thought, a rich terrain within which to examine afresh some intellectual crosscurrents of the Wilhelmian era.

Landauer's work and the various circles and movements of his social milieu after 1900, including anarchist, youth movement, expressionist, and Zionist groups, reveal a convergence of *völkisch* and communitarian ideas with libertarian forms of socialist democracy. The study of this kind of "romantic socialism," in revolt against both industrial modernity and authoritarian government, highlights the inadequacy of viewing *völkisch* themes exclusively in terms of Nazi "roots."

What emerges from this study is the appeal of antiauthoritarian and commu-

nitarian ideas for middle-class Left intellectuals dissatisfied with the official
Social Democratic Party. In the light of
the tragic failures of democratic and
socialist forces to gain middle-class support during the Weimar Republic, and
of the Nazis' antidemocratic uses of
*Gemeinschaft,* this earlier search for a
communitarian democracy gains in importance.

EUGENE LUNN is a member of the History Department at the University of
California, Davis.

# Prophet of Community

University of California Press
Berkeley and Los Angeles, California

University of California Press, Ltd.
London, England

Copyright © 1973 by The Regents of the University of California
ISBN: 0-520-02207-6
Library of Congress Catalog Card Number: 70-186105
Designed by Dave Pauly
Printed in the United States of America

to Myra

# Acknowledgments

I should like to acknowledge the help I have received in the preparation of this book. I owe a debt to the excellent staff of the International Institute of Social History, Amsterdam, especially to Mr. Rudolf de Jong, for assistance in locating materials and for permission to read the manuscripts contained in the Landauer Archives. I would also like to thank Professor Gerald Feldman of the University of California, Berkeley, for the thoughtful advice he offered while this study was in thesis form. At a later stage my work benefited from readings by Professors Robert A. Kann of Rutgers University and Peter Loewenberg of the University of California, Los Angeles. It it a particular pleasure to acknowledge the invaluable guidance I have received from Professor Carl E. Schorske, teacher and friend, currently of the History Department at Princeton University, whose searching and thorough critique of my work included numerous helpful suggestions, especially with regard to questions of method. Finally, my wife Myra provided the moral support that again and again renewed the energies needed to complete, and twice revise, the manuscript. With her help I managed to sustain a lively interest in my subject over a number of years by preventing it from taking over our lives.

# Contents

INTRODUCTION   3

1. THE MAKING OF AN ANARCHIST   17
   Adolescent Romanticism: Völkisch and Nietzschean
      Elements   18
   Berlin and Socialism   35
   The Berliner Jungen: The Education of an
      Anarchist   49

2. CHANGING PERSPECTIVES   75
   The Appeal of Anarchism   75
   Resistance to Social Democracy and Anarchist
      Terrorism   81
   A New Theory and a New Tactic   89
   Idealist, Romantic, and Völkisch Perspectives   101
   Isolation and Withdrawal   118

3. THE CONSOLATIONS OF MYSTICISM   124
   Sources of Mystical Belief: Philosophic and Personal
      Experience   127
   The Emergence of a Völkisch Socialist   138
   Isolation and Mystical Belief: Landauer's *Skepsis und
      Mystik*   150

4. THE ROMANTIC AS SOCIALIST   172
   A Philosophy of History   173
   The Socialist Bund   190
   Landauer and Marxism   200

Anarchosocialist Society    213

The Origins of the State and the Question of Tactics    223

5. THE SOCIALIST AS ROMANTIC    232

World War I: The Response of a Libertarian Romantic    233

Community, Nation, and Humanity    257

The Literature of the Volk    280

6. REVOLUTION IN BAVARIA    291

Landauer and Munich's November: A Democracy of Councils?    292

The Advance of Parliamentarism and the Response of the Radicals    305

Thermidor Deferred: Eisner's Assassination and the Council Republics    317

Thermidor with a Vengeance: Landauer's Failure and Martyrdom    336

CONCLUSION    343

APPENDIX    349

NOTES    351

BIBLIOGRAPHY    405

INDEX    427

# Prophet of Community

This passion for bureaucratization, such as we have heard expressed here, is enough to drive one to despair. It is . . . as though we knowingly and willingly were *supposed* to become men who need "order" and nothing but order, who become nervous and cowardly if this order shakes for a moment and helpless when they are torn from their exclusive adaptation to this order. That the world knows nothing more than such men of order—we are in any case caught up in this development, and the central question is not how we further and accelerate it but what we have to *set against* this machinery, in order to preserve a remnant of humanity from this parcelling-out of the soul, from this exclusive rule of bureaucratic life ideals.

—MAX WEBER, *Gesammelte Aufsätze zur
Soziologie und Sozialpolitik*

It is the fate of our time, with its characteristic rationalization, intellectualization, and above all, disenchantment of the world, that precisely the ultimate and most sublime values have disappeared from public life, either into the shadow realm of mystical life or into the brotherliness of direct relationships between individuals. It is not accidental that our highest art is intimate rather than monumental, nor is it chance that today, only within the smallest circles of community, from man to man, in *pianissimo* does that Something pulsate which earlier, as prophetic *pneuma*, went through the great communities like a fire storm and fused them together.

—MAX WEBER, *Wissenschaft als Beruf*

# Introduction

In May 1919—in the brutal aftermath of the postwar German Revolution—a tall, thin, bearded intellectual was beaten to death outside Munich by White troops of the Reichswehr and the Freikorps. The man, Gustav Landauer, was one of three well-known German-Jewish libertarian socialists who had participated in the revolution and been murdered in the reaction to it; Rosa Luxemburg and Kurt Eisner were the others. Each of them was a powerful critic of capitalism, militarism, and bureaucratic authority. All three were impassioned prophets who fought for an ethically and socially liberated humanity.[1] None of them achieved even an approximation of their goals. Instead, their murders seem in retrospect to have ominously foreshadowed the string of political assassinations in the 1920s and the still heavier darkness of Auschwitz.

Of the three figures, Landauer was the least known in 1919, and this is even more true today. German political historians are acquainted with him as a minor leader of the Bavarian Revolution of 1918–19, and some literary historians know of his critical works on poetry and drama. He is best known, however, to students of the history and theory of anarchism. Landauer was, in fact, the most important German anarchist publicist and intellectual since Max Stirner. It is partly for this reason that he has begun to attract scholarly attention in the past decade.[2] As one German reviewer noted in 1969, "The reemergence of anarchism has coincided with the shaking of all authorities in the West and the East. . . . The rise of an antiauthoritarian student movement and the oppressive growth of the state have lent color once again to the faded writings of Landauer." [3]

The anarchist issue suggests, however, only one side of a much richer activity. Landauer was a man of many talents and interests. To grasp his historical importance, which is a central aim of this book, one must begin by noting the fascinating range of his intellectual and political life in Wilhelmian Germany. A highly regarded literary critic, Landauer published incisive studies of Hölderlin, Whitman, and Shakespeare, as well as of many other figures of world literature. During and after World War I he was in close contact with a number of major writers of the expressionist movement, particularly the dramatists Ernst Toller and Georg Kaiser, upon whom he exerted considerable influence. Yet Landauer's literary work was closely allied with his philosophical studies and his political activity. With his close friend, the great Jewish philosopher Martin Buber, he developed a species of philosophic mysticism which drew upon the German idealist tradition going back to Meister Eckhart. As a socialist Landauer had begun his political career in the 1890s by doing battle with the official Marxist movement in Germany, the Social Democratic Party (SPD). As editor of a Berlin anarchist paper *Der Sozialist*, Landauer developed an antiauthoritarian and idealist critique of Marxism whose positive aspect was the call for a replacement of the state with a decentralized society organized from below. Later, before World War I, he was to utilize the libertarian socialist theories of Proudhon, Kropotkin, and Tolstoi in working out his anarchist notions. Yet from the beginning of his political life in the 1890s he attacked private ownership of the means of production, together with a rejection of all centralized and bureaucratic authority. Unlike the more visible anarchists of his day, however, he totally opposed both violent revolution and individual acts of terrorism, suggesting instead that the state would be destroyed only by building libertarian communities that would gradually release men and women from their childlike dependence upon authority. The heart of Landauer's social thought, as well as the central thread running through much of his lifework, was the attempt to render authority superfluous and unnecessary through the building of radically democratic, participatory communities. The full force of his passionate, sometimes frantic, ethical idealism was directed toward this goal. Landauer was a prophet of *Gemeinschaft*, the German concept whose heavily emotive, almost libidinal, content is inadequately rendered by "community," the closest English equivalent. In his notion of community, libertarian socialism imperceptibly fused with one of the most influential and historically important strains of modern German social thought. Landauer turned not only against bureaucratic authority but also against industrial urbanism. By 1900, and coinciding with a surge of neoromantic sentiment among German middle-class youth, he had begun to argue for communitarian colonies on the land in which the entire German *Volk* would reconstitute itself as a nation of peasants and craftsmen. Following from this, Landauer's mystical philosophy revealed in the depths of each seemingly isolated individual a rich and thriving participation in Gemeinschaft and Volk. For him the libertarian issue was conceived in terms of the famous romantic distinction of "organic" community against atomized, urban society, of Gemeinschaft against *Gesellschaft*. It is not surprising, then, that along with utopian expressionists like Kaiser and Jewish mystics like Buber, both of whom shared his communitarian socialism, Landauer's friends and circles after 1900 included members of the neoromantic Wandervogel or youth movement.

Landauer's use of the *völkisch* and communitarian strain within German romanticism included an emphasis on democratic decision making and socialist ownership. It was also grounded in a universalist view of the Volk: each nation, Landauer insisted with many of the early romantics, contributes to a common humanity. As a Jewish socialist it is not surprising that Landauer resisted imperialist nationalism in Germany. But what was equally important, he was not a "rootless" cosmopolitan. In tirelessly attacking the German war machine in World War I, Landauer did not invoke humanity so much as a humanitarian concept of the Volk. Insisting on his roots in various communities, including German as well as Jewish, Landauer was a cultural pluralist who had no desire to see the disappearance of nations, but only that of states.

It was an antiauthoritarian, socialist, and humanitarian brand of völkisch romanticism which Landauer developed. Its theoretical richness is, I think, obvious. More important, this kind of romantic socialism is rich in historical interest. Efforts to combine radical democratic forms of participation, socialist economics, and völkisch communitarian living patterns were far from unusual in Wilhelmian Germany. Zionist Socialists, left-wing sections of the youth movement, and circles of expressionist writers—groups with which Landauer was directly involved—each exhibited a pattern of middle-class left-wing communitarianism. Other culturally important groups and individuals that revealed different varieties of the same constellation are discussed later. It is in this connection that the study of Landauer's intellectual development is historically illuminating. German romantic political and social thought has often been studied, in the past thirty years, in terms of its alleged value in explaining the triumphs of National Socialism in 1933. As a result, the protofascist, racist, and xenophobic views of reactionary thinkers of 1870–1933 have usually been seen as the only inheritances of the völkisch longing for community first articulated by Herder and later heightened by opposition to industrial modernity. By viewing these currents teleologically, however, historians have tended to overlook democratic and humanitarian versions of the romantic heritage in modern Germany.[4] The example of a libertarian socialist strongly influenced by völkisch thinking—and of his participation in a wide-ranging Left communitarian subculture in the years 1899–1919—should be instructive for those who view political romanticism as a unilinear development to Nazism.

We are now far enough away from the Nazis' use of völkisch and communitarian imagery to gain wider historical perspectives. One of these would seem to be that the fervent desire among middle-class intellectuals, writers, artists, and youth for a revitalized community life in the modern social world of early twentieth-century Germany was a far more widespread phenomenon than any exclusive focus on the intellectual roots of Nazism would disclose. Many of the issues concerning community in modern society, which Landauer and others addressed, are still very much with us. They are serious ones and the discontents that lay behind them should not always be written off as mere romantic escapism or proto-Nazism. This is not to say, of course, that there were no prewar völkisch roots of Nazism, or that critics of urban, industrial modernity always presented realistic and viable solutions; Landauer's communitarian vision, though far more democratic and humane than the reactionary one of Langbehn, is not important primarily because of its direct utilitarian value. For historians of modern German culture, however, the study of Landauer and his social world provides access to a little-noted and significant feature of middle-class intellectual life in Wilhelmian Germany: the convergence, among numerous culturally important groups of intellectuals, of the communitarian impulse with demands for radical and libertarian forms of democracy. Fixation upon the roots of Nazism has obscured this communitarian Left. It has also caused many historians to read back into the German cultural past the total split between democratic and *gemeinschaftliche* ideals which set in only after World War I and the early years of the Weimar Republic. This polarization after 1920 may have had some unfortunate results: it may have played a role in preventing democratic and socialist forces from gaining the pivotal support of the middle classes, enabling the Nazis and their allies to monopolize and manipulate the appeals of Gemeinschaft to their own advantage. In any event, it is one of my main purposes here to study the earlier search for a communitarian democracy through the medium of Landauer's intellectual development and social milieu. In the end this method may provide fresh approaches to the entire issue of antimodern "cultural despair" in industrial Germany.

What sort of a man was Gustav Landauer? We know something now about his intellectual posture and historical interest, but have said little concerning his personal qualities. In this regard, reminiscences by acquaintances, or by close friends, repeat and are insistent upon an important point: Landauer was a gentle, thoughtful, humane man who was not given either to violent behavior or to doctrinaire fanaticism. "His voice was so peaceful and soft," his friend

Eduard von Bendemann wrote, "that from the very first moment one could not help feeling trust and affection for him." [5] As early as 1896, when he was barely twenty-six years old, Landauer appeared to Rudolf Rocker—another leading German libertarian socialist of the period—as a "spiritual giant" whose "thoughtful eyes seemed to look beyond all around him. One felt when he spoke that every word came from his soul, bore the stamp of absolute integrity." [6] The impatience, restlessness, and irritability he displayed, especially during World War I and the Revolution of 1918–19, resulted mainly from an intense ethical fervor that caused him to make heavy demands both upon himself and upon others. Such qualities brought many to compare him with the Prophets of the Old Testament or with Jesus.[7] His physical appearance heightened such impressions: he was thin, narrow-chested, and more than six feet tall; his deep black hair hung down to his shoulders, while his full dark beard framed a long, pale, and even gaunt face. He walked with giant steps along the street, often wearing a long cape and an unfashionable old hat.[8]

Landauer frequently gave the impression of being a combination of seeming opposites: at one and the same time he appeared as a dreamer and a man of great practicality, both the scholar and the agitator, a man who was often "fiery and thoughtful" in the same moment.[9] In 1914, at a time when Landauer was participating in an international circle of pacifist intellectuals just before the outbreak of the war, he was described by the Dutch literary critic Frederik van Eeden: "Landauer, who was the best speaker among us, was a spiritually rich, gentle, and friendly man, with the external appearance of a dreamy idealist and humanitarian; but within this wrapping there was an iron-hard core, a cool, sharp, and critical look, and an uncompromising independence." [10] One has only to read a few of Landauer's published letters[11] to appreciate the acuteness of van Eeden's comments. They reveal a man of both tenderness and uncompromising critical intelligence. Beyond that, however, the letters often assume the tone of a gentle pedagogue. Without pontificating or talking down to anyone, and also with very few traces of humor, Landauer was always a teacher.

As noted above, impressions of Landauer often crystallized into a comparison of him with the Old Testament Prophets. The parallel struck Franz Schoenberner, once an editor of the satirical journal *Simplicissimus*, while listening to Landauer speak before a mass meeting during the Munich Revolution. His "oratory was full of deep and passionate ethical pathos, drawn from the religious genius of his race," Schoenberner wrote, trying to account for the impression Landauer had made on "even a sceptical mind like mine." [12] The judgment was repeated by one friend after another in the eulogies that followed his murder and have been continued by many commentators since that time.[13] It was and is an inescapable analogy. Landauer's use of language drew heavily upon the moral and spiritual lyricism of the Prophets. He once specifically advised the young poet and anarchist Erich Mühsam to use them as a source for his work.[14] Furthermore, Landauer's Christ-like appearance and impassioned pedagogical tone only reinforced the impression.

Yet if the comparison is made, it is worth making with some precision. If Landauer was a prophet, it was not because he correctly prophesied the future, although he longed for a new world of free communities and his diagnosis of Germany and Europe half a century ago may still have some bearing today. To some degree the content of his writing and oratory resembled the actual teachings of the Old Testament Prophets: their common desire to renew their own nation through moral honesty and social justice; the dedication of Isaiah to universal peace above the claims of a narrower nationalism; the insistence of Ezekiel that all renewal requires an inner, spiritual transformation of the individual.[15] There were, however, more immediate and direct sources of Landauer's social thought. Rather than predictive accuracy or overt content of his ideas, it is the form of his life and thought which more directly suggests the comparison. There are a number of points to be made about this. First, as with many other Jewish middle-class socialist intellectuals, Landauer was far more an ethical idealist than a political pragmatist or a disciplined social scientist. Whereas Marx was able more or less to combine all three postures, Landauer had no desire to. Even more than most idealist intellectuals, Landauer found himself unable either to lead or to participate effectively in large organized political movements. Here was a further resemblance to an Isaiah or an Ezekiel: Landauer deeply experienced the agonies of isolation, which his communitarian vision only partly mitigated, and although his friendships and social circles provided companionship and necessary support, he often feared that he might be crying in the wilderness as far as the German Volk as a whole was concerned. After the failures in Munich, anguish and embitterment over his isolation contributed to his death, for these feelings lay behind his despondent refusal to flee the city when White troops descended in April 1919.

Although he was a sensitive critic of poetry and drama, Landauer had little of the purely aesthetic sensibility. As Julius Bab, another drama critic and friend, perceptively observed, Landauer's pathos was that of the morally lacerated prophet: "He was a prophet and not a poet, because instead of simply being delighted by the tremendous possibilities of life, he compared; he compared its possible heights with the baseness, misery, and outrages of the existing world and became embittered through the disunion and contrast he found." [16] Landauer would have well understood these words from Brecht's poem "An die Nachgeborenen":

> Ah, what an age it is
> When to speak of trees is almost a crime
> For it is a kind of silence about injustice!
> And he who walks calmly across the street,
> Is he not out of reach of his friends
> In trouble? . . .
>
> You, who shall emerge from the flood
> In which we are sinking,
> Think—
> When you speak of our weaknesses,
> Also of the dark time
> That brought them forth. . . .
>
> For we knew only too well:
> Even the hatred of squalor
> Makes the brow grow stern.
> Even anger against injustice
> Makes the voice grow harsh. [17]

In the chapters that follow I attempt to present a comprehensive intellectual biography of Gustav Landauer. Instead of tracing any allegedly autonomous development of ideas, however, the narrative follows the shifting interaction of Landauer's active life, historical milieu, and intellectual responses. The primary focus is on the third figure in this triad. Yet a major purpose is to present Landauer's romantic socialism as not simply a body of ideas or a theoretical construct, but rather as an ongoing synthesizing process mediated by historical and personal realities. Among these conditioning realities were Landauer's changing political goals and the problems arising from their attempted implementation in Germany in the years 1891–1919; his reception and reworking of a wide variety of traditions of philosophy and social thought to which he brought a shifting set of social and intellectual priorities; and the manner in which these priorities and goals (e.g., for anarchism as well as socialism, for a communitarian setting and a mystical justification) were influenced by historical options, by prevailing patterns of politics and culture. We shall see, for example, how Landauer's path toward a libertarian and then a gemeinschaftliche definition of socialism was formed, in part, as a negative response to the SPD, the dominant force in Left politics in Germany.

Such a historically grounded intellectual biography is usually possible only when the evidence includes far more than the man's systematic theoretical work, that is, only when there is available a large body of correspondence that spans his career and reveals his life responses to the problems of the day. Landauer, fortunately, left behind a rich correspondence. Although the bulk of letters written after 1900 were posthumously published [18] and have been used by all students of Landauer, the letters of the 1890s—the crucial formative decade in his development—remain unpublished in the Landauer Archives in Amsterdam [19] and have not been studied until now. Chapters 1 and 2, in which Landauer's path toward a synthesis of libertarian socialism and völkisch romanticism is interpreted, have benefited from the use of these previously unexamined materials. The same situation exists with regard to Landauer's important work as a publicist. In addition to his philosophical, political, and literary works, and his letters, Landauer produced a massive number of journalistic articles, many of them as editor of *Der Sozialist*. A number of the most important and interesting ones have been published since his death, but these are only from the years 1909–1915.[20] In chapters 1 and 2 use is made for the first time of his earlier *Sozialist* work of 1892–1899. These articles, together with the letters of the 1890s, other archival materials, and relevant secondary literature on the period, make it possible to understand the historical sources of Landauer's lifework. Careful study of the years 1891–1903 (the latter date saw the publication of his first major work, *Skepsis und Mystik*) illuminates Landauer's mature philosophy and action in a way that has not been seen before.*

* All previous studies of Landauer, including five recent accounts, are based only on his published books and letters and exclude the wealth of materials contained in the Landauer Archives at the International Institute of Social History, Amsterdam, as well as the numerous *Sozialist* articles that were not published in book form. In addition, none of these studies provides an adequate historical framework for the understanding of Landauer's work: an analysis of the main traditions of social thought upon which Landauer drew and which he reworked, and the manner in which this activity was influenced by his response to a changing political and social world around him. Sterling Fishman's "Prophets, Poets and Priests: A Study of the Men and Ideas That Made the Munich Revolution of 1918–19" (Ph.D. dissertation, University of Wisconsin, 1960) provides a sensitive and competent discussion of Landauer's participation in the Bavarian Revolution, but it is not Fishman's aim to trace Landauer's intellectual development or assess his lifework. Thomas Esper's "The Anarchism of Gustav Landauer" (M.A. thesis, University of Chicago, 1961) is based entirely on a few published works and fails to provide the kind of comparative analysis of anarchist theory which his topic requires. A German work, *Gustav Landauer: Kultur Sozialist und Anarchist* (Meisenheim am Glau, 1967), by Wolf Kalz, includes some of the latter but is devoid of historical treatment. Kalz handles Landauer's ideas before 1918 in a hermetically sealed vacuum and presents his work as an abstract system of political theory. He entirely neglects, moreover, whole areas of Landauer's political thought, especially his view of nation and Volk. Kalz's interest is only with Landauer as a theo-

Although Landauer's formative years need to be studied in detail (as is done here in the first three chapters) the full definition of his romantic socialism was spelled out only in the last twelve years of his life, 1907–1919. In the

retician of socialism and anarchism. The long introduction to a new edition of one of Landauer's major works, *Aufruf zum Sozialismus* (Frankfurt am Main, 1967), by Heinz-Joachim Heydorn, although written with far deeper insight into the personality of his subject, also suffers from an exclusive focus on one aspect of Landauer's work. On the basis of very scant evidence, Heydorn argues that Landauer's Jewishness is central to all his work and activity.

Many of the same faults of thin research and narrow focus are found in the most recent work on Landauer, Charles Maurer's *Call to Revolution: The Mystical Anarchism of Gustav Landauer* (Detroit, 1971). In its original form as a literary dissertation (Northwestern University, 1965), Maurer concentrated on the relation of Landauer's mystical philosophy and literary criticism to the language studies of Fritz Mauthner, a close friend of Landauer's. Maurer's research included only published materials and very little reading in history and social theory. His contention was that Mauthner's critique of language was the most important intellectual experience of Landauer's life; as a result, most of Landauer's work is analyzed in connection with Mauthner's. The narrow focus of this interpretation was due, in part, to Maurer's failure to carefully study Landauer's intellectual development in the 1890s, the traditions of social thought and philosophy upon which he drew, and the relation of his intellectual biography to his political activities and the wider social world of Wilhelmian Germany. In the recently published form of his work Maurer has added introductory and concluding statements which emphasize Landauer's significance as an anarchist, but the text does not provide much that is new; except for an occasional mention of some earlier anarchists whom Landauer read, the frame of reference continues to be Mauthner and *Skepsis und Mystik*, Landauer's most ambitious foray into metaphysics. Such an approach allows Maurer to tell us much about this side of Landauer's work and, aside from his exaggeration of its importance, this is to the good. There is, moreover, some good discussion of Landauer's later poetic and dramatic criticism. But the work as a whole still suffers from the author's inadequate research—Maurer, for example, remains unaware of the Landauer Archives—and relative unacquaintance with German history and socialist and romantic theory. More specific criticisms are offered at appropriate places in the reference notes.

study of these prewar, war, and revolutionary years an attempt is made to continue the method of reciprocal illumination—of personal and political activity, cultural and social setting, and their refractions in theory. The reasons for this method are overlapping ones. This is the approach to the writing of intellectual history which I favor. Equally important, however, the subject itself suggests such a method, for only in this way can Landauer's work be understood and his importance be recognized. At the age of twenty-one, soon after arriving in the socially turbulent modern Berlin of 1891, and on the threshold of his emergence as a libertarian activist, Landauer wrote to a university friend:

> I must absorb new worlds into myself; my spirit needs new nourishment. From the depths of the spirit alone nothing can be created, without a steadily increasing fund of experience of the world. Without it one would always only repeat himself; and what does the world of Gustav Landauer have, if he does not have the world in himself? It is from a union and indissolubility of the individual with his surrounding world that what one calls personality emerges.[21]

# 1. The Making of an Anarchist

Landauer's education in romanticism and socialism began at an early age. In his adolescent years he was already an admirer of Schopenhauer's philosophy and Wagner's music dramas, and in his local gymnasium in Karlsruhe he was exposed to the völkisch nationalist education that German schoolboys regularly received. In his early twenties, however, at the University of Berlin, his apolitical romanticism was given a new political thrust by his increasing concern for the plight of the industrial working classes of the German capital city; by the age of twenty-one he considered himself a socialist, having received a superficial education in Marxian philosophy. Landauer's socialism was not materialist, either in these early years or later, however, and his early abandonment of Marxism revealed the ethical-idealist and romantic sources of his socialist commitment. Marxism, moreover, was represented in Germany after 1891 by a mass political party that had no use for the utopian and romantic early Marx but proclaimed instead a species of Marxian philosophy suited to the late nineteenth-century cult of scientific determinism. The German Social Democratic Party (SPD) was a bureaucratic, centralized structure which had little appeal to romantic intellectuals such as the young Landauer. In reaction to the form of socialism the SPD represented, Landauer moved toward an anarchist rejection of all forms of centralized authority in social and political life, aided in his quest for a libertarian alternative to social democracy by a group of SPD dissidents called the Berliner Jungen.

Landauer's path toward anarchism did not begin with his association with the Jungen. Both his romanticism and his short-lived Marxism were strongly colored by libertarian and antiauthoritarian perspectives and were marked by a commitment to the ethical and intellectual autonomy of the individual. The path from adolescent daydreaming to anarchist militancy was, in fact, mediated by the reading of the works of Friedrich Nietzsche; after the world-escaping romanticism of Schopenhauer and Wagner, Landauer received a powerful stimulus toward the "life-affirming" activism that lay at the base of Nietzsche's teachings. In this first chapter I am concerned not only with Landauer's first exposure to völkisch and socialist philosophies, but also with his path toward the libertarian form in which he was to conceive them. The romantic, Nietzschean, and socialist education Landauer received in his early years was all part of his development as an anarchist.

*Adolescent Romanticism:* Völkisch and Nietzschean Elements

Landauer was born in Karlsruhe, the capital of Baden, in April 1870, a few months before the southwestern German state was integrated into the unified German Reich forged by Bismarck's wars of "blood and iron." In later years, however, Landauer did not regard himself as a citizen of Baden, but as a Swabian; his strongest attachments were to the rural and small-town milieu of Swabia, the old medieval duchy and mountain region of modern Württemberg from which his parents came.[1] Here Landauer was taken on frequent summer trips during his childhood and adolescence.[2] Commenting on Landauer's attachment to the Swabian countryside, Theodor Heuss remarked, after Landauer's death, that all three of Germany's followers of the

French anarchist Proudhon—Arthur Mülberger, Ludwig Pfau, and Landauer—were from this same southwestern German region.[3] One glance at the sociological features of this part of Germany may indicate why this was so. As with Proudhon's native Burgundy, which was directly across the French border, Swabia was an area dominated by a system of free peasant proprietorship. Proudhon's ancestors, on both sides, had been free peasants, exempt for centuries from feudal servitude, and he had learned from an early age to sympathize with their passion for equality and independence, their "savage resolution to be each master of his own fields and his own household." [4] A similar attitude prevailed in Swabia. Unlike the situation in Prussia, where large landed estates and a servile and dependent peasantry predominated, rural conditions in southwestern Germany more closely resembled those in France. Whereas emancipation in Prussia created a large landless group of day laborers for the large estates or dwindled the holdings of the few richer peasants, in southwest Germany it gave full title to the small and middle-size holdings of an independent peasantry.[5] Some industrialization occurred in nineteenth-century Württemberg, but it proceeded very slowly, unlike that in northern Germany. Both the countryside and the small towns of Swabia, which tended to predominate over the few cities, were marked by an absence of socially polarized classes; instead of big industrialists and factory workers, small-scale merchants and handicraft workers made up the urban population in the traditional social structure of the area.[6]

It was to this kind of social environment that Landauer was exposed at an early age and to which he remained attached: traditional, völkisch, decentralized, and relatively independent. Although attracted by the intellectual excite-

ment of Berlin in the early 1890s, Landauer never abandoned his sense of the superiority of the Swabian milieu to
the industrial metropolis of modern Germany.[7] In later
years, after the turn of the century, he was to make explicit
his völkisch attraction to the traditional life of the peasantry; yet Landauer always shared Proudhon's streak of
peasant traditionalism, as well as his intense federalism and
distate for modern urban and industrial life. For the development of these views, Landauer's attachment to the
Swabian region was almost as important as Proudhon's
Burgundian background. In a revealing passage he wrote
in 1911, Landauer contrasted the taste of bread produced
by small-scale ovens in Swabian homes with the mass-
produced factory bread of Berlin:

> One has to journey a long way, these days, into remote
> villages, even to foreign countries, in order to get a piece
> of bread between your teeth which is tasty and special. In
> the south German home of my youth, however, one knew
> how the bread tasted in every single village of the vicinity;
> and in the villages, one knew of specific homes where a
> bread was baked which could not be duplicated elsewhere.
> Now baker's bread is consumed even in most villages, and
> in many of them it is factory bread.[8]

Landauer's grandparents on both sides were middle-class
Jews, merchants in small Swabian towns; his father followed suit: Hermann Landauer owned a small shoe store in
Karlsruhe.[9] Although born as a Jew, Landauer grew up
in "an environment indifferent to Judaism," as he wrote
years later.[10] As full civic rights granted to German Jews
in the 1860s had provided legal encouragement to their increasing assimilation into German cultural life,[11] a non-
sectarian education was quite common. Most young German Jews were reared in the late nineteenth century on

German literature and culture in much the same way as other German youths.[12]

Although Gustav was introduced to Goethe and Schiller at an early age, his father had other designs concerning his formal schooling. Favoring a technical education for his son, Hermann enrolled him in the Karlsruhe Realgymnasium. Gustav, however, received only fair grades in science courses, while he excelled in German, English, history, and religion.[13] Disregarding the boy's strong interest in literature and philosophy, Hermann insisted that he prepare himself to study chemistry and the natural sciences at a university so that he could become a dentist. At the age of fifteen, having decided that he wanted to study modern philology, Gustav persuaded his father to switch him to the classically oriented Bismarck Gymnasium in Karlsruhe. Landauer's lifelong struggle against institutions of authority began with a refusal to be led by his father during his adolescence; the slogans the fifteen-year-old Landauer repeated to himself in his diary already indicated a marked concern for independence and autonomy: "Be a man!" and "I will be led by no one."[14] When his father insisted that it was Gustav's duty to obey him, the young Landauer replied, according to his diary: ".... my duty is to protect myself against a profession that someone else wants to force upon me when I have no desire for it."[15] Significantly, the unwanted profession would have been a technical and scientific one. Landauer's early conflict with his father may have encouraged him to associate authoritarian direction and the scientific outlook, an association that later marked his rejection of both bureaucratic and scientific forms of socialism. In reaction to Hermann's wishes, Gustav cultivated an early love for romantic and mystical literature; from his adolescence he came to regard the more intuitive and mystical modes of understanding as a prophylactic against what he took to be unjust authority.

Intuition and mystical experience are private affairs, and Landauer wrote years later that as a boy he had cared little for school and had found his "real education" by himself, in his private world of books, music, and daydreaming. The *gymnasium* represented "a tremendous theft of my time, my freedom, my dreams, my own explorations, and my search for action," he wrote in an article of 1913. "Since outside school I was alone enough, my real experience came from the theater, from music, and above all from books." [16] Besides daydreaming and fantasying about himself in his diary, Landauer wrote poetry, did a great deal of reading, and went often to concert and opera performances. By the age of fifteen he had developed a strong attachment to German romantic music and literature; for his fifteenth birthday Landauer was given a *mittelhochdeutsch* edition of the *Nibelungenlied*, which he devoured along with Wagner's libretto for *Götterdämmerung*. [17] One of the most profound experiences of his boyhood, he wrote years later, was attending performances of Wagnerian operas, at which his "eyes protruded out of [his] head in a Wagnerian manner" and his "lips opened from 'schmerzlicher Sehnsucht' " ("painful yearning"). [18] Wagner, he wrote, had nourished all the "romantic longing of my heart." [19] In the years that followed Landauer began to read works of philosophy, significantly enough, works that appealed to his romantic and mystical predilections: Spinoza and Schopenhauer's *Die Welt als Wille und Vorstellung*. In a 1913 article Landauer wrote on his youth, he linked Spinoza and Schopenhauer with Wagner as characteristic interests of this period of adolescent introspective romanticism. [20] Spinoza, of course, was a rationalist precursor of the Enlightenment and would seem, in certain ways, to be out of place in the company of Schopenhauer and Wagner. German romantic philosophers, however, especially Herder, had been deeply attracted to Spinoza's pantheism, and there is some indication that it was this aspect of his thought which particularly impressed the young Landauer.[21]

Landauer's private experience of romantic philosophy and music was not the only source of his adolescent romanticism. Although he did not care much for school, he was not untouched by the völkisch education he and most other German schoolboys of the time received in the gymnasium. In the Bismarck Gymnasium in Karlsruhe, in the years 1886 through 1888, Landauer was exposed to the same ideology that pervaded the entire educational establishment in Germany in the late nineteenth century. In his study *Das Selbstverständnis des Deutschen* (Stuttgart, 1961), Erich Weymar noted a common trend of thought in German high school history textbooks of this period. In these textbooks there was much talk of a peculiar destiny of the German Volk, of a unique Germanic mission, while the virtues of rootedness in, and sacrifice for, this Volk were praised throughout. Coupled with this was an all but universal condemnation of modernity, which was defined in terms of urban and industrial materialism and the breakdown of community life through the atomization of society. It has proved to be of great importance for the history of modern Germany that this constellation of ideas, which may be called völkisch ideology, did not cease to be taught in German gymnasiums, as well as universities, after the full impact of industrialism was felt. Many decades after the great industrial advances of the late nineteenth century, which transformed Germany from a predominantly rural to a largely urban society, this ideology was still being taught in German schools and was widely held, especially among the middle classes. An analysis of history textbooks in the Weimar period reveals a continuation of the teachings of the earlier period.[22] Speaking of Weimar, as well as of the earlier Bismarckian and Wilhelmian periods, George L. Mosse has written: "Schools dominated by the völkisch ideology were so numerous as to constitute the center rather than the fringe of German education." [23] Moreover, "education pre-eminently institutionalized the ideology. Prior to 1918, no political organization or group of like-minded people were as important as educators in anchoring the Germanic faith within the German nation." [24]

Many völkisch thinkers centered their attacks upon modernity on liberalism, which they sensed, somehow, to be its spiritual and political basis. This was true, for example, of the three figures Fritz Stern has found to be representative, namely, Paul Lagarde, Julius Langbehn, and Arthur Moeller van den Bruck.[25] As a result, it might have been expected that in Baden, where the liberal tradition had been particularly strong—one eminent historian has termed it the "real school" of nineteenth-century German liberalism[26]—völkisch ideology would have had difficulty in penetrating. The liberalism of Baden, however, had a strong völkisch and nationalist stamp throughout the nineteenth century. The first organization dedicated to the goal of German national unification, which published the newspaper *Die Deutsche Zeitung* in Heidelberg from 1847 to 1850, was made up of leading Badener constitutionalist liberals including Karl Welcker, Karl Mathy, and George Gervinus. The prospectus of *Die Deutsche Zeitung* attempted to make nationalism a means of unifying the various divisions within the liberal movement in Germany.[27] The founder of the paper, Gervinus, was an especially fervent German patriot whose *History of the Poetical National Literature of the Germans (1835–1842)* was a classic of romantic nationalist historiography.[28] In the 1860s the Baden tradition of liberal nationalism was continued, on a radical democratic basis, in the establishment of the German People's Party, which lasted from 1865 to 1870 and was first centered in Baden. A number of the features of Landauer's later political orientation were contained in this lower middle-class organization of small-scale entrepreneurs, artisans, and independent peasants: the party was committed to both nationalism and political federalism, to social reforms and radical democracy.[29]

As a center of liberal nationalism, Baden also educated its youth in völkisch and nationalist ideology. The highest award Landauer's gymnasium in Karlsruhe granted its students was a Fichte medal, inscribed upon which, besides a likeness of the philosopher, were the three qualities being honored: "love of the fatherland, a willingness to sacrifice, and truthfulness." [30] The prize was awarded each year for the best student essay on a theme that always focused upon the sacredness and the peculiarity of Germanic traditions and folk heroes. For example, in 1881 the theme was a "eulogy of a German mountain"; in 1885, "Arminius in history and fiction"; in 1891, "The ideal of the hero in the folk epoch of the Greeks and the Germans." In 1888 Gustav Landauer won the silver medal at the gymnasium for an essay on Friedrich von Hohenstaufen (the Holy Roman emperor Frederick I, also known as Barbarossa),[31] a theme dear to the hearts not only of German romantic nationalists, but particularly of Swabians, for Barbarossa and the Hohenstaufen dynasty had derived from the Swabian region of southwestern Germany.

The romantic cult of the medieval emperor Frederick Barbarossa included the myth of his imminent awakening from a sleep of centuries and his call for a renewal of what romantic thinkers took to be the greatness of the medieval German "nation." In one of his early poems, written at the age of fifteen, Landauer had given expression to this folktale when he wrote: "Germany, you beautifully adorned bride, / Still you sleep softly. / If you awake with loud drums / When will you lead her, my Kaiser? / A people who have a good prince / have the most beautiful freedom, the most beautiful equality!" [32]

If such a poem was orthodox enough, Landauer's later essay on Barbarossa, written when he was eighteen, presented a rather unexpected kind of romantic nationalism. The *vaterländisches Thema* that won him a silver Fichte medal combined the cult of Barbarossa with the revolutionary sentiments of the libertarian romantic Heinrich Heine. To the dismay of the assembled students and teachers, Landauer read his essay on the Hohenstaufen which attempted—he wrote years later—"in the spirit of black, red, and gold and under the solemn call of Heinrich Heine, the poet most despised by the teachers," to bring "fatherland, unity of Reich, and revolution into . . . a community with the old Hohenstaufen emperor." [33] After a sharp reprimand by the school's director and a sympathetic handshake from the "good mathematics professor," Gustav was awarded the silver medal, although with "strong reservations." [34] In the boyish formula of Heine and Barbarossa, Landauer gave early expression to the antiauthoritarian manner in which he was to cast the romantic tradition. If he did not reject the völkisch and nationalist education to which he was exposed at the gymnasium, he coupled it with vague revolutionary sentiments, no doubt in order to assert his prized independence from the school authorities. The value of using Heine in combination with Barbarossa, Landauer later pointed out, was that of all German poets he was the "most despised by the teachers."

In the article Landauer wrote in 1913 on his adolescent years, he claimed that before any exposure to anarchist theory he was already, by the time he left the gymnasium, an anarchist, "without calling it that." This unconscious anarchism, he wrote, was his "romantic" rejection of a rigid and "philistine" society around him, his insistence upon personal independence from the customs and institutions of conventional society; it was an anarchism that preceded any form of socialism and was not based upon any knowledge of social, economic, and political problems, any awareness of the suffering of the poor, or any feelings of social solidarity with them.[35] In his first years as a university student, at Heidelberg, and then at Berlin in the years 1888 to 1890, he showed no concern for the social and political environment around him, except as this environment might pose a threat to his personal autonomy and individual freedom. In the spirit of the German *Sturm und Drang*, of the Promethean hero martyred by the earth but attempting to storm the heavens, Landauer wrote the following poem while at Heidelberg in early 1889 (to a close friend, his cousin Siegfried): "In the struggle against superstition and malicious chatter, / against hypocritical foolishness and those who sit on the thrones, / against the oppression of the spirit, / against hobgoblins of the mind, / the complacency and stupidity of the people, / For freedom and justice, for truth and honor, / I stand alone!" [36]

Landauer's religious beliefs reflected a similar romantic individualism. For the nineteen-year-old Landauer, God existed only in the sense that he was embodied in the ideals for which each of us must strive, although they may never be reached. In a letter of April 1889 Landauer wrote to a fellow student at Heidelberg: "God certainly did not exist in the past; he exists now only as a 'becoming'; he is not a person, but *the ideal, which we ourselves steadily approach, without ever wholly reaching it.*" [37] In his letters from Heidelberg, Landauer revealed little interest in his formal studies at the university, although he was an active member of student literary and philosophical societies.[38] He indicated no interest in political or social issues; Gustav's concern was with his own personal struggle *against* society, and for ideals he never clearly defined. His unconscious anarchism of these years amounted to a vaguely conceived apolitical rejection of philistinism.

Promethean individualism, however, was far from the world-escaping aestheticism of Schopenhauer and Wagner. In his early university years Landauer's most significant experiences were still in the private world of his own reading and thinking, yet his reading revealed and encouraged a need for a more active life of individual struggle and not merely aesthetic withdrawal; instead of Schopenhauer and Wagner, Landauer was now absorbed in the works of Ibsen and Nietzsche, two apostles of activist individualism who were then receiving much attention throughout Germany. In the interval between adolescent daydreaming and the anarchist commitments of his twenties, Landauer absorbed a strong dose of individualistic vitalism, a necessary ingredient in the making of an anarchist.

In the late 1880s Ibsen made his first great impact upon young German writers. The dramas of the Norwegian playwright deeply impressed the circles of literary rebels in Berlin and Munich which had begun to define and champion the literature of naturalism.[39] It was not because of the exactitude of his representation of the natural and social world that Ibsen appealed to Landauer, however, but because he expressed the value of the creative individual while placing him in his "real" situation: engaged in a struggle against the ugly and philistine bourgeois society around him. It is significant that Landauer's favorite Ibsen plays were *The Enemy of the People* and *Ghosts*, both concerned with the tyranny of social custom over the aspirations of the individual.[40] In his autobiographical article of 1913, Landauer wrote: "It was Ibsen who . . . with fascinating power forced me not to ignore the real foundation, society and its ugliness, but to become aware and criticize it and set against it the revolt and struggle of the individual." [41] According to Arnold Hauser, such romantic individualism was the real source of Ibsen's appeal to young writers in the 1880s and 1890s, and not the playwright's allegedly scientific naturalism.[42]

In the academic year 1889–90 Landauer attended the University of Berlin, concentrating in his studies on the literature of German classicism and romanticism.[43] He liked Berlin far more than either Karlsruhe, his home, or Heidelberg. The metropolis exhibited modern industrial social struggles more than the smaller towns, of course, and was the political center of the German Reich. Yet Landauer was not attracted to it for these reasons, but because he liked the "freer, less philistine air" that flowed in Berlin more than the stuffiness of provincial Karlsruhe, as he wrote to a friend, Ida Wolf.[44]

By the late 1880s Berlin was indisputably the literary center of Germany, the mecca to which all aspiring young writers were drawn.[45] It was Berlin's burgeoning cultural life that formed Landauer's experience in his first year there. He published his first article in a Berlin literary journal, an essay on different forms of poetry,[46] and sent a play about Karlsruhe and Berlin to the city's leading avant-garde theatrical company,[47] the Verein Freie Bühne, an institution founded in 1889 to support the production of important new dramatic works such as Ibsen's *Ghosts* and Gerhard Hauptmann's first important drama, *Vor Sonnenaufgang*.[48]

In this early apolitical period, when Landauer's outlook was that of a rebellious literary bohemian, he was profoundly moved by the philosophy of Nietzsche. At the University of Strasbourg in the winter semester of 1890–91, in his third year of university studies, Landauer studied Nietzsche's writings intensively.[49] Seen in the perspective of Landauer's intellectual development as a whole, this strong dose of Nietzsche's philosophy provided the necessary bridge from his earlier purely interior and largely passive aestheticism to the anarchist and socialist activism of the years following 1892.[50] In only a limited degree did Ibsen provide this bridge for Landauer; the dramatist's message emphasized the protection and defense of the individual, not his willful self-transformation through active struggle.

For Landauer, Nietzsche's writings encouraged the abandonment of Schopenhauer's pessimistic outlook, a philosophy to which he had been drawn as a gymnasium student. Nietzsche's *Birth of Tragedy* had been concerned with the manner in which the Greeks, who were peculiarly aware of the sufferings and horror of existence, were yet able to avoid pessimism and, through the transforming power of art, affirm life in all its fullness.[51] In February 1891 Landauer wrote from Strasbourg to a friend that Nietzsche had fully "recognized and overcome Schopenhauer's mistakes." Having recently reread *Die Welt als Wille und Vorstellung*, Landauer wrote that he could no longer accept the work "as truth," although he still appreciated it "as a work of art" and as an expression "of a powerful personality." [52] In November 1890, Landauer had begun to outline the plot of a novel which revealed the impact of Nietzsche's philosophy of life affirmation: the hero was to be a man who passed from total despair of life and the longing for death—which made him into a *Todesprediger*, or "Preacher of Death," as the novel was to be entitled— to an experience of the joyous nature of all existence.[53] After reading *Also Sprach Zarathustra* during the winter of 1890–91,[54] Landauer explained the Nietzschean motto of the novel in a letter to his cousin Siegfried: "The motto could perhaps be: first I teach renunciation and love, then I teach death, then I prize life and chaos." Later in the letter he wrote, rather mystically—in an incoherent manner much like the often amorphous *Lebensphilosophie* of German neoromanticism around 1900—that "life and chaos" was "joyous, untroubled, free, the enlightening of everything existing and corrupt, the emergence . . . of all hidden possibilities." [55] Nietzsche's impact on Landauer, as on so many romantic youths after the turn of the century, was to encourage in him a kind of inarticulate cult of experience and life.

At the base of Nietzsche's affirmation of existence was his conception of man as essentially a creature of volition. Such a focus upon human will, upon philosophical voluntarism, was a central conception of Nietzsche's which Landauer permanently embraced. Man was to be distinguished from the animal world through his potential capacity of transforming himself through a conscious act of will. In this process of transformation, or "overcoming," as Nietzsche liked to call it, the individual was to live according to values that could only be self-determined. In an article entitled "Die Religiöse Jugenderziehung" ("The Religious Education of Youth"), published early in 1891, Landauer illustrated the manner in which this philosophy coincided with his thinking about a variety of subjects. God, he wrote, is not a transcendent being who, external to ourselves and to the world, exerts influence upon our lives; he is, rather, the very goals we posit for ourselves. The God we believe in is the "God we want to become and will become." [56] Our development need not be left to chance. The raising of the "human type" would necessitate that our future progress be "foreseen by the spirit and therefore willed." [57] In a letter of this period addressed to an old Heidelberg friend, Landauer emphasized the activism this thinking encouraged, for which he now felt great need: "Without ideals, for which one struggles with all one's strength, life is to me worth no more than a whiff of powder." [58] At the center of Nietzsche's "spiritual universe," Landauer wrote years later, was "activity," which must be "created, formed, destroyed, and transformed." [59]

Although encouraging a life of vitality and struggle, Nietzsche, of course, did not approve of direct political activism and especially not of the socialist cause. To him the socialist demand for equality represented a disguised desire for comfort, security, and the easy life; the complete negation of individuality and culture, it amounted merely to a lust for material possessions.[60] Although not attracted to Nietzsche's thoroughgoing aristocratic elitism, Landauer was still affected in 1891 by his critique of socialist materialism. In the first direct political comment of his correspondence, in February of that year, Landauer wrote to his Heidelberg friend, a certain Herr Moos, that he was "far from socialism or communism" and that "present social democracy [is] . . . indissolubly united with materialism, militarism, puritanism, . . . eudaemonism, and hostility to art." [61]

Although Landauer agreed at this point with Nietzsche's attitude toward socialist materialism, he could never accept Nietzsche's negative attitude toward human solidarity in general. Despite all his youthful concern for personal autonomy and independence from dictatorial authority, Landauer had absorbed the romantic, völkisch view that the individual was rooted in the community and the nation. What is more, on a personal level, Landauer always felt a great need for strong emotional contacts with others, as his adolescent diary reveals. While insisting upon the necessity for independent and individual decisions, Landauer expressed a desire in the diary to "be able to sink myself wholly into the soul of another, to seek to understand how it is possible to realize the universal love of man of which so many have spoken, but which is practiced by so few, a love that is so different from that other, egotistic kind." [62]

In the February 1891 article, "Religiöse Jugenderziehung," Landauer emphasized his view of the individual's ties to all humanity: "Our goal," he stated, cannot simply be the "securing of the well-being of the individual," but must extend to the "education of the human race," the "further development of the human type." For this task the "social problem" must be solved, Landauer admitted; this, however, was not primarily a matter of the economic deprivation of the poor, he emphasized, but the ethical and spiritual elevation of all mankind. "Disgust with forms of labor which are of a purely physical, spiritless nature, and passionate striving for a higher way of life," he wrote, "are the deepest kernels of the social question." One crucial means by which to bring about this spiritual change was through a certain kind of religious education of youth. Instead of sectarian training, religious education should focus upon the fact that "man stands in a completely secure and indissoluble connection with the entire organic and inorganic world" and is, in fact, an "inseparable limb of the world." Equipped with so firm a conviction, Landauer naïvely insisted, mankind would soon be able to emerge from "purely bodily labor" and evolve into an unspecified "higher form" of life.[63]

Landauer's adolescent article on religious education was an early, and peculiarly naïve, example of his tendency to see the solution of social questions in terms of the altering of human consciousness, the necessity for man's mystical education concerning the connection of each individual with the "entire organic and inorganic world." The article also revealed, however, how Landauer resisted the egoistic conclusions that most early readers had drawn from Nietzsche's writings. His thinking at the time, though in a purely philosophical and prepolitical framework, first exhibited the problem of reconciling his desire for complete individual autonomy with his need for commitment to the larger local, national, and general human community, a problem that was to trouble him for many years. Seen in the context of his early intellectual development, it was the problem of fusing Nietzschean voluntarism and völkisch romanticism, the two main sources of his adolescent education. In later years Landauer sought a way of rooting the individual within the larger whole without sacrificing his power independently to transform his life through the power of his autonomous will.

Before such a synthesis was attempted, however, Landauer had learned to conceive of the problem in more political terms; in the years 1891 through 1893, in the turbulent social climate of Berlin, Landauer received his first education as a socialist and an anarchist. When Nietzschean individualism and romantic communitarianism were finally reconciled in his mind, he called this personal synthesis "anarchosocialism"; although it was deeply informed by both Nietzschean and völkisch perspectives, the eclectic mixture was to be framed in far more specific sociological and political terms than he had developed by the age of twenty-one.

*Berlin and Socialism*

In April 1891 Landauer left Strasbourg and returned to the University of Berlin. The intellectual and literary life of the south German city could not long hold his interest; Berlin was exciting, while Strasbourg was "boring." [64] But the Landauer who returned to Berlin in the spring of 1891 was not likely to remain the purely literary bohemian and aesthete he had been during his first stay in 1889–90. "Life," he had written in January 1891, is not worth much if we do not devote ourselves to the struggle for our ideals "with all our strength." Although Landauer was an amateur novelist and poet at the time, it was beliefs, convictions, struggles, and ideals that captured his imagination, no longer simply the reflections on his own sensibilities, or the literary representation of the external world. The industrial metropolis of Berlin would provide him with an opportunity for involvement in current social and political struggles.

When Landauer returned to Berlin in 1891, the Bismarckian era had come to an end. The German Reich—a structure based upon the Prussian military aristocracy and the German industrial bourgeoisie, a union that was co-ordinated by the Emperor, or rather by his chancellor, Bismarck—was to be headed by William II, a pompous, erratic buffoon whose blustering, boastful speeches were soon to alienate public opinion all over Europe. Instead of the coherent direction of Bismarck's leadership, Germany now had little leadership at all, as William's changeability was only "heightened by the numerous influences at his court which were brought to bear upon him." [65] The fault, however, lay more in Bismarck's erection of a merely pseudoparliamentary regime than in William himself; it was Bismarck who "was the architect of the Constitution which placed the destinies of Germany in the hands of William II." [66]

One of the reasons behind Bismarck's dismissal in 1890 had been his strong difference of opinion with William II regarding the proper tactics to be used to fight the increasing electoral strength of the socialists. While Bismarck wanted to strengthen the provisions of the Anti-Socialist Law, thoroughly disillusioned with the attempt to win over the working classes through peaceful methods, the new kaiser fashioned himself as the "king of the beggars" who would wean the workers away from socialism and gain their support for himself and the monarchy through an extension of the earlier body of social legislation. William wanted to care for the welfare of the workers through the paternalistic enactment of such laws as compulsory Sunday rest and control of conditions and limitation of hours of labor for women and children.[67] As a result of the spread of socialist or vaguely socialist ideas, or of the attempt to counter their spread, the solution of the social problem had become a widespread concern.

Such a concern was particularly strong in Berlin, owing to the city's rapid industrialization and the accompanying exhibition of socially polarized classes. For the greater part of the early nineteenth century Berlin's importance in Germany and Prussia had been restricted largely to political and administrative matters. Beginning in the 1840s, however, the quickly growing construction of railroads, the rapid development of machine-building industries in the city, and the increasing importance of the Berlin stock exchange were heralding Berlin's transformation into a *Weltstadt*, a center of industry and trade. By 1890 the electrical and chemical industries and the clothing trades had joined machine building as the main pillars of Berlin's economic life, followed by the developing pharmaceutical and printing industries. Both as a cause and as an effect of the city's industrial development, Berlin's population increased rapidly in the second half of the nineteenth century. The population in 1870 was 775,000, but by 1890, a mere twenty years later, it had doubled to 1,580,000.[68] Of enormous significance for the Berlin labor movement, however, was the fact that after 1890 the rate of industrialization far surpassed the rate of population growth in the city; in such a situation, the standard of living of the industrial working-class population soon rose. In the period 1890–1900, while the population of the city increased by 25 percent, the number of factory establishments almost doubled. At the same time the number of workers in these establishments— machine building, mechanized textile factories, chemical, optical, and graphic industries, and so on—increased by 44 percent, although pockets of old, domestic handworkers still remained, especially in the clothing trades.[69]

Although in the long run the factory proletariat fared much better than the domestic handworkers, especially in the years after 1895, their situation did not improve in the early 1890s. When Landauer returned again to Berlin in the spring of 1891, Germany was in the midst of its third cyclical depression since 1873. The program adopted by the Social Democratic Party at Erfurt in 1891, which emphasized the Marxian prediction of the increasingly devastating character of recurrent economic crises in capitalist society, was in part a result of the industrial slump.[70] The party's development into a mass movement (its Reichstag vote rose from 311,961 in 1881 to 1,427,298 in 1890)[71] coincided with the general economic decline of the 1880s. As George Lichtheim has written, "A fatalistic belief in the imminent collapse of the hated system—which was not clearly distinguished from the prevailing socio-political 'class-rule' in Bismarckian Germany—took hold of considerable strata of the movement, facilitating the subsequent adoption of a Marxist, or quasi-Marxist, platform." [72] The early 1890s in Berlin were marked by frequent protest demonstrations by the industrial working classes against the rising prices of food, at least in part due to the agrarian-favoring tariff policy of the government. In the year 1891, in particular, the price of bread had climbed to its highest point since the mid-1870s.[73] Though eventually eased by the long period of prosperity after 1895, social tensions and antagonism toward the conservative city and state authorities were strong in the first years of the 1890s in Berlin.[74]

Coinciding with the emergence of socialism as a mass movement and its gain, with the nonrenewal of the Anti-Socialist Law in 1890, of freedom to openly propagandize and organize, a concern for the social problem became a strong feature of Berlin literary life. It was the order of the day for a novelist, a poet, or a dramatist to present in his works a "slice of social life." [75] Often this took the form of arousing sympathy for various kinds of social outcasts, including prostitutes and tramps as well as workers.[76] Though naturalistic theory emphasized the detached representation of reality without the imposition of value judgments on the part of the writer, the literary method was not at all unsuited to the problem of evoking moods of social pity in the audience. The reality that was observed was, of course, selected by the artist. He simply had to allow "situation to follow situation; the situation would be vivid because actual, and pregnant with meaning because all life is full of tragic pity." [77]

The heightened awareness of the social question in the Berlin literary world in the early 1890s was reflected in the establishment in 1890 of the Freie Volksbühne, an institution to foster working-class cultural education. Its founder, Bruno Wille, writer and socialist, had sought to enable the working classes of Berlin to see performances of the new drama by lowering ticket prices to a level that most of them could afford.[78] Financed from the first by funds from the SPD, the new movement quickly gained a large following and eventually was to outlast the monarchy. The leaders of the movement included both important writers and socialists; Bruno Wille was joined by Karl Wildberger and Julius Türk of the SPD and the literary figures Otto Brahm, Julius Hart, and Wilhelm Bölsche.[79]

This, briefly, was the literary and social situation in Berlin when Landauer returned to the metropolis in April 1891. Here, for the first time, he was impressed by the discontent of the working classes and the hardships of life in a big industrial city.[80] His letters from Berlin in the spring and fall of 1891 exhibit his change in outlook. In the first letter Landauer wrote upon arriving in Berlin, he noted

that the aesthetic enjoyment of beauty would only pe-
ripherally occupy him now. What Berlin afforded him was
not beauty, but the chance to observe and "experience the
world," in all its fullness:

> You ask why I have come to Berlin. I am really rather ill-
> disposed toward its inflated and hollow drives and the un-
> speakable number of its ugly abuses. Had I wanted to spend
> what one calls a beautiful and serene summer, Berlin would
> be the last place I would go. I find, however, that I no longer
> have time for the enjoyment of beauty and can experience it
> only in passing. My inner life has changed in the last years
> and I have broken away from the picture of the world which
> I had previously acquired in my life. My eyes have learned
> to see things differently; now I must also see things differ-
> ently, I must absorb new worlds into myself, my spirit needs
> new nourishment. From the depths of the spirit alone noth-
> ing can be created without a steadily increasing fund of
> experience of the world. Without it one would always only
> repeat himself; and what does the world of Gustav Landauer
> have, if he does not have the world in himself? It is from a
> union and indissolubility of the individual with his surround-
> ing world that what one calls personality emerges.[81]

Later in the year Landauer wrote that he was learning
"from books and from men," but especially from the "life
of the streets" and from "assemblies of the people." [82] His
encounter with the misery and hardships of the working
classes, moreover, often made it difficult for him to sleep.[83]
The result of Berlin's "exploitative commercial life," he
wrote to his cousin Clara, was the contrast between her
"arrogant riches" and her "horrible poverty." [84] New literary tastes reflected his growing social awareness; he found
time to attend the theater, but he was impressed, significantly, only by the work of the Freie Volksbühne, with

its production of social dramas for largely working-class audiences.[85]

In the first two years after his return to Berlin Landauer lived in Friedrichshagen, the city's literary bohemian suburb. Most of the leading figures of the Freie Volksbühne movement were here; Bruno Wille, founder of the organization, was a close neighbor of Landauer's and soon the two became good friends.[86] Friedrichshagen, Wille wrote some years later, was an "intellectual hotbed" in which there was almost constant debate of the latest literary, socialist, and anarchist ideas (two Berlin anarchists, John Henry Mackay and Benedikt Friedländer, as well as the later utopian socialist Franz Oppenheimer, often joined in the discussions).[87] Here Landauer found others who shared his multiple interests and his independent and antiauthoritarian temperament.

Until the spring of 1892, Landauer once again attended the University of Berlin, taking courses in the history of German literature and art;[88] it was only after he dropped out of school in April 1892 that Friedrichshagen became his primary ambience. During the fall semester of 1891 Landauer became associated with a group of radical students and received his first education in socialist theory, an education for which he was now prepared, given his new concern about the plight of the working classes. Unlike the socialist intellectuals of Friedrichshagen—a number of whom were either anarchists, or ethical idealists such as Wille[89]—these students were orthodox Marxists firmly within the intellectual orbit of the official Social Democratic Party of Germany.[90] Before becoming an anarchist Landauer passed through a short phase in which he expressed his rebellion against bourgeois society and his commitment to the struggles of the industrial working classes in Marxian terms. In view of the fact that his later socialism was to be formed in direct opposition to this ideology, it is of some importance to examine his earlier short-lived flirtation with Marxism.

In the fall of 1891 Landauer was asked by the Marxist students to draft a statement to the International Socialist Student Congress to be held in December of that year in Brussels. Since Prussian law made it impossible for young persons to engage in any concerted political activities,[91] the group would not be allowed to attend the conference. As the Social Democratic paper *Vorwärts* reported in late December, the students had written to the Brussels Congress complaining of the "dissolute and intellectually backward level of German students," most of whom were right-wing nationalists, and of the reactionary German regime which made it impossible for them to send representatives to the international student gathering.[92] Apparently the statement Landauer wrote was to be sent to Brussels as a substitute for actual attendance by the Berlin students.

In his statement Landauer pointed to the tremendous growth of international social democracy and its call for a union of workers of all lands to pursue the class struggle against their bourgeois oppressors.[93] As a means of furthering the cause of social democracy, Landauer stated that if students should find themselves in a position where they were called upon to do service for the state, they should exploit this opportunity to spread socialist ideas and agitate for revolution in the bureaucracy and the army.[94] The focus of his statement, however, concerned the divergent motives that animated workers and students, respectively, in their common fight for socialism: while the proletariat pursued the class struggle primarily out of economic need and for its own liberation, students of bourgeois origin did so in order to work for the proletariat whose liberation would alone constitute the progress of mankind.

> We have turned away from the bourgeoisie, from which we derive, and we despise it. Insofar as possible we want to be worthy followers of the founder and leader of our movement, Karl Marx, who was like us in his bourgeois background. With this we turn ourselves away from our parents, our family, our youthful education, our own generation, and place ourselves in the ranks or at the head of the proletariat. . . . We are bourgeois who have abandoned the bourgeoisie, and we are one with the proletariat in our goal but not in our origin; we have the same will as they, but not the same body and the same spirit. The proletariat fights in the class struggle in the first place out of need and for its own liberation; we struggle in it for the sake of the proletariat and for the progress of all mankind.[95]

In this Marxist-colored statement of late 1891 Landauer failed to emphasize certain central tenets of Marxian thinking. Most notably absent was an emphasis on the historical inevitability of socialism, its necessary emergence from the social relations of production which capitalism had developed. Instead of placing historical inevitability at the center of his analysis, Landauer significantly emphasized the active struggle of renegade idealistic bourgeois intellectuals for the proletariat and the liberation of humanity. Landauer's Marxism slighted Marx's profoundly historical orientation in focusing almost purely upon his ringing call to action.

Interestingly enough, this voluntaristic interpretation of Marx was voiced a number of times at the Brussels Student Congress which Landauer was not able to attend. Although the congress passed resolutions repeating the Second International's judgments against the anarchists in the same

year, and was very concerned to show its Marxist orthodoxy and its "scientific socialism," a number of speakers,
especially from Holland, emphasized that the class struggle
must be carried out not only in economic and political
matters, but in terms of the moral concerns that many students brought to the socialist movement.[96] Landauer's ethical-idealist orientation was far from unique among young
socialist intellectuals in Europe.[97]

Following his eclectic tendencies, Landauer had not rejected Nietzsche in the period of his association with the
group of Marxist students at the University of Berlin. It is
significant, for example, that he chose to emphasize strongly
that aspect of Marxism which was closest to Nietzschean
voluntarism, whereas he de-emphasized the historical materialism that would have been fundamentally irreconcilable
with the teaching of Nietzsche. In certain ways Landauer
was here working toward the kind of theoretical fusion of
Marx and Nietzsche which Georges Sorel was to attempt
in his *Reflections on Violence* a decade or so later. With
Landauer, however, even more than with Sorel, the Marxist
current did not run very deep. His early writings of 1892
indicate that instead of truly synthesizing Nietzsche and
Marx, Landauer was merely adding a socialist component
to Nietzsche. As a residue of his exposure to Marxian ideas,
Landauer now regarded himself as a socialist. To understand what he meant by this term, however, we must examine how he attempted in early 1892 to reconcile the
various currents of thought which he had absorbed in the
course of the past two years.

In the first months of 1892 Landauer reassessed his attitudes on the purpose and function of art in the light of his
new social outlook. Literature, he stated emphatically in a
letter in January to his friend Moos, cannot be viewed as

an autonomous activity. It must be seen against the "entire life of man" and especially in terms of man's whole social and public life. With this point the naturalists would not have argued. Later in the letter, however, Landauer showed his sharp break from naturalism. Hauptmann is not what we need, he emphasized; he is too "mild, too reserved, too much 'tout comprendre, tout pardonner.' There is not enough fire in him: *Die Weber,* though a drama of the weavers' revolt of the 1840s, does not enflame the audience sufficiently." [98] The purpose of art should not be the mere representation of reality, even if it is a reality that has been carefully chosen to arouse the social pity of the reader or viewer. If it is to be socially meaningful art it must be the direct expression of the artist's own values and judgments. In his literary views, as well as in his socialism, Landauer resisted the scientific approach and spoke as an ethical idealist.

In two articles of early 1892 for the SPD organ, *Die Neue Zeit,* Landauer developed these views. In the first piece he wrote that art could no longer be his central concern because "it requires rest; and we need struggle." Appearing to accept the necessity of a representational view of art, he argued that since art "leans back and quietly observes the present," we no longer "have time for art." Whereas art "needs satiation, we have hunger and want to awaken the feeling of hunger." Instead of artists who observe the face of the world around them, "we need prophets who excoriate the present and proclaim the future." [99] One of these prophets, Landauer felt, was Friedrich Nietzsche. In his second article Landauer juxtaposed Hauptmann with Nietzsche and argued that "the younger generation," in Germany and elsewhere, were beginning to turn to Nietzsche because they were fed up with an "ossified and tasteless naturalism." Instead of "objectivity and consistent realism," what is desired now is "unheard-of depth and strength, passionate assault, ability for greatness in pain and joy, independence, and a broad view of things." Nietzsche, Landauer concluded, provides us with all of this and we need not be troubled that the great philosopher was an enemy of socialism. Having understood little about the material-social world, Nietzsche could not see that socialism is, in essence, an attempt to realize his dreams.[100]

In his novel *Der Todesprediger*, which he wrote largely in the spring of 1892,[101] Landauer attempted to fuse Nietzschean vitalism with his new socialist commitments.[102] The main character, Karl Starkblom, questions the purpose of life, but can see nothing but death as its goal. The best that one can hope for, he concludes, is to reach the goal quickly.[103] After hearing some speeches for social democracy and reading Marx's writings, however, Starkblom decides to devote himself to the cause of international social democracy so as to find some meaning in life. Yet the first attempt to avoid pessimism soon fails: Starkblom is quickly disillusioned with the kind of socialism he has been taught. In an essay that clearly reflects Landauer's reading of *Zarathustra* and the Nietzschean critique of the cult of progress as expressed in the concept of the "last man," Starkblom announces his abandonment of socialism and, once again, proclaims death alone to be worthwhile: "Socialism is a lie," he writes, "for it speaks only of the future, and it is a superstition because it calls itself a science." It is pitiable because it is ruled by an abstract idea of the future, instead of making it possible "to dance and sing" in the present. "You men believe that 'future' is something in reality," Starkblom continues, "something that concerns men more than heaven and hell do." [104] Echoing Zarathustra before he

gains the strength to accept the fact of the eternal recur-
rence of all things, Starkblom concludes his essay by asking
for death as soon as possible, since "eternally repeated nonsense is so frightfully boring!" [105]

In this mood of despondence Starkblom is visited by a
woman who, after reading his essay, had decided to attempt
to bring him back to an affirmation of life. This she is able
to do by reawakening in him his natural sensuality. At first
she reads to him at length from *Also Sprach Zarathustra*
in an effort to convince him of the insufficiency of purely
intellectual life. Gradually Starkblom falls in love with the
woman, Marguerite, and through her gains a new love of
life and of humanity. Once again he proclaims himself to be
a socialist because he wants to help create a world in which
everyone will be able to affirm the fullness of life and
humanity. His earlier socialism, he now realizes, promised
little because it was based purely on abstract and cold
reason. How could I not despair of such a socialism, he
writes in a final essay, when I still really regarded life as
a horror and the future only promised more of the same?
The creation of a new world must begin with the individual's personal discovery of the potentialities of a higher
life through the tapping of his own deepest emotions. Attacking the purely rationalistic socialism which he has now
overcome, Starkblom writes:

> I am no moralist, but I ask you: Are you not evil? You have
> gone too far along a false way; if you want to find the right
> point to begin you must trace your steps back a little. Too
> soon you proceeded with naked reason. It is not time to
> allow the soul to freeze. Do not do anything whose end you
> cannot at least have a presentiment of. Beware of intellectual
> spite! From time to time, rather, be still an animal! That is
> what I demand of you, you dreamers and thinkers: *You*

*should have passion!* And that means: You should not be an isolated one, you should join others, you should live actively and leave death to death.[106]

The ability fully to affirm life—which Starkblom gains through the tapping of his natural sensuality and love—had to result in the desire to work for a socialist liberation of all humanity. This vitalistic life affirmation, Landauer held, was the sole basis upon which a meaningful socialism could be built. The kind of socialism that would realize Nietzschean teachings was not one based on rationalistic predictions of the future and "objective" analyses of the present, coupled with the continuing atrophy of the will's capacity to gain love of life in the present; it had to be a commitment of the individual will to struggle for a socialist society which he felt would bring joy and fulfillment to all mankind. Years later, in his *Aufruf zum Sozialismus* (1911), Landauer wrote: "Socialism is possible and impossible at all times; it is possible when the right people are there to will and do it; it is impossible when people either don't will it or only supposedly will it, but are not capable of doing it." [107]

*Der Todesprediger*, which brought together Nietzschean vitalism and a humanitarian commitment to socialism, also reflected the twin concerns of Landauer's life: individual self-determination and community integration. Although he implied in the novel that the two were mutually necessary, there was no attempt to demonstrate the validity of this view, except of course on an emotional, intuitive level. Before Landauer fully developed his synthesis of individualism and communitarianism, however, he had abandoned the Marxist approach to socialism and had become an anarchist-socialist. Having discussed his first exposure to socialist theory, we need now to concentrate on his path from Marxism to anarchism in the years 1892–1893.

## The Berliner Jungen: The Education of an Anarchist

In its plea for a voluntaristic approach to socialism, Landauer's *Der Todesprediger* anticipated his more fully developed assault upon Marxism. Whereas his association with Marxist students at the University of Berlin had been protected by his displacement of historical materialism from the center of Marx's thinking and his emphasis upon the master's activist component, the novel that Landauer completed in the spring of 1892 shows that he was becoming aware of the real distance that separated him from orthodox Marxism. In the years that followed, his criticism of Marxism was to develop into a powerful antagonism toward the ideology. In his *Aufruf zum Sozialismus*, written in the years 1908 through 1911, Landauer wrote that "Marxism . . . is the plague of our age and the curse of the socialist movement." [108]

In Landauer's political and intellectual development, anti-Marxist education coincided with his path toward anarchism. In the year after the completion of his novel *Der Todesprediger* in the spring of 1892, Landauer was to go far beyond the kind of Nietzschean critique of Marxism which had figured in the novel; now he absorbed a political critique of the German Social Democratic brand of Marxism, an attack on the bureaucratic and centralized authority which would allegedly govern the kind of society envisioned by Social Democratic leaders. Through his association in 1892–93 with a group of antiauthoritarian dissident socialists who had been called the Berliner Jungen before they were expelled from the SPD in 1891, Landauer's anarchism developed out of the libertarian critique of German Social Democracy. In Germany it was the SPD, far more than the German Reich, which provided most libertarian socialists with their education in the necessity of anarchism, as Landauer explained in a speech in 1896:

> In Germany, as distinguished from other countries, Social Democracy has been the breeding ground of anarchism. In England and France you have your fill of political democracy and are horrified by its authoritarian institutions. In Germany we gain this knowledge in the organization, tactics, and intolerance of our Social Democratic Party. Almost all anarchists were recently Social Democrats. . . . And it was, first of all, through the insight as to how despotic and intolerant this party was, that they were brought to say: we no longer want to strive for political power, but for the spread of our enlightened view that it is necessary to do away with all authority.[109]

In the spring of 1892 Landauer was already ripe for such an experience. To begin with, the Marxism he had absorbed in the preceding autumn was of a rather superficial variety, one that stressed the idealistic activism of the individual in the service of the class struggle, instead of economic historical evolution and party organization. As a romantic individualist, of course, the latter had little appeal for him. By February of 1892 he was, moreover, already disillusioned with the passivity and tactical reformism of the SPD. Speaking of SPD opposition to massive demonstrations by unemployed construction workers, he wrote during the following year:

> In February 1892 a large part of the Berlin work force proved they were something other than merely passive and scientific Social Democrats. . . . In these days, at least, there was a revolutionary proletariat. . . . [But] since Social

Democracy has been allowed into parliament, it wants to have nothing to do with every outbreak of passion and mass instincts, because the independent actions of the unemployed do not correspond at all to the tame tactics of Social Democracy.[110]

A few years later Landauer noted that he had drawn the following conclusion from the February 1892 event:

. . . all party life leads to such miserable consequences and brings such unscrupulous characters to the fore. . . . Here there is always fear of radical propaganda, which occasions the party to designate the revolutionary temperament as either the creation of police spies, the spiritually ill, or the helpers of the bourgeoisie.[111]

Other socialists in Berlin were drawing similar conclusions from SPD policies in the early 1890s. Through his association in the fall and winter of 1892–93 with these older critics of Social Democracy, who were called the Berlin opposition or the Berliner Jungen, Landauer found the theoretical materials with which to develop an anarchist critique of bureaucratic and parliamentary forms of socialism and to construct a libertarian alternative to the Marxian tactic of the "capture of the state." Before examining Landauer's path from Marxism to anarchism in 1892–93, we need to discuss the development and perspectives of the Jungen.

In the 1880s the split between revolutionary rhetoric and reformist practice, which was to characterize the SPD's stance in the years after 1890, was already visible.[112] In the later years of the decade a left-wing criticism of these reformist tendencies in the SPD leadership developed. Attacking the leadership's abandonment of revolution in favor of vote getting, this left-wing opposition centered in some of the larger German cities, especially Dresden, Magdeburg, and, most important, Berlin. All three were northern industrial cities in which it was more likely for local socialists to emphasize revolution and class struggle than in those in the south where "class lines were not so sharply drawn." [113] Berlin, however, was undoubtedly the center of the opposition—hence the later designation as simply the "Berlin opposition" or the Berliner Jungen. In the period of the Anti-Socialist Law (1878–1890), persecution and harassment had been particularly strong in Berlin;[114] it was here, for example, that the Prussian Interior Ministry under the archconservative Puttkamer had led a campaign against strike leaders.[115] In the late 1880s anarchist sentiment was developing among groups of workers and socialist intellectuals in Berlin.[116]

Many of the most vocal leaders of the Left opposition—Max Schippel, Paul Kampffmeyer, Hans Müller, Paul Ernst, and Bruno Wille, for example—were university-trained intellectuals in their twenties or early thirties, as was Gustav Landauer. Wilhelm Werner and Karl Wildberger, two other leading Jungen, were young Berlin craftworkers.[117] Unlike the older leaders of the party, such as Auer, Bebel, Liebknecht, and Singer, who were all above forty, these Jungen leaders had grown up, as had Gustav Landauer, years after the demise of German democratic liberalism in the 1860s. Bebel's generation could still believe vaguely, owing to their ties with an older democratic liberal faith, that "parliamentary institutions could be democratic and useful to the working class." The Jungen, however, grew up in an environment that did not encourage belief in the efficacy of parliamentary institutions.

The German environment of the Eighteen-eighties was in many ways a wasteland for political inspiration. As the *Jungen* grew up they observed an anemic parliament trying

half-heartedly to preserve some elements of liberal government in a conservative *Obrigkeitstaat*. In such a political
atmosphere they easily learned to scorn and ridicule parliamentary institutions. From their political environment, they
had no source from which to develop an admiration for
democracy and radical liberalism.[118]

The lifting of the Anti-Socialist Law in 1890 had the
effect of bringing the conflict of the Jungen with the party
executive to a head. Whereas under the law the immediate
chances for gradual reform were slight, once the pressure
was removed and the prospects for peaceful, parliamentary
change vastly increased, the advocates of parliamentary reform and those of revolution were far more clearly differentiated.[119] Instead of totally rejecting all activity associated
with elections and parliaments, however, the Jungen never
went further, in 1890 and 1891, than criticizing the party
leadership for shifting the purpose of parliaments from that
of merely being vehicles for furthering revolution by exposing the bourgeois parties, to that of being an end in
themselves.[120] The focus of their attack was reformism, not
parliamentary activity. In early 1891, after the SPD representative Karl Grillenberger publicly disavowed in the
Reichstag that the party intended to work for a transitional
"dictatorship of the proletariat," the Jungen view that the
party had abandoned revolution was strengthened. The
speech by Grillenberger, which clearly had the approval
of the party executive, deeply incensed the Jungen and
brought them to make personal attacks upon the party
leaders themselves.[121] Although emphasizing that they had
only the welfare of the party at heart, representatives of
the opposition, Karl Wildberger in particular, directed
strong personal insults at members of the executive at the
party congress at Erfurt. These attacks were the immediate

cause for the expulsion of the five Jungen spokesmen from the congress.[122] In response to this action against its representatives, the entire Berlin opposition group withdrew from the party.[123]

By behaving as "mutineers rather than merely dissenters," the Jungen had prejudiced their case against the party leaders. The response of the executive, however, seemed excessive to many observers. It is impossible to understand the further history of the Jungen and of Landauer's development toward a strongly antiauthoritarian socialism along with one wing of the Jungen without noting the impression of dictatorial authority which the party executive gave in its handling of the opposition threat. The zeal with which the Jungen "were persecuted by the party committee appeared exaggerated to many observers. Even Engels, who was entirely on the side of the committee, was annoyed with Liebknecht and Bebel because they talked too much of 'throwing out' and wished they would avoid 'the appearance that a dictatorship exists.' " [124]

A number of the Jungen, reading into this experience the message that central, bureaucratic authorities are inevitably dictatorial, sought to work out alternative decentralist proposals for both their political movement and the society they hoped it would create. Although Landauer was not one of the Jungen at the time of their expulsion from the SPD in 1891, he was strongly affected by their views of the experience when he became associated with them in the fall and winter of 1892–93. As a spokesman for those Jungen who had become anarchists by 1893, Landauer was sent to the International Socialist Congress at Zurich, at which he planned to attack the SPD treatment of the Berlin opposition in 1891. In a speech he wrote for delivery to the congress in August, he spoke of the Jungen revolt:

Those who stepped forward to reform Social Democracy, to make it more enamored of revolutionary spirit—for there was nothing else in their striving—were honest and proven men who had worked, struggled, and suffered long years in the ranks of Social Democracy. When they took the liberty to be of another opinion from the party committee in many things, however, this was immediately forgotten. Even worse, though, was the poison of the most disgraceful kind of insinuations which now trickled down from above, down into the masses. No man of independent mind was then secure from being branded as an informer and police agent, a lumpen proletariat, and a betrayer. That the warnings of the opposition were all too correct, however, has been abundantly demonstrated in the past two years. . . . One of the tasks of German Social Democracy is to prevent or to defame every independent and imposing action of the proletariat.[125]

In response to the expulsion of their representatives from the SPD, the entire Berlin opposition withdrew from the party and met to organize their own independent movement in November 1891. The manifesto of their organization, which was called Verein Unabhängigen Sozialisten (Union of Independent Socialists), revealed how their expulsion from the SPD by the party executive had affected their political outlook: now extremely suspicious of all forms of centralized authority, they sought to develop a decentralized structure that would give a greater measure of independence to the various groups within a movement. Although still Marxists, the Jungen, now called Independent Socialists, were moving toward the anarchist position. The manifesto read in part:

> We struggle against every forced centralization, that which hinders the freedom of a movement defined by the various sections of the working class. . . . We are for a completely free exchange of opinions. And since we can

no longer find this within the previous party organization, we must work outside its narrow confines. *We are socialists and stand on the ground of class struggle.* However, since the dictatorship of the present party executive smothers all independent thought and the organizational form of the present party limits the free movement of proletarian social classes, we ask members who are not in agreement with the party executive and its tactics . . . to form a union of Independent Socialists in common with us.[126]

One week after the Verein was organized, the first issue of its weekly newspaper, *Der Sozialist*, appeared. From the beginning it reflected the antiauthoritarian direction of its members' brand of socialism. The newspaper's opening statement of purpose repeated many of the old charges against the SPD executive: it was attacked, for example, for abandoning revolution in favor of opportunistic social reforms, for having deviated from "proletarian ideas," and for having exercised a dictatorship over the party which sought to make of party members "will-less instruments" of their rule. There were increasing signs of anarchist sentiments, however; antiparliamentarism, for example, became one of the cardinal points of *Der Sozialist* and was enshrined in its opening statement of purpose. The statement read, in part: "We are opponents of legislative-parliamentary activity; experience has shown that it leads unavoidably to corruption and possibilism. We must stress the fact that parliament is an institution through which the bourgeoisie exercises its rule over the proletariat." [127] In an attempt to give a strongly antiauthoritarian direction to Marxist purposes, the editors wrote: "Our goal is the economic and social liberation of the working class. We struggle against authority and servitude in every form, the material as well as the spiritual. This goal can be achieved through the negation of bourgeois private property, especially through the socialization of the means of production." Turning to the organization of the proletarian struggle, the editors made it clear, however, that the bourgeois were not alone capable of dictatorial authority and that centralization of any group, socialist or otherwise, would result in the control of the members by the leaders.[128]

Until the spring of 1893, when those who resisted anarchist conclusions left the Independents, *Der Sozialist* contained both purely antiauthoritarian and more orthodox Marxist articles. In the first year of the newspaper, Bruno Wille, Benedikt Friedländer, and Wilhelm Werner represented the anarchist position most strongly, while Max Schippel, Karl Wildberger, and Paul Kampffmeyer continued to argue along more Marxist lines. The movement with which Landauer became involved after mid-1892, although it was united in a common antipathy toward the SPD and the authoritarian centralism it saw in the mass party, was one marked by strong divisions regarding the proper alternative to the SPD. Throughout 1892, however, the tendency toward anarchism was growing.[129]

Landauer knew Wille, Wildberger, and Bernard Kampffmeyer through their common participation in the Freie Volksbühne.[130] Since all these friends were leading figures among the Independents, it is not unlikely that it was through them that Landauer made his first contacts with the socialist group. In August 1892 his first article for *Der Sozialist* appeared: a piece on the libertarian socialist Eugen Dühring.[131]

Before assessing Landauer's initial work among the Independents, some more general comments are in order. Landauer's path toward anarchism in late 1892 and early 1893, in conjunction with the growing anarchist wing of the Independents, can best be seen in terms of a continuing development away from Marxism. In this he was not alone; by the last decade of the nineteenth century those who sought to formulate antiauthoritarian forms of socialism had to do so in terms of a critical assessment of Marxism. As George Lichtheim has pointed out:

> After the collapse of the original Anarchist movement some time in the later 1880's, every other school of "anti-authoritarian" Socialism was obliged to come to terms with Marx, and do so to a greater or lesser extent even when its theorists prided themselves upon their doctrinal independence. The relevant point here is not that these groups held dissenting views, but that they formulated them with reference to the dominant Marxist credo. This was a state of affairs very different from that of the 1860's when Marx was simply regarded as a rival of the more widely known Proudhon; or the 1870's when there was thought to be a choice between an "authoritarian" and a "libertarian" corpus of Socialist doctrine. From about 1890 onward the legitimacy of such a distinction was no longer admitted by the parties and movements which had come together in 1889 to form the Second International; and in 1896 this attitude was formalised by the refusal of the International's third congress to seat the Anarchist delegates.[132]

As we have seen, not all the Independents were willing to ground their attacks upon the "authoritarian dictatorship" of the SPD executive along anti-Marxist lines. A number of the editorial staff of *Der Sozialist*, including Wildberger and Paul Kampffmeyer, were still antiparliamentary Marxists who held that the SPD's fall from grace had come as a result of its deviation from Marx. The other group, however, which included Wille, Werner, and Max Baginski, became more and more interested in anarchist alternatives to Marx, frequently inviting the Dühringian anarchist Benedikt Friedländer to write articles for *Der Sozialist.*[133]

In his first articles for the paper, in the fall of 1892, Landauer sided with the attempts of the Wildberger group to develop a libertarian brand of Marxism. His first article, a piece on Eugen Dühring's "Kursus der National- und Sozial-oekonomie," attempted to develop a qualified defense of the value of Marx's thought. While recommending Dühring's work as a healthy corrective to Marx's tendency toward dogmatism or the "mechanistic transformation of living, fluid realities into dead and fixed concepts and laws," he insisted that independent-minded socialists should not forget the "powerful scientific and agitational service that Marx performed." The conclusion of the rather insubstantial article was the dubious view that Dühring and Marx had arrived at similar results through different methods.[134]

In his second article for *Der Sozialist*, published in October 1892, Landauer clarified his views of Marxism; in so doing he began to formulate his own conception of socialism a bit more carefully. Like the first piece, this second one was a qualified defense of Marx; this time, however, Landauer defended him—or at least the pre-1848 more voluntaristic Marx—against his positivistic followers. By October 1892 Landauer had learned that Marxism had changed since the turbulent 1840s and that contemporary Marxists did not read the master as he had in his statement for the Berlin socialist students the year before; instead of focusing on Marx's passionate activism and the allowance he had provided for the transformation of conditions of existence by human will, as the young romantic Landauer had done, orthodox Marxists of the 1890s stressed the philosopher's "demonstration" of the historical inevitability of the emergence of socialism from capitalism. Marx, of course, was still alive when Engels's *Anti-Dühring* appeared in 1878—the key work in this transformation of Marxism—and it is clear that he had become reconciled to the shift in the view of the socialist revolution from that of a "unique historical breakthrough into the doctrine of a causally determined process analogous to the scheme of Darwinian evolution." [135]

In his article of October 1892, Landauer defended Marx against what he called the "epigones," those who had interpreted Marx's thought as a closed and abstract science instead of a call to fight passionately against the existing order. Landauer began to argue, however, that Marx himself was not entirely free from blame on this score. Reading back into Marx the simple scientific determinism of many of his followers, Landauer unfairly charged that Marx had fallen into the error of believing, in the 1850s and 1860s, that he had an "unquestionable and irrefutable perception of the past and present, from which the future could be predicted with mathematical certainty." But this latent tendency toward dogmatism and the ordering of discrete, living things into mechanistic abstractions had been immensely exaggerated and caricatured by the Marxist epigones, while they entirely neglected his passionate activism. In this way, according to Landauer, the freedom of the individual will had been straitjacketed into a framework of iron determinism.

> It was Marx who, at the end of the 1840s in the Rhineland region, raised the call for freedom and revolution with greater might than anyone else. . . . Marx's gathering of disparate particulars into firm concepts and laws, his dictatorial forcing and murdering of living things, which can never be wholly covered with . . . words and laws, his dogmatism, his mechanizing, his transformation of the great living world of

thought and activity into dead abstractions . . . all this, which he developed later, has been exaggerated in the most unheard-of way and been caricatured, so that a handy and wonderful system has simply been taken over and mechanistically utilized, while the true substance of this form, the real perception of the world, the powerful will of Marx, have not been inherited at all. These bloodless followers have now brought socialism into the danger of being nothing but a cold science, no longer capable of raising men out of old routines and making it possible for them to struggle, as independent free individuals, against the existing order. . . . Their disinclination against the independent acts of the individual proceeds from their conviction of the mathematically ascertainable . . . course of events; human independence no longer has anything to do with it.[136]

In his important conclusion to the article, Landauer's rejection of historical determinism and positivism went as far as an attack on Marx's historical approach itself, in a plea for socialist action based upon the desirability of socialism and not its historical "necessity." As his character Starkblom had concluded at the end of *Der Todesprediger*, Landauer wrote in the *Sozialist* article:

We perceive the coming condition of things as possible or even as necessary because we love it and desire it. Man is the measure of all things and there is no objective knowledge in which concepts are a mirror of objects perceived. . . . It would be much more worthwhile if socialists would first give unconstrained expression to their will and then make clear why they believe that the thing is also capable of realization. But to proclaim the unconditional necessity, founded upon nature, of a definite course . . . is to cripple the driving power of a movement through a . . . superstition that everything will develop by itself.[137]

Landauer's first two articles for the Independents' paper *Der Sozialist* did not concern only Marx and Marxism.

The major purpose of the more detailed and illuminating second piece of October 22, 1892, was to offer an alternative to the mechanistic positivism of contemporary Marxist orthodoxy by citing the work of Eugen Dühring, the socialist philosopher whose ideas had been popular in Berlin in the 1870s[138] and whose work Benedikt Friedländer had recommended to Landauer in the summer of 1892.[139] While defending Marx against the Marxist positivism of the day, Landauer stated in his second article that "Eugen Dühring is a very worthwhile and serviceable comrade in the struggle against the ossified, rigid, and enfeebling direction" of contemporary Marxism.[140] Dühring's work, Landauer emphasized, reacquaints us with the fundamental importance of individual creativity and action for the realization of socialism, for he shows how the "masses can be dissolved into men," that is, into individuals who are capable of self-determined activity. In this connection Landauer quoted the following passage from Dühring's *Kursus:* "Individuals are more than mere atoms of a societal or state body; they are the sovereign bearers of all associations and their political forms. Socialization does not exclude individualization, but includes it, for freedom can be attained only through a real principle of association." In another passage cited by Landauer, Dühring had stressed that the alleviation of the plight of the working classes would not result simply from an increase in their economic standard of living, since the root of their oppression was not in the economic sphere so much as in the lack of individual autonomy and self-determination; the improvement of a worker's economic condition "cannot alter the main problem at all," Dühring had written, "if it is not coupled with an alleviation of the main evil: independence when he suffers and dependence when he is active." [141] Although most of the *Kursus* was taken up with technical discussions concerning the workings of capitalism, the economics of wages, prices, interest charges, finance, and taxation[142] (which, significantly, Landauer entirely neglected in his article), Dühring's socialism appealed to Landauer because Dühring viewed economics in terms of the problem of individual autonomy and self-determination, a question dear to Landauer's heart.

Dühring's focus upon the necessity of individual autonomy and independence reflected his basic assumption that all social and political relations in contemporary society are based on compulsion and force. It was this force theory that appealed to Friedländer and his circle of anarchists among the Independents.[143] In his article on Dühring, Landauer noted that Dühring's main principle was that "capitalist exploitation results from the authority of some men over others." [144] He then quoted Dühring's basic view: "In the process of the development of wealth, political and social oppression is the pedestal on which other more indirect forms of exploitation later develop." [145] Here, of course, was a view that was in direct contradiction to Marxian theory, where political authority is held to be a result of economic property relations and not the other way around. In his article, however, Landauer failed to present a clear argument either for anarchist or for Marxist theory and focused merely on the value of Dühring's philosophy as an antidote to present positivistic versions of Marxism. He had just joined the Independents in the summer; after a few more months of association with them—by the winter of 1892–93—he opted for the anarchist position.

In the fall and winter of 1892–93 Landauer worked directly with the Independents on both cultural and political projects. In October 1892 he joined Bruno Wille and other leading Independents in an attack on the SPD members of the Freie Volksbühne, the theater institution Wille had founded for the education of the working classes of Berlin. Wille had charged that Julius Türk, the leading SPD spokesman on the board of the Freie Volksbühne, and his supporters were betraying the original educational goals of the organization and attempting to make it into a "party political institution," an arm of the Social Democrats. After Wille's attack, Landauer joined with the other Independent Socialists in the organization and with many of the most significant figures in Berlin literary life—Wilhelm Bölsche and Ernest von Wolzogen, for example—in founding a counterinstitution, the Neue Freie Volksbühne. The main difference of the new organization from the original one was its insistence that writers have greater control over the choice of dramatic works to be performed in order to ensure that the cultural level of the working-class audience would be raised.[146] For the next few years Landauer was a member of the five-man "board of artistic experts" of the Neue Freie Volksbühne.[147] Yet the new institution did not function very differently from the old one in the years ahead.[148]

At an early meeting of the Neue Freie Volksbühne, in October 1892, Landauer met and fell in love with a girl named Grete Leuschner, an impoverished needle-trade worker in Berlin's clothing industry.[149] By early November he and Grete had already decided to be married, and they planned to go to Zurich for that purpose.[150] Landauer's father opposed the marriage, possibly because of Grete's social position, and, as a result, they could not be married in Germany since Gustav was still considered a minor.[151]

It was not the first or the last time that Landauer and his father were to come into bitter conflict. Hermann had opposed Gustav's study of literature and his later with-drawal from university study,[152] while Gustav's adoption of radical political sentiments had merely confirmed his father in his refusal to support his son financially.[153] For a number of years, beginning approximately in 1892, Landauer was supported by a close cousin of his, Hugo, who was a watch manufacturer.[154] The estrangement with his father, which was to last until the latter's death in 1900, was merely increased when Landauer was twice arrested for activities connected with the anarchist cause. Such a generational conflict was commonplace, of course, in numerous middle-class German homes in this period preceding the youth movement and the expressionist literary revolt.[155]

To this estrangement Landauer reacted differently at different times. In the spring of 1892, before matters reached the crisis stage because of his engagement to Grete, Landauer was able to write to his cousin Clara of the "inevitability" of a "conflict of cultures" between generations in the contemporary period of rapid social change.[156] By December, however, he was writing to an aunt that he could think of his father only "with bitterness." [157] The time of strongest animosity between them was precisely the time when Landauer was exposed to anarchist theories. While he did not show signs in his correspondence of hating his father and was eventually to attempt to resume a relationship with him,[158] Landauer's total rejection of all forms of authority may have been conditioned by the conflict; the experience of Hermann Landauer's authority may well have reinforced the anarchist arguments of some of the Independents. It is important to bear in mind, however, that for Landauer anarchism was to be an alternative method of restructuring society from below, not a call to acts of terrorism; similarly, it was independence from his father's authority which he sought, not revenge brought on by hatred.

The Landauers stayed in Zurich in December and January of the winter of 1892–93. Much of Landauer's time was spent with those Berlin Independent Socialists who were also present in the Swiss city—Max Baginsky, for example, a leading member of the anarchist wing of the Independents.[159] In Zurich there was also a group of dissident Swiss Social Democrats who were fighting against the executive of the Swiss party. In December Landauer addressed them and attacked the SPD and parliamentarism in his talk.[160] The education of an anarchist was proceeding apace.

Soon after his return to Berlin in February 1893 Landauer finally completed his shift from Marxism to anarchism. Benedikt Friedländer, the leading anarchist theoretician in the *Sozialist* circle, had not gone to Zurich during the winter, yet before he left for Switzerland, and after he returned, Landauer engaged in political discussions with him.[161] These discussions, coupled with the publication and review of Friedländer's new book, *Libertarian Socialism in Opposition to the State Servitude of the Marxists* (Berlin, 1892), in the pages of *Der Sozialist* early in 1893,[162] brought Landauer more and more to the anarchist position. From Zurich he had already written that "for my part you can call the so-called Independent Socialists also anarchists"; on his return to Berlin he began to articulate an anarchist program for the Independents. In February Landauer spoke at a meeting of the Independent Socialists. In his talk he launched the usual attack on the SPD and its trade unions, which he said were "at least as bankrupt as bourgeois society," emphasizing how necessary it was to avoid the centralization of the present SPD organization in a future socialist society. The goal of our direct, economic struggles with the bourgeoisie, Landauer stated—hinting at a syndicalist alternative to SPD parliamentarism—must be a "free organization of society on the basis of independent economic groups." [163] In early April Landauer proclaimed in the pages of *Der Sozialist* that this program was anarchism and that it was this banner that the paper should carry and not the amorphous-sounding phrase, "Independent Socialism." In two articles entitled "What Should We Call Ourselves?" Landauer completed his path away from Marxism and finally embraced the anarchist position.

"Independent Socialism" is a term with little substance, Landauer wrote in April, one that no longer fits the direction of the movement. "At first we conceived of ourselves only as a justified and necessary opposition within the party," Landauer stated, citing the experience of the Berliner Jungen of 1891. "Then, however, during the Erfurt Congress, we noticed that the oppositions were of a deeper kind, even though there were very few who perceived that these were basic principled oppositions." One of the fundamental differences with the SPD was our opposition to parliamentarism, Landauer went on, and our "emphasis on the economic struggle." The position we have developed, one that focuses upon the "necessity of economic organizations" and a future society based not upon the state but upon "free productive groups," has brought us "within a hairbreadth" of the anarchists of Berlin. "The name 'the Independents' . . . does not express anything in terms either of principles or tactics," Landauer wrote; what is it that holds us back "from declaring ourselves in solidarity with those comrades who had seen through the party earlier than we and who before us represented free socialism and struggled boldly for its fulfillment?" [164]

Landauer had now reached the point where he fully grasped the distinction between the Dühringian theory and that of the Marxists, a distinction that failed to emerge from his articles of the preceding fall on Dühring's *Kursus*. The force theory of Dühring had been a restatement of the classic anarchist distinction, first clearly enunciated by Proudhon, between present social organizations, which are based upon authority and political rule, and those based upon the cooperation and association of individuals and voluntary groups. [165] It was on the latter foundation that both anarchism and any meaningful socialism must rest, Landauer asserted. After Herman Buhr, one of the leaders of the Independents, had charged that Dühring was a socialist and not an anarchist and that in Germany the two were not compatible, Landauer countered in his second article of April 1893: "Buhr himself wants a free association of individuals and economic groups in which there would be no authority. He is also an anarchist; . . . Dühring wants the same; . . . from every side of his thought it is clear that for Dühring there exists no opposition between anarchism and socialism." Every anarchist knows that the liberation of the individual can be reached only through the cooperative use of economic goods. The real contrast is between authoritarian and libertarian forms of socialism, Landauer emphasized, and the latter is called anarchism: "One speaks of state socialism," he wrote, "and what is its opposite? What is the opposite of all use of authority? Anarchy! . . . Anarchism and socialism are not oppositions in the least for those who can think only of realizing socialism without the use of authority." [166] Besides Dühring, Landauer went on, we have been shown this by Theodor Hertzka (a Viennese economist whose utopian scheme of a cooperative colony, a "Freeland," was then having a vogue in Berlin socialist circles).[167] Landauer also cited one of the Independents in this connection, Benedikt Friedländer; the recent pamphlet of the Berlin anarchist was being published in *Der Sozialist* at the same time as Landauer's articles of April 1893. It was Friedländer, with whom Landauer had been conversing off and on since the preceding summer, who finally highlighted for him the crucial distinction between force and cooperation which lay at the base of the anarchist vision and the libertarian critique of Marxian socialism.[168]

In his book Friedländer charged that by seeking to utilize political and bureaucratic means to achieve their ends, Marx and his followers would, if they succeeded, only perpetuate the political servitude and economic exploitation they claimed to oppose. By capturing the state and erecting a system of state socialism through the nationalization of the entire economy, the Marxists would merely be "making private wage slaves into public ones."[169] But one need not prophesy about the evil results of a Marxian revolution: prerevolutionary Marxian practice is already a preview of future dictatorial authoritarianism. Building upon the experience of the Jungen in the SPD in 1890–91 and repeating a charge made frequently by the Independents since then, Friedländer argued that the present SPD was merely a microcosmic authoritarian state in itself. In both instances it was dictatorial centralization that was the oppressive organizational principle.[170]

Implicit in Friedländer's charge was the view that bureaucratic parties and states tend to perpetuate themselves. Nineteenth-century anarchists had developed this point before twentieth-century sociologists contended that this process was visible in all modern political life. Anarchists often insisted that the Marxian claim that their "dictatorship of the proletariat" would be temporary was, at best, a self-deception; those who have captured the state so as to introduce a collectivist economy would be no more disposed to oversee the liquidation of that state than those rulers and bureaucrats from whom it had been captured.[171] In his classic sociological treatise, *Political Parties* (1915), Robert Michels developed his concept of an "Iron Law of Oligarchy" with insights gained from earlier anarchist thinking and, in large part, through an analysis of the SPD foreshadowed by the Jungen critique of the early 1890s. "The directors of this revolutionary body existing within the authoritarian state," Michels wrote, "sustained by the same means as that state and inspired by the like spirit of discipline, cannot fail to perceive that the party organization, whatever advances it may make in the future, will never succeed in becoming more than an ineffective and miniature copy of the state organization." [172]

In his *Sozialist* articles on anarchism in the spring of 1893 Landauer embraced Friedländer's critique of state socialism and its Marxian derivation. In his second April article on the subject "What Should We Call Ourselves?" he wrote:

We stand at a most significant moment where revolutionary socialists of all directions and all lands can unite against both the bourgeoisie and the state socialist direction. . . . Social Democracy strives—in part scientifically, in part, unscientifically—for today as for the future, for a dictatorship and a regime of force in which it is aided by the ignorance of the masses. Obviously we do not belong in its ranks. . . . Anarchism will not tolerate the practice of authority either today or in the future. It seeks to make individual men free and independent and strives for this through a socialist economy.[173]

While the articles of April did not focus upon Marxism directly—although they contained an attack on the state socialism of contemporary Social Democracy—in June Landauer made explicit his break from the Marxian approach to socialism. After rereading the Communist Manifesto, Landauer wrote, in a *Sozialist* article of June 1893:

> For Marx the way to a nonauthoritarian society is through authority, the way to statelessness is through the state. . . . That was his great error. Where there are rulers, there are also those who have voluntarily relinquished their power. . . . If I want a society without authority, then I cannot strive for authority. Instead I must strive to destroy all oppressive powers and found a realm for the freedom of individual men.[174]

The practice of Marxian socialist parties, both in the present and the future, only strengthens the authoritarian state, Landauer asserted. Attacking SPD attempts to solve political problems through the machinery of the state, he wrote in June 1893: "Everything that is patched up and reformed within the context of the contemporary state secures the economic and political foundations of this state, solidifies its real character, increases the expanse of its power . . . and weakens the initiative and independence of individuals and groups." [175] The short-lived flirtation with Marxism was over; after close to a year with the Independents, Landauer had joined its anarchist wing.

Landauer's articles of the spring of 1893 called for a fusion of anarchism and socialism as the sole means of bringing about the liberation of the individual and society. In the term "anarchist socialism" Landauer attempted to synthesize individualism and communitarianism, personal autonomy and commitment toward the community of men. In later years his efforts to combine individual self-determination and communitarian "rootedness" were to include currents of mystical philosophy and völkisch romantic social thought, elements of which he had already absorbed by 1893. The synthesis of his early twenties was more limited, an intellectual construct of the currents he had absorbed in Berlin from 1891 to 1893: the individualist need was satisfied by the term "anarchism" and the communitarian one by "socialism."

Landauer's insistence in April 1893 that the movement of the Independents adopt the anarchist label brought the conflict between its libertarian and Marxist wings to a head. By late 1892 the conflict between the antiparliamentary Marxists and the anarchists among them had already reached a point where the two factions no longer found it possible to cooperate. With the Marxists Karl Wildberger and Hermann Teistler in control of the editorial board of *Der Sozialist* at the end of 1892, all articles with a clear anarchist position were rejected.[176] After Landauer returned to Berlin in late February 1893 he was asked by Wildberger to join the editorial staff, since the latter was unaware of Landauer's development away from Marxism.[177] By February 1893 the ban on anarchist articles had to be lifted because groups outside Berlin, which had previously been active in spreading the newspaper in Mainz, Stuttgart, Frankfurt, and Cologne, among other cities, had refused to perform this service until the former editorial policy was resumed.[178] This stand made it possible for Landauer to publish the articles of early April, unleashing an open debate in the pages of *Der Sozialist* regarding the proposed adoption of the "anarchist" label.

In May 1893 the matter was settled at a conference of the entire editorial staff; when the anarchist group around Bruno Wille, Wilhelm Weise, Max Baginski, Albert Weidner, and Landauer outvoted the Wildberger group, the latter withdrew from the movement.[179] Landauer was then asked to become editor in chief of the newspaper. His article had brought the conflict to a head. According to the anarchosyndicalist Rudolf Rocker, however, the Independents had been moving in the direction of anarchism throughout 1892 and withdrawal of the Wildberger group had been only a matter of time.[180] A number of the Marxist Independents were eventually to find their way back into the SPD, many attaching themselves to the party's right wing, for example, Max Schippel, Hans Müller, and Paul Kampffmeyer.[181] The attempt to fuse libertarian, decentralist ideas with Marxism had failed (although it was later to turn up again among some SPD radicals, especially Rosa Luxemburg). The movement of many of the Marxists among the Independents to the right wing of the SPD completed the polarization process dramatized in the conflict of April and May 1893. The Jungen had split, by the mid-1890s, into a group that had moved to the left—the anarchists whose leader was now Gustav Landauer—and a group that had moved, after 1893, to the right wing of the official socialist party.

Before the final split of May 1893, however, the Independents had exercised an important formative influence upon Gustav Landauer's political and intellectual development. As a dissident group that felt persecuted by the SPD central executive, the Independents had sought to find alternatives to what they regarded as the authoritarian and oligarchic results of organizational centralization. In his association with the Independents after mid-1892 Landauer inherited this interpretation of their experience in the official socialist party in the years 1890 and 1891 and absorbed the anarchist views of Eugen Dühring and Benedikt Friedländer, ideas that appealed to a growing number of Independents in the course of 1892–93. In April 1893 Landauer stated that he was now an "anarchist-socialist."

The tension between Nietzschean and Völkisch romanticism in his adolescence, which revealed and developed his attraction to both individual self-determination and communitarian integration, had been provisionally overcome in the anarchist-socialist synthesis. Apolitical romanticism had been given a political stamp in the years 1891–1893 in Berlin. Yet the synthesis of 1893 was inadequate for Landauer, and the reason for its inadequacy was precisely its exclusive focus upon political ideologies: it failed to give expression to Landauer's literary and philosophic interests, which were largely those of the German romantic and idealist tradition.

Although by the age of twenty-three Landauer had already absorbed a number of elements of his later romantic socialism, he was too preoccupied with the political struggles of the day to engage in much philosophic reflection. After 1893, however, political disappointment was to throw him back upon isolated reflection. In the years 1893–1898, to which we now turn, Landauer's anarchist socialism began to develop the explicit idealist, völkisch, and romantic strains that later marked his mature intellectual synthesis.

# 2. Changing Perspectives

In the middle years of the 1890s Landauer began to frame his anarchosocialism in terms of romantic and idealist philosophy. At the same time his attention began to shift away from the problems of urban, industrial society and, in an attempt to escape the dominance of the Social Democratic Party among the proletariat, toward such social groups as handicraft workers and peasants, the traditional social heroes of völkisch ideology. Attempting to build alternatives to both the ideological materialism and the industrial urbanism of the Marxist SPD, Landauer's philosophic and social reorientation developed simultaneously in the years 1894–1897. Whereas in the year following his adoption of anarchism in April 1893 he attempted to compete with the SPD on its own ground—within the proletarian labor movement—after 1894 his approach shifted toward the building of countertactics and counterphilosophies outside that movement. As Landauer's reorientation after 1895 had little to offer to the urban proletariat, however, he lost the support of most of his following in the Berlin anarchist movement; in the late 1890s Landauer's social base was to become narrower and narrower, and by the end of the decade he found himself in political isolation.

*The Appeal of Anarchism*
Before turning to Landauer's political and intellectual development in the years of his participation in the Berlin anarchist movement, from 1893 to 1898, it seems worthwhile to pause for a moment and ask: Why did Landauer

become an anarchist? To answer this question it is not enough to examine his formative years, as I have done in chapter 1; we need to understand why this particular ideology appealed to a certain group of individuals in Germany during and after the 1890s.

The word "anarchism," which is widely understood to mean the advocacy of terrorism and chaos, derives from the Greek word *anarchos*, which means merely "without a ruler." Proudhon, in using "anarchism" as a label for a positive social doctrine in his work of 1840, *What Is Property?* had chosen the word with full knowledge of the meaning of the original Greek; by using this word he sought to make it clear that the attack upon authority in which he was engaged need not necessarily imply an advocacy of disorder. "As man seeks justice in equality," he wrote, "so society seeks order in anarchy. Anarchy—the absence of a master, of a sovereign—such is the form of government to which we are every day approximating." [1] If we seek a working definition of the often misunderstood term we may accept the one offered by George Woodcock in his recent reliable work on the subject: Anarchism is "a system of social thought, aiming at fundamental changes in the structure of society and particularly—for this is the common element uniting all its forms—at the replacement of the authoritarian state by some form of non-governmental co-operation between free individuals." [2]

Landauer became an anarchist in 1893 in a country that had one of the weakest anarchist traditions in all Europe. [3] In the 1840s there had been the individualist anarchist thinker Max Stirner and some followers of Proudhonian mutualist schemes, such as Karl Grün and Moses Hess. [4] Before the Anti-Socialist Law of 1878, however, there was no real anarchist movement in Germany. In that year anarchist factions began to develop within the Social Democratic Party. Johann Most, a bookbinder who had been a member of the Reichstag, became converted to anarchism and with some other anarchist converts was expelled from the SPD in 1880 after his campaign against all participation in parliamentary activities. At the height of his influence, Most—who advocated terrorist "propaganda by deed" tactics—had no more than two hundred followers in Germany, mainly in Berlin, Hamburg, and Magdeburg. Constantly infiltrated by the police, these anarchist groups lost many of their members in the early 1880s; anarchist influence among socialists and workers was almost gone after 1884.[5] By 1891 small anarchist circles had again developed in such cities as Berlin and Hamburg, but their only activity seems to have been the spreading of exile newspapers such as the London *Autonomie*.[6] A more significant development of the early 1890s was the direction taken by a number of the Berliner Jungen toward anarchism. In 1893 *Der Sozialist*, now under the direction of Gustav Landauer, was the only anarchist newspaper published in Germany; though its circulation probably did not exceed a thousand, a number that large represented a definite upswing in anarchism in the early 1890s.[7]

In a sense the anarchist movement had developed too late in Germany to become a mass movement. The appeal of anarchism was strongest, in the nineteenth century, among pre- or nonindustrial sectors of society, such as the landed and artisan classes;[8] and it was precisely these sectors that were shrinking in the late nineteenth century as Germany experienced decades of rapid industrial growth. The concentration of large masses of workers in urban centers and in factories favored the development of disciplined political parties and trade unions, not decentralized anarchist groups.[9] At the same time the cult of the nation-state had spread outward from the educated middle classes to almost all levels of the German population, further limiting the appeal of anarchism. The beginnings of social legislation and social security programs under Bismarck, moreover, may have had the effect of blunting the anarchist attack upon the state as a purely oppressive institution.

Anarchism, however, did not lose all its appeal in advanced industrial societies in the early twentieth century, and it has not lost all its appeal in these societies today. Although mass political parties have predominated in industrialized nations and anarchism has had almost no chance of becoming a mass movement, the libertarian ideology attracted, and still attracts, large numbers of *freischwebende* (free-floating) intellectuals and artists who are in rebellion against the regimentation and bureaucratization of modern industrial and political life. So it was, for example, in France in the 1890s and in England and the United States in the 1940s,[10] as it is in these countries today. Especially in the years since World War I and the demise of a large-scale anarchosyndicalist movement, anarchism as an ideology of class politics has given way in advanced industrial societies to anarchism as a form of "personal-moral redemption," [11] as a form of conduct for the disaffiliated intellectual. It is for this reason that one American sociologist has spoken of the anarchism of many west European and American intellectuals as a peculiarly twentieth-century form of anarchism:

> The rebirth of anarchism in the twentieth century has been due to a general disaffiliation of "intellectuals" and "professionals" from the general celebration of the affluent society. This portion of society, while enlarged as a consequence of the growing need for expertise and exact knowledge, has

also been the most defeated victim of overdevelopment. . . .
Modern society has created the first collectivity of natural
anarchists, people who are resistant to absorption within the
Establishment and whose rejection of affiliation is part of the
self-definition of an intellectual.[12]

Although it would not become an important social and
political movement in industrialized Germany, anarchism
had a strong appeal for a number of free-lance writers and
artist-intellectuals in the period after 1890 and especially
in the first decades of the twentieth century. Besides such
figures as Bruno Wille and Gustav Landauer, who were
anarchists in the early 1890s, there were, after the turn of
the century, a number of anarchist intellectuals among the
expressionists (especially around the journal *Die Aktion*)
and among the leaders of the Bavarian Revolution of 1918–
19.[13]

In view of this appeal of anarchism to the marginal intel-
ligentsia, it may be worthwhile to consider the relevance of
Landauer's Jewish background for an understanding of his
adoption of the libertarian socialist ideology. Jewish intellectuals often occupied a marginal social position in central
Europe in the late nineteenth and early twentieth centuries.
In Germany—but also of course in eastern Europe—there
was a disproportionate number of Jews on the political
Left; this was true among socialist leaders, but especially
among anarchist leaders.[14] Many of the limited number of
German anarchists were Jews—Gustav Landauer, Siegfried
Nacht, Peter Ramus, and Johannes Holzman,[15] for example
—as well as three intellectuals who were associated with
Landauer at different times in his life: Benedikt Friedländer;
Stefan Grossman, a Viennese Jewish writer who worked on
*Der Sozialist* with Landauer in the 1890s; and Erich
Mühsam, a Jewish poet who was one of the leaders of the

Bavarian Revolution of 1918–19. If, as I have said, marginal intellectuals have the strongest tendency toward anarchism in highly industrialized societies, then it was far more likely for a Jewish intellectual to become an anarchist in Germany than for a non-Jewish one. One reason was the fact that a disproportionate number of German Jews were free-lance writers, artists, and private scholars, which may have been partly owing to the discrimination against them in the established judicial, administrative, and educational fields.[16]

Statistical considerations, however, are not entirely adequate to answer the question. One cannot neglect the fact that as far as the attraction of European Jewish intellectuals for socialism is concerned, there may be something to the often made contention that the "classless society" or the social "brotherhood of all men" offered a new means of integration for secularized Jews who felt they were outside both the traditional religion and the country of their birth. Through this search for reintegration they may, of course, have become avid assimilationists or Jewish nationalists; on the other hand, they might well have sought to dissolve all barriers of nation and religion, making all men part of an ingroup.[17] The quasi-religious ethical idealism of many Jewish socialist intellectuals is another point not to be overlooked, especially as our concern is with so excellent an example as Gustav Landauer. In his recent study of the politics of German Jewry, Jacob Toury has noted that among German socialists it was often the Jewish figures who wrote and spoke in the tones of a religious and humanitarian spirit; the idealist passion for social justice and international peace is not an insignificant part of the Jewish cultural heritage.[18]

While our concern here is with the anarchist appeal, it is important to consider it in the context of this general ethical-idealist attraction of Jewish intellectuals to socialist ideas. This would seem to be particularly germane in situations—such as in the 1890s in Germany—when official socialism ran the risk of appearing to place parliamentary expediency above idealist principles. As in the roughly analogous contemporary European student revolt, the anarchist interpretation of socialism may then become attractive to idealist intellectuals. Here a free-floating marginal position is the sociological context of an equally important temperamental refusal to compromise. Landauer's ethical absolutism was not likely to have allowed him to feel comfortable within the structure of a mass bureaucratic party such as the SPD.[19]

## Resistance to Social Democracy and Anarchist Terrorism

Landauer's activity within the Berlin anarchist movement in the 1890s may be divided into two phases. In the first period, which lasted only from 1893 to late 1894, he attempted to compete with the Social Democratic Party within its own social base, the urban, industrial labor movement. The alternative to the SPD which he offered to the Berlin working class at this time was not that of anarchist terrorism, but what was later to be called anarchosyndicalism: workers would engage neither in parliamentary activity nor in bomb throwing, but would begin building trade unions to serve as models of a later nonauthoritarian, decentralized, socialist society, a society that would succeed the revolutionary take-over of the urban factories by the unions. Landauer hoped in 1893–94 to be able to reorient Berlin workers toward a program of workers' control of industry.

With the failure to implement this program, however—

the SPD clearly had the allegiance of the mushrooming Berlin labor movement—Landauer's anarchist activity moved into a second phase which lasted from 1895 until 1897. In this period he sought to build an anarchist alternative to the SPD outside the urban industrial labor movement. He now focused upon the building of producer-consumer cooperatives as a means of withdrawing from the capitalist system and then concentrated on handicraft workers and peasants, social groups the SPD had shunned because they represented pre- or nonindustrial functions in the economy. In this second phase Landauer began to move toward the anti-industrial, antiurban social perspectives of völkisch ideology and away from the quasi-Marxist syndicalism of the first period.

The orientation of the first period was largely urban. Still apparently under the influence of certain Marxist ways of thinking, Landauer wrote in June 1893 that "modern large industry has taken thousands of men from the peasantry, who then, as a result of taking part in the life of the city, have the possibility of escaping from rural stupidity and ignorance, from the insane narrowness of village and farm." [20] In another article of 1893 he wrote that revolutionary trade unions of urban industrial workers should prepare for an eventual take-over of factories, while the unions themselves, in their day-to-day work in the present, should become the bases of a true nonauthoritarian, socialist society which would result from the working-class capture of the industrial apparatus.[21] Here was one means by which to apply anarchist teachings to the problems of contemporary industrial, urban society.

The future for such a doctrine did not, however, look auspicious in Germany in the 1890s; trade unions, which developed rapidly after 1896,[22] when a long-term economic upswing began, were a major factor in the process by which German socialism and the German industrial worker were "domesticated," and the unions came to seek only benefits and reforms within the existing capitalist structure. In France, where economic development was much slower and hence the expectation of economic betterment through capitalist evolution was less pronounced, and where the continued prevalence of small workshops made possible a more decentralized trade-union organization, revolutionary syndicalism had a better chance of success.[23] Although the prospects for a large syndicalist labor movement in Germany were not good in the 1890s, Landauer's advocacy of the cause in 1893–94 and his abandonment of it in favor of the cooperative movement in 1895 are not difficult to understand. In the early 1890s, when there were frequent mass demonstrations in Berlin owing to widespread discontent over high food prices and unemployment, it was easier to believe in the revolutionary élan of the working classes and the possibility of a radical transformation of the existing social order than in the period after 1894.

Syndicalism, like Landauer's other projects in the 1890s, offered a possible alternative to SPD orthodoxy. Fighting the latter occupied more of his time in 1893–94, however, than working for the former; in the early years it was one of the primary concerns of the editors of *Der Sozialist* to attack the theory and practice of the SPD. In the second month of his editorship of the paper, for example, in June 1893, Landauer charged that in attempting to solve social problems through parliamentary legislation the SPD was only helping to strengthen the power of the state, just as in attempting to reform the army of the Reich it was perpetuating the very forces that enable states to carry on wars of aggression.[24]

In July 1893, at a meeting of anarchists in Berlin, Landauer and Wilhelm Werner were chosen to go to the meeting of the Second Socialist International at Zurich as representatives of German anarchism.[25] At the congress Landauer hoped to be able to deliver a report he had written on the state of German socialism. In the report, which, though never delivered, was published later in the year, Landauer argued first of all that the huge vote amassed by the Social Democrats in Germany did not by any means represent a gain for the socialist cause. The Social Democrats were in no way really distinguishable from the other opposition parties in the Reichstag; like the others, "they want reforms within the context of the bourgeois state and bourgeois society" and their voters want nothing else.[26] In the remaining pages of his prepared statement Landauer argued that the SPD was in practice strongly opposed to a real revolutionary proletariat because under such conditions these parliamentarians would then lose all their control over the German working class. As evidence of this assertion he cited an action of the SPD which had made a great impression on him at the time: when mass demonstrations of unemployed construction workers were held in Berlin in February 1892, *Vorwärts* had withheld support from the workers with the rationalization that they were not true workers but only a "lumpen proletariat." [27]

Landauer was unable to deliver his prepared report to the Zurich International Socialist Congress because one of the first actions taken by the congress was to expel all the anarchist delegates. At a preconference held in Brussels it had been proposed that only "trade unions and socialist parties and groups that recognized the necessity of worker organization and political action" be eligible for admittance to socialist international congresses. The Zurich meeting began with a debate on this motion, designed largely to exclude the anarchists from various countries. Introduced by Paul Singer, one of the leaders of the SPD, the motion was resisted not only by the anarchists but also by a large group of delegates representing the British trade unions who opposed the political action stipulation because they feared that it might eventually be used against them. Landauer spoke at some length against the motion. He argued first that the concept of "political action" was meaningless, as it stood, and that if "parliamentary action" was the tactic intended then this matter had yet to be settled by the congress. The real issue, he emphasized, was whether the anarchists whose admittance was in question were truly socialists. Since they were in fact socialists they should be admitted.[28]

Bebel responded with a vilification of the anarchists. Aside from general abuse he argued that in the existing situation it was essential for socialists to take "political, as opposed to direct, action"; they must "use political rights and the legislative machinery as much as they can or seek to conquer them in order to enhance the interests of the proletariat and win political power." A motion was then carried to limit membership to groups and parties that recognized the necessity of political action. In the midst of great commotion Werner and Landauer were forcibly removed from the meeting as they shouted, "We protest!" [29] In a later article for *Der Sozialist*, Landauer expressed his anger at the fact that the German and Swiss Social Democrats did not allow them to leave of their own power, but "pushed and shoved" them out.[30] From incidents such as these—which were to be repeated in later years—Landauer gained a lifelong hatred of German Social Democracy.

After their expulsion from the Socialist International

Congress the anarchists decided to set up their own conference which would meet in the Kasino Aussersiehl in
Zurich and would cover a wide variety of topics. Included
on the agenda were addresses on parliamentarism, war, social democracy, revolutionary propaganda, and other subjects, with anarchist and revolutionary socialist speakers
from England, Switzerland, Italy, and Germany.[31] Sixty
persons attended the congress. As with other international
anarchist meetings, it accomplished little beyond providing
an expression of mutual solidarity.[32] Landauer spoke on the
general strike and called for direct, industrial action by
worker associations for "economic struggles of a revolutionary nature" and not for wage increases. He emphasized
that these economic struggles would lead to a general strike
which would begin the social revolution, by which he apparently meant the change from capitalist to worker control
of industry. The general strike should be organized through
trade unions that would, in addition, be the kernel of the
future socialist society.[33] Such a course of action had already
gained a large following in France, where anarchists were
influential among the syndicates. In 1888 a congress of syndicates at Bordeaux had decided to reject political action in
favor of direct action by means of the general strike.[34] Unfortunately, as in his other pronouncements in favor of syndicalism in 1893, Landauer failed to specify concretely how
the course of action he had recommended should, or could,
be implemented. We have seen, for example, how out of
touch he was with the realities of German trade unionism.

Although Landauer framed his early anarchist stance in
opposition to the SPD, it was not only the parliamentarians
that he resisted. While he sought an anarchist alternative to
Social Democracy, he opposed attempts to implement this
goal by way of terror or political assassination, tactics that

the general public associated with the anarchist movement. Anarchist socialism, for Landauer, had to avoid the terrorist bomb as well as the ballot box.

In the years 1892 through 1894 French anarchist groups unleashed a wave of terrorism in Paris which included eleven bomb explosions, one of them in the French Chamber of Deputies, and culminated in the assassination of Carnot, the president of the republic.[35] In Germany these events were greeted with demands from the Kartell parties for strong repressive measures against anarchists within Germany. While such laws were being debated in the Reichstag, the last months of 1893 and the year 1894 saw a concerted police and court campaign against anarchist propaganda in Germany, especially in Berlin.[36] Two months after he returned from Zurich, in October 1893, Landauer was arrested and sentenced to two months in prison for having written an article advocating "disobedience of the law." Before his term had been completed, however, Landauer was charged with having agitated for the violent overthrow of existing political institutions and, in December 1893, he was sentenced to another nine months in prison.[37] Concentrating upon the staff of the openly anarchist newspaper that Landauer had edited before his arrest, the police campaign led to the arrest and imprisonment of sixteen other writers for *Der Sozialist* before the end of 1894.[38]

All the charges against the staff of *Der Sozialist* were for incitement to revolutionary actions, not for actual deeds.[39] In fact, the newspaper continually deplored the use of terrorism as a means of achieving the desired political and social changes. Unsigned articles appearing in 1894 emphasized that terrorism was in no way a necessary and logical consequence of anarchist teaching; if anything, violence was held to be in contradiction to the anarchist society of voluntary association. While it was pointed out that acts of terrorism arose from the desperation created by miserable social conditions, anarchism was seen as a humanitarian, peaceful world view which regarded "violence and freedom as opposites." [40]

While in prison from November 1893 to October 1894 Landauer kept a diary from which extracts were later published.[41] In the diary he set down his personal reactions to the current wave of anarchist terrorism in Europe. Expressing horror at bomb throwing and assassinations, Landauer was nevertheless convinced that such desperate actions only revealed how wretched the conditions must have been which gave rise to them.[42] He concentrated, however, on the reasons that he could not accept them. "Our world view is not science, not theory, not merely a matter of the head," he wrote; "it is life, love arising from the soul." He reread Nietzsche and found him wanting on this score. Particularly upsetting to Landauer was the passage in the *Fröhliche Wissenschaft* which read: "Who will achieve something of greatness if he does not feel the strength and will to inflict great pain?" Greatness, Landauer felt, did not come from such strength but from a feeling that was apparently very foreign to Nietzsche. This feeling, which made Landauer reject the use of violence against his fellowmen, was the experience, "in all embracing love, of oneness with the entire world." Such an experience of "free reconciliation" (*freie Versöhnung*), as he called it, had always meant a great deal to him, but especially now, in prison.[43]

The concept of free reconciliation was, in a sense, a demonstration of Landauer's contention that anarchism and socialism were mutually dependent doctrines, if rightly understood. The phrase amounted to a definition of his anarchosocialism: "free" for the anarchist meant "voluntary" and "self-determined," not the result of dictation, forcible or otherwise, from institutions ruling "from above"; "reconciliation," on the other hand, in terms of the union of humanity, was the expressed goal of socialism.

Although critical of some of Nietzsche's statements, Landauer continued to be interested in certain Nietzschean perspectives, as shown in the short novel he wrote while in prison in late 1893 and 1894. The main character of the work, Arnold Himmelheber, insists that one must go beyond good and evil in order to grasp the fullness of life, by which he means essentially the fullness of love. Murder and incest are committed by Himmelheber so as to allow for a totally unimpeded relationship of love with his daughter. "There are no sins," he cries. "I am the eternal pagan! I should like to drink from the cup of life for all eternity as I drink this wine here. There are no sins, there is only life." [44] Such ideals apparently still fascinated Landauer, although *Arnold Himmelheber* remains a rather weak literary investigation of amorality. The prison diary, however, indicated that Landauer strongly opposed the use of violence for the attainment of any ends, no matter how noble.

## A New Theory and a New Tactic

By the end of 1894 Landauer's articles and talks in favor of the anarchosyndicalist approach had brought no results; the anarchists could not compete with the Social Democrats for the support of the labor movement in Germany. Surprisingly enough, Landauer never made contact with one source of potential support among German factory workers for anarchism, the so-called localists who favored decentralized trade unions. The localists and their intellectual spokesman, Dr. Raphael Friedeberg—a propagandizer for the general strike—were clearly moving in the direction of anarchosyndicalism in the 1890s.[45] In a country where industrial concentration was proceeding rapidly, however, the localists stood little chance of winning the battle against the unions, which stood for the centralization of labor organization.[46]

In late 1894 and 1895 Landauer reflected upon the fact of SPD dominance of the German proletariat. A new theory of authoritarianism began to take shape in his mind, one that focused upon the obedience, inertia, and dependence of the working masses and not upon the usual anarchist assumption of the usurpation of authority by external institutions. The new theory, however, called for a new tactic. Capitalism, Social Democracy, and the state cannot be attacked directly, Landauer concluded; their roots in the obedience and dependency of the masses must first be eradicated. In what proved to be the first stage of Landauer's withdrawal from the proletarian labor movement, he was still attempting to recruit industrial workers, but the enterprise for which he recruited them was one that called for the eventual building of socialism outside the industrial, capitalist system; in 1895 Landauer hoped to be able to root out the dependency of the masses by developing their capacities for self-help through economic cooperation. The new tactic of 1895 was the building of producer-consumer cooperatives.

Soon after his release from prison in October 1894, Landauer was asked to write an article on the nature of anarchism for Maximilian Harden's journal *Die Zukunft*. Published in January 1895, the article was a clarification of Landauer's position in the light of the recent incidents of anarchist terrorism. It was also his most ambitious attempt, to date, to relate his sociopolitical stance to more grandiose conceptions of human development through history. The main task, the main characteristic, of culture, he began his essay, is the "conscious, willed, purposive formation . . . of smaller or larger communities. . . . The previous history of the human race is composed of innumerable instances of unconscious, dull, blind development." [47] Up to this point Landauer's position had been in harmony with the classic, idealist philosophies of history of Kant and Hegel. Unlike the two great German philosophers, however, Landauer did not regard struggle as a prime force for human progress. On the contrary, according to him, the struggle of man against man had prevented unity in the human struggle against the forces of nature. Cooperation and association are needed, not struggle and the resulting oppression of some by others. The task of anarchism, he insisted, is to bring about the cessation of such conflicts and the development of human fraternity without which man will be unable to move from the realm of unconscious necessity to the realm of conscious self-determination.[48] The tactic of ruthless class struggle was clearly inconsistent with this goal. Although the proletariat should form the bulk of the anarchist movement, Landauer went on, individuals from all social groups are welcome. Such individuals can be recruited through the spread of enlightenment by anarchist "preachers" into "all levels of the population." [49] What is truly important, Landauer emphasized, is the changing of human attitudes, their intellectual and spiritual transformation as a vital prerequisite to meaningful social change. What is really needed, he wrote, is a "rebirth of the human spirit." [50]

Reflecting the idealist tone, Landauer contended that the source of the state's power, the great obstacle to human freedom in the anarchist view, was not so much the privileged economic position of the ruling classes as the "blind belief of the masses in authority." [51] Here was a main reason for the past failure of the human race consciously to "make its own history." Such a position, moreover, made Landauer's rejection of an allegedly necessary class struggle more understandable. The real enemy, according to this view, was not the bourgeoisie, but the present condition of the human spirit, a condition characterized by routine, inertia, and dependence.

Unlike many other anarchist thinkers, Kropotkin and Bakunin for example, Landauer had never idealized the lower classes. "Conditions of exploitation and servitude," he wrote in a letter of September 1893, have bred "in the great mass of workers much brutality and hatred." [52] In 1895 his observations on lower-class beliefs played an important part in the shift of his thinking about man, state, and society.

After his release from prison in the fall of 1894, Landauer visited Bregenz, Austria, a center for textile manufacturing, and spent some time observing the city's workers. He was particularly struck by what he called the "spiritual degeneration accompanying their economic misery." In discussing what he regarded as a comparable situation in Berlin, Landauer provided a clarification of his expression "spiritual degeneration." The mentality of the lower classes in both locales was highly superstitious, he observed; in both cases there existed an almost mystical faith in their salvation through social democracy. Such a faith was marked by the conception that "from some secret place," outside themselves, "everything was being prepared" for their inevitable victory. [53]

From these comments it would appear that what Landauer meant by "spiritual degeneration" was a condition of faith in, and dependence upon, forces external to the individual. Conversely, a condition of "spiritual health" might be defined as one in which the individual was capable of self-reliant and self-determined action. In his *Zukunft* article on anarchism, published in January 1895, Landauer used this distinction throughout. Whereas "the previous history of the human race" has been marked by an "unconscious, dull, blind" development, he observed, the task of culture is the "conscious, willed, purposive formation of communities." The distinction found its way also—and here for the first time in all his writings—into his views of political oppression: the power of the state, he emphasized, is based upon the "blind belief of the masses in authority," a belief nurtured by human routine, inertia, and dependence. The analysis of SPD strength was here transferred to that of the state. The first objective of a libertarian socialism could not be, in his view, the frontal attack upon the state; it must be the attempt to root out the human dependence and resultant belief in authority which made the state possible. In October 1895 Landauer wrote:

> In order to reach our goal we must, in the first place, spread our ideas into all circles of the population, above all among the ranks of the oppressed. We must destroy the thoughtless respect before the old and the traditional; . . . the belief in God, the state and authority must be fundamentally shaken and the new, lasting belief in a free humanity and in the right of every personality, no matter how low and crushed he may be today, must be spread. . . . The dependence of the human masses upon their masters must be destroyed.[54]

Although he did not mention Kant in this connection, Landauer's view of the problem represented an extension of Kant's view of "enlightenment." We shall have occasion later to discuss Landauer's philosophical idealism; it is sufficient to point out here that the moral concern that informed Kant's epistemological argument—the necessity to affirm the autonomy of the human will [55]—was a concern that Landauer deeply shared. For Landauer, man's "blind belief in authority" resulted from a condition of dependence and an incapacity for self-determined and independent action. Similarly Kant wrote:

> Enlightenment is man's leaving his self-caused immaturity. Immaturity is the incapacity to use one's intelligence without the guidance of another. Such immaturity is self-caused if it is not caused by lack of intelligence, but by lack of determination and courage to use one's intelligence without being guided by another. Sapere Aude! Have the courage to use your own intelligence! is therefore the motto of the enlightenment.
>
> Through laziness and cowardice a large part of mankind, even after nature has freed them from alien guidance, gladly remain immature. It is because of laziness and cowardice that it is so easy for others to usurp the role of guardians. It is so comfortable to be a minor! [56]

After his short stay in Bregenz in late 1894, Landauer returned to Berlin early in 1895,[57] where he immediately found himself without a job. As a result of a stepping up of the police campaign against *Der Sozialist*, a campaign that in the last months of 1894 extended beyond the arrest of members of the staff to confiscation of manuscripts and, more important, of the financial donations upon which the paper depended, the newspaper was forced to close down in January 1895.[58] Landauer had to find some alternative means by which to support himself and his family. In an attempt to secure permanent financial independence Landauer applied, in March, for admission to the medical faculty of the University of Freiburg. Because of his previous prison term his application was promptly turned down.[59] Later Landauer realized that even if he had succeeded in entering medical school and in becoming a doctor, this career would not have been what he wanted because such work would have left no time for other studies, writing, and activities.[60] His letters of this period were often requests to his cousin Hugo for financial assistance, pleas that his need for independence made very painful for him indeed.[61] In May he returned to Bregenz and edited a journal there for a few months.[62] By August, however, Landauer was back in Berlin, editing and writing frequent articles for *Der Sozialist*, which had been able to begin publication again in that same month. Unlike the early *Sozialist* there was little concerning the SPD in the new one; besides frequent theoretical discussions of, for example, the relation between anarchism and socialism, between anarchism and natural science, and so on, the new *Sozialist* concentrated upon a new tactic: the creation of producer-consumer cooperatives as a small beginning of an anarchosocialist society. Cooperatives were Landauer's absorbing interest in 1895 and 1896.

Cooperatives had already been developing in Germany for at least thirty years. Although they had little to do with socialism, credit and marketing cooperatives had for years been used by farmers and shopkeepers. In the 1860s Schulze-Delitzsch had founded a consumer cooperative movement in the hope of gaining working-class support for political liberalism. His real interest, however, did not lie with the industrial proletariat; his cooperatives were much more credit cooperatives for small shopkeepers. Until 1890 the legal stipulation of unlimited liability of each single member for all debts incurred by a cooperative strongly limited the growth of the movement. With the change of the law in 1890, however, cooperatives developed rapidly and began to attract many industrial workers.[63]

Early in 1895 a member of the *Sozialist* staff, the construction worker Wilhelm Weise, became convinced that the only way a true anarchist-socialist society would be achieved was through the building of self-sufficient producers' cooperatives which might eventually draw large groups of workers away from the capitalist system. Weise had come to this conclusion as a result, in part, of studying the history of the English cooperative movement and the writings of the German Proudhonian Arthur Mülberger.[64] The main influence upon Weise, however, was the work of Ernst Busch who, in *Die Soziale Frage und ihre Lösung* (1890), had advocated the creation of producers' cooperatives with the financial base acquired as a result of a prior building of consumer cooperatives.[65] Under Weise's direction a small group of thirty-three Berlin anarchists founded a cooperative—the Arbeiter-Kongsumgenossenschaft Befreiung—in April 1895, with the intention of beginning operations in October of the same year; in the intervening months a campaign would be undertaken to attract a large membership. For the purposes of this propaganda campaign a pamphlet was produced in May, entitled *Ein Weg zur Befreiung der Arbeiterklasse* (Berlin, 1895), and ten thousand copies of it were printed.[66] The pamphlet was written, although not signed, by Gustav Landauer.[67]

In early 1895 Landauer was particularly receptive to the new tactic of developing cooperatives. For one thing, he had been impressed, in the course of 1894, with the utter futility of seeking to overthrow the state through the use of individual acts of terrorism. Moreover, his new view of the sources of state power—the incapacity of the masses for independent and self-determined action and their accompanying reliance upon external authorities—necessitated a reassessment of the usual anarchist position regarding the overthrow of the state: if servitude is based upon an interior deficiency of men which facilitates their manipulation by external powers, then this deficiency must be eliminated before anything else can be done. If the state is directly attacked before any of these great human imperfections have been reformed, then it is more than likely that a new state will arise, since the same human dependencies will continue to make men receptive to authoritarian guardianship. The only way to permanently destroy the state was to obviate it; mutual self-help organizations of cooperatives appealed to Landauer as a potentially effective means by which to educate workers in the independent action that alone could eliminate the causes for the present system of capitalism and the state. He was to hold to this line of reasoning until the end of his life. His pamphlet of 1895, *Ein Weg zur Befreiung der Arbeiterklasse*, and his work during that year for the Befreiung cooperatives were his first attempts to put it into practice.

Landauer began his pamphlet with the argument that under present conditions in Germany, and especially owing to the strong allegiance of the army to the government, any attempt at the violent overthrow of the existing social and political order would lead only to the massacre of the rebels.[68] Even if it were possible, however, to overthrow the government forcefully, he continued, such an event would not lead to socialism: "From force one can expect nothing, neither the force of the ruling classes of today nor that of the so-called revolutionaries who would perhaps attempt . . . through dictatorial decrees to command a socialist society, out of nothing, into existence." [69] The crucial words are "out of nothing"; Landauer was now convinced that an immediate beginning, no matter how small, had to be made in the construction of a socialist reality instead of awaiting the day, which might never come anyway, when a revolution would prove barren of socialist-anarchist results because the human roots of authoritarianism and exploitation would still remain. The real revolution, Landauer emphasized, is man's education in self-help which can be provided by cooperative organizations begun in the present.[70] In an article in the fall of 1895 Landauer wrote: "It is finally time to stop attempting mechanistically and slavishly to imitate earlier revolutions. . . . I say not: First destroy, then build up! . . . Our solution is much more: First build up! In the future it will be apparent whether there still remains something that is worth destroying." [71]

Landauer's main concern in his pamphlet was to demonstrate that the power of industrial workers as consumers far exceeded their power as producers. As a result of this fact it was necessary, under current conditions of industrial life, for workers first to harness their consumer power so that they might soon have the financial independence to become their own producers. To substantiate his point—which was in fact the view, as we have seen, of Wilhelm Weise—Landauer sought to demonstrate that the main economic weapon of the workers as producers, namely the strike, was a hopelessly inadequate one. In the strike, he argued, the employer will more and more have the upper hand: "Through experience the employers have learned to mutually support one another, in the midst of strikes against one of them; moreover, while the strike goes on, the worker, not the employer, goes hungry." [72] Drawing upon Ernst Busch's *Die Soziale Frage und ihre Lösung*, he insisted that the liberation of the workers could be accomplished only through the utilization of their power as consumers. If the middlemen who stand between the workers' production and their consumption were eliminated by the collective direct purchase of goods by the workers, then the money saved could be used to begin independent production.

To illustrate the practicality of this suggestion Landauer cited the huge success of the English cooperative movement,[73] although he failed to mention that producers' cooperatives played a very small part in it. England, he asserted, has a much greater degree of socialism, because of its widespread workers' cooperative movement, than Germany has; real socialist activity is what matters, not votes for a parliamentary party.[74] For Landauer, cooperative production would ensure that socialism would involve the active participation of men, not their dependence on, and obedience to, external authorities.

With the spread of consumer cooperatives, Landauer continued, the various organizations could in turn cooperate among themselves in the purchase of the more expensive products necessary for the beginnings of independent factory production, and eventually even in the building of houses for the members. Since workers would be producing for their own consumption there would be no incentive to cheat those who consume, as under the present economic system, and therefore no need for any state intervention in the form of the inspection or control of production. In this way, Landauer emphasized, an anarchist-socialist society could be developed, because both the bourgeois and the socialist state system would be obviated.[75]

The response to Landauer's pamphlet was disappointing. In October the membership of the Befreiung cooperative had increased only to sixty-five. Nevertheless, the earlier plan to begin operations in October was carried out, for the members reasoned that only a practical demonstration of the effectiveness of the idea would attract a larger follow-

ing. The first business local was set up and goods were purchased on credit. At the end of the first year of operation the cooperative could show a small net profit and a large membership increase to 240. For the purposes of attracting these and future new members the cooperative had decided to give back 30 percent of the net profit to its members, retaining 70 percent for future expansion of the cooperative's activities in the direction of independent production of goods.[76]

Although enjoying moderate success in its first year or so of operation, it is uncertain whether the Befreiung cooperative was in fact able to expand itself into a producers' as well as a consumers' cooperative. I have been unable to find evidence concerning its activities beyond the second year of operation. Landauer wrote years later, however, that it had been sufficiently successful for the Social Democrats, after having ridiculed the undertaking,[77] to imitate it on a large scale.[78] The participation of Social Democratic workers in the cooperative movement did, in fact, expand a great deal in the years after 1895; the Zentralverband deutscher Konsumvereine, established in 1902, was an organization whose cooperatives were almost all led by Social Democrats.[79] Landauer's contention that all this activity amounted to an imitation of the Befreiung cooperative seems, however, to have been little more than an expression of his resentment against the SPD.

Although it was not marked by more than moderate success, Landauer's work for the cooperative movement in 1895 was of considerable importance in his intellectual and political development. Based on an idealist theory of political authority and economic exploitation, and involving an attempt to bring socialism by means of action outside both the state and the industrial, capitalist environment, the new tactic proved to be a first step in Landauer's shift away from the mainstream of the proletarian labor movement. By late 1896 Landauer's socialism, no longer oriented toward urban industrialism, began to draw heavily upon idealist, romantic, and völkisch currents of thought.

## Idealist, Romantic, and Völkisch Perspectives

If the year 1895 saw Landauer develop a new theory and a new tactic, the following year brought a more fundamental philosophic and sociological reorientation. Beginning in the fall of 1895 with the renewal of his active work for *Der Sozialist* after an interval of close to two years, Landauer began to formulate basic alternatives to Social Democracy, in the realm both of social theory and of social practice. The new theory and new tactics of early 1895 had begun this reorientation with their focus upon the immediate need to develop human capacities for autonomy, self-determination, and voluntary cooperation; now the reorientation broadened into a basic restatement of anarchosocialism. In the year following the reappearance of *Der Sozialist* in August 1895, Landauer moved a long way toward his later synthesis of völkisch romanticism and libertarian socialism.

In the first issue of the new *Sozialist*, which appeared in August 1895, Landauer continued the line of thought expressed in his *Zukunft* article of January; rejecting the Marxian concept of class struggle, he proclaimed the solidarity of *Der Sozialist* with what he called the "progressive elements in the middle classes." By this designation he did not necessarily mean middle-class socialist intellectuals. As a result of the new idealist focus that informed his thinking in 1895, Landauer was increasingly receptive to the work of various kinds of ethical reformers who had very little to do with socialism. In the article he mentioned, besides the followers of Hertzka's Freiland schemes, such groups as the Ethical Culturists and the followers of a certain Moritz von Egidy, a former army officer who preached a mystical doctrine of ethical Christianity and humanistic pacifism in the Berlin of the 1890s.[80] In both instances the inspiration came from the ethical idealism of Kant. The historian George L. Mosse has written of the Ethical Culturists whom Landauer had in mind, the members of the Ethische Gesellschaft founded in 1892: "Wilhelm Förster, its moving spirit, expanded the doctrine of the primacy of ethical behavior into a pantheistic humanism embracing all of mankind. Inspired by Kantian precepts, his society presupposed a goodness in man which obviated any reference to mysterious and occult elements."[81] Concerning von Egidy, who became more and more antiauthoritarian in the course of the 1890s and frequently addressed anarchist meetings in Berlin,[82] Landauer wrote that the Kantian categorical imperative was at the basis of his ethical idealism and of his slogan, "Peace is possible, because it is necessary."[83]

Förster and von Egidy, however, were not the only followers of Kant in Germany in the 1890s. Neo-Kantian and neoidealist currents were very strong in the work of Dilthey and Simmel as well as in the southwest German philosophic school around Wilhelm Windelband and Heinrich Rickert; such currents were closely related to the revolt against positivism in the 1890s.[84] Kantian moral philosophy, moreover, was adopted by a number of socialist thinkers and an attempt was made by the so-called Austro-Marxists, but also by a number of German socialist scholars such as Max Adler, to reconcile the teachings of Kant and Marx, in part by concentrating on the ethical-idealist aspects of Marxian thought.[85] In redefining his social thought in 1895 and 1896 on the basis of idealist philosophy, Landauer merely reflected one of the dominant trends in the intellectual life of the period.

The structure of idealist social thought is based uopn the premise that there exists a radical cleavage "between the phenomenal and the spiritual world, between the world of natural science and the world of human activity." [86] Rickert, Windelband, and Dilthey had each attempted to delineate a method of understanding which was held to be peculiar to the study of human affairs: the suggestion that the historian's work is a reliving or a reexperiencing of the past was one formulation of this allegedly unique methodology which the social scientist does not share with the natural scientist.[87] The basic premise was the conviction that human society does not, or need not, operate according to laws that apply to the world of nature, but is capable of arrangements based upon conscious human choice. It is important to remember that German idealism was born as a response to the British empiricists' claim that all human ideas are merely the result of custom and habit. Kant's epistemology was a way out of the implications of empiricism. Herbert Marcuse has written of the problems facing Kant and Hegel:

> If men did not succeed . . . in creating unity and universality through their autonomous reason and even in contradiction to the facts, they would have to surrender not only their intellectual but also their material existence to the blind pressures and processes of the prevailing empirical order of life. The problem was thus not a merely philosophical one but concerned with the historical destiny of humanity.[88]

It was this concern that Landauer expressed at the outset of his *Zukunft* article of January 1895, when he wrote that the task of culture is the "conscious, willed, purposive formation of smaller or larger communities . . . [while] the previous history of the human race has been composed of

innumerable cases of unconscious, dull, blind development."
It was also as a philosopher in the tradition of German idealism that Landauer reacted against the doctrine of social Darwinism. In an article written for *Der Sozialist* in August
1895 he attempted to counter the view that human society is
necessarily an arena for violent struggle and ruthless competition since, as a part of the natural world, society was
only following the laws of nature. Man is capable, he argued, of perceiving that his best interests lie in his cooperating with his fellows and peacefully building a free, nonauthoritarian community. If the natural world is dominated
by violent struggle and force there is all the more reason for
men to exercise their capacity for autonomous development
and build a society that runs counter to "blind" nature.[89]
Whereas Kropotkin's refutation of social Darwinism in his
work *Mutual Aid: A Factor in Evolution* (London, 1902)
upheld the positivists' assumption that human society necessarily follows laws that are discovered in nature and argued
that nature is itself a field more of cooperation than of competition, Landauer insisted that mutual aid and cooperation
are desiderata of the human will, not natural laws that operate in human life.

Landauer's statement that mutual aid and cooperation between men were in man's best interest was an uncharacter-
istic way for him to formulate the issue. He had never
regarded man's so-called self-interest as the basis of human
solidarity. We have seen how he refused to accept Nietzschean and Stirnerite egoism. At the Zurich International
Socialist Congress in 1893 Landauer had insisted that anarchists were also socialists, and in August 1895 he continued
to dwell upon this point by giving his newspaper a new
subtitle, *Organ der Anarchismus-Sozialismus*. In the first
issue of the new *Sozialist* Landauer defended the suitability

of the title and subtitle against the charge by the SPD paper *Vorwärts* that the name was inappropriate and that the paper should be called simply "Der Anarchist." Landauer replied that he had not given up the position he stated at the Zurich Congress; the new subtitle underlined this position.[90] His personal need for both individual autonomy and social commitment had taken the theoretical form of an attempt to demonstrate the mutual interdependence of anarchism and socialism.

In the months from November 1895 through February 1896 Landauer published a series of articles he had written as a comprehensive justification of the anarchosocialist label. The articles were directed toward both the Social Democrats, who had denied that anarchists were socialists and had therefore excluded them from the International Socialist Congress, and the anarchist followers of Max Stirner whose theoretical position of absolute individualistic egoism provided ammunition for the Social Democrats' contention. The Stirnerites, such as John Henry Mackay, also denied that anarchism and socialism were interdependent: "humanity," "class," and other collective nouns were all purely mental abstractions and "fixed ideas"; the "I" alone was real. Landauer's defense of anarchosocialism was an attempt to refute the Stirnerite conception of the atomistic, absolute individual whose liberation necessitated the destruction of his commitment to such allegedly unreal fixed ideas. This series of articles, "Toward a Developmental History of the Individual," proved to be the basis upon which Landauer's later philosophical position was built, a position most clearly and comprehensively defined in the works *Skepsis und Mystik: Versuche im Anschluss an Mauthners Sprachkritik*, first published in 1903, and *Die Revolution*, published in 1908.[91]

"Is there such a thing as an individual in an absolute sense?" Landauer asked. Are "anarchy, the self-rule of the individual," and "socialism, the integration of the individual into the community," compatible or do they exclude each other? In answering his second question Landauer immediately rejected the English utilitarians' argument that individual and community are reconcilable through the fact that the community is a sum of individuals and can be sustained through an appeal to each man's rational self-interest. Community is possible, he argued, only because the individual understands that there are community interests, in addition to individual ones. It is significant here, of course, that Landauer used the word "Gemeinschaft" and not "Gesellschaft," which is the German equivalent of the Benthamite "society." In the tradition of German romantic social thought the word "Gemeinschaft" meant to Landauer much more than the mechanistic "sum of individuals" which "society" was judged to be. "Gemeinschaft" or "community," in contrast with "Gesellschaft" or "society," was understood as a living, independent organism and "personality" which represented something above and beyond the mere sum of individuals who composed it. His argument against the Benthamites was, in part, tautological: to a thinker in the tradition of German romanticism the very definition of the word "community" excludes the view that it is a "sum of individuals."

The "community" is not a mere abstraction, a construct of the human brain designed to deal with discrete, individual phenomena, Landauer insisted; it is a "concrete reality" and an "organism." But just as the individual is part of the community, so the community is, in turn, part of a larger sum of organisms that make up the largest one, "humanity." [92] Stirner would argue that "humanity" is a mere mental construct; Landauer argued, however, that it is quite real and that each man is indissolubly bound to humanity, in both a physical and a spiritual sense. On the physical side, each man is a limb of humanity through the "invisible chains by which his body is united with that of his ancestors," the chains of "heredity." Following the social thought of the romantic organicists, Landauer wrote that the multitude of human physical forms that have lived upon the earth do not together constitute merely a sum of separate individuals, but form, rather, a "real physical community, an organism." Through the sexual drive and the hereditary transmission of our physical characteristics we are bound to succeeding generations in the same way that previous generations are bound to us.[93]

In these articles Landauer contended that on the spiritual side, also, man is but a "limb of the world." "There is no absolute, independent individual, there are only psychic [*seelische*] forces as there are material ones; one of these forces is consciousness. . . . Through these forces an indissoluble connection is made between the individual soul and the rest of the world. As the individual organism is only a part of a great, real physical community, so the individual soul is a part of a great, real spiritual community." [94]

On this point, unfortunately, Landauer's argument was particularly obscure and unsubstantiated. It was a position he *wanted* to hold, and at this early stage of his life he had yet to find some respectable philosophic formulation within which his assertion might sound more convincing. We know, however, that Landauer had read a critique of Schopenhauer and copied out passages from the philosopher's writings in the prison months of 1893 and 1894, the same time that he was reflecting upon these matters.[95] There are, moreover, a number of crucial passages in the articles which appear to be directly based upon Schopenhauer. For example, the statement that represents the most extreme antithesis to the Stirnerite conception of the individual reads as follows: ". . . humanity is not a dead, abstract concept; humanity is real, particular men are only emerging, changing, and again disappearing phantoms through which humanity is visible." [96] (Conspicuously absent from Landauer's argument was the Schopenhauerian injunction that the negation of the individual will would alone provide escape from the pains of individuated existence.) Although Schopenhauer played a part in helping Landauer to formulate some of his conclusions, Landauer did not attempt to build a consistent philosophic underpinning for his assertions. When he did attempt a comprehensive substantiation, in *Skepsis und Mystik*, first published in 1903, Landauer was able to formulate his beliefs as plausible deductions from the analysis of language worked out at length by his friend Fritz Mauthner. Mauthner's work was to provide a respectable framework within which to state beliefs that Landauer had held, and apparently needed to hold, for many years. At the beginning of *Skepsis und Mystik* Landauer stated that the perception by the individual that he is not a separate atom, but one manifestation of humanity, is a "necessity" of life.[97]

In the concluding part of the series of articles Landauer focused directly upon Stirner's views. He convincingly demonstrated that Stirner had ended only with an abstraction, the allegedly absolute and separate "I," although it had been his intention to overthrow all abstractions. While Stirner had discovered that human oppression is based upon the respect for, and the worship of, concepts such as "God," "Morality," and "State"—a view that supported the new conception of authority which Landauer had developed in

1895—the concept of the absolute ego was only another phantom idol; the individual is himself not an undifferentiated "I" but the scene of perpetually conflicting emotional battles. In place of "individual" Landauer emphasized that we should substitute the concept of "individuality"; in each man, he argued, there is a unique "individuality," a different picture of humanity.[98]

Landauer's distinction revealed that he was not arguing against individualism, but against the atomistic individualism of the eighteenth century. It was not simple collectivism that he defended, but a notion of "individuality" which had been developed by the early German romantics. The distinction here between *Individuum* ("individual") and *Individualität* ("individuality") is clarified by Robert W. Lougee in a recent article:

> Romantic individualism must be sharply distinguished from atomistic individualism. The social contract theories prevalent in the eighteenth century generally assumed that the individual in nature enjoys a position of independence from his fellows, and that he has natural rights which do not derive from any association. But to be independent is not to be unique, and these theories assumed that all individuals behave more or less in the same way, and, therefore, like atoms, respond alike to general laws or forces. Romantic individualism, on the contrary, stressed the uniqueness of individuals, a uniqueness which placed them beyond conformity to any general law or principle. . . . The same age . . . reacted against the isolation of the individual. From the mid-1790's romantic writers more and more stress the role of the individual as a vital part of a larger organic whole. This stress did not aim at subordinating the individual to the group but rather at coordinating him with it. . . . The group was thought strong according to the uniqueness and diversity of its elements. The assumption was that the individual by being completely true to himself would best represent and

contribute to the character of the whole. As Schleiermacher wrote, ". . . it has become clear to me that every man ought in his own way to represent mankind." [99]

Instead of the concept of the isolated atomistic individual Landauer substituted the romantics' view of the unique personality that is a "vital part of a larger organic whole" and is, in its own way, an image of humanity. "Humanity," he wrote, "is visible" through "emerging, changing, and again disappearing" particular men. In this way Landauer felt that he had demonstrated that self-reliant individualism and social commitment were not irreconcilable, that "anarchism and socialism" were, in fact, interdependent. The basis of his demonstration was a restatement of the organicist philosophy of romanticism. In the year 1896 Landauer coupled this philosophic reorientation toward romanticism with a shift in his social and political activity; he began now to move toward the social groups celebrated in völkisch ideology.

In the years 1893 and 1894 Landauer and the other anarchists associated with *Der Sozialist*, encouraged by frequent industrial working-class demonstrations in Berlin in a period of lingering economic slump, had attempted to compete directly with the SPD for the support of the Berlin proletariat. The economic upswing after 1894, however, which was to be the beginning of a tremendous twenty-year boom,[100] began to remove the most fertile sources of working-class discontent in the city. As mass demonstrations and restiveness among Berlin's factory workers diminished, so did the hopes of the *Sozialist* circle of gaining their allegiance. Landauer's work on cooperatives was an early response to the more quiescent situation. Beginning in 1896, however, he became more and more involved with nonfactory workers—first urban, handicraft needleworkers and then rural agricultural workers—in attempts to build a movement from social groups both spurned by the SPD and not in a position to benefit from an industrial upswing. Landauer's path away from the struggles of the urban, industrial environment toward the traditional social groups of concern to völkisch thinkers was a process mediated by the conflict with the theory and practice of German Social Democracy; the search for alternatives to the SPD finally resulted in the synthesis of anarchosocialism and völkisch romanticism.

The largest group of domestic handworkers in Berlin in the 1890s comprised the needleworkers of the large Berlin clothing trade. Numbering 50,000, 70 percent of them women and only 2.5 percent of them organized into unions,[101] this was one large group in the Berlin working-class population whose situation did not improve in the course of the 1890s. Frequently performing their handwork in their own homes from materials supplied by entrepreneurial middlemen who were able to keep wages very low, the needleworkers suffered severely in the 1890s from the competition of factory-produced clothing from abroad.[102] In January 1895, at a conference of delegates from among the clothing workers, a commission of five, including the Social Democrat Johannes Timm, was selected to work for the improvement of conditions by "propagandizing for the workers." In October large protest assemblies were held by Berlin clothing workers and in January 1896, at a meeting with more than 200 employers, the commission of five demanded wage increases, improved working conditions, and abolition of the middleman system. The demands were flatly turned down, and on February 11, 1896, 20,000 to 30,000 needleworkers went out on strike in Berlin.[103]

A few days after the beginning of the strike the employers stated that they were willing to grant concessions; as it turned out these concessions amounted to minor pay increases, yet left the middleman system intact. The commission of five immediately accepted the concessions and called for the end of the strike. An opposition group of locally organized tailors, however, claiming that the commission did not truly represent the workers, called for the continuation of the strike. Landauer, who was the leading spokesman for the opposition group, immediately wrote a pamphlet attacking the commission and demanding that the strike be continued until much more substantial gains were made. At numerous assemblies of needle-trade workers the issue was noisily debated; the outcome, according to the Social Democrat Eduard Bernstein, was that a majority of the assemblies voted to end the strike.[104] In mid-April, however, the employers declared themselves no longer bound by the compromise and retracted the concessions they had granted during the February strike. The commission of five, feeling that the almost totally ununionized workers could not sustain themselves through another strike, advised the workers to remain at their jobs and prepare themselves for a possible walkout in the future.[105]

In the aftermath of the February strike Landauer was attacked in the Social Democrats' paper *Vorwärts* for having attempted to exploit the misery of the needle-trade workers for his personal gain; the attack was repeated by Wilhelm Förster in his journal *Ethische Kultur*. The argument used in both papers was that the slightest success in the strike had to lead to an immediate settlement because the clothing workers were too poorly organized and organizable and thus had insufficient funds to continue a strike. Landauer, Förster claimed, had called for the continuation of the strike without informing himself of the strength of sources of aid.[106]

Landauer replied to the charges by saying that the settlement had gained nothing, not even pay increases, for most of the workers and that the action of the commission had "ruined the tailors' movement for years." The strike, he argued, should have been continued even without large supporting funds. (Though he did not mention it in his defense, Landauer had attempted to raise funds through contacts in the Berlin literary community.)[107] Before writing the pamphlet attacking the commission he had gained the strong impression, from the attendance at large meetings of needle-trade workers, that it was the overwhelming desire of the exploited domestic workers to continue the strike even if it meant that they would go hungry. Timm and his associates on the commission had betrayed the workers by settling with the employers before consulting them.[108] Landauer failed to mention that a majority of the workers voted with the commission after it had called for an end to the strike. If presented with this point, however, he would probably have argued that they were misled by the commission and suffered only from the termination of the strike. After the retraction in April of concessions earlier granted by the employers, Landauer argued that he had additional evidence of the betrayal; in *Der Sozialist* it was claimed that the hasty ending of the strike had proved to the employers that they had the power to withdraw the compromises without risking a new strike, while the workers, thoroughly demoralized, sustained their expectations.[109]

Undoubtedly Landauer had been guilty of some impracticality. In fact, the needle-trade workers would not have been able to improve their conditions until they were better organized. His "all or nothing" attitude, moreover, was in some degree the stance of a radical intellectual out of touch with the simple desires of hungry working people. At the same time, however, he may well have sensed that the SPD and the free trade unions connected with it had done little work in attempting to organize the workers because they had felt that the cause of an atomized, preindustrial group of exploited handworkers was hopeless. To feel that a certain group is unorganizable—as had been suggested in *Vorwärts*—and to call off a strike because of insufficient unionization was to condemn that group to continued economic misery. Looking for direct contact with lower-class social groups outside the hold of the SPD in Berlin, Landauer had attempted to organize the needle-trade workers for a long battle with their employers; when it failed, he blamed the failure entirely upon the commission of five, even though the failure was traceable to the weakness of the handworkers' position.[110] In any event, Landauer had begun, still within the confines of an urban metropolis, to champion the cause of social groups that were outside the party and trade unions of the SPD, at least in part because they were outside the process of modernization and industrialization. In his search for alternatives to SPD practice. Landauer had taken a small step away from the modern, industrial world. At the Socialist International Congress held in the summer of 1896 in London, he was to take another.

Although the anarchists had been formally excluded from the Second International at the Zurich Congress in 1893, anarchist and syndicalist currents were sufficiently strong in the French and Dutch labor parties for the issue to be raised again at the London Congress which met late in July 1896.[111] Many of the leading anarchists of Europe, including Peter Kropotkin and Errico Malatesta, were present at the London Congress in order to seek admission and, in the event that they were excluded, to set up their own congress.[112]

Again Landauer prepared a report on German Social Democracy which he had hoped to be able to deliver at the socialist congress. In the essay, published later in the year in English under the title *Social Democracy in Germany*, Landauer repeated many of the attacks that he had made in the earlier report of 1893, such as the charge that the SPD feared independent action by the masses only because it would then be unable to dominate "from above" and that its parliamentary work merely helped to strengthen the power of the state. The attack of 1896, however, incorporated some of the new directions in Landauer's thought: he placed strong emphasis this time, for example, upon the dependence and obedience of the oppressed classes as a major reason for the dominance of authoritarianism both in the general political life of Germany and in its official socialist movement. "Germany," he wrote, "enjoys the doubtful honor of being the home of monarchism and militarism. This imperialist and military spirit, this dependence and obedience of the masses exists, we are sorry to say, also in the poorest classes of the people, which are socially, politically and economically oppressed to the utmost—and the German Social Democratic party in the most shameful way uses this reactionary tendency of an oppressed people, this dependence of the masses, as the basis upon which an extremely strict party rule can be constructed, strong enough to crush on every occasion the rising germs of freedom and revolt." [113]

The question of admitting the anarchists was brought up on the first day of the congress. Paul Singer, the SPD leader, tried to have the vote taken before any of the anarchists were allowed to speak. As, however, the deputy chairman of the day was Keir Hardie, the leader of the British Independent Labor Party, who was not by any means a representative of orthodox social democracy, both sides were given a chance to state their case. Nieuwenhuis, Malatesta, and Landauer each spoke for the right of anarchist admission.[114] Landauer emphasized, once again, that anarchists were socialists and therefore belonged in the Second International; since we do not seek to exclude parliamentarians from the congress, he went on, "why, then, is our right not to serve parliamentarism denied?" In the account of Landauer's speech contained in the official protocols of the Second International it is stated that "after the translation of his talk Landauer climbed on a table and attempted to continue speaking after another speaker had already been called." [115] In the report of the proceedings in *Der Sozialist*, however, Landauer said that he was attempting to correct a mistranslation and climbed on the table to continue speaking only after he was denied the chance to do so.[116] Whatever version of the incident is correct, the result of the debate turned out as expected; on the second day of the congress, on a motion that again exempted trade unionists, the anarchists were expelled from the congress. Except for the Dutch delegation and the syndicalist faction in the divided French delegation, all the various national groups voted for expulsion.[117] The London Congress of 1896 was the last time the anarchists sought admission to the meetings of the Second International.

As they had done in Zurich, the anarchists held their own assembly after their expulsion from the London Congress. William Morris sent a message of support to the anarchist assembly and Keir Hardie and Tom Mann made speeches on the rights of minorities.[118] The anarchists themselves discussed numerous topics in the course of their three-day meeting. The topic that received closest attention, however, was the role of the peasantry in the creation of a free society. On this issue, of course, the anarchists were sharply divided from orthodox Marxists. In the view of the latter the proletarianization of the peasantry represented an inevitable and progressive development which would constitute a stage in the realization of socialism.[119] Anarchists, on the other hand, as George Woodcock has written, "have placed great hopes in the peasant. He is near to the earth, near to nature, and therefore more 'anarchic' in his reactions. . . . The peasant, moreover, is the heir to a long tradition of co-operation forced upon him by historical circumstances." [120]

Landauer had never addressed himself to the question of the peasantry. At the anarchist assembly in London in July 1896, this was the major topic, however, and he responded to the occasion with one of the major speeches of the meeting. After Malatesta and Nieuwenhuis had spoken generally about the importance of enlisting the peasantry in any attempt at social transformation, Landauer emphasized how cooperative enterprises, if sharply expanded among the peasants, could provide them with economic independence from the great landlords and be the beginning of real socialist activity.[121] Framing his argument as an alternative to Marxian thinking on the peasantry, Landauer said that

> Anarchists no longer believe in the fatalistic and jesuitical teaching of Marx which regards the concentration of capital and the destruction of the small peasant as necessary preconditions for the realization of socialism. . . . We desire that peasants prevent their proletarianization; as they unite with farm laborers in agricultural cooperatives, so the growth of large landed estates will be averted and organizations will be created which will serve as the kernel of a socialist society.[122]

In his search for social groups for which the SPD could have little appeal, Landauer had now found the small peasant in addition to the small handworker. His social thinking, however, was not fixed only upon new groups. The reorientation was more profound: he had begun to see the expansion of the urban, industrial proletariat through the absorption of the independent peasant and artisan as a process that must be resisted. Whereas earlier he had attempted, through the advocacy of workers' control of industry and other means, to work within the context of proletarian, urban, industrial growth—although hoping to direct it into anticapitalist and antiauthoritarian channels—Landauer now began to see industrial modernity as an essentially noxious world. The year 1896 saw his last attempt to seek entrance for the anarchists into the Second International; his relinquishment of such attempts, however, merely symbolizes the fact that after 1896 Landauer did not compete with the Social Democrats on their own ground. In the building of a world view that would contrast with that of the hated Social Democrats, Landauer had begun to add the anti-industrial social views of völkisch romanticism to his previously held anarchist beliefs.

## Isolation and Withdrawal

In the year and a half after the London Congress there were additional developments that isolated Landauer from the urban proletariat and, indeed, from almost all of Berlin's small anarchist movement, except for a diminishing circle of intellectuals. The crisis that cut off his active political life by 1898 began with a struggle within the editorial staff of *Der Sozialist*.

Up to 1897 the staff had been made up of a mixture of

intellectuals of middle-class background, such as Landauer and Stefan Grossman, the Viennese writer, and a number of self-educated workers, such as Paul Pawlowitsch, a metalworker.[123] For a number of years there had existed a conflict between the two groups concerning the proper function of the paper, a conflict that began as early as July 1893 when a group of "proletarian" (they are not further defined) readers wrote to *Der Sozialist* and complained of their difficulty in understanding the confusing array of viewpoints expressed in the newspaper.[124] From the beginning of his editorship in May 1893 Landauer had attempted to make *Der Sozialist* a paper in which discussion of varying viewpoints and a consistently high intellectual level would serve to educate the reader and encourage him to think for himself. In the years of militant struggle against the SPD by the Independents (1891–1893), and later against the Berlin police (1893–1894), *Der Sozialist* was by and large sufficiently entangled in the numerous struggles of the day for Landauer's hopes to be only partly realized. After August 1895, however, Landauer directed the paper into more theoretical channels; many philosophic questions were raised which were not systematically answered. The workers on the staff, led by Pawlowitsch, then demanded that the paper follow a more simple party line which would be less confusing to its readers; they argued that under Landauer's direction the paper had lost its propaganda value for the spread of anarchism, that its indefinite, many-sided approach and philosophical tone frightened away numerous potential adherents to the movement.

Conflict between the two groups continued because there were insufficient funds to produce two papers, one representing Landauer's thinking and the other a propaganda sheet. In August 1896 Landauer agreed to publish a small propaganda paper, named *Der Arme Konrad*, but it was not enough to satisfy Pawlowitsch and his group.[125] In May 1897 Landauer's opponents withdrew from *Der Sozialist* and began publication of a rival paper. Entitled *Neues Leben*, the new paper was written in a much simpler style and established a definite program; within months it had begun to draw away large groups of working-class readers from *Der Sozialist*: from a high point of 4,000 the number of readers soon dropped to less than 2,000. The financial help *Der Sozialist* had previously commanded now frequently went to the rival paper.[126] The effects of the split were politically disastrous for Landauer. As Rudolf Rocker wrote years later,

> . . . Landauer's "Sozialist" slowly died. Its death was a severe blow to the intellectual German movement. [Rocker apparently means the movement of intellectual anarchism.] The new paper [*Neues Leben*] was poorly edited and badly written, and it was little consolation to plead that it was produced entirely by ordinary working men. For Landauer it was a tragedy. It deprived him of a valuable activity, for which he was supremely fitted, and in which he rendered splendid services. It made him feel isolated and solitary.[127]

Because of dwindling readership and funds *Der Sozialist* was finally forced to cease publication in 1899. Before that, however, Landauer had another experience that revealed to him the extent to which he was isolated from both orthodox socialist and anarchist working-class groups. In the same month that the Pawlowitsch group withdrew from *Der Sozialist*, he set out on a speaking tour through Germany to gain new anarchist supporters. In travel reports he sent back to *Der Sozialist*, Landauer wrote disappointedly that in numerous cities his talks were attended almost entirely by curious SPD officials, "bourgeois" elements, and students and professors; a very small part of his audiences consisted of "working-class people." [128]

Landauer was not opposed to working with middle-class groups, of course, especially the intellectual and professional elements that might be attracted to social reform activity. He had, however, always expected that his social base would be predominately from the lower classes, and in the years before 1897 his frequent speeches at radical meetings in Berlin had indeed had a noticeable effect upon the predominately working-class audiences, as a fellow anarchist, Albert Weidner, wrote years later.[129] Nonetheless, as we have seen, in 1896 he had begun to seek out contacts with nonfactory workers and even small peasants because industrial proletarian groups were more and more controlled by the SPD and its gradualist unions. Now, in 1897, he was losing his former working-class readers and was unable to attract substantial numbers of new ones, either factory workers or urban handworkers.

In response to his increasing political isolation Landauer turned once again to the study of literature and philosophy. In 1892, after his first exposure to socialist ideas and the social struggles in Berlin, he had written that art could no longer be his central concern because "it requires rest; and we need struggle." Six years later, after the passing of the more turbulent early 1890s and the loss of contacts with the urban working classes, Landauer saw little point in continuing the "struggle" and withdrew into private study. In March 1898 he gave a series of twenty-one public lectures on the history of German literature; the lectures, significantly, were delivered at a Berlin concert hall and were not addressed to specifically working-class or socialist audiences. In an article announcing the series, Landauer wrote that he had abandoned the world of art six years before because he mistakenly had had a "limitless" faith in the ability of the proletariat to achieve its immediate liberation through revolution. He now saw, however, that "those among the proletariat who are interested in building socialism are today a disappearing minority"; the revolution is by no means at hand and he did not intend to be a useless martyr, for "there is nothing more useless than to play the martyr a few decades too early." As a result, he concluded, we now have time for "our inner liberation, the development of our spirit; . . . once again we have time for art." [130]

In 1898 Landauer withdrew from direct participation in the Berlin anarchist movement. The next ten years were to be devoted largely to private study and writing. In place of his dual life in 1893–1898 as political actor and political thinker, Landauer withdrew into philosophic reflection. Yet the comprehensive world view he began to develop after 1900, which incorporated mystical philosophy as well as libertarian and völkisch social thought, represented an enlarged and integrated version of many of the ideas he had developed in the 1890s. The idealist conception of authority which formed the basis of Landauer's anarchism after 1895 —the view that political authority and social oppression result from the dormancy of man's capacity for self-determination and voluntary cooperation—was broadened after 1900 into a vast idealist metaphysical system. The romantics' view of the individual as a unique reflection of community and humanity, which Landauer had developed in his *Sozialist* articles of early 1896 as a justification of anarchosocialism, was deepened through a study of mystical philosophy. Finally, the sociological reorientation of the mid-1890s, the shift from the urban industrial scene and the proletarian labor movement to such preindustrial social groups as handicraft workers and peasants, was developed into a völkisch antiurban conception of anarchism in the years after 1900. Although Landauer moved from political involvement to private study, the attitudes developed in the earlier activist years had left their mark.

# 3. The Consolations of Mysticism

Although in the years 1898–1903 Landauer began explicitly to ground his socialism in völkisch terms, he was primarily engaged in this half decade in more abstract metaphysical questions. His preoccupation with the problem of coping with his new political isolation led Landauer to mysticism; in these years he attempted to demonstrate the validity of the mystical doctrine that humanity and the universe lie within the individual soul. Mystic consciousness, however, was not to be separate from the fight to liberate social humanity; Landauer's mysticism figured in many aspects of his romantic socialism.

In June 1900, a few months after the demise of *Der Sozialist*, Landauer gave a lecture entitled "Through Isolation to Community" in which he stated:

> Monstrous and almost inexpressibly huge is the distance that now separates us—we who consider ourselves the advance guard—from the rest of humanity. . . . What is decisive here is not greater knowledge or ability but different interests and views of life. With ardor we have gone into the Volk in order to raise it, awaken it, purify it, stimulate it to anger and rebellion, call it to beauty and greatness, finally to organize it into new social and economic associations. . . . Now we, who have gone into the Volk, have returned from our migration. A few of us have been lost, either to a party or to our own despair. We have brought something back with us: isolated men. Isolated men we have fished out of the sea of everyday life; more we have not found. Through pain and struggle, however, we have gained this knowledge: we have gone too far in front to be understood by the masses. . . . Our realization is that we should not go down to the

masses, we must lead the way for them, and that will seem for the time being as if we are going away from them. The community we long for and need we will find only if we separate ourselves as individuals; then we will at last find, in the innermost core of our hidden being, the most ancient and most universal community: the human race and the cosmos. Whoever has discovered this joyous community in himself is enriched and blessed for all time and is finally removed from the common accidental communities of our age.[1]

Faced with the collapse of *Der Sozialist* after the decline of its readership and the depletion of its financial resources in 1897 and 1898, Landauer attempted to change his political isolation from a liability into an asset; true community, he argued, must first be discovered in the soul of the individual. Mystical belief, the conception that within the spiritual interior of the individual, humanity and the universe are contained, was called upon to mitigate the pains of isolation. Landauer was quite aware that this mystical view provided philosophic compensation for him:

. . . my inner feeling that I am an isolated unity can be false, and I declare it to be false because I cannot be satisfied with this horrible isolation. I must, however, know what I should do with this feeling. I abandon the feeling of being a single one, of which I seemed to be sure, and I drive out into the heights, into the wild sea of postulates and fantasies. I renounce the certainty of my "I" so that I will be able to bear existence. I build myself a new world with the consciousness that I have no basis upon which to build except necessity. . . . The "I" kills itself so that the "World-I" may live. . . . We allow the world to go through us, we create the conditions of readiness to feel it in us, we allow ourselves to be grasped and seized by it.[2]

After 1897, as political isolation grew, the attractiveness of personal mysticism grew with it. Only now was Landauer fully receptive—given his feeling that "monstrous and almost inexpressibly huge is the distance that now separates us . . . from the rest of humanity"—to teachings that stressed the indwelling nature of community, humanity, and cosmos. Besides *Skepsis und Mystik* (1903), the major effort of these years of political inactivity, Landauer's personal contacts and reading attest to this direction of interest.

By the late 1890s Landauer's earlier hope in the possibility of imminent radical social change had vanished. He was aware that the economic upswing after 1895 had eliminated, at least for the time being, much of the proletarian discontent that had marked the Berlin of the early 1890s. "We live in the stage of reaction, which has become unbearable for only relatively few persons from the various levels of the population," he wrote in 1899. "The passionate resistance against existing conditions is on the decrease, not the increase, among the great masses of the industrial proletariat. . . . The economic upswing has done its work; the hunger question is no longer so pressing, while the enthusiasm for cultural ideals has never been very strong among the masses." [3] Within the Social Democratic Party Eduard Bernstein began to raise much the same issue at this time. For the revisionists, however, the refutation of Marx's predictions concerning the inevitability of revolution as the result of increasing social polarization constituted the negative argument for a positive defense of the parliamentary road to socialism. Landauer commented on the similarity of his observations to those of the revisionists in the following way: "The exploitative society and the authoritarian state will not die by themselves. At this point, where the new Social Democrats and the anarchists are united, the two part company. Therefore we should direct ourselves into this society and state, they say. Therefore we should destroy them, we say." [4]

How does one begin to destroy them, however? The answer cannot be through direct, violent assault; it must be through the discovery of an alternative community: ". . . if we sink down deep into ourselves as individuals, then we will at last find, in the innermost core of our hidden being, the most ancient and most universal community: the human race and the cosmos." For the sources and development of this view it is necessary to examine Landauer's personal life and philosophical interests in the years after 1897.

## Sources of Mystical Belief:
### Philosophic and Personal Experience

In March 1899 Landauer was sentenced to six months in jail for having written a "libelous" attack on the Berlin commissioner of police in the pages of *Der Sozialist*. In the preceding year Landauer had become involved in the campaign of Moritz von Egidy, the ex-officer turned Christian pacifist, to free a certain man named Ziethen from jail. In the hope of gaining a retrial for Ziethen, who had been sentenced to life imprisonment for the alleged murder of his wife, Landauer wrote a lead article in *Der Sozialist*, in February 1898, accusing the police commissioner of having falsified documents in his effort to prove the case against Ziethen. Six months later Landauer repeated the charges in a circular that he sent to members of the Reichstag and the state attorney's office. When a trial was finally held, in March 1899, Landauer was convicted of libel and sentenced to six months in jail.[5]

Despite his conviction Landauer's spirits were high in

March 1899. A month earlier he had met a young, sensitive poetess named Hedwig Lachmann and immediately became infatuated with her. His life with his first wife had for some time been unbearable for Landauer. In October 1898 he had written to his cousin Hugo that his wife Grete was jealous of every moment spent away from her and "needed a husband who could not live for a second without a wife." His relationship with her "could not go on." [6] Since Grete became very ill in the early part of 1899, however, Landauer's concern for her precluded an immediate divorce.[7] Yet by March he was in love with another woman. Two days after his jail sentence was handed down, he wrote Hugo: "It's not my fault that in the midst of all this misery I cannot destroy an uncommon inner happiness, . . . the rare joy that I have finally found an intellectually accomplished, spiritually mature feminine creature." [8] In the months ahead Landauer's emotional attachment to Hedwig grew; in August, immediately before beginning his prison term, he wrote Hedwig of the emptiness of the life of human isolation and of his need for profound involvement with others: "I just read a statement of Nietzsche's: 'Do not remain attached to a person, even the most beloved —every person is a prison.' Oh God how I need this prison! And what is freedom but an empty, brutal thing if we do not surrender ourselves with our whole soul a thousand times!" [9]

Hedwig was born in Krumbach, a village in Swabia, in 1865, the daughter of a cantor in the predominantly Jewish town. In the years preceding her connection with Landauer she had gained some recognition as a lyrical poetess and translator. She had a deeply withdrawn personality and it was not until 1901 that Landauer was able to convince her to live with him. In 1903 Landauer was finally divorced from his first wife and soon after married Hedwig.[10] According to Stefan Grossman, one of Landauer's closest associates in the last years of *Der Sozialist* in the late 1890s, Landauer's separation from his first wife and his relationship with Hedwig after 1899 had "symbolic, ideological significance which went beyond his private life." Grete was a "proletarian" and Landauer's separation from her symbolized, according to Grossman, the fact that Landauer had abandoned the struggles of the urban working class and had withdrawn, with Hedwig, into personal mysticism. Grossman illustrated his point by comparing the content of *Der Sozialist* in its second appearance after 1909 with that of the first *Sozialist* in the years before 1899: "The newspaper had shifted more to questions of the soul [*Seelenfrage*]; no longer was Landauer tied to a young proletarian woman but to the tender breath of a lyrical artist." [11] Hedwig was certainly more attuned to, and may indeed have contributed to, Landauer's mystical, romantic views after the political failures of the 1890s.

While in prison in the fall and winter of 1899–1900, Landauer wrote a short novel which he entitled *Lebendig tot* ("In Living Death"). In this partly autobiographical work —Landauer wrote later of having "set down [his] *Seelenleben* in it" [12]—the main character is a man who passes from a purely sensual, physical relationship with a woman to one based upon love. When the second woman dies bearing his child, however, the man, now condemned to a "living death" in spiritual isolation from others, interprets the fortuitous event as the result of a curse laid upon him through his earlier addiction to purely animal instincts. Speaking of his relationship with his first wife, he says: "I lived all those years with a woman whom my senses loved and almost constantly desired, but who was to me almost nothing,

nothing at all; . . . we hated ourselves and had to hurt each other." [13] In his actual life, however, Landauer had "finally found an intellectually accomplished, spiritually mature" woman with whom he lived happily until she died in the influenza epidemic of 1918, one year before his own death.

With a strong relationship already established with Hedwig by the time he entered prison in August 1899, Landauer was able to bear the lonely existence of a prison cell with considerable equanimity. He wrote to Hedwig, for example, that the modern prison afforded him the same kind of inner peace that the cloister offered the medieval man.[14] The long hours were spent by Landauer in various literary tasks. Besides writing the short novel, *Lebendig tot*, Landauer performed the large task of carefully arranging the manuscripts of his friend Fritz Mauthner's massive language studies so that they would be ready for publication.[15] These studies were to provide for Landauer a point of departure for his own major philosophical work, *Skepsis und Mystik*, on which he worked in the two years after his release from prison early in 1900. Other work in prison was of greater importance, however, in developing the mystical philosophy expressed in *Skepsis*: in the months of cloistered isolation, Landauer studied and translated the sermons of the medieval German mystic, Meister Eckhart. When his Eckhart translations were published in 1903, Landauer wrote in the notes that his own study, *Skepsis und Mystik*, "comes back again and again to Eckhart." [16]

Meister Eckhart, who has been called the "father of German idealism," [17] taught that man cannot find God and truth either through the use of his physical senses or through external activities, but only through an awareness of their presence in the interior reaches of the soul. In one sermon translated by Landauer, Eckhart wrote:

> St. Augustine says: "There are many people who have sought light and truth, but they look for it outside themselves, where it is not." And then they finally get so far off the track that they cannot find their way back to the care of their souls and they never discover the truth, for truth is at the core of the soul and not outside the man. To be enlightened and discerning, cherish the birth of God's Son in the core of the soul and then the soul's forces will be illuminated [*alle Kräfte . . . erleuchtet*], and the outward man as well.[18]

In order to find the Kingdom of God in the soul it is necessary, at first, to withdraw completely from the external world; to the degree that this is accomplished will one be able to perceive the truth within. In the sermon that Landauer entitled "On Silence," Eckhart had written:

> When all the faculties are withdrawn from all action and ideation, then this word is spoken. Thus he spoke: "In the midst of silence was a secret word spoken to me." The more you can withdraw all the faculties and forget things and images you have received before, . . . the nearer you are to this [word] and the more sensitive to it you will be; . . . so should man escape his senses and introvert his faculties until he achieves forgetfulness of things and self.[19]

Translated into the language of a more secular mysticism, one that substituted "humanity," "cosmos," "Volk," and the like for Eckhart's "God," these sermons provided for Landauer a comforting view of his relation to the world. His apparent isolation disappeared when he believed that community and humanity could not first be found in the external world, which was obviously a frustrating disappointment, but must be discovered in the interior of the individual soul; here, beyond the reach of the "accidental" institutions, parties, and economic relations of the day, dwelt eternal humanity and the world. A few months after his release from prison Landauer wrote to Hedwig of this conception, which he called his "favorite idea" (*Lieblingsgedanken*), one that substituted the humanity within for the chance institutions of the state and capitalism without:

> . . . next to the authoritarian chance communities that surround us, there is something that is different, and greater, something that coincides with the deepest essence of the individual. . . . The deeper we climb down into the tunnels of our individual life, all the more are we in a real community with the race, humanity, the animal world, and finally, if we withdraw from conceptual thoughts and sensate appearances and sink into our most hidden depths, we are participant in the whole unending world. For this world lives in us, it is our origin, that is, it is continuously working in us; otherwise we cease to be what we are. The deepest part of our individual selves is that which is most universal.[20]

In this connection Landauer wrote years later to Julius Bab: "From the outside, of course, the sequence is viewed: individual–Volk–humanity; internally, in my own individuality, on the contrary, I am . . . first an animal, then a man, then a Jew, German and south German, and then this special I." [21] Landauer often called himself a mystic,[22] yet his mysticism was terrestrial. Eckhart's Christianity was not for him; Landauer sought union with secular humanity.

Landauer shared his interest in Eckhart with many other romantic idealists in Germany. Eugen Diederichs, for example, the publisher of Landauer's lecture "Through Isolation to Community," who was an important figure in the transmission of mystical, völkisch ideas to the more sophisticated reading public in Germany after the turn of the century, was profoundly concerned with Eckhart and published his complete works.[23] Interest in Eckhart tended to fuse with the cult that was developing around the similar mystical theories of the eighteenth-century Swede, Emanuel Swedenborg. The man who possibly more than any other exerted the widest influence in the 1890s in the spread of völkisch views, Julius Langbehn, whose *Rembrandt als Erzieher* was read by millions, "transformed [Swedenborg] . . . into a German mystic whose function was equated with that performed by the medieval mystic Meister Eckhart"; these two thinkers "became pivotal" for Langbehn "in providing the Volk with the spiritual mysticism that would lead it to its goal." Landauer's mystical belief that the "world lives in us, it is our origin, . . . it is continuously working in us," which he found in Eckhart's sermons, closely paralleled Langbehn's views based upon Swedenborg.[24]

The ideational parallel between Landauer, the anarchist, and Langbehn, the völkisch thinker of the extreme Right, is only part of the story; for Langbehn, Swedenborgian mysticism provided comfort for an even more isolated social existence than Landauer's. According to his most recent analyst, Langbehn "alternately cherished and resented his self-constructed isolation. . . . Gradually he faded into a phantom world of his own, remote from reality, surrounded by books, pictures, fears, and day-dreams, obsessed by thoughts about himself." [25] Even in the years after 1898 Landauer's life was never cut off from others to such an extent; his isolation was a matter of political failures, not of private life. This may explain, in part, the fact that Landauer's mysticism was dedicated to the service of humane goals while Langbehn's overall social views have earned him the designation of "proto-Nazi." [26]

In later years Landauer discovered many other poets and philosophers whose views of man as a microcosm were similar to those of Meister Eckhart. In an essay on Walt Whitman, written in 1913, Landauer stated that "the idea that man bears the entire world in his inner spirit, that the world is an unending wealth of microcosms, is only a new form of an eternal teaching of philosophers and mystics, Indian, medieval, Renaissance—all the way to Berkeley and Fichte." [27] It was precisely because of this shared belief that in later years Landauer felt himself to be akin not only to Walt Whitman, but also to the great German poet Hölderlin and the Russian Tolstoi. The latter figure, however, was particularly important for Landauer because Tolstoi had utilized this mystical belief as the theoretical basis upon which to build the argument for a nonviolent, pacifist anarchism.

As we have seen earlier, Landauer could not accept terrorist violence. With his separation from the Berlin anarchist movement in the late 1890s, he renewed his attack upon it; this time, however, his argument was built upon ethical and mystical beliefs he had developed through contacts with the thought of Eckhart and Tolstoi. The link between Eckhart's mysticism and Landauer's defense of pacifism centered upon Eckhart's notion of the "eternal moment" as the locus of the religious experience. In a sermon that Landauer entitled "On the City of the Soul," Eckhart had said:

> If the spirit were only always united with God . . . a man could never grow old. For the Now-moment, in which God made the first man, and the Now-moment in which the last man will disappear, and the Now-moment in which I am speaking, are all one in God, in whom there is only one Now. Look! The person who lives in the light of God is conscious neither of time past nor of time to come but only of the one eternity. In fact, he is bereft of wonder, for all things are intrinsic in him. Therefore, he gets nothing new out of future events, nor from chance, for he lives in the present moment.[28]

Stated simply, this mystical belief had political significance as a refutation of the common separation of ends and
means in which statesmen, parties, and revolutionaries indulged. Landauer found this refutation in the political
thought of Tolstoi. Although it is uncertain if Landauer
read Tolstoi at this time, his frequent allusion to the Russian
writer in the years 1898–1901 is not surprising, since Tolstoi's anarchist pacifism was widely discussed in libertarian
circles in Germany in the late 1890s,[29] and frequent articles
on his views appeared in the pages of *Der Sozialist* in 1898
and 1899.[30] After an anarchist assassinated America's President McKinley in 1901, Landauer wrote an article on the
subject of terrorism for Maximilian Harden's *Die Zukunft.*
Here he echoed Tolstoi's stress upon the necessity of ethical and nonviolent activity in the present, the refusal to
separate future ends and present means, in a thorough condemnation of revolutionary violence:

What has the murder of persons to do with anarchism, the
teaching of a society without the state and without authoritarian force? Nothing at all. . . . The anarchists are, for
me, not anarchistic enough; they are still a political party.
. . . That is the great error of the revolutionary anarchists,
with whom I have participated long enough: the idea of
being able to reach the ideal of powerlessness through power.
. . . These are self-deceptions; every act of force is dictatorship. . . . The anarchists must realize that a goal can be
reached only if the means to this goal are already bathed in
the color of it. One will never arrive at nonviolence through
violence. Anarchy is there, where there are anarchists, real
anarchists, men, that is, who no longer practice force. With
all this I am saying nothing new; it is the same thing that
has been said for a long time by Tolstoi. . . . Anarchy is
not a thing of the future, but of the present; not a matter of
demands, but of living.[31]

In a piece written in 1912 Landauer continued his argument by contrasting Kropotkin's future-oriented suspension of present moral absolutes with Tolstoi's injunction to live morally in the here and now, for this alone would constitute a revolution:

> Tolstoi seems to say: . . . you men think too much about the environment, the future, and others; you separate means and ends too much, as if an end could be gained in this way. You think that questionable means are justified by a noble goal. For us, however, the moment alone exists; do not sacrifice reality to a phantom! If you want the proper life then live it now. . . . Tolstoi brings the absolute into life; Kropotkin is a positivist and therefore a relativist and allows for the revolutionaries, even violence, if it must be.[32]

What, however, was one to be conscious of in this present? Landauer felt certain that if man recognizes, right now in the present, before any social or institutional changes have been made, that he is fundamentally rooted in humanity, that the deepest part of his soul contains the whole world, then he will be "reborn," will cease to ape the behavior of the authoritarian state, and will begin to build community with his fellows. Mysticism and nonviolent, communitarian anarchism are fused in Landauer's conception of "spiritual rebirth," the political romantic's translation of Eckhart's view of religious conversion. In the *Zukunft* article of 1901, written within two years of his intensive study of Eckhart, Landauer wrote:

> If all the anarchists knew how their ideas touch the deepest soil of the essence of man, . . . they would shudder in recognition of the chasm that yawns between their action, their shallow behavior, and the depths of their *Weltanschauung*. . . . Whoever kills, dies himself. Whoever wants to create life must live anew and be reborn again from within. . . . The way to a new, higher form of human society leads

through the dark, fateful gate of our instincts and the *terra abscondita* of our soul, which is our world. Only from within to without can the world be formed. . . . There will be anarchists and anarchy, here and there, separate and dispersed; they will find each other; they will kill nothing but themselves in a mystic death that leads through the deepest contemplation to rebirth. . . . Not to kill others, but rather one's own self: that will be the characteristic of the man who works with his own chaos in order to find what is best and most primeval in him so that he may be mystically one with the world, so that what he effects in the world seems to have flown into it from an unknown world within him. . . . To him the world will be as himself and he will love it as himself. These men will live with one another in community, as fellows. This is anarchy, . . . not more war and murder, but rebirth. Whoever awakes to the passing world in himself, to a new life, to individual life, whoever feels himself as a ray of the world [*Strahl der Welt*], does not feel that he is a stranger [*nicht als Fremden*].[33]

Landauer's social and political thought now included perspectives derived from religious mysticism. According to Hans Kohn, Landauer's conception of revolution was directly related to a religious view of conversion. "In Landauer's view," Kohn writes, "the moment of religious belief was to be felt more strongly; in the midpoint of his social philosophy stood the religious message of spiritual convulsion [*Erschütterung*] and conversion."[34] Mystic awareness, not rationalism, was for Landauer the cure for terrorism, either by the state or by violent anarchists. Whereas for most observers anarchist terrorism was the result of emotional fanaticism born of irrationality, Landauer placed the blame upon the terrorists' addiction to a mechanistic and cold logic; the problem was not that they were too emotional but, on the contrary, that they were too much given to purely mental abstractions:

Anarchists have been, up to now, too much the systematizers and have been constricted in fixed narrow concepts; this is, finally, the last answer to the question as to why anarchists regard killing men as something worthwhile. They have accustomed themselves to living with concepts, no longer with men. There are two fixed, separate classes for them, who stand opposed to each other as enemies; they don't kill men but the concept of exploiters, suppressors, state representatives. . . . They have cut themselves off from the life of feeling; they exist as beings of pure thought, who are dependent, like Robespierre, on the goddess of reason, who separates and passes judgment. From the judgments of a cold, inwardly unaware, unliving logic, one that is an enemy of life, are these cold death sentences declared which please these anarchists. Anarchy, however, is not the distinct, cold, and intelligible thing that these anarchists are accustomed to; if anarchy would become for them a dark, deep dream, instead of a conceptually accessible world [*eine begrifflich erreichbare Welt*], then their ethos and their action would be consistent.[35]

Landauer had concluded by 1901 that mystical consciousness of the existence of humanity in the individual soul was an essential component of any nonviolent society. Developed under the influence of Eckhart's sermons and Tolstoi's pacifist teachings, Landauer's mystical beliefs were to form a permanent part of his social philosophy. Before Landauer attempted, in *Skepsis und Mystik* (1903), to demonstrate the validity of these beliefs, however, his social thought developed the distinctly völkisch romantic cast in which he was to frame them.

## The Emergence of a Völkisch Socialist

Landauer's social contacts in the years after 1898 both reflected and contributed to his development of a socialist philosophy framed in the antiurban, anti-industrial terms of the völkisch, romantic tradition. In the year before he entered prison in the summer of 1899, this shift in orientation had been strengthened through his involvements with both Hedwig Lachmann and Moritz von Egidy, the man with whom Landauer had worked in the Ziethen affair.

In the last year of his life von Egidy made a very strong impression on Landauer. In January 1899 an entire issue of *Der Sozialist* was devoted to him as a memorial. In it Landauer wrote of von Egidy: "I have lost more in this man than I may ever hope to gain again in life. I loved and respected him as scarcely any man has been loved and respected." [36] When von Egidy died, Landauer wrote a year later, he "still had so much more to offer to our Volk." [37] What had he already offered, however? What did Landauer find valuable in von Egidy's life and thought? The passages Landauer selected from von Egidy's writings for inclusion in the *Sozialist* memorial issue provide a clue to this question. All of these gave expression to von Egidy's anarchist pacifism and völkisch mysticism. A former army officer, he was profoundly opposed to the use of force and violence in human affairs. In one passage selected for inclusion in the memorial issue, von Egidy had written: "Unthinking men connect the idea of 'Anarchie' with the idea of disorder; that, however, is contained neither in the word nor in the strivings of those who call themselves anarchists. On the contrary: a more complete order, an order that rests upon self-discipline and self-rule; an order without force." [38]

Pacifist anarchism was, however, only one aspect of von Egidy's social thought. A different component revealed his connection with the ideology of völkisch romanticism; the proper units of a social "order without force," von Egidy maintained, were the family, the local community, and the Volk. In another passage selected by Landauer for inclusion in the *Sozialist* tribute, von Egidy had written:

> What is required is that each individual free himself from every association—whether it be an economic, political, or confessional one—which sets up doctrines of force or in some other way sets him against a *Volksgenosse*. . . . We must remove ourselves from every unnatural union—family, *Gemeinde* [local community], and Volk are natural unions —and come together voluntarily under this view: to serve the whole and every individual within the community with precisely the same fidelity and love. . . . The real idea that is at the basis of present efforts at transformation is the desire for the independence and autonomy of the individual, the local community, and the Volk.[39]

Von Egidy's religious, pacifist anarchism was not directed to any specific social groups within German society; it was aimed, rather, at both the individual and the Volk as a whole. In view of the fact that Landauer's thought was developing in the direction of a fusion of anarchist and völkisch currents, it is significant than von Egidy's impact in Berlin in the 1890s was precisely in these two directions. His association with the anarchists of *Der Sozialist* had begun with his participation in the Befreiung cooperative in 1895 and 1896[40] and had continued through his talks at their public forum, the Freie anarchistisch-sozialistischen Vereinigung in Berlin.[41] His closest friends, however, were not anarchists but a group of young men who were later to play important roles in the process by which völkisch ideology was institutionalized in early twentieth-century Germany. According to a leading student of the völkisch movement, von Egidy, "by gathering around him in his Berlin apartment a small circle of friends, . . . exerted an influence on the völkisch movement that made it more readily acceptable to more sophisticated young people. . . . Hermann Lietz, one of Egidy's closer disciples, played a key role . . . in institutionalizing völkisch thought through education."[42] Two other disciples of von Egidy, Ferdinand Schöll and Kurt Wilhelmi, were leaders of the movement to actualize völkisch thought through the establishment of separate, utopian communities on the land; Wilhelmi was the founder of the utopian colony Eden, and Schöll was the leader of another "Germanic utopia," Vogelhof.[43]

In von Egidy's teachings Landauer found the view that the proper units of social life are not classes, but rather the family, the Gemeinde, and the Volk. In addition, von Egidy held the view that the reconstruction of social life must begin with the individual's own change of perspective. Atomization and social isolation, which Landauer had known only too well, were seen here as necessary momentary prerequisites for the construction of a freely chosen social reintegration. If social life was to be noncoercive, it must be based upon the decisions made by the individual on his own; atomization was seen as a transitional stage necessary to assure the fact that community, when it develops—and von Egidy, like Landauer, felt that it must—would be built, unforced, from below. "We must disorganize, we must atomize ourselves," Landauer quoted from von Egidy; "we must remove ourselves from every unnatural union—family, Gemeinde, and Volk are natural unions—and, after free self-determination, come together in this view: to serve the whole and every individual within the community with precisely the same fidelity and love."[44] Von Egidy's view prefigured Landauer's statement in his talk, "Through Isolation to Community," delivered in 1900, that "the community we long for and need we will find only if we separate ourselves from the old communities, . . . if we thoroughly isolate ourselves."

While Landauer had cited von Egidy's social views with approval, later experiences, in 1900 and 1901, were to be of more lasting significance in developing his völkisch socialism. It was only after participating in discussions among the so-called Neue Gemeinschaft circle of young Berlin intellectuals that Landauer explicitly framed his anarchism in these terms. His participation in this circle reflected again his withdrawal from the struggles of the working-class socialist movement, as Max Nettlau, the historian of anarchism, has pointed out. Noting that Landauer's participation in the Neue Gemeinschaft brought him into contact primarily with middle-class idealists, poets and writers, Nettlau writes: "At that time, after the experiences in the milieu of *Der Sozialist*, Landauer moved into a circle of ethical and humanitarian strivings and poetic-artistic expression . . . [connected with the literary figures] Heinrich and Julius Hart." [45] In May 1900 Landauer wrote to Hedwig that his "solitary life [had been] . . . interrupted" through meetings with this group.[46] It was to them that he was to deliver his important talk, "Through Isolation to Community."

Landauer's participation in the circle was not based upon any deep respect for its founders, Heinrich and Julius Hart. He regarded the books of these former literary critics, who now described themselves as philosophers of a "new humanity," as abstract and empty word games. In a review of the Harts' *Die Neue Welterkenntnis* ("The New Perception of the World"), Landauer wrote that "in piling up words upon words they have lost all relation to reality; where they are ecstatic, . . . to me it is a matter of empty playing with words." Instead of their sophistry what is needed is that "Our will form a picture of the world which it can comprehend and love and, in harmony with this picture, form our life and our institutions." [47]

The circle attracted Landauer because it provided an escape from his political isolation. Here at least he had an audience for his views. He still hoped to resume his journalistic activity,[48] but in the meantime participation in the Neue Gemeinschaft would have to suffice. The group interested Landauer also because it attracted numerous idealistic young persons to its meetings (which were held, significantly, in a home on Uhlandstrasse, a street in one of Berlin's middle-class districts).[49] It was Landauer's hope, no doubt, that after his failure to retain contacts within the Berlin labor movement he might be able to rally groups of the new generation of young intellectuals. He was overjoyed, for example, at the enthusiastic response that greeted his "Through Isolation to Community" lecture. After the dismal failures of the late 1890s, Landauer was only too happy to find a receptive audience among the younger generation. He wrote to Hedwig concerning the reception of his talk:

> There were perhaps sixty persons there, writers, artists, musicians. . . . The impression seemed to me to be strong and sustained. . . . Naturally I am not allowing myself any illusions; there were many there who were merely drawn by the sensation, . . . but it is beautiful to see in others that they have come to what is in the air. A young generation is there which can form a point of crystallization.[50]

Landauer's reception by these young bourgeois intellectuals reflected the fact that he was very much in step with the neoromantic mood that was spreading among the younger generation around the turn of the century. The revolt against positivism, which for the past decade or so had been primarily an enterprise of some leading German professors, was now showing signs of becoming a mass phenomenon. Three years before Landauer joined the circle of the Neue Gemeinschaft, for example, the German youth movement had its beginnings among middle-class students in the humanistic gymnasium of Steglitz, a bourgeois suburb of Berlin. The movement, which spread rapidly after 1901, although it did not go much beyond the organizing of hikes in the woods and the singing of folk songs, represented a revolt against the cramped life of the German authoritarian public school, as well as against parental authority. The desire to escape from the cities, moreover, as well as the cultivation of a mystical language focused on an ineffable and irrational *Erlebnis*, revealed how closely the movement was tied to the current of neoromanticism. The bourgeois youths who joined the Wandervogel, as the various groups were called, were united in a common dissatisfaction with modern urban and industrial civilization and the dull parliamentary liberalism that was one of its symbols.[51]

What were the political implications of this youth movement? Especially after 1912 or so the youth movement exhibited some anti-Semitism, and many veterans of the movement were associated largely with the political Right during the later Weimar Republic. The opposition to urban, industrial civilization which the youth movement represented might conceivably have moved more in the direction of the organized political Left, however, if this part of the spectrum had not been solely represented in Germany by a party that seemed to have lost all revolutionary élan and was engaged in the same unromantic parliamentarism as the despised liberals.[52] The mood of the early youth movement was antiauthoritarian and antiparliamentarian; such trends did not preclude left-wing groups, which in fact existed within it.[53] The organized political Left suffered so much in

Germany from the neoromantic mood of the young after
1900 because the political Left in Germany was the SPD.
SPD dominance on the Left was due largely to Germany's
rapid industrialization and urbanization after 1870, developments that favored the kind of mass, bureaucratic, and centralized party that emerged; but this is a matter that concerns Germany's social history, not neoromanticism as such.

To Landauer the young intellectuals of the Neue Gemeinschaft might be able to "form a point of crystallization"
precisely because it was unlikely that they would be absorbed within the SPD, as had most of the Berlin proletariat
in the course of the past decade. Among those for whom
Landauer was a "leader and teacher" in the Neue Gemeinschaft were Erich Mühsam, poet and later anarchist leader
during the Bavarian Revolution, and Martin Buber, the
great Jewish philosopher and formulator of a libertarian,
religious socialism.[54] Neither the youthful neoromantics of
the Neue Gemeinschaft, nor those of the Wandervogel,
joined the orthodox political Left in Germany. In his discussion of factors that limited SPD strength after the turn
of the century, Carl Landauer has written:

> In the period preceding the First World War, the direct
> numerical effect of the antirationalistic trend was not great.
> The young workers were not yet much affected by the
> *Wandervogel* spirit, and there was hardly a trace of anti-
> rationalism in the "adult" party, or among the voters who
> cast the party ticket. But the new antirationalism reduced
> further the small but highly important influx of idealistic
> young intellectuals into the ranks of the Social Democratic
> party. The number of young people who joined the liberal
> parties decreased even more.[55]

Through their common participation in the circle around
the brothers Hart, Landauer exercised a strong influence
upon the young neoromantic intellectual Martin Buber.

According to Hans Kohn, "the meeting with the friend who was six years older was a landmark in his [Buber's] life. From that point until Landauer's death, a close friendship bound these two men. Buber's views concerning man's life in community were decisively influenced by Landauer." The two shared, first of all, a lively interest in mysticism. While Landauer had been working intensively on the writings of Eckhart, Buber lectured in the Neue Gemeinschaft circle on Jacob Böhme, and soon after began work on the Chasidic Jewish mystics.[56] The social philosophy Buber developed in later years was, like Landauer's, intimately connected with his philosophic idealism and mysticism and, in many ways, closely resembled Landauer's.[57]

Besides the talks on mysticism presented by Landauer and Buber, the discussions in the Neue Gemeinschaft were largely concerned with the question of how to begin the building of a new community outside the institutions of the present. When inviting Erich Mühsam to the circle, Heinrich Hart had communicated to him the desire to found a small communitarian settlement on the land, to "acquire a piece of land and there set an example as a forerunner of a socially united, great working commune of humanity." [58] Within the Neue Gemeinschaft a degree of communal living was soon in operation. Landauer, who was living apart from his first wife and had not yet begun to live with Hedwig, joined Mühsam and a number of other young poets and writers in what Mühsam called a "Tischgemeinschaft," or boarding community, as all of them lived and cooked together. The similarity of this life to the spirit of the Wandervogel is quite obvious. Moreover, according to Mühsam, the young intellectuals in the Neue Gemeinschaft spent much of their time debating the precise arrangements that would prevail in the *Siedlung,* or settlement, they would set up on the land.[59]

For Landauer, however, a friendly community debating society was not enough. He was gradually convinced that the will for concrete action was very weak in the group and that the mood was created by the empty pomposity of the brothers Hart.[60] The Neue Gemeinschaft, Martin Buber wrote years later, taught Landauer "how community does *not* originate." [61]

Nonetheless the discussions concerning the beginning of a Siedlung away from the life of the modern city had an important influence on Landauer's social thought. By the late 1890s he had become disillusioned with the Berlin labor movement. The full shift from an urban to a rural orientation, however, was mediated by Landauer's contact, after 1898, with primarily middle-class intellectuals. Among this group völkisch thinking was becoming increasingly pervasive. Through the public schools and the universities of Germany, the sons and daughters of professional and business people, who made up the bulk of the students in these educational establishments, were educated in the tradition of German idealism in connection with the völkisch rejection of urban and industrial modernity.[62]

A few months after he left the Neue Gemeinschaft circle Landauer made explicit his reformulation of the nature of anarchist society. It was not to be a victory of certain classes, but the emergence of a new organic Volk which would migrate from the cities and establish communitarian Siedlungen on the land. In the same article in which Landauer developed a mystical basis for the rejection of force and violence, his path toward a völkisch socialism was culminated:

Anarchy is not a thing of the future, but of the present; not a matter of demands, but of living. It is not a matter of the nationalization of acquisitions made in the past, but of a new Volk which, through internal migration and in the midst of other Völkern, forms itself into new communities out of small beginnings. Finally, it is not a matter of a class struggle of nonpossessors against possessors, but the union into new structures of free, inwardly strong, and self-ruled beings who have disengaged themselves from the mass. . . . All will work together, for a communal socialism, for consumer and living cooperatives in the settlement [Siedlung]; public gardens and libraries will be founded, cities will be abandoned, one will work with spade and shovel as the external life will be simplified to gain space for the luxuriant life of the spirit.[63]

Landauer did not give full expression to his antiurban social views until 1907, when he began to concentrate once again upon questions of a directly social nature. In 1901 he was primarily concerned with the elaboration of the mystical philosophy that resulted in his work, *Skepsis und Mystik*, published two years later. Nevertheless, there is evidence of an increasing völkisch emphasis in the first years of the decade. Besides his advocacy of rural communitarian colonies, he himself abandoned the big city: in 1903 he moved to Hermsdorf, a small, old village outside Berlin.[64] According to his associate Stefan Grossman, "Landauer, who stemmed from the Swabian area, always required a sense of stillness. He could never bear the big city. Moreover, he had a preference for work in a small Gemeinde." [65] In the year 1903 Landauer participated in meetings of the Deutsche Gartenstadt Gesellschaft,[66] an organization based upon the English Garden City Association and founded by Landauer's old acquaintance, Bernard Kampffmeyer, and Adolf Otto, the brother-in-law of Hedwig Lachmann.[67] The organization, which included a number of figures directly connected with the völkisch movement, such as the painter Fidus and the land reformer Adolf Damaschke, as well as the utopian socialist Franz Oppenheimer,[68] was concerned with replacing the mass metropolis with smaller model cities located in the rural countryside. Here it was expected that workers and other residents could occupy inexpensive but attractive, hygienic, and comfortable homes, each with its little garden and all to be surrounded, if possible, by a belt of agriculture.[69] The focus of the association was the integration of small workshops and factories with agriculture; yet, even if it steered clear of total archaism, it was not without a strong element of romantic antiurbanism. In the first pamphlet of the German society this idea was expressed in the emphasis upon the need for a strong reintegration of man with the land: "Man needs the lasting contact with the mother earth," it stated, "with nature, a life in the pure air and bright light, if he is not to atrophy and decline." [70]

In the Deutsche Gartenstadt Gesellschaft Landauer saw the prospect of a beginning of small rural communities which would be based upon a voluntary, "an-archic" union of men. According to Max Nettlau, who was close to Landauer in these years, Landauer "saw in it [the Garden City Society] an argument for voluntary, cooperative strength, very organized, which effectively broke the evil of cities of stone and made men alive to the necessity of a life closer to nature. It confirmed Landauer in his confidence in voluntary cooperation and in action in the here and now and not only in the society after the revolution." [71] The appeal of the society was limited for Landauer, however, because the association tended to attract "only people with a fair amount of capital, not poor people." [72] Romantic antiurbanism had appeal largely for the middle classes.

Despite his reservations about the Neue Gemeinschaft and the Garden City Society, Landauer's involvement in these two groups was to leave a lasting imprint upon his social thought. By the time his major philosophical work, *Skepsis und Mystik*, appeared in 1903, Landauer's anarcho-socialism had been restated in völkisch terms. We shall return in chapter 4 to the elaboration of this social philosophy after 1907, but here we need to examine in some detail the philosophy that was Landauer's main concern in the years 1901–1903: his attempt to demonstrate the mystical belief in the existence of community within the interior of the self.

*Isolation and Mystical Belief: Landauer's*
Skepsis und Mystik

Before Landauer's move to Hermsdorf in 1903, he and Hedwig spent close to a year in England. They left Germany reluctantly and only because they felt that it would be easier to begin living together in a country far from their former lives.[73] First in London and then in the suburb of Bromley, Landauer worked intensively on the elaboration of his mystical philosophy, but he also had the opportunity to meet and converse with some leading European anarchists. The most famous of these was the Russian, Peter Kropotkin, who lived close by in Bromley. Landauer and Kropotkin, however, did not spend much time together after a few initial conversations. Nettlau later wrote of the failure of a closer association between the two:

> Landauer knew little of France and Russia; Kropotkin knew little of Germany and was not interested in German questions and German culture. In economics, the exclusive communism of Kropotkin was not shared by Landauer. . . . For Landauer, moreover, what he took from Ibsen and Nietzsche in the course of his development was as important as what

he took from Proudhon, Bakunin, and Kropotkin. He felt
the necessity of not excluding from the continuous development of his personal individuality any influence, so long as
it seemed worthwhile. For Kropotkin, however, individualism was an enemy. . . . As a result, although Landauer and
Kropotkin were close to each other geographically in Bromley, soon they had very few things to say to each other.[74]

Frustrated by his lack of contact with a movement in
which he could believe, Landauer was never really able to
feel at home in a large movement; he valued individual
autonomy far more than did Kropotkin. After his dissoci-
ation from the Neue Gemeinschaft, he wrote to Mühsam, in
a spirit more of depression than of elation, that "it is already
always my fate merely to pass through such movements." [75]
In his impressions of Landauer, Rudolf Rocker discusses
the question of political isolation:

I hadn't much opportunity to get to know him during the
London Congress, but I had another occasion later, when
he lived for a time in London; I learned to know him well.
Landauer was a mild-natured man, with a deep sense of
justice. It did not prevent him being sometimes harsh in
his judgments and even unjust. But he was always ready to
admit that he had made a mistake. He demanded the highest
standards from himself; he was always searching for the
truth, and therefore kept himself far away from all dogmas.
As he expected the same from others he often found himself
in conflict with his closest comrades. Though he was all his
life actively engaged in social movements he was never a
man in a movement. His influence extended therefore only
to a small elite who could understand his thought, and were
devoted to him.[76]

Although Landauer made acquaintances with other anarchist intellectuals, it was in England that his isolation
reached its peak. By April 1902 Hedwig and he had decided

to return to Germany because they did not want to live completely separate from others, as they were doing to a considerable degree in England. "We have here not the slightest circle," he wrote, "within which we can work or which could demand something of us; the prospect for one is also very slight. We are homesick in a spiritual sense and in every other sense. We are also too happy together to want to be isolated; we want to be able to bring others into our *Bunde*." Also, living was too expensive for Landauer in England, and he saw no prospect of employment that he would find compatible.[77] After returning to Germany late in 1902 Landauer was able to find some work in translating[78] and, after 1904, in the Hermsdorf bookshop of the Axel Juncker publishing firm.[79]

The return to Germany provided the Landauers with employment opportunities and the more comfortable milieu of their friends. The feeling of political isolation, however, did not cease after 1902; it was to remain with Landauer for the rest of his life. In *Aufruf zum Sozialismus*, begun in 1908, Landauer wrote that "we are the Volk, now downtrodden, the pioneers and harbingers of whose reawakening are disgusted with our age of stupid force and with the infamous isolation and surrender of the individual man." [80] To alleviate his frustration Landauer developed a mystical philosophy of the self. Near the conclusion of the same work he wrote: "We cannot wait for mankind; we can also not expect that mankind will develop a communal economy for itself, a just exchange economy, as long as we do not find and re-create humanity in our individual selves. Everything begins with the individual, and in the individual lies everything." [81]

In *Skepsis und Mystik* (1903), which was based upon an elaboration of the lecture "Through Isolation to Community," Landauer gave the fullest expression to this mystical philosophy. Although subtitled *Versuche im Anschluss an Mauthners Sprachkritik* ("Essays Arising out of Mauthner's Language Criticism"), Landauer's *Skepsis und Mystik* utilized Mauthner's studies of language, which Landauer examined in manuscript during his prison term of 1899–1900, as an epistemological scaffolding for the defense of ideas that appear in embryonic form in Landauer's articles of 1895 and 1896, "Zur Entwicklungsgeschichte des Individuums." [82] In these articles Landauer attempted to refute the Stirnerite and classical liberal conception of the atomistic individual, substituting the view that the individual is "indissolubly bound" to the entire past and present of humanity; the individual is, in fact, a "phantom through which humanity is visible." Landauer thus replaced the concept of the isolated, atomistic individual with the early romantics' view of the unique personality who is a "vital part of a larger organic whole," that is, in his own way, an "image of humanity." [83] Such views Landauer found, in the year 1899, in the mystical, theological writings of Meister Eckhart, where, of course, in place of Landauer's "humanity" a pantheistic conception of God appeared. By the turn of the century, moreover, this mystical view of the individual had an even stronger appeal for Landauer than it had had five years earlier; it was especially comforting to one who had found himself increasingly isolated as a political actor.

In the months after his talk "From Isolation to Community," Landauer studied the works of the great period of German idealism in order to clarify and deepen his own philosophical thinking. In August 1900, while still a member of the Neue Gemeinschaft, he wrote to Hedwig that he was "buried" in the study of Berkeley, Kant, Fichte, and Schelling.[84] In his return to the early idealist and romantic philosophers Landauer was reflecting one of the leading intellectual currents in Germany at the turn of the century. The conception of the individual as a microcosm of the world, which made it possible to entertain simultaneously the belief in individual self-determination and the belief in communitarian integration, was a commonplace of early romantic philosophy in Germany. At the turn of the century it formed one of the bases of neoromanticism. In his study of Martin Buber, Hans Kohn writes of this movement:

> For the early romantics . . . the life struggle was recognized as a structural principle of the personal world. The new philosophy revived this basic idea. . . . The individual in his deepest essence, expressed only through his full concentration, and the general appear now only as dialectical variations in one unity in which the general expresses itself in the individual. Here the new philosophy takes over and widens the kernel ideal which appeared in Herder, Schleiermacher, and Fichte. In the first decade of the twentieth century the interest in the romantics awakened again.[85]

Fritz Mauthner's studies of language, as we have seen, provided Landauer with a support for his own previously developed mystical conceptions. Years later, however, he regretted having mingled with his own thoughts frequent references to Mauthner in *Skepsis und Mystik*: "If I were able to write a second edition," he wrote in 1910, "I would transform the whole composition and abandon the mixture of reference to Mauthner and continuation of my own thoughts. That would change nothing, however, which is essential and which already stands in it." [86] *Skepsis und Mystik*, nevertheless, does utilize Mauthner's *Beiträge zu einer Kritik der Sprache*; in order to understand why Landauer found Mauthner's work useful, it is necessary to discuss some of the latter's views on language.[87]

Mauthner's three massive volumes on language were written in an attempt to demonstrate that language—which is the same as thought—is useless as a means for the perception of reality. Knowledge is impossible because all we arrive at in each step of our investigation of reality is words. Mauthner, who was a radical empiricist, held that all knowledge comes from sense experience. This experience is then deposited in memory or in language, which is exactly the same thing. When we order these experiences we do not do so on the basis of so-called innate mental categories, such as causality, as Kant held, but on the basis of previous sense-data; so-called categories are merely words which are the memory of previous sense impressions. The fundamental point, however, is that thought and language are precisely the same thing. When we speak we are not "expressing" concepts; these concepts, which we delude ourselves into thinking are descriptions or explanations of reality, are nothing more than words. In his paradoxical style Mauthner wrote: ". . . men all believe that they think while they only speak; students of thought or emotion speak of a thought for which language should be an instrument or a dress. That is, however, not true; there is no thought without speech, that is, without words. Or better: there is no thought, there is only language." [88]

Since thought is the same as language or, more precisely, the use of language, man can never know reality. The reason for this fact Mauthner finds in his analysis of language itself. In his recent discussion of Mauthner's *Sprachkritik*, Gershon Weiler writes:

> Mauthner held that language is essentially misleading. The most obviously misleading characteristic of language is its inherent substantivizing tendency. Where our senses record only qualities or changes of qualities, we are inclined to talk

about things, about entities which exist in a self-contained manner. The process of abstraction, by which we reach these substances, is essentially nothing but the consistent use of the grammatical substantive. In fact, there is no limit to the use of substantives. This is how we find ourselves talking about values, laws or other most general concepts as if they *were there* to be discovered and talked about. It is easy to see how the concept of causality comes to be rejected on the basis of these considerations. . . . From Hume Mauthner has learnt the criticism of the notion of causality and from Kant its categorical inevitability. Mauthner interprets Kant in a psychologistic manner and causality as a category becomes for him an unavoidable feature of human thinking. . . . The relation between cause and effect is, according to Mauthner, the basic hypothesis of our whole *Weltanschauung* (*Beiträge*, I, p. 279), a kind of linguistic prison in which we are held without a hope of release. Hume's "custom" and "habit" are turned by Mauthner into customs and habits which cannot be avoided as long as we think.[89]

Mauthner is led by this analysis into an attack on all abstract concepts. All universals, he argues, are "abstractions"; they are meaningless, though inevitable, tendencies of thought:

As the content of a concept stands in the same relation to its range as the numerator to the denominator, so if the denominator extends to infinity, that is, if the concept includes everything that exists, then the value of the numerator related to the infinite must be zero; the content of concepts like "something," "substance," "being," and so on, equals zero.[90]

Mauthner's radical skepticism does not end with his critique of universals. He not only views collective concepts as mere words, but believes that separate individuated existence may well be another mistake, another mere "linguistic abstraction without perceptual substance." [91] It may be that the feeling of human isolation is merely a deception of our senses which originates in us as a reflex of some wholly unknown unity of all life.[92] The study of language may lead, according to Mauthner, to the view that the mental life of the individual, rather than isolating him from humanity, makes him only one link in an unending chain of human history, for each individual is entirely dependent upon the cultural traditions that he and millions of others have inherited from the past. Mauthner arrives at this speculation after considering the fact that language, words that we have inherited from the past, is the same as our cultural inheritance, our "traditions," the collective memory of our culture. "Tradition is not only set down in language," Mauthner writes, "but is, moreover, language itself." [93]

How did Landauer utilize these studies and speculations of his friend Mauthner? First of all, they provided ammunition for his analysis of the sources of authoritarian oppression. As early as 1895 Landauer had concluded, as we have seen, that the origins of the power of the state lay in man's incapacity for self-determined action and his accompanying dependence upon authority. Stirner had held a similar position and Landauer praised Stirner's analysis of the state as a mere phantom in the human brain, a "fixed idea." [94] With Mauthner's *Sprachkritik*, however, this view might be given a philosophic basis. Landauer could now argue that the "state" was nothing more than a word men use in an attempt to transfer what is essentially an internal experience of spiritual atrophy and dependence onto an allegedly separate and externally operating material construct. As Julius Bab, the theater critic and friend of Landauer, wrote:

> . . . capitalism lives only through the power of the state that protects it. But who protects, supports, and enlivens the power of the state? Nothing at all, so sounds Landauer's answer, only our illusion, only the superstition of men, only the senseless worshiping of large-sounding words. The libera-

tion of the human self from this superstition is in Landauer's judgment the first order of business. This is the reason that Fritz Mauthner, the critical destroyer of linguistic superstitions, was so invaluable an ally, because here concepts that would otherwise have been enthroned with religious power over the spirit were dissolved into the nullity of mere linguistic habits.[95]

Schooled in the voluntarism of Nietzsche and the idealism of Kant and Fichte, Landauer writes, utilizing Mauthner's attack on word superstitions:

> . . . we speak, for example, of the state, without thinking that this word designates nothing but a definite condition of a public-legal nature in which we persist with our wills. This convenience is a blessing for our common understanding, which would not be possible without this reification [*Verdinglichung*] of what are, in fact, fluid and spiritual relations; it does injury, however, to our perception, because we take an expedient for a naked reality.[96]

If Landauer had not been so concerned with differentiating his own conceptions from Marxian terminology he might have spoken of the "fetishism" of the state and revealed his relationship to the left-wing inheritors of the German idealist tradition in the 1840s, such as Feuerbach, Moses Hess, and Marx himself.[97] Just as Feuerbach, in *The Essence of Christianity*, had provided Marx with an approach that could be utilized for the ideological unmasking of all human social idols, so Mauthner provided Landauer with the same in his *Sprachkritik*.

Landauer, however, like Feuerbach and the other young Hegelians, did not regard all social collectives as mere word fetishisms or linguistic superstitions. The use of Mauthner's skepticism for the purposes of unmasking the cult of the state was dictated by Landauer's prior commitment to the anarchist world view. *Sprachkritik* might just as logically have been applied to the "Volk," or to the conception of "Gemeinschaft" which Landauer cherished. He used Mauthner's skepticism very selectively, of course, and for his own purposes. When it came, moreover, to a positive social doctrine with which to replace the state-oriented view, Mauthner's work was only loosely connected with Landauer's purpose.[98] Mauthner's *Sprachkritik* did not make Landauer an anarchist or a representative of völkisch romantic conceptions.

The possibility of certain mystical beliefs was suggested in Mauthner's work—such as the speculation that the individual may be only a passing moment in an unending stream of human cultural evolution—but Landauer saw that Mauthner was essentially a thoroughgoing skeptic whose random mystical speculations were not assimilated structurally into his work. Soon after studying Mauthner's manuscript, Landauer wrote to Hedwig in September 1900:

> Just as Kant was followed by the romantics, so, in the same way, will Mauthner's question mark not be an end, but an entrance into a new mysticism. All this lies in his book, almost said with words; but, as it sometimes happens, the Mauthner who comes to expression in the best places is much greater than the usual Mauthner; he has not grown into his own thoughts, and, as it is, they even threaten to substantively destroy him.[99]

Landauer's mysticism soon left Mauthner's radical doubt far behind. Mauthner remained his whole life a skeptical philosopher who despaired of the senses but could never renounce empiricism. The difference between the two men was symbolized years later in an exchange of letters on Judaism; whereas Landauer proclaimed his spiritual tie with Judaism, Mauthner could do no more than admit that

Judaism was a regrettable "cerebral duct." [100] According to Hans Blüher, with whom he spoke during World War I, Landauer "called himself a mystic, and his friend Fritz Mauthner, the skeptic, he called a wanderer through the night." [101]

At the outset of *Skepsis und Mystik,* Landauer contends that skepticism and nihilism would have no value at all if they did not prepare the way for a newly created mysticism. In a manner strongly reminiscent of Nietzsche, of whose "vital significance for the present" he had spoken in the Neue Gemeinschaft circle in 1901,[102] Landauer asserted that new self-created "illusions" are justified because they are necessary for the revitalizing of one's life activity. All culture and life require illusion; the function of negation and skepticism, then, must be to clear the ground for a new mysticism:

> What, then, would be the great value of the act that destroys all absolutes and annihilates every truth, if this irony and nihilism were not the path to a play of life, to brightness, and to previously unbelieved illusions? Illusion—an idea in which we believe, a holy goal—has up to now created the spell of all Völker, of all *Kultur.* . . . From every great despair a new, greater hope grows in the end, . . . for where nothing more stands firm and there is no ground left, we will drive our stakes down. . . . As Kant's *Critique of Pure Reason* stands for me in a causal connection not only with the romantics, but also with the revolutionary transformations of 1830 and 1848, so the great work of skepticism and the most radical negation, which Mauthner has practiced, is for me the preparation for a new mysticism and for new, strong action.[103]

For the purpose of affirming life and facilitating activity within it, Landauer felt that it was necessary for his will to posit a conception of reality in which he could believe. Fol-

lowing Kant's *Critique of Practical Reason*, Landauer held
that all matters concerning ethics must be conceived of in
terms of the choices made by man's autonomous will. "We
know nothing of the purpose of our life," he wrote in 1903,
"therefore we want to set ourselves purposes! . . . You see,
I am also ethically oriented; only I would rather translate
*Ethik* as *menschliche Willkür* ["human volition"]—naturally whoever wants to be big about it will not see this in
the petty sense of *willkürlich* ["arbitrary"]. And likewise
I naturally admit that this 'volition' is determined; but it is
nonsense, therefore, because one *must* want—to no longer
want to want! We have to want—therefore, one is free!" [104]
Here Landauer went beyond Kant. Whereas Kant
strongly differentiated desire and practical reason and held
that morality consists in freely choosing to follow the dic-
tates, not of personal desire, but of a universal, rational,
moral law, Landauer's views were much closer to those of
the voluntaristic followers of Kant—Schopenhauer and
Nietzsche—who conceived of "will" as something more
akin to "desire" than to rationality. The basis of the world
view that Landauer constructed in *Skepsis und Mystik* was
nothing but desire and need. Mauthner's *Sprachkritik*
"cleared the ground" for these beliefs by asserting that the
feeling of personal isolation, of the separate "I," may be a
misperception of reality owing to its dependence upon mis-
leading descriptions of the self contained in language, a
view Landauer had asserted as early as 1895 and wanted so
much to believe. In *Skepsis und Mystik*, Landauer wrote:

> . . . my inner feeling that I am an isolated unity can be
> false, and I declare it to be false because I can not be satisfied
> with this horrible isolation. . . . I renounce the certainty of
> my "I" so that I will be able to bear existence. I build myself
> a new world with the consciousness that I have no basis upon

which to build except necessity. The force that is practiced by all powerful life, however, has a liberating strength in itself which creates affirmation [*befreiende, jauchzenschaffende Kraft in sich*]; I know from now on that it is my own self-created world into which I look, in which I work.[105]

Whereas empiricism—reasoning upon external sense-data— led to the feeling of individual isolation and the sense of the separation of things, internal, mystical contemplation afforded Landauer a sense of community with the world.

The "I" kills itself so that the "World-I" may live; . . . in the place of abstraction, the deadening, depleting, and desolate diverging of things, we set contraction, the drawing in of the whole world into our sphere. This is worthwhile, for abstraction and conceptual thought have arrived at a terminus; Mauthner's blow has felled it. . . . We allow the world to go through us, we create the conditions of readiness to feel it in us, we allow ourselves to be grasped and seized by it. . . . The way in which we must proceed, in order to come to community with the world, leads not toward the external, but toward the internal; . . . we return wholly into ourselves and there we find the living world.[106]

Landauer was an immanent idealist who was attracted to the writings of Meister Eckhart not only because the medieval preacher affirmed the primacy of spirit over matter but because he taught that the world of the eternal spirit is born only in the deepest part of the individual soul. For German romantics such as Herder and Schelling, however, the immanent spirit—of which each individual and each Volk was a microcosm—was an organically developing, temporal affair. In following them on this score, Landauer departed from the metaphysics of both Eckhart and his earlier teacher, Schopenhauer.

Up to this point Landauer's formulation is strikingly similar to Schopenhauer's. For Schopenhauer, the thing-in-itself, the World Will, appeared in the phenomenal world as separate individuated existences; since individuation is the source of pain the solution must be to go beyond phenomenal reality to the nondifferentiated, noumenal World Will. In *Skepsis und Mystik*, Landauer, continuing the thought of his "Entwicklungsgeschichte" articles, argued that Mauthner's *Sprachkritik* allowed him to say much the same thing:

> Individuals are only phenomenal and transitory points, electric sparks of the whole, the greater; . . . it seems that the world has had to isolate us and create individuals in order to be able to be visible and apparent in us. . . . Because the world has fallen into pieces and has, as a result, been differentiated and separated from itself, we must flee into mystic seclusion in order to become united with it.[107]

At this point Landauer diverged from Schopenhauer. For the latter the World Will was completely timeless and was outside temporal, historical change; for Landauer, on the other hand, the world with which we must unite was "eternally alive," by which he meant eternally "developing." He recognized this departure from Schopenhauer and tried, unsuccessfully, to patch it over: "The eternally living, . . . eternity, is also a temporal process. Even if Schopenhauer says 'timeless' he means nothing other than the unending process of time." [108] Schopenhauer's rejection of history, however, was too fundamental an aspect of his thought for Landauer to gloss over in this way. Landauer's mysticism concerned union with temporal humanity; the mystical experience was a vital moment in the remaking of historical society. In a letter of 1910 to his friend Ludwig Berndl, Landauer recognized this sharp difference from Schopenhauer.[109]

Landauer followed Eckhart and Schopenhauer in regarding the phenomenal world as an objectification of spirit[110] (for Schopenhauer, the World Will). Unlike them, however, he attempted to demonstrate this view by arguing that the sense of space, which is entirely dependent on sense impressions, resolves itself into the sense of time, which is inherent in the soul. Basing his speculations on Bishop Berkeley's efforts to refute empiricism, Landauer argued that the external world is merely a "sign" of the internal world because we can explain all seemingly spatial developments as moments in the flow of time which we experience without reference to phenomenal reality. "Consider the dial of a clock," he wrote in a letter of 1902. "The movement of the pointer in the calibrated space is only a symbol, a sign, for the passage of time. So, I think, all our external world is a sign of the hidden life, which we know directly only in our self-consciousness; the proceedings in our consciousness, moreover, are of a purely temporal nature, the sense of space is not involved. So, I think, all space and, with it, all matter are only a sign language between our senses and other psychic systems." [111]

In the completed *Skepsis und Mystik*, Landauer developed this view: "Time is not merely perceptual, but the very form of our experience of self; therefore it is real for us, for the conception of the world which we must form from out of ourselves. Time is real, just because it is subjective. Space, however, is merely the result of our perceptions." [112] The argument for the derivation of the external world from our internal experiences followed: ". . . there is no space as such: what appears to us as spatially solid is a temporal transformation; what appear to us to move in space are the changing qualities of temporal proceedings. . . . If we had no eyes then the difference between myself and the world would never originate." Without the sense of sight I would not feel that I touch something hard, but that "my finger-tips become hard." [113]

Although Landauer insisted upon the historicity of *Geist*, the word he now used for the "living world" that we may experience internally, it did not follow that he abandoned the sense of "present consciousness" which is so vital a part of the mystic outlooks of Eckhart and Schopenhauer. To do so would have meant to undercut his own argument for nonviolent anarchism, the refusal to suspend the ethical imperatives of the present for the purposes of their future realization. Landauer attempted, rather, to incorporate Eck-hartian present consciousness into his view of the world as time. In the very first sermon Landauer translated from Eckhart, the view is presented that the rebirth of man—his experience of God in his soul—is not an event that can occur at one point and then spiritually sustain the individual thereafter, but that "this birth is always happening" or else it is not present.[114] Landauer introduced this emphasis upon the eternal present into his own thought by arguing that what exists in the present has not originated in the past; the existence of anything means that it is "continually originat-ing," is always being created anew. History and time can-not be divided into past, present, and future; the only exist-ence is the eternally present. "What sterility and prepost-erousness," he wrote in *Aufruf zum Sozialismus* a few years later, "to ask for the original cause of something as an occur-rence which happened once in the past. Nothing has origi-nated once; everything is continually originating, and there is no original cause." [115] That which obtains in the world does so by virtue of the fact that it presently exists in man's soul. Landauer's view was here strikingly similar to the his-torical methodology of Dilthey, possibly the leading figure of the neoidealism of the age; the concept of *Verstehen* connoted the view that the past can be known only through its reexperiencing in the present.[116] For Landauer, the voluntarist, the past does not exist unless we choose to have it operate in the present.

These were the mystical and idealist conclusions of Landauer's *Skepsis und Mystik*. Mauthner's nominalist attack on empirical truths as mere word superstitions, and especially his questioning of the belief in the empirically observed isolated self, had provided Landauer with a useful basis upon which to defend his own mysticism: the belief that the historically developing, continually reborn world is to be experienced within the interior of the individual soul. What relevance, however, did all this philosophical discussion have for Landauer's social thought? The answer is that Landauer conceived of the mystic present consciousness of the endlessly developing *Weltall* as a consciousness of the individual's rootedness in the "inherited," developing communities that make up humanity. In enlarging on this point Landauer was only restating the position he had argued as early as 1895 in the "Zur Entwicklungsgeschichte des Individuums" articles written for *Der Sozialist*. In the earlier presentation of this view, however, Landauer tended to give much weight to man's physical indebtedness to the past history of humanity, his inheritance of common biological characteristics which rendered human evolution as something more than a "succession of distinct individuals." In the years between 1895 and 1903, as we have seen, a more mystical, spiritual orientation came to predominate, and it was this framework that Landauer continued in *Skepsis und Mystik*; the rootedness of the individual in the eternal flow of humanity was now described more as an awareness of the human community in the individual soul.

The shift was very significant. At a time when reactionary völkisch thinkers were developing a pseudoscientific biological orientation for their view of the individual's rootedness in the community or the race—as can be seen, for example, in the influential work of Houston Stuart Chamberlain, *The Foundations of the Nineteenth Century* (1900) [117]—Landauer's communitarianism was focused upon a mystic growth of consciousness which was accessible to all men, regardless of their allegedly fixed, physical characteristics. Whereas the racist doctrine was based upon a vulgar materialist view, separating men in terms of their fixed biological makeups, Landauer stressed that man grows spiritually through a deeper consciousness of his roots in community and humanity.

Eckhart's sermons provided the proper focus. Their emphasis upon the spiritual discovery of God in the soul,[118] however, had been updated, for Landauer, by the Nietzschean stress upon the creation of a new world from out of the self. At the beginning of *Skepsis und Mystik* Landauer had written, "I know from now on that it is my own, self-created world into which I look, in which I work." Here was another crucial distinction between Landauer's thought and that of most right-wing völkisch thinkers in Germany. For Landauer, as for all völkisch thinkers, the individual was rooted in community; but community was entirely dependent, for its existence, according to Landauer, upon the self-created communitarian consciousness of the individual.

The earlier emphasis upon physical heredity was not entirely lacking in *Skepsis und Mystik*: "The individual bodies, which have lived on the earth from the beginning," Landauer wrote, "are not merely a sum of separate individuals; altogether they form a great, thoroughly real *Körpergemeinschaft* ["bodily community"], an organism that is eternally changing and that manifests itself eternally in new individual forms." [119] Here Landauer clearly distinguished this view, as he did not do in the "Entwicklungsgeschichte" articles, from one of a physical evolution that operates, outside human consciousness, as an allegedly deterministic, natural law. "We must remember," he emphasized, "that there are, for us, no longer any former causes and no natural laws, no transcendent principles. We know only immanent life, present effectiveness." Heredity was given a spiritual, mystical interpretation:

> There is neither an abstract heredity nor a concrete individual. "Heredity" is a decayed and earlier word for something that is very much alive and present. . . . Heredity concerns itself with a very real and continually present power which functions so that the ancestral world is continued in new forms and structures. The individual is the spark of a spiritual stream which is called the human race, the species, the cosmos. [120]

What is inherited, however? Landauer's self-created world was one in which the inherited communities of the past—which, in the *Zukunft* article of 1901, he identified with the various Völker and regional Gemeinde—were felt to exist within the recesses of the individual soul, unlike the "thin influences" of the surrounding state and society. The way we may begin to obviate the present authoritarian state and capitalist economy is to proceed, through isolation, to the awareness of community within:

> The great inherited communities are real; for this to be so, however, the ancestral world must be alive in the present. . . . The closer an individual comes to himself, the deeper he draws back into himself, the more he separates himself from the impressions of the surrounding world, all the more will he converge with the world of the past and with that which is fundamental. What is fundamental in man, what

is most essential and most hidden, his inviolable property, is the great community of the living which exists in him; . . . the community, when it is found by the individual in himself, is more powerful, nobler, and more ancient than the thin influences of state and society. The deepest part of our individual selves is that which is most universal. The deeper I return into myself, all the more do I become participant in the world.[121]

The man who is peculiarly equipped to realize and express this mystic awareness, Landauer made clear in his later writings, is the artist. Sharing the common view of most other völkisch thinkers, Landauer held that the mythos of the Volk was to be provided, not by its politicians, or by its scientists or businessmen, but by its poets and artists; it is they who are best able to create the awareness of the self as a microcosm of the Volk. In his essay *Ein Weg deutschen Geistes*, written during World War I, Landauer wrote: "The Völker no longer know . . . that they are called to realize in the living, material life of men and conditions what the poet sees, loves, and foreshadows in his spirit. . . . The men of our age do not know that the mythos stems from the poet." [122] In *Skepsis und Mystik* Landauer provided a basis for this viewpoint by arguing that it is the artist who is most capable of contact with the reality behind the sensate, empirical world, the objective world which he knows to be an externalization of the inner world of spirit.

Mauthner's critique of language was particularly helpful in this connection. Mauthner had concluded from his attack upon linguistic superstitions that the mystic and the poet may be much closer to reality than the scientist, since language, which both must use, is itself metaphorical and hence appropriate for poetic, not scientific, expression.[123] The purpose of art, in this view, was not to reproduce external reality, which according to Mauthner was impossible anyway, but to provide symbolic communication of inner feelings, an aesthetic stance that Landauer had held as early as 1892 when he attacked the naturalist position. Utilizing Mauthner's analysis, Landauer concluded his *Skepsis und Mystik* with a celebration of symbolic poetry and music, two forms of communication which were free, he felt, from the taint of our deceptive sense impressions. "Is it not true," he asked, "that language is so unfruitful because it is too material, and not, on the contrary, because it is too immaterial? Why should it be tied to the alleged reality through the metaphors of our senses, only in order to babble away about what other similarly mistaken means have babbled about? . . . Would it not be possible and fruitful to express the world in new metaphors?" [124] The purpose of art, he held, was to create symbols in which we can believe, creations without which, following Nietzsche's *Birth of Tragedy*, he felt life would be unbearable.[125] Since, however, the spatial, external world was to be experienced merely as temporal changes of which we are internally aware, symbolizing art must express the internal experience of the "world within." By living in the symbols created by art we are able to experience the world internally; through it, "we win and create worlds and lose ourselves within them." Only in this manner, Landauer concluded in *Skepsis und Mystik*, may "words and concepts . . . lead us to the rhythm, the inexpressible, which vibrates within us and allows us to vibrate with it." [126]

The mystical outlook of Landauer's first major philosophical work was to remain a basic ingredient of his thinking until the end of his life. Before any real community can be built, he always emphasized, we must realize that "the world has had to isolate us and create individuals in order to be visible and apparent in us. . . . We must flee into mystic seclusion in order to become united with it." [127] The political isolation that was to plague Landauer for the rest of his life[128] was here transmuted, on a theoretical level, into an experience reputed to be vital for the growth of communitarian consciousness. "We cannot wait for humanity," he wrote in his main political work, *Aufruf zum Sozialismus* (1911); we must "ourselves find humanity within us and then create it anew. From the individual begins everything, and in the individual lies everything." [129]

For Landauer, as well as other völkisch romantics,[130] mysticism had provided the theoretical means by which to proceed "from isolation to community." In the same years that he developed this mystical philosophy, however, Landauer had begun to clarify the nature of the community disclosed by mystic awareness. Rejecting the urban orientation and the class categories of the Marxists, Landauer's socialism in the early years of the new century called for the creation of an anarchic community of the entire Volk living in decentralized cooperative settlements on the land. If such a community was not in evidence in 1903, it was because man had become unaccustomed to searching within himself for the sources of his social life; after discovering the community within, man would be equipped to begin the construction of a new Volk without. The purpose of Landauer's *Skepsis und Mystik* was to demonstrate how this community was to be discovered. In the years that followed, Landauer was to define more precisely the nature of that community and the means by which it could be realized.

# 4. The Romantic as Socialist

In the decade preceding his involvement in the Bavarian Revolution of 1918–19 Landauer comprehensively articulated his intellectual synthesis of romantic and socialist thought. It was in these years that he produced his most substantial works of social philosophy and literary criticism. The prolific decade began in the fall and spring of 1906–07. During that year Landauer wrote two important works: *Die Revolution*,[1] an interpretation of the history of Europe which combined romantic medievalism with libertarian perspectives derived from Kropotkin's great work, *Mutual Aid*; and "Volk and Land: Thirty Socialist Theses," [2] an essay in which Landauer focused his völkisch socialist conceptions upon present society.

The intellectual stance of 1906–07, however, included only certain facets of Landauer's mature synthesis. In the years ahead he was to further develop this synthesis through books and articles on some of the major political issues of the day—the question of the viability of Marxian socialism, for example, as well as the problem of an impending war between the major European states—and to attempt to implement his theories through the construction of a socialist Bund, an organization that grew out of the "Thirty Socialist Theses." To each of these problems Landauer responded both as a libertarian socialist and as a völkisch romantic, working out, in each instance, the fusion of the two traditions he had been developing in the preceding decade and a half.

## A Philosophy of History

In the years 1902 through 1908 Landauer withdrew almost entirely from public activity and indulged his strong appetite for private study. His social milieu was reduced to a small circle. Significantly, Landauer shared his philosophical and literary interests with his friends much more than he did his anarchosocialist political stance. Erich Mühsam and Martin Buber, young intellectuals whom Landauer had befriended in the Neue Gemeinschaft circle, were anarchists; yet Landauer was never very close to Mühsam[3] and his relationship with Buber was based as much upon the similarity of their mystical philosophies as upon their political affinities. Most of Landauer's letters to Buber in the prewar years were concerned largely with Landauer's reactions to Buber's writings on Jewish mysticism.[4]

With Landauer's other friends the nonpolitical side was even more pronounced. Two of them, with whom Landauer had become acquainted in the years of the Neue Gemeinschaft (1901–1902), were literary figures: Julius Bab, a prominent Berlin theater critic, and Auguste Hauschner, the cousin of Landauer's old friend Fritz Mauthner and a popular novelist.[5] It was the sharing of common philosophical interests which brought Landauer together with still two others. In 1908 he was befriended by a young philosopher from Austria by the name of Ludwig Berndl, who was particularly interested in Indian thought; in the years ahead they carried on lively and intense debates both in person and in correspondence.[6] The most significant relationship Landauer established after he and Hedwig settled in the Berlin suburb of Hermsdorf in 1903 was with Constantin Brunner, a Spinoza scholar and philosopher whose massive epistemological study, *Die Lehre von den Geistigen und vom Volke* (1908), Landauer read in manuscript.[7] In time Brunner, who was first drawn to Landauer after reading his translations of Meister Eckhart in 1903,[8] became one of Landauer's three closest friends, the other two being Mauthner and Buber.[9] Landauer's social ambience reflected an apolitical existence in the half decade after the appearance of *Skepsis und Mystik* in 1903.

From Landauer's perspective, however, these friendships were not apolitical. The only political action he considered worthwhile was the building of communities from below, and for this project the best beginning was the collection of a circle of friends.[10] These men and women were of great importance to Landauer; he had for years insisted that community can begin only in the immediate experience of one's private life.[11] In his relations with his various friends he invested much of his energies and talents, as is eloquently attested by his letters. The intensity with which he pursued these relationships led to some conflicts which were usually touched off by Landauer's occasionally strident criticisms;[12] the sometimes bitter disagreements were to increase over the years, especially after the outbreak of World War I. But, whereas after 1914 relations between Landauer and some of his friends were deeply strained by their different views of the war, in the preceding decade he regarded disagreements as healthy signs of real diversity in his circle. He did not want his friends to be his "followers." "I do not want to proselytize for myself," he wrote in 1912. "[I am] heartily contented if my friends understand in what way I differ from them." [13]

By 1904 Landauer had to concern himself with supporting a family. In 1902 Hedwig had given birth to a daughter, Gudula, and a second daughter, Brigitte, was born two years later.[14] Writings and translations in the years 1903 and 1904 provided some money for his family; besides *Skepsis und Mystik* and the Eckhart translations, Landauer's *Der Todesprediger* was republished in 1903 and translations of Oscar Wilde and Kropotkin were published the following year.[15] This source of income was insufficient, however.

To further support his family Landauer took a job in a bookshop in Hermsdorf in 1904, a shop connected with the Karl Schnabel publishing house, and remained there until 1906. Although it provided financial security, the job left little time for Landauer's own work, and in late 1906 he resigned "in order to be able to sit at a writing table." [16] Landauer had been asked by Martin Buber to contribute a volume on revolution to the series Die Gesellschaft which Buber edited. In the fall and spring of 1906–07 Landauer returned, once again, to the writing table and produced his most important work of history, *Die Revolution*, which Buber published in 1908. Instead of studying the nature of modern political revolutions, Landauer had written a treatise on European history since the Middle Ages. The years of political withdrawal and private study had brought Landauer to an interest in the past.

Why did Landauer turn toward history in 1907? In one sense *Die Revolution* represented a continuation of the ideas of *Skepsis und Mystik*. The latter work had emphasized that the Geist that man discovers within his soul is not timeless, but is a historically developing phenomenon that unites the individual not only with contemporary humanity but with the historical past. In this sense *Die Revolution*, which focused upon the past, was a logical development from the earlier work. Yet there were other possible continuations of Landauer's work on mysticism. An important clue is contained in the body of *Die Revolution*, in which Landauer recommended three works to his readers. Besides

Mauthner's *Kritik der Sprache*, he cited Kropotkin's *Mutual Aid*, which he had translated in 1904, and Constantin Brunner's *Die Lehre von den Geistigen und vom Volke*, which he had carefully studied in 1905 and 1906.[17] These two works encouraged Landauer's turn toward history in *Die Revolution* and directly influenced the historical perspectives he developed in that book; both *Mutual Aid* and Brunner's *Die Lehre* focused upon the contrast of medieval and modern civilizations which formed the basic subject matter of Landauer's book. Before examining *Die Revolution* it is necessary to consider those aspects of Brunner's and Kropotkin's works which interested Landauer.

In the history of anarchist thought Kropotkin's *Mutual Aid* occupies a fundamental position. Besides being the classic defense of voluntary cooperation as against centralized authority, it was the first systematic attempt to base this defense upon historical grounds. In *Mutual Aid* Kropotkin argued that mutual cooperation is not only natural to man and animals and is the foundation of all of man's ethical urges, but is also biologically and historically effective. Those species that cooperate among themselves have the most promising chance of continued survival and evolution.[18] To counter the social Darwinians, Kropotkin had argued with them on their own grounds: in terms of natural evolution. The importance of Kropotkin's work for Landauer's development, however, was not in any scientific refutation of Darwinism; to Landauer, the philosophical idealist, Kropotkin's attempt to make "mutual aid" into a natural and scientific principle merely represented a projection of his will upon the external world.[19] What captured Landauer's imagination was Kropotkin's demonstration that voluntary cooperation was a powerful historical current in European social life; in advocating mutual aid

and not authoritarian rule, Landauer could point to a significant, continuous tradition of decentralized, communitarian
life in the European past. The greatest period of voluntary
cooperation in the European past, according to Kropotkin,
was the Middle Ages, and in *Die Revolution* Landauer referred to Kropotkin's detailed study of medieval life in
*Mutual Aid*.[20]

Predictably, Kropotkin's focus was upon the medieval
city. Admitting that cities in the Middle Ages constituted
an "oasis amidst a country plunged into feudal submission," [21] Kropotkin presented evidence that urban life, from
about 1100 to 1500, was marked by various forms of voluntary association and mutual aid. "The medieval city . . .
appears as a double federation," he wrote, "of all house-
holders united into small territorial unions—the street, the
parish, the section—and of individuals united by oaths into
guilds according to their professions." [22] Kropotkin saved
his most fervent panegyrics for the medieval guild which,
he said, was "not a body of citizens, placed under the control of state functionaries; it was a union of all men connected with a given trade. . . . It had its own self-juris-
diction, its own military force, its own general assemblies,
. . . its own relations with other guilds of the same trade
in other cities: it had, in a word, a full organic life which
could only result from the integrality of the vital functions." [23]

While Kropotkin chose to emphasize the libertarian aspects of medieval society, his treatment of modern history
in *Mutual Aid* made no claims about the dominance of
voluntary cooperation in the centuries after 1500. The sixteenth and seventeenth centuries, far from being an age of
renaissance, were marked by cultural and social degradation
and decline. The growth of the centralized state had de-

stroyed the libertarian social fabric of the medieval city and the rich communal culture that was the expression of urban society.[24] The growth of authoritarianism, however, did not entirely destroy the historical evolution of mutual aid. Concluding his study with a survey of modern institutions of voluntary cooperation—including urban and rural producer cooperatives, trade unions, village communities, and the like[25]—Kropotkin emphasized that "neither the crushing power of the centralized state nor the teaching of mutual hatred and pitiless struggle which come, adorned with the attributes of science, from obliging philosophers and sociologists, could weed out the feeling of human solidarity, deeply lodged in men's understanding and heart, because it has been nurtured by all our preceding evolution."[26] Driven underground but not destroyed, the tradition of mutual aid had survived as a countercurrent beneath the regimen of modern capitalism and the authoritarian state. In *Die Revolution,* which Landauer wrote two years after translating Kropotkin's *Mutual Aid* in 1904, Landauer was to reproduce the outlines of this anarchist philosophy of history.

Although Kropotkin's work presented a favorable view of medieval civilization, the other work that directed Landauer's attention to the past contained a denunciation of that civilization. Constantin Brunner's *Die Lehre von den Geistigen und vom Volke* was a work of philosophy which in certain ways paralleled Landauer's own *Skepsis und Mystik.* Brunner taught that science does not provide real knowledge of the world, but only knowledge that serves us in our practical life; ultimate knowledge, which concerns such questions as the origin and cause of the world, the purpose of life, and so on, is not accessible to man's rational faculties and can be divined only through intuition or spirit.[27]

Here, of course, was an idealist position consistent with Landauer's own feelings. But Brunner's conclusions about the nature of science, which took up most of *Die Lehre*, were even more interesting to Landauer. Brunner argued that science, if understood properly, must discard the notion of cause and effect and perceive that physical reality is marked by endless movement. Things are not what they seem—firm, solid, unchangeable—but are in continuous, never ceasing motion.[28]

In an article on Brunner which Landauer wrote a year after *Die Revolution*, in early 1908, he commented that *Bewegungslehre*, the "theory of motion," was the central conception of Brunner's work.[29] Significantly, however, he obscured the fact that for Brunner it was science that could yield this theory and not the process of introspection, as he himself had argued. He tended here to assimilate Brunner's view to his own concept of "Geist": "The unending nature of movement and the eternity of the spirit are the same," Landauer wrote, commenting inaccurately on Brunner's thought.[30]

What had all this discussion of science to do with Landauer's turn to history, however? The answer is that in tracing the history of philosophy in *Die Lehre* in terms of his doctrine of motion, Brunner presented an interpretation of the Middle Ages and the Renaissance which infuriated Landauer, hence encouraging him to correct Brunner's version. In *Die Lehre* Brunner continued the familiar eighteenth-century view that the Middle Ages were marked by darkness and superstition. The essence of the superstitious nature of the age was its failure to distinguish relative thought, which pertains to physical reality and is the proper activity of reason, from absolute thought, which pertains only to spiritual questions. The failure to separate the two realms had resulted, Brunner contended, in the inability of medieval men to attain to either true scientific or true spiritual understanding, since they insisted upon confusing the physical world with such spiritual abstractions as the "will of God," "virtue and sin," and so on.[31] Only in the period of the Renaissance were the two realms separated, to the advantage of both.[32]

In his first letter to Brunner about *Die Lehre*, Landauer bitterly criticized this view of European history. Giving voice to the romantic medievalism he had imbibed as a schoolboy and later developed with the assistance of Kropotkin's anarchist researches, Landauer wrote to Brunner in July 1905:

> What you say . . . about the practice and work of what you call the barbaric Völker of the Middle Ages is false and even revolting. . . . What you say about a dead hand at play there is false. Indeed there was much life, and blissful life, in the monasteries and institutions, and there was noble labor in the great work of the guilds and brotherhoods. But I am also opposed to what you say, in an entirely protestant manner, about the Renaissance, humanism, and the Reformation, which you see, with the professors of history, as the rebirth of scientific life. . . . What you have so quickly and falsely asserted remains a problem, even in terms of your observations: Why didn't the people of the Middle Ages, who had been such excellent masons, coopers, carpenters, cabinetmakers, weavers, and artists, develop natural science and natural laws? And why did their great thinkers—which they had—not direct themselves toward physical reality but toward the spirit and toward symbolism? Whoever has the proper love for these Völker, a love such as you have for classical antiquity, would find the answer.[33]

Armed with Kropotkin's historial schema, to which he added his own idealist, völkisch perspectives, Landauer proceeded in *Die Revolution* to construct a philosophy of his-

tory which directly contrasted with Brunner's denigration
of the medieval world. In Landauer's turn toward historical
questions in 1904–1907, when Kropotkin's *Mutual Aid* had
been a positive influence, Brunner's *Die Lehre* had operated
as a negative incitement. Landauer here began to develop
his synthesis of libertarian socialism and völkisch romanticism through a description, not of a future ideal community, but of the historical traditions from which that
community might be built.

Reflecting his roots in the German historicist and idealist
tradition, Landauer began *Die Revolution* by sharply differentiating historical from natural science, asserting against
Comtian positivism that history cannot and should not be
an exact science, since science leads "from experience to
mental abstractions," to mechanical "laws," while history
always remains on the level of the immediate "datum of
experience." [34]

In the early pages of the book Landauer attempted to
demonstrate the inadequacy of viewing history in terms
of scientific laws by trying to develop a consistent law of
historical development which would be adequate to the
multiplicity of historical data; in a manner reminiscent of
Saint-Simon, he presented a possible scientific explanation
of history in terms of a fluctuation of historical states of
"utopia," which are marked by individualism and social
instability, and of "topia," which are characterized by social
cohesion and stability.[35] In this view "revolution" is regarded as the period between the stabilization of successive
"topias," another name for "utopia." Such a view of history—which Landauer mistakenly called "inductive" and
scientific,[36] thinking only of the positivistic historical philosophies—was inadequate as a means of approaching historical experience, Landauer contended. The idea of pre-

senting history as a fluctuation from topia to utopia, he wrote in a letter of 1907, was done at least in part as a joke,[37] and his intent seems to have been satirical. There have been no successive interchanges of revolution and order in history, in which historical development follows some ineluctable scientific law; there has in fact been only one revolution in European history, the one that began with the dawn of the modern era around 1500 and was still continuing in his own day.[38] From the conception of alternating topia and utopia, which Landauer had used as a straw man with which to satirize what he alleged to be the scientific approach to history, we arrive at the romantic philosophy of history in which medieval spirituality is contrasted with the long downward path of modernization.[39]

For Landauer, ancient Greece had very little relevance and was not part of "our history"; the ancient Greeks, Romans, and Jews are "neighbors of the Völker of Europe," he wrote, "but not its ancestors or models."[40] As was so common among German romantics, Landauer found his central historical model in the local communities and guild associations of the Middle Ages. Our real ancestors, who according to Landauer's mystical philosophy are part of "our past" because they are "alive within us," are the men of the new Völker of the early Middle Ages:

> The breakdown of Greco-Roman culture, the origins of Christianity and the new Völkern . . . in the context of the so-called Völkerwanderung ["migration of the peoples"], signify a break of a special kind and a new beginning. . . . Our feeling is that we belong with the so-called medieval age, above all in contrast with the Greco-Roman world. . . . In this Christian world of man we find our soul and in the classical period, stately death and strange rigidity.[41]

In Die Revolution Landauer returned to the romantic medievalism that had attracted him as a boy, the world that had been introduced to him in the operas of Wagner and the patriotic education of the Karlsruhe gymnasium where he had written his "Germanic" theme on Frederick Barbarossa. In the 1890s, however, he had become an anarchist. In his mature conception of the Middle Ages, antiauthoritarian and völkisch elements were combined. He now viewed the period as an age of rootedness and spirituality, of "organic community" and völkisch art, but also as an age in which social organization was allegedly not imposed by centralized authorities, but resulted, as Kropotkin had argued, from the cooperation of a profusion of independent and autonomous guilds, associations, and corporations.

Landauer's medievalism did not reflect the views of a feudalist, like Adam Müller, or an ultramontane, like de Maistre, and it was not religious unity that attracted him as it did Novalis in his *Christendom or Europe*. Unlike conservative romantics, Landauer included in his idealization of the Middle Ages his commitment to anarchistic decentralization and a social cohesion born of cooperation, instead of force. Like all other romantic medievalists, Landauer made his picture of the period more a projection of personal values than a detached historical assessment,[42] but it was precisely because of this projection that his conception of the Middle Ages exhibited the viewpoint of an antiauthoritarian romantic. In *Die Revolution*, Landauer wrote:

A degree of high culture . . . arises when the unity pervading the various forms of organization and the supraindividual formations is not the external bond of force, but a spirit dwelling in the individuals themselves and pointing beyond earthly and material interests. . . . This principle of the Middle Ages is in opposition to the principle of centralism and state power which always develops when the communal spirit is lost. . . . We do not mean that there was no state in the Christian age . . . but that there were no all-powerful states, no state as a central organization taking over from all the remaining forms of community; the state was at most an incomplete, stunted structure in the midst of a multiplicity of community forms. . . . The Christian age was not represented through the feudal system, not through the village *Genossenschaft* ["cooperative society"], the imperial assembly, . . . the Church, and the monasteries; not through the guilds, corporations, and fraternities, the towns with their own jurisdiction . . . , not through the city leagues and chivalric orders—and how many more exclusive and independent forms could one mention. The Christian age was characterized by this totality of independent units which mutually interpenetrated. . . . The form of the Middle Ages was not the state but society, the society of societies. And what united all these variously differentiated forms and bound them together at the apex into a higher unity, a pyramid whose point was not power and was not invisible in the clouds, was the spirit streaming out of the characters and souls of the individual men and women into all these structures, drawing strength from them and streaming back into the individuals.[43]

If Landauer's view of the Middle Ages was marked by an antiauthoritarian, cooperative socialism, it was also the conception of a völkisch romantic; in his description of medieval culture, for example, Landauer predictably contrasted the communitarian art of the period with the modern isolation of the artist from the Volk. The contrast was symbolized by the Gothic cathedral, on the one hand, a social art having a living purpose in the daily life of the Volk, and the museum on the other hand, the modern showplace of socially superfluous art, a special "place for art" which no longer bears any relation to community life.[44] Medieval community, moreover, not only was rooted in a common spirit and in a völkisch communal art, but was based upon what Landauer alleged to be the peculiarly medieval form of Christianity: the fusion of spirituality and natural sensualism, both of which are vital in the binding together of men. With the Reformation attack on man's natural senses, Landauer wrote a few years later, this kind of fusion was destroyed.[45]

For Landauer the question posed by studying the Middle Ages was how to revive its communal spirit in the modern world, an age of "unspirituality and therefore of violence . . . , of individualism and therefore of atomization, the masses uprooted and drifting like dust." [46] The retreat from medieval spirituality and social multiplicity, the "society of societies," set in fully around 1500, the date that, according to Landauer, marked the beginning of the long revolution that is still being experienced today. In contrast with medieval community and decentralization, the central trends of modern European history since 1500 were defined by Landauer as social atomization and authoritarian centralization.[47]

By so characterizing modern history Landauer left little doubt about his views on alleged historical progress in Europe's development since the Middle Ages; like other romantic philosophies of history, those of Novalis or Wagner, for example, Landauer's presented a view of historical degeneration since 1500.[48] Landauer gave this degeneration the völkisch and libertarian formulation of an increasing substitution of state tyranny for communal cooperation, a substitution made possible, however, by the prior decay of medieval spirit and community. The societal atomization, capitalist exploitation, and political absolutism which took tremendous strides in the fifteenth and sixteenth centuries merely reflected the decay of medieval self-governing communal organizations and community spirit. This decay Landauer decried in the destruction of the medieval Christian "power of the mythos" through the sterile academicism of late scholastic theology and late medieval church organization.[49] Instead of symbols alive in concrete reality—the mythos of high medieval art and philosophy—late medieval scholasticism and church dogmatism were marked by the destruction of spirituality through an obsession with literal representations and descriptions.[50] In Landauer's analysis, so strikingly similar to Huizinga's *The Waning of the Middle Ages*, written a few years later, the decay of medieval *Geist* and community was revealed in the rampant realism of late medieval culture.[51] Whereas for Brunner this realism represented a cultural rebirth after the reign of medieval superstition, for Landauer it entailed the decline of medieval spirituality.

While Brunner upheld the conventional Enlightenment view of the Renaissance as the dawn of modern scientific rationalism, Landauer countered with his communitarian, romantic interpretation. Renaissance culture, in Landauer's view, began the fateful split between art, philosophy, and science, on the one hand, and the masses on the other. This separation between *Kunst* and *Volk* was one of the characteristic features of modern spiritual decay. In the medieval world art was an expression of the entire community, but during the Renaissance it was the creation of an educated, intellectual elite with no roots in the *Volk*.[52]

There was more, however, to the watershed of 1500 than the separation of art from community life. In Landauer's view, so consistent with those of the romantics Novalis and Friedrich Schlegel,[53] it was the religious and political developments of the Reformation of the sixteenth century which fully ushered in the modern age of spiritual decay and social atomization. With the romantic "historical school of law," Landauer distinguished the medieval freedom of

Germanic federalism from the authoritarian centralization imposed by Roman law. Although he admitted that the Germanic Middle Ages were not free from "Roman Caesarism," Landauer emphasized that it was only in the period of the Reformation that Roman law was fully utilized as a rationalization for the replacement of corporate and local independence by authoritarian centralization.[54]

Absolutism was facilitated by developments within Christian theology, Landauer contended; Luther's tendency to separate private religiosity and public social life, and his abandonment of the latter to the will of the existing political authorities, were prime forces in the development of the absolute state in the sixteenth and seventeenth centuries. "Luther completed with fearful sharpness," Landauer wrote, "what had already been developing in this century: the separation of life from belief and the substitution of organized power for Geist." [55] The Lutheran Reformation was fundamental to the development of the twin evils of modern life, "infamous isolation" and "stupid force," social atomism and political authoritarianism. The puritanical Reformation, Landauer wrote in an essay in 1911, by capping the destruction of the medieval unity of spirit and nature, encouraged man's "natural sensuality" to be driven toward guilt-ridden self-seeking instead of toward a natural sympathy among men. Man's spirituality, moreover, was then driven upward to an empty otherworldliness which abandoned the present world to social and political injustice.[56]

If the sixteenth century ushered in the long period of modern spiritual decay, it was not barren of positive elements. In Landauer's philosophy of history, dialectical without being determinist, the long revolution that began around 1500 bred its own antithesis, a spirit of revolutionary revolt against the oppressive social and political order. Following the line of argument in Kropotkin's *Mutual Aid*, Landauer emphasized that Geist and community did not die with the Middle Ages; they had merely been forced to go underground, forced to coexist with modern centralization and isolation as subterranean countercurrents. Periodically these countercurrents would burst forth, only to be suppressed and drawn upon in later attempts to revitalize man's social life. The anarchist revolution that must be made in the present would not be merely a return to the distant past, but a continuation of the revolutionary countercurrents that had developed beneath the "accidental institutions of our age": the community, Volk, and humanity which Landauer claimed to discover through mystic consciousness of the spiritual world within. "Each revolution," Landauer wrote, ". . . remembers all its ancestors, earlier revolutions, and regards itself as one of their children." [57]

Whereas Kropotkin had studied the evolution of the countercurrent of voluntary associations since the Middle Ages, Landauer focused in *Die Revolution* on the development of radical republicanism in the era of the absolute state as evidence of the continuing presence of communal Geist beneath the absolutist facade. Besides the sixteenth-century political theorist Étienne de La Boétie, whose attack on the "voluntary servitude" of the masses paralleled Landauer's own view of authority, Landauer pointed to the developing current of republican sentiment among Huguenot opponents of political absolutism such as François Hotman and Hubert Languet, the author of the famous *Vindicae contra Tyrannos*.[58] In this republicanism of the early modern era Landauer cited the continuing importance of federalist sentiment, coupled with the resistance of parliamentary estates to the process of state centralization, as evidence of a countercurrent that might replace absolutist *raison d'état* with a "comprehensive political community of the nation." [59] Again, however, Landauer was projecting his own sentiments onto others; he neglected to point out the extent to which parliamentary estates sought aristocratic privilege and autonomy more than community decision making, and the degree to which Huguenot republicanism merely reflected Catholic control of the monarchy and little of a substantive commitment to the celebrated *res publica*.

Whereas the republican movements of the sixteenth century were based upon a conception of *Ständesverfassung*, an arrangement of society into a number of graduated estates, Landauer observed, the French Revolution and the revolutionary movements of the early nineteenth century were in favor of social democratization as well as being opposed to political absolutism. Failing to sort out liberal and democratic-republican elements in these developments, Landauer asserted that modern political revolutions have sought both democracy and social atomism, seeking to dissolve the earlier estates society in favor of an atomistic equality under the law, guided by "an ordered administration of an impersonal kind," the state.[60] Landauer here revealed an ambivalence toward the French Revolution. Although he admired the federalist organization of the Parisian "sections" and applauded the initial destruction of political absolutism, he condemned the renewal of political centralization and tyranny under the Jacobins, blaming it on the attempt to solve social problems overnight by means of the state. Such attempts, Landauer asserted, invariably become, as in 1793-94, a mere matter of perpetuating the power of the rulers.[61]

Having examined his analysis of European history, we

need to turn now to Landauer's socialist activities and theories in the years after 1907. Whereas *Die Revolution* had focused Landauer's völkisch anarchosocialism on the past, he was to be occupied in the years 1908–1911 with developing a theory and a practice to begin implementing it in the present. The early phase of this period was taken up with the building of a socialist Bund in 1908.

## The Socialist Bund

A few months before Landauer wrote *Die Revolution*, in the fall of 1906, he composed an article entitled "Volk and Land: Thirty Socialist Theses," which was published in *Die Zukunft* in January 1907. The article generated sufficient interest to bring about the establishment of an organization to realize the program contained within it. That organization, the Socialist Bund, which occupied most of Landauer's time in 1908 and 1909, was launched on its career by Landauer's article.

Landauer began his short piece by once again comparing contemporary European society unfavorably with the medieval world. While "Christianity was the spirit of the Völker in the Middle Ages," he lamented, because it "gave to the social life of men a supernatural, a spiritual, sense," no spirit now infuses our life.[62] In adding substance to this statement Landauer focused on the problem of what he took to be the modern substitution of the state for the imagined medieval existence of the Volk community, of the state bureaucracy for voluntary cooperation, and of human drudgery for creative labor. The state isolates men; the Volk represents their binding together. The state is a centralized, bureaucratic structure; the Volk is tied to localities, to the land, and to the remnants of village communities.[63] If socialism is ever to emerge, Landauer insisted, it must be built outside the state, in the context of a reemergent Volk organism. "This new Volk must be there," he wrote, "before socialism can live anywhere but in the minds and in the desires of individuated, isolated men. Socialism can live, really live, only . . . in the newly evolved organism of the Volk." [64] This new organism must begin to replace the state or else all attempts at socialist construction will be in vain. The form of the organism, Landauer emphasized, had to be the local Gemeinde, or community. The only way to replace the state with a self-determining, socialist Volk community is to begin, on a local level, with the formation of voluntary associations among men. [65]

Published in January 1907, Landauer's article stimulated interest in his ideas among some Berlin anarchists and independent socialists. In May 1908 he was invited to speak to these groups at a public assembly. His talk, which was to form the basis of his major socialist tract, *Aufruf zum Sozialismus* (completed in 1911), met with an enthusiastic response. Two weeks later, returning to speak to the same groups, he outlined a plan for a new organization by reading the "Twelve Articles of the Socialist Bund." [66] With this second meeting, in June 1908, the first group of the Bund was set up. [67] Landauer wrote to his friend Fritz Mauthner that a new beginning had been made, one that enabled him to satisfy his "need for an immediate contact with men," freeing him from the secluded existence of the past few years. [68] The period of withdrawal had ended; it was time to build externally the community that Landauer had insisted must first be experienced internally in isolation.

In August 1908 Landauer traveled to Bern and Zurich, Switzerland, to help bring new Bund groups into existence. [69] In October he had printed 10,000 copies of a brochure entitled, "What Does the Socialist Bund Want?" in order to further implement his purpose.[70] More important, in January 1909 the first issue of a newspaper appeared, with Landauer as editor; entitled *Der Sozialist*, as his paper of the 1890s had been, the new one was to be the organ of the Socialist Bund. In Switzerland, in the preceding summer, Landauer had met a certain Margarete Faas-Hardegger, with whom he immediately fell in love; it was she who had encouraged him to revive *Der Sozialist*.[71] Margarete, who had previously been secretary to the Swiss Social Democratic Trade Unions,[72] was deeply impressed by Landauer's ideas and became a leader of the Bund in Switzerland. In the first year of the new organization Landauer wrote to her often, composing letters that combined politics with protestations of love. After a year, however, in which time his relationship with Hedwig seems not to have suffered, his infatuation with Margarete had subsided, along with his most active campaigning for the spread of the Socialist Bund. The two involvements, to some degree, seem to have gone hand in hand.

The new *Sozialist* was rather different from the earlier one; this time Landauer was the sole editor, and every bimonthly issue during its six-year existence contained his own articles and translations. According to Max Nettlau, who studied every anarchist paper in Europe and America in these years, Landauer's *Sozialist* (1909–1915) was the most distinguished anarchist paper in the world, "tirelessly seeking in all fields of socialism for any libertarian kernels to develop, any number of various possibilities of action to follow." [73] The paper was an ideal vehicle for Landauer's myriad interests in world literature, philosophy, and current social and political problems. Its wide range and its theoretical focus, however, created a handicap for the development of the movement whose organ it was: the Socialist Bund tended to attract largely middle-class intellectuals, instead of elements from all sections of society as Landauer had hoped.[74] Almost all the leading members of the Bund were from this social group. The outstanding figures in the Berlin group were Landauer's friend Martin Buber[75] and Landauer's brother-in-law Adolf Otto;[76] another friend, the poet Erich Mühsam,[77] and Franz Jung, a young bohemian writer,[78] were leaders in the Munich group.

The purpose of the Socialist Bund, following consistently from Landauer's social and political theories, was to begin the immediate construction of socialist enclaves outside the authoritarian state and centralist, urban capitalism.[79] If the state and capitalism are merely reflections of the disappearance of communal spirit, then the way to attack them is to begin replacing them with real libertarian, cooperative communities; it is only when men form just associations with other men, Landauer wrote in "Volk and Land: Thirty Socialist Theses," that the state will gradually disappear.[80] The viewpoint embodied in the Socialist Bund was that an immediate beginning of socialist construction is an absolute necessity if socialism is to develop; it will not develop out of a political revolution, since direct attacks upon the state fail to eliminate the sources of authoritarianism and thus merely perpetuate centralized authority.[81]

To ensure that the socialist settlements begun by the Bund would not be centrally controlled, but would be autonomous and self-governing, Landauer developed an organizational scheme based upon the structure of the independent group. In June 1908 he wrote of the proposed decentralized structure of the Bund:

> The Socialist Bund is composed of groups. These groups join a union of groups and participate in smaller or larger collective meetings depending upon the requirements of each

situation. Federation: No central court of appeals. Each person can approach every group or larger meeting with proposals. The model of this organization, which has often been successful, . . . is the organization of sections and districts of French cities at the time of the great revolution, above all in Paris. . . . Each person who is seriously interested should win a few others and collect a group, or more, around himself. The groups give themselves statutes and define the manner and degree of member contributions; . . . and whoever needs the means and support to enable him to work for the S.B. . . . should turn to the groups.[82]

Intended to form a federation, in actual practice the various groups of the Bund seem never to have participated in the larger association Landauer had envisioned. I have seen no evidence that the Bund was anything other than a collection of separate groups in various parts of Germany and Switzerland, each reading *Der Sozialist* but each entirely independent, and never coming together to so much as a single general meeting.[83] By February 1912 there were eighteen groups in all. To the first group, called "Gemeinschaft," which had gathered around Landauer in Berlin after June 1908, were added other groups in Zurich, Lucerne, and Bern, three more in Berlin, one in Munich, and ten others located mostly in northern and southwestern Germany.[84]

As a whole the Bund contained at its height no more than a thousand members.[85] Landauer was much less concerned, however, about its small membership than about the narrowness of its social appeal. Distinguishing his views from those of the Marxists and many anarchists, Landauer sought to make the Bund into a heterogeneous mixture of elements from all social groups; announcements of lectures to be given by Landauer were addressed to "men and women of every class." [86] The program of the Bund, however, and the intellectual sophistication of its organ, *Der Sozialist*, tended to limit the appeal of the organization to the educated middle classes.[87] Those groups that did contain more than a few workers frequently complained to Landauer about their difficulty in comprehending *Der Sozialist*. His answer was that, although "we want to speak to the broad masses," there was little purpose in repeating to them what they want to hear; the paper should be educational and not imitate the SPD policy of cultivating "mental sluggishness" among the proletariat.[88] The articles are not "really incomprehensible to the workers," Landauer wrote to Margarete Faas-Hardegger, who had written to him from Switzerland about the problem; intellectuals and workers should "work out the sense and meaning of the articles together."[89]

Landauer's advice did not solve the problem. A year after the founding of the Bund, in the summer of 1909, Landauer attempted to attract more industrial workers to the organization by taking a propaganda tour through the industrial region of Rhineland-Westphalia. As with a similar tour of the late 1890s, however, Landauer reported in *Der Sozialist* that his speeches had attracted only very small groups of industrial workers.[90]

More interesting than Landauer's own personal recruitment drive was the one attempted by Landauer's associate in Munich, Erich Mühsam. In 1909 Mühsam, the leading figure in the Munich group Die Tat, had been able to attract groups of déclassé "vagabonds and lumpen subproletarians" to some meetings. Mühsam was convinced that the "tramps and vagabonds" despised by the SPD, as well as by bourgeois society, were potential socialist "rebels" and "new friends" for the work of the Socialist Bund.[91] When the Social Democratic paper *Münchener*

*Post* attacked the Bund as a collection of tramps from the local taverns, Mühsam replied at a meeting of Die Tat that these people were just as respectable as any others and just as capable of socialist work.[92]

Mühsam's short-lived attempt to organize the taverns failed to erode the predominance of the educated middle classes in the Bund. It was, moreover, not only a socialist organization with few workers; it was also an antiurban organization with no peasants. Such was the appeal of Landauer's völkisch socialism, a constellation of ideas grounded in the anti-industrial, antiurban feelings of the left-wing romantic intellectual of the modern city.

Since the Bund was a strictly decentralized organization, its projects were the projects of its independent groups. Besides putting on recruitment drives and establishing funds for the founding of Bund settlements, or Siedlungen, Landauer's Gemeinschaft group in Berlin was occupied for a time in 1910 with the founding of a "free school on a communitarian basis," one that would aid, as Landauer put it in *Der Sozialist*, in "the renewal of our Volk . . . by struggling against uniformity and discipline." [93] Free from state influence, these schools would be locally controlled by parents and teachers.[94] It does not seem, however, that any such schools were actually set up.

The desire to establish libertarian, cooperative schools was not the only one that lacked implementation. Not one group of the Bund seems to have progressed beyond the stage of setting up a Siedlung fund; not one seems to have begun to build an actual communitarian colony away from the cities. Although Nettlau claims that "real beginnings" were precluded by the Bund's sense of proportion, since any such settlements would have been dwarfish affairs, given the limited membership of each group,[95] this explanation would seem to contradict Landauer's insistence that any beginning, no matter how small, was preferable to the endless postponement of socialist construction. Landauer, unfortunately, was not particularly candid about the matter of implementation, except to rationalize at one point, to his literary friend Auguste Hauschner, that what concerned him was not reaching the goal so much as working for what he believed in.[96] With a program like his, such rationalizations were necessary, for Landauer's Socialist Bund was a pretty unrealistic affair.

Besides left-wing middle-class intellectuals, to whom would the Bund appeal? Völkisch ideas in themselves—the desire to leave the city and develop a close community on the land, and so on—had considerable appeal to the middle classes in Germany, and a völkisch utopian movement was gaining momentum in the prewar decades in Germany. But in the long run the Germanic utopia movement tended more toward nationalist and even racist ideologies of the Right[97] than to any anarchosocialist theories to which Landauer tied the Bund.[98] Socialism, on the other hand, while it attracted numerous intellectuals, especially among the Jewish middle classes, had a mass base only in the industrial proletariat; by advocating a völkisch antiurban and anti-industrial socialist program, Landauer made it impossible to make inroads into SPD strength among the urban work force. Few workers, especially in the years of economic improvement from 1895 to 1914, would be interested in "returning to the land." As an intellectual construct völkisch socialism might have appeal for middle-class intellectuals, but as a social movement in Germany it did not have much of a chance. As we shall see in the discussion of Landauer's thought in the period 1908–1911, he had failed to adjust his socialist thinking to historical realities.

The völkisch utopianism of the Bund was unpalatable to most German anarchist groups of the pre–World War I period. Unlike Landauer, most German anarchists still placed their faith for socialist liberation in the urban proletariat and viewed the state, pure and simple, as a manipulative institution based upon external coercion. In 1909 Landauer came into direct conflict with the majority group of Berlin anarchists connected with the publication *Der Freie Arbeiter* when he refused to publish their publicity notices in the pages of *Der Sozialist*. For Landauer, *Der Freie Arbeiter*—which stood essentially for the anarcho-syndicalist tactic, directed toward the urban proletariat, of the general strike[99]—was "closer to Marxism than to anarchism," especially as he noted a strong trend toward centralism among its anarchist followers.[100] Asked to speak at a congress of German anarchists held at Halle in 1910, a meeting directed by the so-called German Anarchist Federation, Landauer attacked the federation on similar grounds as a bureaucratic, centralist institution which destroyed individual initiative.[101]

In 1912 more conflicts between Landauer and other German anarchist groups flared up. Whereas *Der Freie Arbeiter* had accused Landauer of destroying the solidarity of the anarchist movement because of his refusal to publish their notices,[102] in 1912 the Leipzig paper *Der Anarchist* attacked Landauer's brand of socialism as a philosophy directed purely to "intellectuals moving rather freely on the heights of theory," with no meaning for the worker who is directly involved in the "miserable conditions of the capitalist war economy." Landauer was working for the development of a community aside from the state and capitalism so as to render these evils superfluous, but *Der Anarchist* insisted that a direct battle with these "external" institutions could not be avoided: ". . . even if a socialist city with 100,000 inhabitants could be set up," the editors argued (as Marx had with the utopian socialists), "it would still be surrounded by the capitalist war economy and would have to reckon with it in a decisive struggle." [103]

The crucial distinctions between Landauer's social theory and that of the majority of German anarchists were his völkisch antiurban orientation and his conception of the state. In an extended article on Landauer's Socialist Bund, published in 1912, Pierre Ramus, the German anarchist-communist, attacked Landauer's view that the entire Volk must liberate itself; Ramus insisted that the "proletariat alone has the will to overthrow the existing system." Landauer's Bund, Ramus continued, will have no effect upon the capitalist world since it disregards the roots of capitalist power in the state; the only way to build anarchism is to destroy the state and expropriate the means of production.[104]

Landauer insisted, in opposition to most anarchists, that the state is not something "external," to be destroyed by a revolution; it can be destroyed only through the immediate building of socialist communities. Was this anarchism, however? The reaction of the German writer, Oskar Maria Graf, to Landauer's *Aufruf* is interesting in this connection; in his autobiography Graf writes:

> I buried myself in Landauer's "Call to Socialism." . . .
> I began to see what it was driving at. But what had it to do
> with anarchism? There was nothing at all in it about bombs
> or murdering princes. It only repeated quite innocently:
> "The Socialist Union is a community of those who want to
> create a new economic system inspired by an ideal." Further
> there was talk of groups which were to build up this com-
> munity, this new human society, step by step; of the dis-

tribution of land, of revolutionizing our whole manner of life by the power of the spirit; and so on.[105]

Graf's reaction to the Bund was, in fact, very similar to that of most anarchists. Landauer's reorientation of anarchist theory and practice in the direction of idealist and völkisch thought was often incomprehensible to the more traditional libertarians, and in the period of the second *Sozialist* Landauer no longer felt entirely comfortable with the simple "anarchist" label. For Landauer anarchism and socialism had always been different expressions of the same view; now he regarded anarchism as "merely the negative side of what is positively called socialism." "Anarchy," he continued in an article of 1911, "is the expression for the liberation of man from the idols of the state, the Church, and capital; socialism is the expression of the true and genuine community among men, genuine because it grows out of the individual spirit." [106]

Landauer's anarchosocialism, and the Socialist Bund that was its expression, were incomprehensible to the more traditional anarchists because Landauer blamed the existence of the state on the atrophy of communal life. Actually, his largely futile activities as leader of the Bund in the years 1908–1911 occupied him less than the theory of socialism which lay behind the organization. Although no longer engaged in purely private study, Landauer remained primarily a theorist. It was in these years, in numerous theoretical articles for his paper *Der Sozialist* and in the major work of the period, *Aufruf zum Sozialismus*, that Landauer fully developed his anarchosocialist position.

### Landauer and Marxism

Landauer's socialist education began with a short flirtation with Marxism, while his later development as an anarchist represented a continuing reaction against Marxist theory and practice. In his earliest articles for *Der Sozialist*, in 1892, he tended to take the position that the SPD had falsified Marx. In later years, however, after numerous battles with the SPD in the 1890s, Landauer came to emphasize the continuity of Marxist theory and SPD practice. His earlier attraction for the activist and voluntarist aspects of Marx had been forgotten through the long experience of what represented to him the endless inactivity of the SPD Marxists. At the outset of his major statement of socialist belief, *Aufruf zum Sozialismus*, written in the years 1908–1911, Landauer wrote that "Marxism . . . must be told to its face that it is the plague of our age and the curse of the socialist movement!" [107] Given such a judgment, it is not surprising that Landauer's entire socialist outlook was consciously framed as a sustained rejection of Marxist orthodoxy.

In the first place, Landauer's revolt against positivism, like that of many other neoromantics and neoidealists around the turn of the century, took the form of a rejection of the Marxist doctrine of historical materialism.[108] Landauer argued that scientific socialism was an impossibility in the sense that men do not desire and act on the basis of previously gained "objective knowledge"; the desires of our will dictate both that which we strive for and that which we choose to call objective knowledge. The voluntarist teachings of Schopenhauer and Nietzsche form Landauer's rejection of Marxist "social science":

> What we take to be a necessity is, of course, not something that comes to us in the form of a natural law, but as a moral necessity. . . . What we make of our body and life, . . . everything that we call the future, cannot be given to us in the form of science, that is, in a body of facts that have al-

ready been ordered, but only in the form of accompanying feelings, of disposition, of an inner pressure, of longing and desire; . . . that means the gamut from desire, the feeling of moral obligation and of presentiment, to prophecy, vision, or artistic construction. . . . History, therefore, and political economy are not sciences. . . . Judgments in them will always be based upon valuations that one can cover with the higher or lower name of prophecy or professional babbling; they will always depend upon values that are derived from our essence, our character, our loves, our interests.[109]

The focus upon human will, instead of historical necessity, did not mean that Landauer discarded all concern for historical development. In *Skepsis und Mystik* he had argued that time and historical change were actually rooted in internal experience, in the recesses of the soul. The future cannot be predicted from the past, he asserted against Marxist scientism, because my will is the filter through which the past must go, and I can decide, in the present, which aspects of the past I choose to have continue in the future.[110]

Although Landauer missed the fact that Marx and Engels never contended that ideological currents could have no reciprocal effect upon social developments,[111] he argued that the scientific approach to socialism made it impossible to value the full creativity of the autonomous will. In an article, "Socialism and Science," which appeared in 1912, he asserted the dubious conclusion that his view of the mutual interaction of social and spiritual life could never be advanced by a scientist: ". . . certainly we can and must speak of a defining influence of conditions on views, thoughts, religions, arts, and so on [an admission that his metaphysical philosophy in *Skepsis und Mystik* did not, in fact, allow]. Yet we should not overlook the contrary side: that these thought forms become complex, firm, and lasting and that we must speak of the continuous effect, for example, of Christianity on the economy, as of the contrary relation. In science there is no sense of mutual interaction." [112] In fact Marx and Engels spoke often of an influence of the superstructure of ideas upon the substructure of economic and social relations. It is not this view that separated Landauer and Marx, but the fact that the idealist tended to view matter and spirit as separate and distinct with the spiritual world autonomously derived, although admittedly influenced thereafter by material factors. Landauer could never accept the designation of ideational life as a "superstructure," no matter how much autonomous existence it might take on after its initial derivation from social reality. More often than not, he argued—as the whole of *Skepsis und Mystik* had endeavored to prove—that the external world is a reflection of the interior one.

There was something more, however, which Landauer seems to have missed in Marx's historical materialism. Reading Marx, at least after the mid-1890s, through the eyes of the positivistic Marxists of his day, Landauer failed to understand what Marx had meant by material "existence." While Engels had attempted to make of historical materialism a kind of social aspect of the laws of physical matter, Marx, though he may not have resisted the trend, had understood materialism in terms of man's active, social behavior, that is, not as a doctrine of life as "matter in motion." Landauer's attack upon Marx exhibits no knowledge, for example, of the *Theses on Feuerbach* or the *German Ideology*, an acquaintance with which would have shown him that Marx spoke of the derivation of consciousness from man's social existence, not from physical matter.[113]

Landauer missed all this, ascribing to Marx many of the

wooden views of Marxism which have survived down to our own time. The crucial attack of *Aufruf zum Sozialismus*, however, was more accurately aimed. Whereas Marx had attempted to show scientifically that socialism would necessarily emerge from the historical conditions created by capitalism, Landauer contended that socialism would come only if people desire it and build it; left to itself, capitalism would survive. From the vantage point of a more advanced stage of industrial capitalism than Marx was to see—the same vantage point as Bernstein's revisionism—Landauer found a historical basis upon which to defend his essentially ethical argument for socialism:

> Capitalism need not be changed into socialism. It need not perish. Socialism need not come. Also the proletarian-state-capitalist socialism of the Marxists need not come—and that would be no great misfortune. For no kind of socialism *has to come*—that we will now show. But socialism can come and should come, when we wish it, when we create it—that also will be shown.[114]

In order to base his argument for socialism upon its ethical necessity, Landauer, like the Kant-oriented revisionists, such as Bernstein, sought to undercut Marx's historical arguments by refuting them on their own ground. Unlike the revisionists, however, Landauer had no allegiance to Marxism whatsoever and he spoke not only of capitalism's holding power but of the fact that capitalism might never collapse. Bernstein still maintained that "capitalism, no matter how resilient, could never solve its own problems";[115] Landauer was "convinced that capitalism, the state, and the worker have found remedies with whose help capitalism can thwart the prophecy of its destruction." [116] First of all there was the fact that increasingly devastating economic crises had been averted, and possibly eliminated, through the monopolization process which effectively curtailed the destructiveness of unlimited competition. Capitalist entrepreneurs, recognizing the dangers to themselves of a totally unregulated battle for the economic survival of the fittest, had learned to cooperate, as Landauer put it, "against the consumers." [117] The social policies of the state, moreover, had helped to blunt the insecurities felt by the industrial worker; paternalism, which was of course particularly strong in Germany, had done its job to increase the strength of capitalism and the state and to "weaken the revolutionary mood of the masses and the political parties." [118] The number of industrial enterprises and bourgeois capitalists had, in fact, not decreased, Landauer continued, repeating the familiar revisionist point, but had increased with the proliferation of new industries to satisfy new needs and with the growth of a new rentier and managerial middle class.[119]

Far more important than these matters concerning the empirical revision of Marx's *Das Kapital* was the problem of the allegedly progressive nature of capitalism. For Marx, who had fully absorbed Hegelian dialectical thought and the notion of the "cunning of reason," capitalism would succumb to its own internal contradictions, most notably that represented by the dialectical struggle between private ownership and socialized production. For Landauer the real danger in the Marxist conception was the view that in the socialization of production and the creation of a socialized class antithetical to itself—the proletariat—capitalism had been developing socialism all along in its own "womb." Refusing to accept the premise of the necessarily progressive character of historical development, Landauer insisted that both capitalist ownership and capitalist production were antithetical to, not historical prerequisites for, socialism.

The argument, of course, turned upon one's definition of "socialization." Landauer wrote:

> Within capitalism, says Marx, we have arrived at the "centralization of production" and the "socialization of labor"; . . . "cooperation" and the "common possession of the earth" are already achievements of the capitalist era. The great, huge, almost unending human masses, the proletarianized, have really almost nothing more to do for socialism; they only have to wait until it is ready. . . . The form of work present in the capitalist enterprise, the factory system in which thousands work in a narrow area, the accommodation of the worker to the machine tools and thus the increasing division of labor in the production of goods for the capitalist world market—this Karl Marx calls cooperation, which should be a part of socialism. . . . Marx is shown the economic conditions of England in the middle of the nineteenth century, with its wasteland of factories, its devastation of the land, the uniformity and misery of the masses, an economy for the world market instead of for real needs, and he finds there socialized production, cooperation, and the beginnings of common possession.[120]

Thus, for Landauer, capitalism could never be regarded as historically progressive because he did not regard socialism as merely a transfer in ownership of the same mode of production operative under industrial capitalism. Private proprietorship was not the only problem; it was the whole process of industrial centralization which he found to be inimical to what he defined as "socialism": the abandonment of the mass, urban factory and the return to a decentralized economy based upon an integration of agriculture and craft industries. In Aufruf zum Sozialismus, Landauer attacks Marx for his readiness to accept what seem to be the main directions of modern technology.

Landauer's Aufruf of 1908–1911 was written after a decade and a half of steady economic improvement of the

German working classes, massive trade-union growth, and increasing trade-union influence over the SPD. Although consistent with his statements of the late 1890s concerning the proletariat, Landauer's argument in *Aufruf* showed an even sharper disillusionment with the industrial working classes. Trade-union reformists had captured the executive of the SPD in the years 1906–1909,[121] and it was now more evident than ever that the official labor movement in Germany was concerned largely with working for parliamentary democracy and social reform within the context of capitalist development. Outside Germany, however, these years fashioned a rather different working-class posture. Industrial workers had been in the forefront of the Revolution of 1905 in Russia, and radical anarchosyndicalist tactics were increasingly utilized by French and British workers in the years when Landauer was working on *Aufruf*.[122] Yet Landauer was so mesmerized by the conditions in Germany that he failed to be influenced at all by the experience of foreign labor movements. Whereas SPD radicals, such as Rosa Luxemburg, were inspired by the Russian events of 1905 to launch an offensive against the revisionists in the SPD,[123] Landauer's *Aufruf zum Sozialismus* exhibited no awareness of events outside Germany. Riveted to German experience alone, Landauer concluded that the industrial working class, since it was directly concerned with the capitalist system by laboring in its factories, was incapable of working for socialism; participation in the capitalist process, either by the entrepreneur or by the worker, serves only to perpetuate capitalism. As in his view of political oppression, Landauer held that the only way to destroy capitalism was to obviate it through withdrawal from capitalist factories and the beginning of socialism outside the capitalist system:

. . . the worker is not part of a revolutionary class, but of a crowd of poor wretches who live and must die in capitalism. . . . All this is necessary under capitalism, so long as the worker does not understand that he must exclude himself from it. . . . Everything that happens within the context of capitalist production leads him deeper and deeper into this system, not out of it; . . . in his role as a producer for the capitalist world market the worker is engaged in nothing but the capitalist process. . . . All that can be seen here is that the working class becomes acclimatized to its situation and to the general conditions of this society.[124]

On the basis of German labor history in the decade and a half after 1895, Landauer argued that through his trade-union activities the industrial worker loses any desire for structural change in society: "In their trade unions they are organized within capitalism; . . . through its funds and the workers' increased social security, through the improvement of their circumstances, their standard of living is soon cared for and the worst horrors are mitigated, which permits the continuation—of what? Of capitalism!" [125]

Landauer refused in these prewar years to recognize the possibility of radical industrial working-class organizations. The period in which he wrote *Aufruf zum Sozialismus*, 1908–1911, was a time when a person preoccupied with the current German situation might understandably have predicted the increasing domestication of the industrial work force under conditions of advanced capitalism; from an opponent of historical determinism, however, this was a surprisingly dogmatic prediction of the future, especially as the years after 1905 saw working-class radicalism increase in other European countries. Landauer's abandonment of the cause of the industrial proletariat, and his injunction to workers, after 1901, to rejoin the peasant-artisan world, did not equip him very well for the period of working-class radicalization which preceded and propelled the revolutions of 1918–19.

Socialism, Landauer argued, must be constructed outside the existing capitalist process. Marx's historical analysis of capitalism, as well as the parliamentary activities of the SPD, Landauer concluded, show only that what the Marxists really want is not socialism, but a capitalist economy in their own hands, instead of in those of the present exploiters. As Benedikt Friedländer had contended in Landauer's early anarchist days, Landauer claimed that Marxists wanted only to substitute a more efficient and bureaucratic state capitalism for bourgeois capitalism. The Marxist state would merely enhance the most stultifying conditions of the contemporary world, that is, economic and political centralization and the dominance of great factories and massive bureaucracies:

> There are now different kinds of centralization: economic centralization, . . . technical centralization of enterprise, and . . . the centralization of the state, bureaucratism, and the military. . . . All these forms of stultifying, odious, homogenizing, narrowing, and oppressing centralism have been models for Marxism, have had influence upon its origin, development, and spread. . . . This kind of socialism does grow from the undisturbed further development of capitalism! . . . The future state of the Marxists: the blooming of the tree of state, capitalist and technological centralization. . . . The organizational forms of capitalism are good (the Marxists say); but they lack order, regimentation, strict centralization. Capitalism and state must come together: then there is, we would say, state capitalism; the Marxists would say, socialism. . . . From the proletariat of the capitalist enterprise emerges the proletariat of the state, and proletarianization, if this socialism begins, will proceed as they

have predicted: extended on an immense scale so that all men, without exception, are small economic officials of the state.[126]

Landauer argued that in the process of pursuing means incommensurate with ends—either parliamentary activity or the attempt to capture the state through political revolution—Marxists will seek to perpetuate the power they have gained and the end will come to resemble the means. He felt that he had learned this crucial fact about Marxism from the behavior of the SPD. It was for this reason that he said, in 1896, that Social Democracy was the school that Germany provided for many of its anarchists. In 1909 he wrote, concerning the bureaucratic, "political" road to socialism: ". . . we are not going to found a party in which what is a mere instrument toward an end becomes an end in itself." [127]

Marxists "will not transform the state into socialism," Landauer wrote in an article of 1911; rather, "the state [will] transform these socialists into state worshipers!" [128] Through its absorption into the parliamentary game, Landauer charged that the SPD had come to feel more and more responsible for the state.[129] On this basis he correctly predicted, in 1911, that the Social Democrats would support the German government if a world war broke out.[130] Support by the SPD for the authoritarian state would not be difficult, Landauer further argued; the party is a small-sized despotic, bureaucratic state in itself. "Whoever knows the reality of the Social Democratic Party and the centralized trade unions," Landauer wrote in the pages of *Der Sozialist* in the same year, "knows that there is no genuine democracy in them, only parliamentary demagogy and rule by officials." [131]

The historical theory of Marxism, in which socialism

was reputed to be developing within the capitalist process, was according to Landauer a necessary consolation for the atrophy of the Marxists' own powers of construction and activity. Of the Social Democrats he wrote in 1913: "The inactivity in the camp of these socialists is so great and the obstacles to be found are in themselves so powerful that a theory must be found, the developmental theory of the Marxists, so that . . . they can bear their own pseudo life." [132] As Marx had unmasked the fetishism of commodities under capitalism, Landauer argued, in effect, that he had unmasked the fetishism of history under Marxism; as individual vitality, defined in terms of an immediate beginning of social reconstruction, decreases, so the Marxist transfers all creativity to impersonal historical laws.

To the follower of Landauer or of Marx, however, the other one appears utopian. For a Marxist, Landauer's flight from the struggle for political power and from the urban, industrial scene ensured his historical irrelevance.[133] For Landauer, on the other hand, the Marxist fixation upon the necessarily progressive character of historical change merely reflected his inability for socialist construction and rendered utopian his predictions of postrevolutionary qualitative change. "Only the present is real," Landauer wrote, "and what men do not do now, do not begin to do immediately, that they will not do in all eternity." [134] To the Marxist position, the ethical vitalist and idealist responds:

. . . the realization of socialism is always possible if a sufficient number of people want it. The realization depends not on the technological state of things, although socialism when realized will of course look differently and develop differently according to the state of technics; it depends on people and their spirit. . . . Socialism is possible and impossible at all times; it is possible when the right people are there to will it and to do it; it is impossible when people either don't will it or only supposedly will it, but are not capable of doing it.[135]

Marx's approach was, of course, more historical than Landauer's; the historical revision of Marx's analysis of capitalist development provided Landauer only with a historical justification for the flight to ethical idealism: "Socialism need not come. . . . But socialism can come and should come, when we wish it." Nevertheless, Landauer's view of Marx was strongly conditioned by the positivistic brand of Marxism which was prevalent in his own day, especially in the SPD, and this blinded him to certain Marxist views which he shared. It is for this reason that Landauer neglected the fact that Marx did not turn his back upon the tradition of German humanism and idealism which he had absorbed in his youth.[136] Although they undoubtedly had different tactical approaches, the two men shared a similar conception of the necessity of the return of joy to human labor, the view of man's self-realization through creative activity. In concert with Marx's view, Landauer emphasized that workers should be concerned with transforming the nature of their labor into a joyous, creative activity; they should not merely clamor for shorter working hours to free them from labor.[137] For both thinkers the emphasis on creative labor was based upon the idealist conception of the externalization of the human essence in the objective world.[138]

Certain similarities aside, however, the fundamental distinction remained: Marx saw sociohistorical transformation as the necessary prerequisite for the liberation of the individual; Landauer insisted that social and historical reconstruction had to be preceded by the rebirth of the individual in the unregenerated world of the present.[139] The mystic experience of the existence of community and humanity within would provide man with the will for real change; without this spiritual renewal all attempts at socialist construction would be in vain. "No progress, no technology, no virtuosity will save us," he wrote, "only out of the spirit, out of the depths of our inner need and our inner riches will the great change come which we call socialism." [140] The desire for a socialist community without had to be nurtured through the rebirth of the community within.

## Anarchosocialist Society

The libertarian socialism of Landauer's writings of 1908–1911 was conceived with the aid, primarily, of three other anarchist thinkers: Proudhon, Kropotkin, and Tolstoi. Tolstoi's pacifism had deeply impressed Landauer in the years after 1899 when he was attacking anarchist terrorism. As for Kropotkin, although Landauer was familiar with some of his writings as early as 1893, he did not fully incorporate any of Kropotkin's ideas into his own thinking until after 1904 when he translated *Mutual Aid*. Finally, of the French anarchist Proudhon, whose writings were translated in almost every issue of the new *Sozialist* after 1909, Landauer wrote in 1910: "Proudhon had nothing to do with the origin of my views and tendencies. I became acquainted with him after I was finished, and was happy, of course, that such a totally different spirit had arrived at similar results." [141] In the writings of these years, all the same, Landauer drew upon Proudhonian mutualist schemes for the formulation of his own doctrine.

Landauer was not a disciple of any of these three figures; rather, he selected those details that had the most appeal for him. Proudhon's theoretical approach derived from the rationalism of the Enlightenment,[142] and Kropotkin attempted to develop an empirical, scientific basis for anarchist ideas,[143] but Landauer rooted anarchist belief in his mystical, idealist philosophy of the self. Proudhon and Kropotkin conceived of sociability and voluntary cooperation as scientifically verifiable in the external world; Landauer, breaking, with Tolstoi, from the traditional rationalist approach of philosophic anarchism, argued in *Skepsis und Mystik* that the libertarian community must first be experienced within the recesses of the human interior.[144] Yet, while they differed in philosophic approach from Landauer, Proudhon and Kropotkin were nevertheless of great value for his socialist writings of 1908–1911.

In line with his earlier work in the building of consumer and producer cooperatives, Landauer conceived of socialism as a system of social relations based upon mutual exchange of products. As he had argued as early as 1895 in the pamphlet *Ein Weg zur Befreiung der Arbeiterklasse*, Landauer held that the organization of consumption, by enabling workers to hold down prices while wage increases tended only to raise them, would provide workers with the economic independence gradually to withdraw from the capitalist economy. In the years after 1908 he formulated these schemes with the aid of Proudhon's mutualist writings.

Landauer's interest in Proudhon—whom Landauer once called "the greatest of all socialists" [145]—centered on Proudhon's writings during and after the Revolution of 1848 when Proudhon published a series of very successful anarchist periodicals.[146] In these journals, the most important of which was *Le Representant du Peuple*, Proudhon concretized his earlier advocacy of a mutualist-anarchist society by developing the idea of a people's bank which would enable independent producers to gain cheap credit for the production of goods. Such a bank would facilitate the just exchange of products by granting credit notes that could be exchanged for consumable products.[147] The point was to eliminate the usurious credit rates of capitalist banks which Proudhon held to be the most pernicious feature of capitalist exploitation. It was not property that determined class exploitation, according to Proudhon, but rather the interest charged for credit.[148]

With Landauer's reliance upon Proudhon in his mature writings on the nature of socialist cooperation, a strong emphasis was now placed upon problems of money and credit. Parallel with the theories of another German Proudhonian anarchist, Sylvio Gesell, whose free-land and free-money ideas have earned him a place in a recent comprehensive history of völkisch ideology,[149] Landauer attacked the "slavery of interest charges" which he and other völkisch thinkers held to be at the basis of capitalist exploitation. By shifting socialist advocacy away from the attack on all forms of private ownership to the question of the evils of a parasitical finance capitalism and its multiplication of unearned money, Landauer accomplished the same avoidance of both capitalism and communism which Proudhonian anarchism shared with the völkisch tradition in Germany.[150]

Under capitalism, according to Landauer, the original function of money is distorted. From an accepted "sign" of mutually accepted credit for the purposes of the exchange of products, money under the capitalist system becomes "interest-bearing capital . . . which gains products of labor and services without having performed any work itself"; from a "relative" position comes "absolute money," and the "exchange of this absolute money, which has broken away and been disengaged from the circulation of goods, for products means the exchange of nothing for something, of work for no work." [151]

Drawing upon Proudhon, Landauer argued that mutual credit would provide the basis upon which to build a mutualist, exchange economy. For Proudhon, prices in a mutualist society would be arrived at through an actual higgling of the market"—the "chaffering in the village square between the man selling a cow and the man selling fodder"—and upon this theory of the just price all production could be organized "on a basis of mutuality, when producers agree to be consumers of the goods produced by each other." [152] The economic basis of social reciprocity, however, would be the organization of consumption and credit, facilitated by the exchange bank. As Landauer put it:

> Carpenter, you have no bread? Of course you can't go to the baker and offer him stools and cupboards he doesn't need. Go to the exchange bank and leave your services, exchanging them for all-purpose checks. . . . Do you have no customers? Why not sell your products among all the mutually cooperating workers, without the intrusion of an exploiting intermediate? [153]

Unlike his view in the earlier period of involvement in the urban cooperative movement, Landauer's view of a mutualist society was a decidedly antiurban conception after the collapse of the first *Sozialist* in 1900. In his mature conception of socialism, Landauer saw the organization of workers' consumption and the resulting increase of credit as merely stepping-stones for the purchase of land and liberation from the "smoke of the cities." [154] A withdrawal from the entire urban factory system was needed, along with the construction of rural, mutual-aid settlements.[155]

In these years Landauer dismissed all methods of accommodating anarchist doctrine to the urban present, such as anarchosyndicalism. His rejection of syndicalist notions was based upon his view that mutual exchange was incompatible with the modern urban and industrial system, so incompatible that after the workers had succeeded in seizing factories after a general strike they would proceed to engage in production for profit on the world capitalist market.[156] If a proletarian wants to become part of a cooperative socialist society, he must prepare to abandon the big city and begin the reintegration of small-scale industry and agriculture in federalized communities on the land.

Landauer's antiurban celebration of peasant life was directly in line with the tradition of völkisch romanticism in Germany. His increasing idealization of peasant life in the first decade of the new century brought him also toward the kind of anarchist position represented by Proudhon.[157] Landauer's early impressions of Swabian peasant life parallelled Proudhon's childhood world immediately across the French border. After 1903 Landauer lived in the semirural Berlin suburb of Hermsdorf and, beginning in 1907, he spent all his summers surrounded by peasants in the small town of Krumbach in Swabia,[158] where Hedwig had been born. In one of the pamphlets he wrote for the Socialist Bund, a pamphlet entitled *Die Siedlung,* Landauer wrote:

Society can be capitalist only because the masses are without land; . . . the land, from which everything comes, all that is reworked by industry, and out of which all our means of life come, is a piece of nature like the air we breathe, like the life and the warmth without which there is no life. . . . The uprooted and unsteady proletariat of today need land, character, responsibility, nature, and love of labor and freedom.[159]

Elsewhere Landauer spoke of "land and spirit" as the "solution of socialism": "The struggle for socialism is a struggle for the land; the social question is an agrarian question." [160]

Landauer was not so much in favor of setting up model communities on the land, however, as in reawakening what he held to be the dormant memories of communal life which still existed among the peasants in the rural Gemeinden. One vital link between the future socialism and the peasant past were the vestiges of communal life remaining in the rural countryside. In *Aufruf zum Sozialisums* Landauer wrote:

> There is so much to which we could add whatever outward forms of life still contain living spirit; there are village communities with vestiges of ancient communal property, with peasants and laborers who remember the original boundaries that have been in private possession for centuries, communal institutions embracing agricultural work and the handicrafts. Peasant blood still runs in the veins of many city proletarians; they should learn once again how to listen to it. [161]

Although a worshiper of the land, Landauer did not envision a purely agricultural livelihood in the rural Gemeinden. For the sketch of his ideal community he drew upon Kropotkin's *Fields, Factories and Workshops*, which he had translated in 1904, with its practical demonstration of the effectiveness of an integration of decentralized industries and agricultural production. He insisted that he was not opposed to advanced technology as such but rather to its previously debilitating effects in the massive centralized industrial system of the cities. [162] Kropotkin had shown, Landauer felt, that it was possible to achieve a balanced and integrated economy of agricultural and industrial production in smaller regional operations where each individual would be able to engage in both endeavors. The watchword of Kropotkin's approach was "integration," the recombining of man's mental and physical skills:

> We proclaim *integration;* and we maintain that the ideal of society—that is, the state to which society is already approaching—is a society of integrated labour; a society where each individual is a producer of both manual and intellectual work; where each able-bodied human being is a worker, and where each worker works both in the field and the industrial workshop; where each aggregation of individuals, large enough to dispose of a certain variety of natural resources —it may be a nation, or rather a region—produces and itself consumes most of its own agricultural and manufactured produce.[163]

In the article "Die Siedlung," which appeared first in *Der Sozialist* in July 1909, Landauer outlined his conception of a rural socialist community based upon the traditional village and, drawing heavily upon Kropotkin, characterized by the integration of fields, factories, and workshops, of peasant, craftworker, and intellectual:

> The peasants need men: men who will settle with them, who will help them to carry out the intensive cultivation of their lands; in the winter months to work together in handwork and industries; men who learn practical things from them and teach them practical things. . . . Our settlement will be finest if it is not traditionless and constructed from the thoughts and theories of those outside, but if it grows from the connection of the settlers to the existing village . . . and seeks to awaken the old, firm, forgotten communal institutions to new life. . . . A socialist village, with workshops and village factories, with fields and meadows and gardens, with large and small livestock and poultry —you proletariat of the big cities, accustom yourself to this thought, strange and odd as it may seem at first, for that is the only beginning of true socialism, the only one that is

left us. Socialism is the return to natural labor, to the natural union of all activities, to the full exchange of these activities, to the community of intellectual and physical, of handicraft and agricultural work, the union also of education and work, of play and labor.[164]

A careful reading of Kropotkin's seminal work shows, however, that Landauer was little concerned with the real thrust of Kropotkin's argument. Although Kropotkin was of course interested in improving the aesthetic qualities of labor by his schemes of industrial decentralization and the diversification of man's economic activities, his primary aim in *Fields, Factories and Workshops* was the increase of productivity, especially that of food. His pragmatic concern for productivity led, among other things, to the advocacy of intensive scientific methods of food production.[165] For Landauer, however, Kropotkin's researches were primarily useful in terms of demonstrating the plausibility of engaging in the kind of economic arrangements which Landauer held to be most conducive to the spiritual rebirth of the individual and the community. Here Landauer the idealist diverged from Kropotkin the scientist.

As advocates of administrative and political decentralization, anarchists often emphasize that if communities are to be self-governing they must be economically self-sustaining; for Kropotkin as for Landauer, one of the primary purposes of a reintegrating of industrial and agricultural production was to promote the economic independence of local and regional communities. Such an arrangement would not mean the isolating of each locality, however. Entire regions would be made up of cooperating local towns and villages which would engage in the mutual exchange of products that the other might lack. Each locality would be sufficiently equipped, however, to free itself from excessive dependence upon other communities.[166]

In line with his concern for decentralization and regional independence, Landauer advocated the federal union of local communities as the basis of any meaningful unity in Germany. When asked to comment, in 1910, on the three-class voting system in Prussia, Landauer replied by arguing that a centralized system of parliamentary democracy would be no improvement over the present system; only an electoral structure rooted in a Prussia of federalized Gemeinden would constitute progress toward a free society. Decisions affecting all Prussia could be reached through the agreements of the various regions and localities, but they were decisions that would not be binding on any local community. If there need be any representational or administrative apparatus beyond the Gemeinde, Landauer insisted that it must be one that is completely dependent upon the local unit from which it is derived. [167] For him, mankind "must have its kernel and its roots in the unique individual, in the couple, in the house, the village, . . . in the Gemeinde." [168]

In Kropotkin's socialist scheme—which was the most influential in anarchist circles in the decades following the 1880s—the means of production were to be owned by "associations or communes of producers, organized on a voluntary basis and connected federally, in which each man would do whatever work he could and receive from the common pool goods sufficient to provide for his needs without exchange or money." [169] Communism would not be introduced and controlled from above but would develop on the initiative of the cooperative "people." Proudhon, on the other hand, although he favored various forms of economic cooperation, was strongly opposed to all forms of cooperative production and communized property. The latter he saw as the replacement of private exploitation by public tyranny.[170]

In his views of property Landauer tried to reconcile individual possession—which, following Proudhon, he strongly distinguished from inherited property worked by wage laborers—and mutualist cooperation. Unlike Proudhon, however, Landauer did not feel that all possessions need be in private hands, although he desired that all individuals have some possessions of their own. The future Gemeinde, he held, should be marked by a "profusion" of forms of possession—individual, communal, and cooperative—with the balance periodically worked out by the members of the community.

> Property is something other than possession; and in the future I see private possession, cooperative possession, and communal possession in rich profusion; not merely possession of the things of immediate use or of the simplest instruments, but also the possession, superstitiously feared by so many, of means of production of all kinds, of houses, and of land. No final precautionary securities should be made for a thousand-year Reich, or for eternity, but a great and comprehensive equalization [Ausgleichung] should be carried out and the will created to bring about new settlements periodically.[171]

The ideal of a periodic redistribution of possessions was meant to ensure that socialism would be something "continually being created," not absolute and fixed. All formulas for the eternal elimination of exploitation and injustice Landauer branded as chimerical, as absolutes that were no more than "words." [172] Socialism must be an endless restructuring of society accomplished by succeeding generations in accordance with what is immediately desirable and possible. Much more in line with romantic organismic theory than with the utopianism of Fourier, Saint-Simon, and the Marxists, Landauer held that history "knows no absolute fulfillment of an ideal" but is a continual process of struggle toward a goal that will never be fully realized.[173]

This was the anarchosocialist society that Landauer envisioned in 1908–1911. Its cooperative economic relations were defined largely in terms of Proudhon's conceptions of mutual credit and exchange, and the nature of its enterprises was based on Kropotkin's plea for integration of crafts, small industry, and agricultural pursuits. With his anarchist mentors, Landauer also conceived of socialism in strictly decentralized, federalist terms, befitting the anarchist cast of his socialist theories. In terms of the problem of property, Landauer attempted to combine Proudhon and Kropotkin: there would be individual and communal possessions, with redistributions to be periodically worked out by the community. Instead of a socialism directed from above, by the authoritarian state, Landauer envisioned a community held together by mutual cooperation from below.

In what way, however, was this ideal to be realized? How was the state to be replaced by a cooperative community of self-determining individuals? The answer to this question lies in Landauer's discussion of tactics.

## The Origins of the State and the Question of Tactics

Aside from Bakunin, the major anarchist theoreticians and philosophers have not been celebrants of violence. Before Tolstoi, however, and Landauer who followed him, anarchist thinkers had not dealt systematically with the problem of the effectiveness of political revolution and violence as a means of attaining a nonauthoritarian end. Neither Proudhon nor Kropotkin provided a systematic critique of the problem of political revolutionary means and nonviolent, decentralized ends, although, at the end of his life, Proudhon wrote bitterly, after having been a lifelong worshiper of the French Revolution, that "it is the revolutionary struggle that has given us centralization." [174]

At the heart of the matter was the question of the origins of political authority. Proudhon's and Kropotkin's view of the state as an external "usurpation" based upon nothing but force[175] continued to commit them to the position that revolution was capable of finally destroying the state, that prerevolutionary anarchist beginnings were possible, but not absolutely necessary; if all the human potential for an anarchist society exists now and the evils of authoritarian oppression are seen to originate in political institutions that are not derived from existing human failings, then the revolutionary overthrow of the state is possible.

As Martin Buber has shown, it was at this point that Landauer made an original contribution to anarchist thought:

> . . . there are in Kropotkin's teaching fundamental elements which point to the significance of prerevolutionary structure-making . . . he stresses that the future he wishes to see "is already possible, already realizable." From there it is only a step to demanding that an immediate beginning be made with the restructuring of society—but that step is decisive. . . . Landauer's step beyond Kropotkin consists primarily in his direct insight into the nature of the State. The State is not, as Kropotkin thinks, an institution which can be destroyed by a revolution. "The State is a condition, a certain relationship between human beings, a mode of human behavior; we destroy it by contracting other relationships, by behaving differently." (*Beginnen*, p. 53)[176]

Deviating from Marx's socialism, and from the traditional anarchist directions, Landauer held that a real anarchistic social order had to be begun before any revolution, or else revolutions would lead to nothing but increased state power and the perpetuation of an authoritarian bureaucracy. The Revolution of 1848 in France, for example, had resulted in the increase of "state tyranny and spiritual servitude under Napoleon III" because it had not been preceded by the concrete development of a social order representing an alternative to capitalism and the state.[177]

The state, Landauer held, is not an external force that operates upon man, but a mere "name for what man allows," [178] an "illusion" or "phantom" (in the terminology of Mauthner), or a "spook" or "idol" (following Stirner's terms).[179] Here Landauer was in the idealist philosophical tradition, relating the seemingly external environment to its origin in man's mental apparatus. Landauer, however, followed the voluntarist direction that Fichte, Schopenhauer, and Nietzsche had stamped upon German idealism. All political and social institutions, he held, depend for their existence on the decision of the individual's will to lend them support; withdrawal of this voluntarily given support can alone bring change.[180] Capitalism and the state are voluntarily chosen by men because their capacity to live independent, self-determined lives has atrophied.

In developing this voluntarist view of political authoritarianism Landauer drew, in the years after 1907, upon the ideas of the sixteenth-century political theorist Étienne de La Boétie. In opposition to the apologists of absolutism of his day, La Boétie had argued that the primary source of political authority lay not in God or the monarch but in the "voluntary servitude" of the masses, a servitude that could end only through the decision to withhold support. In 1907, in *Die Revolution*, Landauer wrote of La Boétie:

Where does the tremendous power of the tyrant derive from? It does not come from external power; . . . no, its power comes from the voluntary servitude of men. . . . But, asks La Boétie, what is to be done against the tremendous servitude that has come over men? . . . there is nothing more than the desire to be free. . . . "Decide to be slaves no longer and you are free." I do not seek to chase the tyrant or throw him from his throne; do not support him any longer . . . and he will be destroyed. . . . If one gives nothing more to the tyrant and ceases to listen to him, then men stand naked without a struggle and without a blow; they stand destitute and are nothing, as a root that can find no moisture and nourishment becomes a dry, dead piece of wood.[181]

For Landauer the authoritarian state was nothing more than an artificial surrogate for *verbindender Geist*, the spirit of community, which had been ossifying since the Middle Ages. The voluntary acquiescence in dependent lives controlled by parties such as the SPD and states such as the German Reich merely reflected the dormancy of the capacity to build without the community that men felt within.[182]

The power of the state would become weaker and weaker . . . if the Volk would begin to constitute itself aside from the state. But the Völker have not grasped the fact that the state has a task and is an unavoidable necessity until there exists that which may replace it: socialist reality. One can throw away a chair and destroy a pane of glass; but those are idle talkers and credulous idolators of words who regard the state as such a thing or as a fetish that one can smash in order to destroy it. The state is a condition, a certain relationship among human beings, a mode of behavior between men; we destroy it by contracting other relationships, by behaving differently toward one another. . . . We are the state, and we shall continue to be the state until we have created the institutions that form a real community and society of men.[183]

Landauer's theory of authority tended, to some degree, to reflect conditions in Germany in the decades before

World War I. Especially in the years after 1895, when German industrialization had begun successfully to emasculate oppositional sentiment among the largest section of the urban masses, there was more reason for a German anarchist to speak of the inertia and the dependence of the masses, of their "blind belief in authority," than a French or Russian one, such as Proudhon or Kropotkin. In 1898 Landauer wrote in the earlier *Sozialist* that among all the peoples of Europe the German is the most obedient of subjects; all of us are subjects, he wrote, in willing obedience to our officials, our party leaders, and our king.[184] Since libertarian currents and movements were particularly weak in Germany, it is not surprising that he should have been less of a populist than either Proudhon or Kropotkin, or anyone in the anarchist tradition, for that matter, and that he should have blamed the existence of the state on human passivity and dependence, instead of seeing it as an externally imposed tyranny.

Landauer's view of authority ruled out appocalyptic change and the separation of means and ends which such a goal necessitates. This view was represented most forcefully in his time by Leo Tolstoi. For Landauer, Tolstoi embodied the ideas of Eckhart and La Boétie, the mystical philosophy of the indwelling of God and the political philosophy of passive resistance to authority.[185] In a 1912 essay Landauer used Tolstoi to distinguish his own tactics from those of Kropotkin and other political revolutionists:

> Tolstoi seems to say: You men think too much about the environment, the future, and others; you separate means and ends too much, as if an end could be gained in this way. You think that questionable means are justified by a noble goal. For us, however, the moment alone exists; do not sacrifice reality to a phantom! If you want the proper life then live it now. . . . Tolstoi brings the absolute into life; Kropotkin

is a positivist and therefore a relativist and allows for the
revolutionaries, even for violence, if it must be.[186]

According to Landauer, "no one has hammered into our
heads with such force and such irrefutable simplicity, once
and for all, what Tolstoi has finally demonstrated: that the
goal, powerlessness, is at the same time the means to reach
that goal, that coercive rule breaks down, and that the tor-
ment of injustices expires if subjects cease to practice
force." [187] Tolstoi's importance in the history of anarchism
was his exemplary consistency, his reasoned refusal to sub-
ordinate means to ends. Until April 1919, when, in a mood
of desperation, he entered a revolutionary government,
Landauer followed Tolstoi's consistent anarchist pacifism.

Landauer's view of authority leads to a crucial question
about his tactics. For one who was so free from the common
anarchist naïveté about the "people" as Landauer—a thinker
for whom the spiritual atrophy of the age included the voluntary servitude of the "bourgeois, the petit bourgeois and
the worker, the liberal and the Social Democrat, the communist and the individualist anarchist," [188] and who spoke
of the "present stupidity and inertia of the masses" [189]—how
was it possible to avoid the conclusion that the masses must
simply be led, be "forced to be free"? The answer, though
difficult to implement in practice, was at least satisfying in
theory: Landauer's mystical belief that humanity is born in
the soul of the individual and that this birth could take place
in any individual provided a theoretical solution. As with
most pacifist theories, this one depended upon the power of
example of the few:

One has always turned to the community, all have done this,
all have engaged in mass politics as if we had a high and
noble Volk to which one merely had to speak the truth.
. . . For the first time, however, the watchword has been

given: through isolation to community. To the question—Where are the human beings who can do no other than create the new forms of union among men?—we answer: the few are there! . . . It is only in this way that the whole has ever gone into movement.[190]

Landauer appealed to those few, usually middle-class intellectuals, whose willingness to set up cooperative settlements on the land would serve as a beginning, as a demonstration of a movement that would be sure to spread. If these few resolve to dissociate themselves from the capitalist process and the working of the authoritarian state, then they will serve to arouse the masses from their passivity and their dependence: "Although we are few, we must begin; because we are few, we must begin in a small way. Once we have begun, however, we will be able to show all those who can see, what socialism, joy, and community really are! Then we know: *we will soon be many*." [191] The masses would not be "forced to be free"; they would gradually be encouraged to be free, not by moral preaching, but by the spreading example of an alternative social order, one based no longer upon voluntary servitude but upon voluntary cooperation.

In a letter to Max Nettlau, Landauer complained that most anarchists spent all their time "contemplating" their enemies and all obstacles to freedom which exist; what is needed, Landauer argued, is that we learn to speak a new "language: the language of example and of beginning." [192] According to Julius Bab, Landauer was thoroughly unlike the "wild-eyed fanatic" who sought to remake the world overnight, a socialist who was always ready to utilize the concrete materials of the past and present if they could be directed toward certain definite, and at first very limited, goals.[193] Although Landauer insisted that we turn our backs on the state and the urban factory, he focused upon potentially libertarian and cooperative social institutions present in contemporary society which might furnish the needed structures for the development of real socialist activity. Besides the "remnants of old communal possessions in old rural villages" across the German countryside, Landauer called for the redirection of the German consumer cooperative movement away from its recent tendency toward centralizing bureaucracy,[194] and for all trade unions to withdraw from the capitalist system by operating as organs of a self-sufficient economic life for its members, through the use of the union funds at their disposal.[195] Instead of a negative general strike in which mass work stoppages would precede the capture of urban factories, Landauer called for an active general strike in which workers would cease to labor for the capitalist market and begin producing goods for their own use.[196]

Such suggestions for the utilization of existing social materials in the building of anarchosocialism made up a part of what Landauer had called the "language of example and of beginning." Yet Landauer's primary attention was not focused upon existing trade unions and cooperatives, at least not urban ones, but upon the immediate beginnings of socialist settlements on the land, settlements that would draw upon whatever traditional communal patterns of rural life were still in existence alongside the present regimen of bourgeois, individualized, private property. To implement this völkisch socialist philosophy, Landauer had created the Socialist Bund, whose unsuccessful career has been examined earlier. In the years 1908–1911 Landauer had combined activity for the Bund with the writing of *Aufruf zum Sozialismus* and numerous articles on socialism. In these years he had developed a conception of libertarian socialism which included romantic and völkisch elements, such as the worship of the medieval past and the rural present. In opposition to Marxian socialism, moreover, he had developed an idealist critique of historical materialism. In the years after 1911, however, Landauer's attention shifted in some degree from the socialist question to the national one; with the intensification of European tensions in 1911 and the threat of a massive war that would embroil the great nations, Landauer's völkisch socialism developed in new directions.

# 5. The Socialist as Romantic

In the years 1911–1918 Landauer's preoccupations were different from those of the preceding decade. Whereas his social thought had earlier been marked by a call for co-operative settlements away from the smoke of the cities, after 1911 Landauer directed his attention much more to the national question, the problem of the relation between each Volk and the rest of humanity. The reasons for the shift in emphasis are not difficult to find. It was in response to the second Moroccan crisis of 1911, with its aftermath in Germany and France of intense mutual hostility and nationalist frenzy, that Landauer began to develop a humanitarian and pacifist conception of the nation.

In the three years preceding World War I and in the first three years of the war, imperialist and chauvinist sentiment was at a height in Germany. To this situation Landauer responded as an anarchosocialist, calling for an end to the system of states which he regarded as the cause of war; he also responded, however, as an heir to the century-old völkisch romantic tradition in Germany. In the years after 1911 Landauer utilized the cosmopolitan, cultural nationalism of the early romantics in Germany against the state worship and the xenophobia of later right-wing völkisch thinkers. Each Volk, Landauer insisted, is a reflection of and a contributor to universal humanity; it is a community of peace as distinguished from the state, which is a structure of force and violence. Landauer repeated this message over and over again in these years: at first, from 1911 to 1915, in his private correspondence and in numerous articles for

*Der Sozialist* and other journals, and later in the works of literary criticism he wrote during the war years. While he did not abandon his earlier interest in libertarian cooperative communities, Landauer's völkisch socialism developed after 1911 largely in response to the threat, and then to the actuality, of a war involving the great nations of Europe. A necessary prelude to an examination of his cosmopolitan nationalism, both in his political commentaries and in his literary criticism, is a consideration of his response to the tragic events of these years.

## World War I: The Response of a Libertarian Romantic

In the years preceding World War I, Germany had been led by Wilhelm II and his top policy advisers into a situation long dreaded by Bismarck; after 1905, three of the major powers—England, France, and Russia—were allied against her and Germany was forced to become dangerously dependent on the shaky fifth power, the Austro-Hungarian monarchy, whose battle with its subject Slavic nationalities was bound to result in a war with Russia. The carte blanche that Bismarck had never given to the Habsburg monarchy was given by his less astute successor in the years after 1907; this dangerous development, which would bring Germany into any war between the Habsburgs and the Romanovs, was to a large degree a reflex action of earlier blunders by William and his advisers, especially the solidifying of the Anglo-French Entente Cordiale after the Moroccan affair of 1905.[1]

Landauer reacted to these developments by focusing upon the internal, domestic causes of Germany's isolation from the rest of Europe. In a 1907 article Landauer argued that the autocratic, feudal, and militarist condition of German society was isolating the country from political developments in the rest of Europe, especially as Russia seemed to Landauer at that time to be taking a progressive step away from autocracy after the Revolution of 1905. Condemning a recent unanimous Reichstag resolution against moving for disarmament at The Hague peace conference of 1907, Landauer charged that Germany's diplomatic isolation was of her own making; the paranoiac state of mind in Germany, he added, might well lead to war. The basic cause of isolation was not that others sought to encircle her, but that Germany seemed peculiarly resistant to calls for peace, a resistance that rested, in turn, upon the authoritarian nature of her political institutions and the "tutelage" and passivity of the masses from which the institutions gained their strength.[2] In this earliest phase of Landauer's war prophecies, the burden of guilt in his indictment fell upon Germany alone, but it was conceived in terms of his view of the state as a reflection of the voluntary servitude of the masses.

After Landauer's 1907 article on German foreign policy, he dropped such questions and, in the years 1908–1911, as we have seen, concentrated upon his Socialist Bund and the development of his anarchosocialist theories. After the summer of 1911, however, Landauer became increasingly concerned about the threatening European situation. The second Moroccan affair and a dangerous turn in German public opinion brought Landauer to a preoccupation with the threat of a European war.

If the first Moroccan crisis of 1905 had done much to isolate Germany and further divide Europe into two suspicious armed camps, then the second Moroccan affair of 1911 made a mockery of Landauer's hopes for international cooperation and resulted in increasing pressures for war on both sides. "On 1 July 1911 the cruiser 'Panther' sailed into the harbor of Agadir to protect German interests in Morocco. Under the strange illusion that this show of force would result in a speedy and mutually satisfactory accord with France, Germany's foreign office therewith unleashed a diplomatic crisis which solidified the Entente Cordiale, increased Germany's isolation, and strengthened the war parties of both France and Germany." [3] In the second Moroccan crisis the German foreign ministry engaged in a far wider propaganda campaign in the press than it had after the crisis of 1905 or after the one following the Austrian annexation of Bosnia in 1908.[4] It is little wonder that Landauer's attention was drawn toward the question of nationhood and humanity after 1911; never before had chauvinist and imperialist sentiment been so widely expressed in Germany as in the wake of the second Moroccan affair.[5] Such sentiments only became more strident with the disappointment over the results of the incident. Instead of "receiving the French Congo as the cornerstone of the future, great, continuous colonial empire in Africa"—as numerous German publicists had demanded—"Germany was fobbed off with the meagre strips of land on the Congo and Ubangi." [6] Frustrated by these disappointments, pressure groups such as the Navy League, the Colonial League, and the Pan-German Association fanned public discontent and demanded increased armaments and imperial expansion.[7] Numerous imperialist pamphlets poured from the press after 1911. In General Frederick von Barnhardi's *Germany and the Next War*, for example, which appeared early in 1912 and went through five editions by the end of the year, a preventive war against France was urged for the purposes of facilitating the acquisition of new colonies and the securing of German hegemony in Europe.[8]

The crisis strengthened the militant anti-imperialist Left

radicals within the Social Democratic Party; Karl Lieb-knecht's isolated crusade against war was generalized beyond a small circle of Cassandras prophesying disaster for an assault by the SPD Left and left Center against the increasingly reformist party executive.[9] Agadir also fully launched Landauer's personal campaign against the war hawks. In the months following July 1911 Landauer wrote numerous articles in *Der Sozialist* in which he prophesied that a European war would soon result if the anxieties of the "armed peace," largely created by Germany, continued.[10] Later he cited the evidence, presented by Liebknecht, that the arms industry was of great importance in encouraging war through its influence on the government and the press.[11]

In his attack on German policy, however, Landauer did not merely blame the industrialists, the military, and the autocracy. If the Moroccan crisis did not lead to a war, Landauer wrote in September 1911, it was not because the masses opposed it and stayed the hand of their governments; earlier fears of war among "the peoples" had now turned into hysteria for war, and "if it had been up to the Völker then a European war would have broken out over Morocco." [12] Landauer's anarchism had never been based upon a naïve populism. Reflecting in 1913, however, on the state of German public opinion, Landauer withdrew his earlier judgment and claimed that it was only the political immaturity of both German and French peoples which made them clamor foolishly for increased armaments out of an anxiety for peace.[13] All this time Landauer must have known, although he did not emphasize, that there was at least some link between popular war hysteria and the tremendous influence on the press exercised by those who imagined that their interests would be advanced by war.

As a champion of national self-determination for all Völker—that is, as a consistent Herderian romantic—Landauer was particularly disgusted by the Austro-German alliance, an accord that after 1907 committed Germany to any war the Habsburgs might wage against any of the emerging nations over which they ruled. "We do not want any war!" Landauer wrote in the fall of 1911. "Above all, we do not want a war for the support of the most ruthless and rotten of states, the Habsburg monarchy!" [14] "You Germans who shed crocodile tears over the struggle for national liberation of the Boers against the English," he continued, "why do you not see that the Serbs are in the same situation against the Austrians?" [15] In the same vein, Landauer championed the cause of the Albanians, an "independent" but "suppressed community," against the imperial domination of the crumbling Ottoman Empire. [16]

Yet Landauer's commitment to national self-determination was for him, as for Herder and the early romantics, only a first step in the development of a united humanity of diversified Völker. The way toward a united Europe lay through the prior "bottom-up" groupings of culturally similar nations. In 1912 Landauer called for what he regarded as the first step toward a potential "united Völker of humanity," a union of Swiss, Belgian, Alsatian, and Dutch "nations" as a neutral Völkerbund based on geographical and historical-cultural unities. [17] In Landauer's view the way to humanity lay through differentiated nationalities whose unity was to be made up of cooperation from below, not of imposed centralization from above. In May 1912 he wrote in Der Sozialist: "The brotherhood of Völker is not something that can come vaguely and all at once for the whole of humanity, but something that results from the definite conditions . . . of time, geography, and history, a brotherhood that is to be created in a variegated and manifold way." [18]

In his *Sozialist* articles of 1911–1913 Landauer did not attack merely the German and the Austrian states. In the struggle against war, as so often in the past, he saved some of his choicest invectives for the German Social Democrats, the party that had used its power in the Second International to prevent the adoption of various motions calling for an international general strike in the event of war and had even "pressed for a fuller acceptance of colonialism." [19] Failing to take sufficient account of the differences among the various Marxist parties, however, as well as the divisions existing within each, Landauer's attack on SPD policy followed the monolithic anti-Marxist stand of his recently published *Aufruf zum Sozialismus*. Arguing that Marxists see national wars in terms of the historical-progressive value of destroying outmoded social and political systems, Landauer contended that they have no ethical basis upon which to build a campaign against militarism.[20] In response to a speech by Bebel in December 1911, Landauer remarked that it was impossible for Marxists to take a negative view of a massive military struggle since they regarded a European war as a final deathblow to capitalism, a welcome historical occasion for the socialist revolution. "Socialism," wrote Landauer, "does not come through waiting and an expectation of downfall." [21] In 1913 he predicted that "if the regimes should come to war, the German Social Democrats will scarcely play a larger role than they did in 1870, in spite of their many voters. . . . The dear German Volk, as a whole, and to be sure with enthusiasm and devotion, will do what the officials command." [22] Here, of course, was a prophetic estimate of the *Burgfrieden* of August 1914 and of the unanimous vote of the SPD Reichstag delegation for the war credits asked by the government. With all his idealism, there was often a shrewdness in Landauer's political judgments.

If parliamentary socialists were not going to avert a war, how was it to be averted? After 1911, in order to prevent the fulfillment of his warnings, Landauer advocated the political strike tactic developed by the French syndicalist Gustave Hervé. A majority of the French delegation to the Stuttgart Congress of the Second International of 1907 had supported this tactic; it was debated—but not passed—at both this meeting and the one in 1910 at Copenhagen.[23] In the fall of 1911, immediately after the Agadir crisis, Landauer wrote a pamphlet entitled *The Abolition of War through the Self-Determination of the Volk* in which he called for a massive general strike of workers to force the government to abandon its present direction toward war. Emphasizing that such a political strike must be launched immediately and not wait for the outbreak of hostilities, Landauer called for grass-roots selection of working-class representatives to be sent to local, then regional, conferences, and finally to a national workers' conference to plan the strike. The present socialist party and trade-union officials must be replaced by delegates who are fully controlled by the groups that elect them; decisions should be arrived at through federalist cooperation and not imposed by bureaucratic fiat.[24]

Combining these libertarian elements with his antipolitical cultural nationalism, Landauer argued—rather pathetically, given the state of popular sentiment at the time—that the "socialist-feeling German worker" will support such an antiwar project since he "knows" that governmental struggles have nothing to do with the "land, language, and customs" of the nation to which he is tied.[25] Such predictions, however, were of little more than academic interest after December 1911. Landauer's pamphlet was never distributed; before the 100,000 copies that had been printed were mailed out, the Berlin police confiscated them, aided in their seizure by the release of a copy by a police agent working on *Der Sozialist*.[26] Later, in the courts, the confiscation was defended on the basis of a statute against the spreading of writings that call for disobedience to the law.[27] Landauer's Tolstoian attempt to bring about a mass disaffiliation of workers from the war economy and the state had been nipped in the bud. If the pamphlet had not been confiscated, however, it would, no doubt, have fallen upon deaf ears; Landauer's attempt to prevent the war, as well as so many other of his political activities, was carried out in isolation from any real mass base.

In August 1914 the European war, long dreaded by Landauer, erupted. The division of Europe into two armed camps had brought about the immediate generalization of a local conflict between the Habsburg monarchy and Serbian nationalism. Besides a small number of pacifist intellectuals such as Hermann Hesse, Martin Buber, Gustav Landauer, and the professors who later formed the Bund Neues Vaterland in 1915 to work for a compromise peace, as well as a few Marxist revolutionaries such as Rosa Luxemburg and Karl Liebknecht, the war was met in Germany with high enthusiasm and often exaltation, offering, ironically enough, a kind of release from the tension of the preceding years.[28] SPD members, of course, outside the right-wing group of imperialists, did not greet the war with enthusiasm; yet almost all of them rallied to what they regarded as the defense of the fatherland against the czarist oppressor. Such motivation for national defense tended to diminish as they became aware that much of Germany's struggle was against the Western democracies and, after the overthrow of Russian czarism in March 1917, even the Majority Socialists were moved to support a Reichstag peace resolution.

For the first two years of the war the so-called Burgfrieden reigned. Domestic political struggle was voluntarily suspended by the various parties, while all military and political authority was abdicated to the army and the government. In addition the trade unions called off all strikes so as not to cripple the war effort.[29] The overwhelming majority of German writers and academic intellectuals did not merely participate in the Burgfrieden, but were among those groups that were most enthusiastic about the war, feeling, as Friedrich Meinecke recollected, that the collective exaltation of August 1914 promised a "spiritual renovation of our state and culture." [30] As Fritz Stern has written, the "spontaneous experience of unity found intellectual embodiment in the 'ideas of 1914,' in the wartime literature in which some of the best German minds sought to prove Germany's cultural apartness from, and superiority to, the West. Those were the years in which Ernst Troeltsch and Thomas Mann, among many others, grappled with the antithesis of German *Kultur* and Western *Zivilisation* and in which lesser minds simply polemicized against the West." [31] Most intellectuals in Germany regarded the war, as Mann did in his *Betrachtungen eines Unpolitischen* (1917), as a defense of German Kultur and idealism against the shallow commercialism and materialism of England and France.[32]

Landauer was one of the few German writers who opposed the war, from the first, on moral grounds.[33] He reacted to it both as an anarchist and as a cosmopolitan, cultural nationalist. Immediately after the assassination of Archduke Francis Ferdinand in late June 1914, Landauer wrote that if war soon comes, as is likely, it will be the product, not of one state such as Germany—here Landauer altered his earlier emphasis upon Germany's prime responsibility—but of the entire system of states. With Tolstoi, to whom he referred specifically, Landauer argued that there can never be lasting peace between states: "It is the mistake of all peace movements not to see with Tolstoi that the struggle against war is a struggle against the state; whoever gets involved in politics of the state, even from the standpoint of revolution, is a party to the war." [34] Two years before the war, in 1912, he had written in much the same vein:

> War is an act of power, of murder, of robbery; . . . it is the sharpest and clearest life expression of the state. It is a dangerous self-deception to protest against the horror of war of a definite state in the name of national sympathies or the economic interests of one or another Volk. . . . War and its horror do not depend on the characteristics of some nation, but rather on the entire situation and on the power of states.[35]

While most anarchists agreed with his view of the European war, Landauer was distressed to find that one of his great teachers, Kropotkin, had deviated so far from the anarchist position, because of his hatred of Germany and his admiration for "progressive" England and France, as to side with the Entente.[36] Kropotkin did not see, according to Landauer, that war could never help, and could only hurt, the libertarian revolution.[37] Yet Landauer's view of the war was not entirely compatible with that of most anarchists. As we have seen, Landauer regarded state power as the result of the voluntary servitude of the masses. For this reason he placed much more emphasis than other anarchists did on the submission of the public, its chosen involvement in the bloodbath.[38]

As a völkisch libertarian and German cultural nationalist, Landauer regarded the war not only as a crime against humanity but as a crime against the various Völker which reflected mankind in their unique ways. The crucial point to be driven home to the public of the different nations, Landauer wrote in 1915, is that only "states are natural enemies, but the nations are not." [39] Whereas war propagandists and chauvinist intellectuals utilized the romantic conception of cultural uniqueness in conjunction with later social Darwinist views of the necessity of conflict and struggle between nations, Landauer emphasized that "differentiation" and "opposition" should not be confused; the essence of every "unique" nation is the peculiar contribution it can make to a peaceful mankind.[40] Late in 1914 Landauer wrote to Fritz Mauthner, who had begun to side with the German armies: "I know myself to be wholly German and yet I do not have the slightest feeling of association with the policies and actions of the German Reich." German identity need not vitiate one's commitment to humanity, Landauer declared; "I sympathize with foreign nations as much as I do with the Germans." [41]

In the months after the outbreak of the war Landauer attacked the war enthusiasm of the German intellectual community in the name of the völkisch romantic tradition. The idealist and romantic traditions had been utilized for the purpose of defending German imperial expansion as a spreading of Kultur, but Landauer countered such uses by quoting Herder against his right-wing distorters: "Why must Völker fight each other and disturb their peace?" Landauer quoted from Herder's *Briefe zur Beförderung der*

*Humanität*: ". . . it is said that this is done for the sake of the continually growing Kultur; but history tells us a different story! . . . Livonians and Estonians now curse their oppressors, the Germans. . . . Kultur has not been brought to them; only the kernel of their own Kultur was destroyed." [42]

Closely watched by the authorities after August 1914, *Der Sozialist* found a ready form of opposition to the war in the writings of the very fathers of German nationalism lauded by the academic war hawks. Late in 1914 Landauer reproduced selections from the writings of Fichte, Herder, and other early romantic cosmopolitan nationalists in *Der Sozialist*. His purpose was to demonstrate how the proper view of the German nation was one that recognized its roots in, and its duty toward, a mankind of autonomous, self-determining Völker. Whereas chauvinist intellectuals merely follow and sanctify government orders, Landauer wrote in *Der Sozialist* in October, the intellectual defenders of the German resistance to Napoleon sought to "create" a nation.[43] Landauer, of course, knew that it was not only German intellectuals who were narrow chauvinists and war propagandists. In December he translated extracts from Romain Rolland's writings condemning the war and its intellectual defenders: Hauptmann and Lamprecht (the Germans), D'Annunzio (the Italian), Bergson (the Frenchman), and others.[44]

Translating Rolland and reproducing the humanitarian sentiments of Herder must have been comforting for Landauer during the first year of the war. He was now experiencing the deepest sense of isolation in his life, as friend after friend, first the poet Richard Dehmel, then Fritz Mauthner, chose to support the policies of the Reich.[45] As his bitterness increased, he became petulant and brusque with those who did not share his views of the war. He defined his position rigorously and was often wounded and pained by the apostasy of friends whom he had trusted.[46] A good example was Landauer's participation in a discussion circle that had met in Potsdam in June 1914, just before the outbreak of war. Conceived as a small attempt to further international cooperation, the group of eight was made up of German, French, and Dutch intellectuals, included Buber and Theodor Däubler, and was soon to be joined by Romain Rolland.[47] The person who seems to have initiated the circle was the Dutch literary critic and pacifist, Frederik van Eeden. In his diary van Eeden described the group's meeting in June 1914 as warm, inspiring, and intense.[48]

With the outbreak of war, however, the group not only was prevented from meeting, but found it difficult to communicate by mail, as disagreements over the war increased. At the same time as a number of non-German intellectuals began to side with the Allies, two German writers, Erich Gutkind and Florens Christian Rang, interpreted the war as a fight for German spiritual values against French and English commercialism.[49] Landauer reacted bitterly to such spurious idealizations of the slaughter. While van Eeden and Buber attempted to patch up the quarrels, Landauer wrote to the Dutch pacifist that he could not participate in any group with men like Rang and Gutkind; as a German, Landauer commented, he could not view them with the same serenity as van Eeden did.[50] Since it was clear that no one would be expelled from the circle, even though the original purpose of the group had been subverted, Landauer wrote to Buber as early as October 1914 that he could no longer participate. He was particularly incensed, he told Buber, by Gutkind's assimilation of a war between states to an alleged battle between spiritually opposed Völker.[51] He continued to exchange letters with the pacifists in the circle for a number of months, but in August 1915 he more or less formally took his leave from the group.[52] With the exception of his old friend, Fritz Mauthner, whose relationship with Landauer remained warm although strained by the former's chauvinism,[53] Landauer found it extremely difficult to associate with those he regarded as political opponents.

At one point the war even brought Landauer into conflict with his closest political ally, Martin Buber. Both were libertarian socialists, völkisch communitarians, and strong opponents of the war. But Landauer's critical eye had been sharpened as never before by the events since 1914. In 1916 he attacked Buber for implicitly defending a German mission in the war in one of his articles for his journal, *Der Jude*. In the piece, entitled "The Spirit of the Orient and of Judaism," Buber had argued that Germany is unique in the West in being able to save the oriental spirit from extinction in the world, owing to its close relationship with Jewry, an oriental Volk.[54] In a letter to Buber of May 1916 Landauer attacked this position. He contended that to defend the German spirit at this time as in any way superior to that of other European nations, without at the very least differentiating it from the imperialist policies of the German Reich, was to indulge in the war propaganda of state officials. If anything, Landauer continued, it might well be argued that the Russian spirit is closer to Judaism; Germany, he alleged, had produced Jewish socialists such as Marx and Lassalle who were ready to eliminate all traces of the Jewish heritage. Buber's position, Landauer concluded, was "very painful, offensive, and almost inconceivable to me."[55] Buber quickly replied. Denying that he had defended the German war policies, he claimed that Landauer had read his article "with the eyes of a fanatic" and had imposed a political meaning that was foreign to it.[56] Landauer, in turn, concluded the exchange by saying that Buber, whether he wanted to or not, had played into the hands of the imperialists, although he saw Buber's position as an unfortunate effect of the agony of the war.[57]

Landauer's pugnacious independence went so far during the war that he refused a request by Erich Mühsam to sign a protest letter against the arrest of Karl Liebknecht in the spring of 1916. In his reply to Mühsam's invitation Landauer wrote that he would not sign a letter in conjunction with leading members of the official socialist party and especially not with the SPD radicals. Landauer called the radicals the "stupidest" group of all in their efforts to turn the war into a revolutionary overthrow of the government without a prior beginning of socialist construction.[58] In the specious reasoning of Landauer's reply there appeared the resentment of one who had been forced out of congresses of the Second International and had long attacked Marxist socialism, but also exhibited was the commitment to a pristine independence which had long marked Landauer's political activities. "It has always been difficult for me," Landauer wrote to Mühsam, "to adopt others' plans and to carry them through. . . . I want to remain pure for future tasks. . . . I do not want to go into the circle of such people as Gerlach, Haase, and Bernstein . . . where I must bend down and conform. . . . It suits me to hold myself actionless now and to do as an individual whatever can be done." [59]

It was usually "as an individual" that Landauer articulated his protest against the war. Resisting participation in the overt political acts of the antiwar movement within the SPD, the groups that were to form the USPD in 1917, Landauer gave veiled expression to his political sentiments in the literary lectures he delivered in Berlin in 1916 and 1917.

*Der Sozialist* had been forced to cease publication in April 1915—the immediate cause was the drafting of the printer[60] —and the lectern was Landauer's only platform from which to express his views publicly. In 1916 and 1917 he presented lectures on Goethe, Hölderlin, and Georg Kaiser in which he sharply distinguished German cultural contributions to mankind from its political dealings with other nations.[61] In opposition to the xenophobic defenders of Germany's cultural uniqueness and its war for Kultur against nations of both East and West, Landauer focused upon the *Humanitätsideal* of German literature, tracing its development from Goethe's *Iphigenia* through Hölderlin's poetry to Kaiser's contemporary pacifist drama, *Die Bürger von Calais;* the great German cultural contributions to humanity constituted "Ein Weg deutschen Geistes," Landauer emphasized, making it clear how he interpreted the political relevance of German Kultur. In a series of lectures on Shakespeare, on the other hand, Landauer emphasized the conflict between man's ethical and intellectual development and his destruction by such lower drives as power and ambition.[62] For Landauer, national Geist and Kultur, far from being advanced by the military exploits of states, were jeopardized by such authoritarian power plays. His German nationalism was pacifist, antiauthoritarian, and cosmopolitan and was of the purely cultural variety.

Never relishing his own isolation—although insisting upon personal self-determination—Landauer was very happy to cooperate with the few individuals he could find during the war who shared his views. He was an endorser, though not an active member, of the Bund Neues Vaterland, a left-leaning pacifist organization formed in 1915 by a number of intellectuals in an effort to coordinate activities for an immediate compromise peace. Numbering among its members outstanding antimilitarists such as the Munich professor Friedrich Wilhelm Foerster, the historian Ludwig Quidde, and Albert Einstein, the Bund was an organization whose activities were drastically curtailed by the military authorities.[63]

Although Landauer endorsed the liberal, pacifist Bund Neues Vaterland, in later 1915 and early 1916 he was far more actively involved with another group: a discussion circle that had been set up in a settlement house in Berlin by a pacifist university student by the name of Ernst Joël. It was the one group in which Landauer fully participated during the war years. Largely occupied with a radical journal entitled *Der Aufbruch* (published by Eugen Diedrichs Verlag, the source of many völkisch publications),[64] the circle brought together important figures from two cultural movements whose social views were very close to Landauer's: literary expressionism and left-wing sections of the German youth movement. The Aufbruchkreis included the writers Kurt Hiller and Rudolf Leonhard, both of whom were founders of the activist wing of the expressionist movement.[65] Joël, on the other hand, had been prominent since 1913 in the attempt to turn the Wandervogel in a socialist direction.[66] Another member was one of the leading intellectuals connected with the youth movement as a whole: Hans Blüher, the historian of the Wandervogel, whose völkisch concept of a communitarian Bund closely resembled Landauer's. On the periphery of the group was a third figure connected with Joël and Blüher, Gustav Wyneken, a libertarian educational theorist who had taught in the experimental völkisch school of Hermann Lietz.[67] Wyneken's fame rested on his powerful speech at the "Hohe Meissner" gathering of Wandervogel groups in 1913, in which he called on the youth movement to turn its back on narrow chauvinism, delete all traces of anti-Semitism, and embrace the humanity celebrated by the German romantics.[68] Wyneken had become interested in the Wandervogel through Blüher's writings.[69] He had also worked with and exercised a major influence on Joël's prewar radical publication *Der Anfang*, with its advocacy of a libertarian and socialist "youth culture." [70] Here was a circle in which Landauer could heartily participate; not only was the group occupied with publishing antiwar articles in *Der Aufbruch* (because of these articles the journal was banned by the authorities after four issues),[71] but it seems to have shared many of Landauer's left-wing communitarian perspectives.

Since Landauer's participation in the Aufbruchkreis highlights his relation to the German cultural scene in these years, it is worth digressing a moment from the immediate subject of the war. In a sense the Aufbruchkreis serves as an interesting example of the ideological fluidity of this period in German culture. Although it helped to encourage the growth of more left-wing groups in the youth movement,[72] its impact was not substantial. There were only 450 subscribers to the journal.[73] At the same time it reflected a number of crosscurrents which seem to have frequently overlapped and combined within Landauer's social world. Landauer wrote articles outlining both his anarchist view of communitarian colonies and his humanitarian view of nationalism.[74] Other pieces in *Der Aufbruch* included Joël's and Hiller's attacks on German militarism; translations of Whitman and Fichte; Hans Blüher's provocative view of an organic socialist community bound together by male libidinal ties; and Joël's call for a libertarian educational system to give expression to socially conscious "bourgeois youth." [75] In the discussion circle itself a number of different "free university" projects were debated, including those of Joël, Wyneken, Rudolf Leonhard, and Martin Buber.[76] Although Landauer did not always approve of the views of all the others in the group—he objected particularly to Blüher's disparaging view of women and to Hiller's tendency toward intellectual elitism—the association of these various intellectuals is of importance in itself. Landauer participated in the circle with "hearty joy in true comradeship," as he wrote to Rudolf Leonhard in October 1915.[77] His connection with these students and intellectuals seems to have been the one cheering experience of the war years. Here opposition to the policies of the Reich was combined with many of the social views that he himself had championed for years. In December 1915 Blüher suggested to Landauer that they combine with Wyneken and Hiller to edit a *Kampfschrift*.[78] Had it materialized it would have provided an even more explicit conjunction of völkisch and socialist crosscurrents than that represented by *Der Aufbruch*.

Landauer's participation in the Aufbruchkreis does not, however, exhaust his connections with the expressionist and Wandervogel movements in these years. With regard to the latter it should not be overlooked that there were important Jewish, Zionist, and socialist groups within the youth movement, altogether numbering about 25,000 members in 1914. To a greater or lesser degree such groups represented a kind of bourgeois communitarian socialism similar to Landauer's.[79] An even closer connection with Landauer's ideas was exhibited by the Hashomer Hatzair youth movement, centered in Vienna at this time. Today in Israel seventy-five kibbutzim owe their existence to it. Combining Zionist with communitarian socialist ideas, and expressing itself in the quasi-religious language of ethical idealism, the Hashomer movement was deeply influenced in the period

1913–1920 by the work of Blüher and Wyneken, as well as of Buber and Landauer.[80]

The question of the relation between the Wandervogel and the expressionist movement in the arts is an involved one and need not be discussed at any length here. There is a parallel, however, to be drawn between much of the thrust of the youth movement and the important utopian and communitarian phase of expressionism in the years 1917–1919. In these years many expressionists attempted to submerge their feelings of isolation and rootlessness and, in anticipation of a postwar revolutionary upheaval in Germany, directed their art toward the creation of a new free cultic community. Envisioning this community as the outgrowth of a spiritual transformation within the individual, such writers as Kaiser and Toller also called for a new humanity which would break from the debilitating industrial and urban present and return to its natural roots.[81]

The similarity between all this ferment and Landauer's social thought does not need to be emphasized. During this period, moreover, Landauer was directly associated with a number of the most important expressionists. We have noted his relations with Kurt Hiller, for example, who later was to credit Landauer with directly influencing the political activism of his group of expressionists.[82] Landauer was in touch with another activist, Ludwig Rubiner, the editor of the *Zeit-Echo* literary journal.[83] In 1919 Landauer's wife, Hedwig, was to publish some poems in Rubiner's collection, *Kameraden der Menschheit*,[84] one of the most significant documents of utopian expressionism. In addition, Landauer was to be a political ally of Ernst Toller during the Bavarian Revolution of 1918–1919; the two were friends in the last year of the war.[85]

Landauer's most important relationship, however, was

with the outstanding expressionist playwright Georg Kaiser. After reading Landauer's *Ein Weg deutschen Geistes*, Kaiser wrote to him in March 1916 that he alone had fully understood *Die Bürger von Calais*.[86] In the next two years monthly letters were exchanged, largely concerning Kaiser's new dramatic works. In these letters Kaiser often showed deep concern for Landauer's critical judgment, and by late 1917 the playwright was asking Landauer to look at his dramas in manuscript and began visiting him in his new home in Krumbach, Bavaria.[87] Landauer wrote at this time to a director of the Neue Freie Volksbühne that Kaiser was the only great dramatist then working in Germany and that the theater organization should "move heaven and hell in order to perform his work." [88] Landauer's greatest enthusiasm, however, was saved for *Gas*, today Kaiser's most famous play, which was written in early 1918. Here Kaiser's work moved very close indeed to Landauer's social views; the anti-industrial communitarianism of the play, and especially its call for a socialist community based upon the Siedlung, were taken by Landauer as a reflection of his own influence upon the expressionist.[89] Kaiser, in addition, had hinted at this fact in one of his letters.[90] *Gas* actually marked the highpoint of the messianic phase of expressionism, a mood with which Landauer was very much in step.

The environment within which this mood developed was that of the last two years of the war. Events of the first half of 1917—the overthrow of the czarist autocracy in Russia and the American entrance into the war in the name of "peace without victory"—alleviated some of Landauer's earlier despair. Although he was mainly concerned with conditions in Germany, Landauer had written a letter to Wilson late in 1916—it was probably intercepted by the authorities—in which he laid the primary responsibility for the war on the armaments race begun by Germany and called for Wilson's sponsorship of an international congress of states which would have jurisdiction over armaments, naïvely concluding that such a plan could be enforced through the moral pressure of peoples freed from the tutelage of the era of secret diplomacy.[91] In March 1917, without explicitly endorsing the Allied cause, Landauer implied such an endorsement when reacting very positively to Wilson's statement of American war aims, the postwar erection of a league of nations to prevent future wars, an aim that would not be implemented in the event of a German victory.[92] Wilson seems to have been the first statesman in whom Landauer placed any trust.

Toward the other great aspirant for the allegiance of world pacifist sentiment in 1917, Lenin, Landauer did not show the same trust. Whereas the overthrow of the autocracy in Russia had been greeted with enthusiasm by Landauer, as well as by all others on the European Left, he was at best unimpressed by the Bolshevik victory of October 1917. At the end of the following year, in his first mention of this world-shaking event, Landauer wrote that the Bolsheviks are "working for a military regime which will be much more horrible than anything the world has ever seen. Rather Napoleon than the dictatorship of the armed proletariat!" [93] With such a revolution occurring in Russia, one universally condemned by anarchists, Landauer turned his attention back to Germany by late 1917, hoping to see a very different kind of social transformation there.

By early 1918, when American troops arrived in Europe and Russia left the war after Brest-Litovsk, the German Burgfrieden had long since disintegrated. A Reichstag coalition of Social Democrats, Progressives, and the Center had existed since July 1917, countering the demand of big industrialists and the Prussian nobility for a victorious peace with their own demand for a negotiated peace without annexations and the introduction of parliamentary government in Germany.[94] The annexationist peace of Brest-Litovsk in January 1918, however, revealed the weakness of the peace parties. In the same month massive working-class strikes broke out in Germany; directed against the war and the military government, these strikes have been called a "dress rehearsal for the November Revolution." [95]

Because of growing dissatisfaction with a long, brutal war and hopes for a new kind of postwar society, Landauer began to find a larger audience for his views. Publishers became very interested in his work and by December 1917, after receiving many requests for copies of his fundamental statement of social philosophy, *Aufruf zum Sozialismus*, Landauer started planning a new edition of the book. The last two years of his life marked Landauer's emergence into the public eye in Germany, at least among the reading public. Late in 1917 he wrote:

> It is not my fault that before the outbreak of the war my socialist publications had almost the character of private printings; I had stood up a little too early. In the course of these war years . . . things have changed; the seekers have found me. It is not a question of coming toward the public as a new figure, now in almost my fiftieth year, but of making my previously hidden work public through new, firm activity.[96]

With the emergence of mass pacifist and revolutionary sentiment in Germany early in 1918, and with his increasing eminence, Landauer could look forward to a more promising future in the months and years ahead. In the midst of this period of growing confidence, however, the greatest tragedy of Landauer's life occurred. In February, nine months after he and his wife had moved from Berlin to the small Swabian town of Krumbach, where she had been born, Hedwig became a victim of the influenza epidemic and died.[97] According to Hans Blüher, who visited him soon after, Landauer's first reaction to this tragedy was to contemplate suicide; he was a "broken man." After sitting at his wife's bedside for days, however, he resolved to go on living both for the sake of their children and because he was convinced that he would be of use in the coming "erection of a 'new Germany' on an anarchosocialist basis" for which he had always worked with his wife.[98] Yet any reader of Landauer's collected letters must note that Landauer never fully recovered from Hedwig's death; an earlier stability and strength were now often missing from his personality. We shall see what effect this change had in the difficult days of the Munich Revolution.

Landauer sat out the rest of the war in Krumbach, unable or unwilling to join in any overt political activities against the war. He was "reserving his strength," he told the visiting Ernst Toller, for the time when the imminent collapse of the monarchy occurred. With strikes revealing the deep rift in German society, destroying the short-lived facade of a monolithic Germany, Landauer expected a social revolution to come within a matter of months. The working classes, for Landauer dormant, passive, and malleable since the economic upswing after 1895, had begun to show signs of life; when the community showed signs of life, the völkisch libertarian had written, the death knell of the state would be sounded. In the spring of 1918 Toller asked Landauer why he was not then participating in any political efforts against the war. Landauer answered: "All my life I have worked for the downfall of this social system, this society founded on lies and betrayals, on the beggaring and

suppression of human beings; and I know that this downfall is imminent—perhaps tomorrow, perhaps in a year's
time. And I have the right to reserve my strength until
that moment. When the hour strikes I shall be there and
ready." [99]

With the coming of the November Revolution of 1918,
Landauer was to emerge from the near total isolation that
had marked his political life for two decades. In chapter 6
I examine his involvement in that revolution and his return,
once again, to the problem of implementing an anarchosocialist theory in modern Germany. The preceding seven
years, 1911–1918, had seen a shift of focus away from that
primary concern and the development of certain new di-
mensions of his völkisch socialism. It was not World War I
that caused this shift to a new concern for a humanity-
oriented cultural nationalism and a stress upon the unique
value of each Volk in the human community; August 1914
had, for Landauer, been merely the culmination of three
years of war hysteria and unparalleled militaristic and chauvinist sentiment in Germany. His intellectual response to the
pervasive belligerence and chauvinism of the German public
in the years 1912–1918 was based upon the same romantic
tradition arrogated by authoritarian völkisch spokesmen on
the Right.

*Community, Nation, and Humanity*

In the years after 1911, in response to the increase of militaristic nationalism in Germany, Landauer wedded his libertarian socialism to a humanitarian conception of the nation.
As a pacifist and an anarchist Landauer conceived of the
nation as a peaceful community. In the fall of 1912 he
wrote: "Every nation is anarchistic, that is, without force;
the conceptions of nation and force are completely irrecon-

cilable." [100] The nation, moreover, which was to be sharply distinguished from the authoritarian state,[101] was the form through which each individual was tied to the rest of humanity. "The goal of humanity," Landauer wrote to Julius Bab in 1913, "is the outer structure for which we strive; the way toward this goal, however, does not lead merely from our own humanity, but above all through our differentiated nationality." [102] It should be clear from this comment that Landauer's "nationalism" was not a rejection of socialist universalism; unlike most völkisch thinkers of the late nineteenth and early twentieth centuries, especially those on the Right, Landauer kept his romantic nationalism consistent with the cosmopolitan framework of the early romantics.

A short summary of the historical development of the German word "Volk" may be useful at this point. In the late medieval and early modern period the word denoted a band of warriors; later it came to mean the servants of a prince. In the course of the eighteenth century "Volk" gradually acquired the sense of the English expression, "the common people"; interestingly enough, however, it first gained this meaning through a pejorative contrast with the educated and the aristocratic. It was the two early romantic figures, Justus Möser and especially Johann Gottfried Herder, who in the last decades of the century accepted this meaning, but they placed a new positive construction upon it. Whereas Möser saw in peasant proprietorship the basis of a true "people" or "Volk," and not the officials and scholars of the court, Herder celebrated the creative genius of primitive and poor Völker and upheld their superiority to the cultural life of the social elites. "Nationalism," a word already used in Herder's writings, was conceived of as a defense of a pluralistic humanity of unique Völker; each

Volk, moreover, was based upon the peasant-craftsman community.[103]

In the early nineteenth century the nobleman Achim von Arnim was to attempt to bridge the gap between populist and elitist concepts of the nation and to define "Volk" in terms of a union of educated intellectuals and the simple poor,[104] a version that was very close to Landauer's understanding of the word. Herder, however, had given more than a merely populist connotation to it. "The *Volk* is not simply the people of a country," K. R. Minogue has recently written of Herder's view, "but a metaphysical entity defined relationally as *that which* produces particular language, art, culture, set of great men, religion and collection of customs. All of these things are taken, not as the products of individual men but as *manifestation* of the spirit of the people, or *Volksgeist.*" Cultural nationalist, populist, and romantic motifs are here interlaced; for Herder, "the lower orders are seen as being not simply primitive peasants but as a source of national creativity." [105]

By 1806, the year of the Prussian defeat at Jena, the word had clearly become associated more and more with the concept of a German nation. The völkisch idea in the nineteenth and twentieth centuries always carries this national connotation, either in its right- or left-wing form. It must be remembered, however, that the early romantics conceived of the "nation" almost always as a cultural, rather than a political, entity. The idea of a nation-state is, of course, not foreign to the writings of Fichte or his contemporaries. They used the word "Volk" far more frequently, though, and meant it to apply to German language, customs, folklore, and general cultural life, as distinct from the state. Often the connotation of völkisch ideas was distinctly antipolitical and antibureaucratic.[106] In this sense the notion was clearly in line with Herder's original view. According to Isaiah Berlin, Herder's enthusiasm for folk culture was "not only anti-dynastic and anti-élitist, but deeply anti-political, directed against organized power, whether of nations, classes, races or parties." It was based upon a "belief in loose textures, voluntary associations, natural ties, and [was] bitterly opposed to armies, bureaucracies, 'closed' societies of any sort." [107]

While much of the original antistatism of Herder's conception was retained in theory by right-wing völkisch thinkers of the late nineteenth and early twentieth centuries,[108] another crucial feature of early romantic nationalism was not. When Landauer argued that each Volk has a unique task to perform for all humanity he was far more in tune with the early romantics than were the völkisch chauvinists of the Right. As Friedrich Meinecke showed as early as 1908 in his pioneering study *Weltbürgertum und Nationalstaat*, nationalism and cosmopolitanism were twin faiths for Herder, Novalis, Schlegel, Fichte, and many other nineteenth-century romantics. In the period of great intellectual and political ferment in Germany, from 1792 to 1815, nationalism was not substituted for the Humanitätsideal of the Enlightenment; rather, the earlier universalist heritage was focused upon the subject of the nation. Novalis, for example, wrote that the German nation was a unique and individual expression of universal culture.[109] Although Meinecke's own purpose was far from humanitarian—he actually wanted to show how the correct view of the nation emerged only in the Bismarck era—his evidence illustrates the fact that the cosmopolitan framework of Landauer's nationalism followed consistently from the romantic heritage; the chauvinist imperialism of the volkisch Right did not.[110]

After the rapid onset of industrialization in Germany in the 1850s and 1860s, the völkisch constellation of ideas was focused upon the resistance to urban and industrial modernity. This feature was, of course, merely an accentuation of earlier romantic attitudes. During Landauer's own lifetime, however, the word "Volk" gained another connotation which deviated from early romantic humanitarianism. Although, as I have attempted to show, there were important völkisch groups that were not anti-Semitic and racist in the Wilhelmian period (1890–1918), racial notions were increasingly added to the völkisch tradition. Houston Stewart Chamberlain and others began to us the word "Volk" in connection with pseudoscientific notions of biological racism.[111] By the time of the rise of the Nazi movement, of course, this was the predominant meaning most Germans attached to the word "völkisch." As George Mosse has recently written, however, there is no necessary connection between völkisch and racist ideas: the youth movement, for example, was "völkisch but not racist in the majority of its Bünde."[112] It is well to bear the following in mind when considering Landauer's own concept of the Volk: while various kinds of anti-industrial, populist, and cultural nationalist meanings are inherent in the völkisch current of German romanticism, racist sentiment is not.

Landauer's nationalism was, indeed, directly in line with the cosmopolitanism of the early romantics. In the years 1913 and 1914 in *Der Sozialist*, for example, Landauer quoted Herder and Fichte against the aggressive chauvinists and imperialists of the day. After the outbreak of World War I, Landauer reproduced sections of that bible of German nationalism, Fichte's *Reden an die deutsche Nation*, in an effort to show how the very figures whom the imperialists used to justify their wars held the conviction that humanity was one and nations were different expressions of it. If Landauer conceded that Fichte erred in regarding Germany as the purest *Menschheitsnation*, instead of seeing each and every Volk as having a unique service to render mankind, he countered by referring, significantly, to other romantic thinkers to correct Fichte on this point, namely to Herder and Jean Paul.[113]

Herder, the real father of völkisch thought, was the most serviceable figure for Landauer's humanitarian campaign. In opposition to those many intellectuals who supported Germany's war in the name of Kultur, allegedly basing their arguments upon Herder's concepts, Landauer published Herder's *Briefe zur Beförderung der Humanität* (1795), as we have seen, in the pages of *Der Sozialist* in November 1914. Although avoiding direct condemnation of the war in the closely watched *Sozialist*, Landauer cleverly supported his cause by quoting Herder against the völkisch imperialists; the basic point of the Herder selection was that wars of one Volk against another which are justified because they are alleged to spread "Kultur" have always meant the suppression of one indigenous Kultur by another. Herder, who was so important for the development of German nationalism, was a very poor support for "Teutonic" imperialism.[114]

If diversity and uniqueness were two of the essential features of romantic thought,[115] they were also the characteristics of Herder's and Landauer's view of humanity. Mankind was made up of unique Völker. On the other hand, "each Volk in its special nationality . . . represents a unique contribution toward mankind," as Landauer wrote to Frederik van Eeden two weeks after the outbreak of World War I.[116] Nationalism or patriotism is not the problem; universal homogeneity is neither possible nor desirable. The root cause of the present nationalist hatreds, Landauer wrote in 1915 to Bernhard Reichenbach, a participant in the Aufbruchkreis, is the confusion of cultural differentiation and opposition:

> Why should one . . . preach the ending of all bonds and therefore of all differences in the world? . . . I am happy about every imponderable and ineffable thing that brings about exclusive bonds, unities, and also differentiations within humanity. If I want to transform patriotism then I do not proceed in the slightest against the fine fact of the nation . . . but against the mixing up of the nation and the state, against the confusion of differentiation and opposition.[117]

Those who confused variety and diversity with the alleged necessity for struggle and opposition were ignorant of the real roots of the unique, but integrated, nation. In his comments on Fichte's *Reden*, Landauer emphasized that for the early nationalist the Volk was one reflection of its "father" which is humanity. Landauer wrote that for Fichte each individual had his roots in the Volk, but his deepest roots were in humanity itself: "Mankind, which itself is founded upon the unswerving humanity that is within our inner selves, is older than all our *Volksthum* and not the product of some externally united nations, but is the father of all Völker." [118] In a letter to Mauthner, which focused on the question of their respective commitments to Judaism, Landauer put the matter most succinctly by replying in the following way to Mauthner's contention that Jewish "nationality" would vitiate his commitment to humanity: "Differentiating among nations, nationalities, or other natural, social, and historical groups no more negates what is common to all humanity than the distinguishing among various species of mammals effaces mammalian characteristics held in common." [119]

Landauer's conception of the Volk contained both the cosmopolitan emphasis of the early romantics and the later völkisch, neoromantic concern for the necessary "myth." With the neoromantics, Landauer conceived of the Volk as not merely a developing historical organism, but as a living creation of the human spirit, as an illusion or *Wahn* or mythos without which there could be no active existence. "The nation," Landauer wrote in 1915, "is the peculiar manner in which, on the basis of the cohesion resulting from a common historical development, the generally human and the individual express themselves at the same time." [120]

As a mystical idealist and student of Nietzsche, Landauer did not regard historical truth as something that operates outside the human will. With Nietzsche, the neoromantics Sorel and Vaihinger, as well as the völkisch Nietzsche scholar Karl Joël, Landauer held that truths were myths created by men to enable them to lead lives of great vitality.[121] The early nineteenth-century focus on the discovery of natural truths had been replaced in the neoromantic view, which predominated after 1900, by the conception that truths are created. As a communitarian anarchist, however, Landauer had to distinguish between such false creations as the state and life-giving illusions such as the community and the Volk. The distinction between the state and the Volk, according to Landauer's Nietzschean formulation, was that although both were created illusions, one was life-giving and encouraged self-determined activity while the other reflected man's passivity and perpetuated it:

A truth that is ripe and pricelessly and deeply felt—that is a living illusion. How does it die? . . . It dies because it is no longer serviceable to life. It dies because life, changing and ongoing life, has killed it. It dies because life has created its successor. . . . And what do we call these truths that seek to destroy the state and its wars? They are called the Volk, socialism, and anarchy. The Volk or the nation is an older, more genuine illusion which must be liberated from its coupling with the lie, . . . the state.[122]

In line with the tradition of romantic historicism derived from Herder, Landauer viewed the nation and the Volk as an organically developing community that has always existed beneath the thin veneer of mechanistic society and the state.[123] We must "bring forth once again the truly living which had seemed completely dead," he wrote. "Everything good that comes into the world does so because it is already there—in the world, in men." [124] On the other hand, Landauer contended with the other neoromantic völkisch thinkers such as Langbehn that the Volk was not so much to be discovered in natural evolution as to be created as a necessary, illusionary mythos: ". . . each great form of the communal life of men," he wrote, "has shone before as an illusion [Wahn]; it has only been through Wahn that men have bound themselves to one another." [125] "It is only where there is a mythos that a new Volk evolves." [126] The völkisch opposition to industrial, urban modernity tried to have it both ways: we must create the mythos of the Volk and cannot rely upon historical inevitability, yet when we do so we are merely uncovering what has all along existed underneath what Landauer liked to refer to as the "accidental institutions of our age." Here Nietzsche's call to the individual to "become who you are" was given a communitarian direction.

We have already noted the völkisch tendency to attack the bureaucratic state in the name of the German cultural community. Disappointment with Bismarck's fusion of German "nation" with Prussian "state" accentuated this tendency in the late nineteenth century.[127] Völkisch anti-

THE SOCIALIST AS ROMANTIC

statism was even more emphatic, of course, in the anarchist hands of Landauer. One aspect of this attitude was anti-parliamentarism, a stance shared by both left- and right-wing völkisch circles.[128] Left and Right divided, however, on the purpose of eliminating parliamentary bodies. Landauer's antiparliamentarian sentiments reflected a decidedly libertarian völkisch outlook: parliament served to strengthen the state and emasculate the socialist desire to build a stateless society, as well as to divide the German Volk into competing, selfish interest groups.[129] His opposition to parliamentary divisiveness was not for the purpose of imposing unification of the German nation through an extraparliamentary and authoritarian mass movement.

Unlike völkisch thinkers of the Right, such as Lagarde, Landauer's concept of the nation was specifically framed as an antiauthoritarian alternative to the state. His distinction between nation and state not only incorporated the romantic separation of organic community and materialistic society, but also rested upon the anarchist distinction between cooperation and force: "National differentiation is a thing of prime significance for the coming realization of humanity," Landauer wrote in 1915, "for those who separate the beautiful, thriving, peaceful fact of the nation from the ugly violence of the state." [130] The nation was conceived, unlike the state, as a free union of self-determining individuals: "Nation is an equality of individuals—a feeling and a reality—which is brought in free spirit to unity and to union [zum Bunde]. Every nation is anarchistic, that is, without force; the conceptions of nation and force are completely irreconcilable." [131] Cosmopolitan and libertarian, Landauer's völkisch nationalism was very different from Lagarde's protofascist interpretation of the German romantic heritage.

Cosmopolitanism and antiauthoritarianism were not the only features that distinguished Landauer's nationalism from that of the völkisch Right. In the same prewar years that saw Landauer turn his attention to the question of the nation and humanity, he also developed a much stronger sense of his own Jewish nationality, as well as his German one, and was thus clearly in opposition to the growing anti-Semitism of much of the völkisch movement. In January 1913 he spoke of himself as a "threefold nationalist: a German, a south German, and a Jew." [132]

Landauer's intellectual outlook has frequently been related to the Jewish heritage and specifically to the prophetic tradition of the Old Testament. His oratorical style often brought Isaiah or Ezekiel to mind.[133] Some of the key words of Landauer's vocabulary, such as "Geist," "renewal," and "rebirth," were in one sense secular equivalents of the kind of intense ethical religiosity found in the prophetic books. Heinz-Joachim Heydorn has even asserted recently that "the Jewish heritage" was the source of many of Landauer's fundamental beliefs. Heydorn points to Landauer's deep concern for the "redemption" and "purification" of man, as well as his conviction of the binding power of "spirit" in the human community, as evidence of his profoundly Jewish outlook.[134] Although one might quarrel with this judgment insofar as some particulars are concerned—we have seen how Landauer's language turned in this direction under the impact of Moritz von Egidy's and Meister Eckhart's writings, both of them non-Jewish mystics—there is little doubt that the tradition of Jewish prophecy formed a component of his thought.

It was not until the years 1913 through 1916, however, that Landauer showed deep concern for questions relating to Judaism. In the preceding five years there had been passing references to Jewish matters in his correspondence, but before 1908 he had only rarely exhibited such an interest.[135] The reasons for the change in Landauer are not difficult to find. Beginning in 1908 he became fascinated with Buber's work on the Polish Jewish mystics, the Chasidim, whom Buber regarded as the true bearers of the Jewish mythos.[136] In that year he read Buber's *Legend of the Baal-Shem* and his *Tales of Rabbi Nachman* with great enthusiasm, and in 1912 he was delighted by Buber's *Daniel: Dialogues on Realization*.[137] The latter demonstrated to Landauer, as he wrote in an essay the following year, that Martin Buber was an "apostle of Judaism before mankind." [138] Buber's evocation of the mystical strain in the Jewish cultural tradition encouraged Landauer to concern himself much more closely with the question of the nature of Jewish identity, as his essay on Buber reveals,[139] especially as he was speculating, in these same years, upon the problem of nationality and humanity.

Other influences conditioned Landauer's new interest. In 1913 Landauer was deeply affected by two incidents of anti-Semitism, one in Russia and one in Germany. After the Russian government attempted, in the Beilis trial, to pin the old charge of "ritual murder" upon Russian Jewry, Landauer responded with an impassioned defense of his eastern coreligionists in an article for *Der Sozialist*.[140] Closer to home, sections of the German youth movement were also exhibiting a tendency toward anti-Semitism. When asked to support a projected federation of all German youth movements, which assembled in October 1913 at the Meissner meeting, Landauer answered that he could not cooperate with those sections of the youth movement made up of racist anti-Semites. Such groups "proscribed and 'outlawed' another human group on the basis of an

THE SOCIALIST AS ROMANTIC

'ineradicable quality,' its Jewishness"; only if the anti-Semitic groups were not invited, Landauer wrote, would he be willing to attend.[141] Landauer not only attempted to define German nationality against the imperialist sentiments of these years, but he also focused on the question of Jewish nationality in response to contemporary anti-Semitism.

Rejecting the assimilationist tendency of most German Jews, as well as the anti-Semitism of much of the völkisch movement in Germany, Landauer insisted that both Jews and Germans were Völker with unique contributions to make to mankind, as he stated in his 1913 essay on Buber.[142] The issue was joined in a controversy of 1912 in *Die Freistatt*, a Jewish literary journal. Julius Bab, the theater critic whom Landauer had known since the Neue Gemeinschaft days, had written that German Jews were rooted in German culture alone. The cultural productivity of European Jews, he asserted, did not mean that they constituted a separate nation; there was no need, therefore, for Jews to feel that way. Focusing particularly on Bab's disparaging comments on the quality and distinctiveness of Jewish poetry, Landauer replied by insisting upon the unique value of Old Testament and modern Jewish lyrics. "From what traditions do Buber's Chasidic tales come?" he asked. "Is the book of Esther . . . and the Psalms and so much in other books great poetry or not?" Herder, Landauer noted, had great understanding for the special lyric power of Hebraic poetry. The Jewish Volk, like every other, Landauer concluded, has its own original poetry, music, and dance.[143]

An individual, Landauer emphasized, is capable of entertaining commitments to various national groups or Völker without one doing harm to the other. When Mauthner, a

thoroughgoing assimilationist, wrote to Landauer late in
1913 that he felt no commitment to Judaism because it
represented nothing more than a "cerebral duct," Landauer
countered: "I do not find in our day so many communal
relationships that reach back for thousands of years that
I should gladly dispense with one of them, especially when
I have no reason for doing so. And a relationship that is
recognizable as a 'cerebral duct,' to use your terminology,
is indeed real enough." [144] In an article from the same year
Landauer wrote:

> . . . I am, the Jew, a German. The expressions "German Jew
> or Russian Jew" are as obtuse as would be the terms "Jewish
> German" or "Jewish Russian." The relationship is not one
> of dependency and cannot be described by means of an
> adjective modifying a noun. I accept my fate as it is. My
> Germanism and my Jewishness do each other no harm but
> much good. As two brothers, a first-born and a Benjamin,
> are loved by a mother—not in the same way but with equal
> intensity—and as these two brothers live in harmony with
> each other whenever their paths proceed in common and
> also whenever each goes his own way alone, even so do I
> experience this strange and intimate unity in duality as some-
> thing precious and I fail to recognize in this relationship
> that one is primary and another secondary. I have never had
> the need of oversimplifying myself or seeking a fictitious
> unity. I accept my complexity and hope to be a unity of
> even greater complexities than I am aware of.[145]

Here was a major reason for Landauer's faithfulness to
Herder's conception of a humanity of united, yet differentiated, Völker; feeling himself to be both a German and
a Jew, it was natural for Landauer to emphasize the necessity of a unity constructed out of plurality and not homogeneity. Socialist universalism was not, for Landauer, an
attempt to escape from anti-Semitism into a humanity

where differences of nation would disappear, as it was for many other radical leftist Jews. His was not a kind of rootless cosmopolitanism, an attitude frequently found among those radical Jews who show traces of anti-Semitism themselves.[146]

As a consistent cosmopolitan nationalist, Landauer felt that Zionism was inadequate because it allegedly negated the contributions that Judaism had to offer in the Diaspora. Had he lived through the Nazi period, of course, he might have argued that these contributions to humanity could be made only within the context of a separate Jewish nation which would alone safeguard the threatened existence of the Volk. In an essay written on Zionism in 1913, entitled "Are These the Thoughts of a Heretic?" Landauer criticized, especially, those political Zionists who were far more concerned about the nature of the future Jewish state than with the special "calling for humanity" which was the task of the Jews. The sign of this Jewish "task toward all of humanity" was that all Jews bear "their neighbors in their own breasts." [147]

Here was a special feature of Jewish consciousness. Instead of being threatened by the narrow chauvinist sentiments that moved other Germans, Russians, or French away from their proper commitment to humanity, Jews, Landauer hoped, would be consistent universalists owing to the variety of nations in which they were rooted. Another special feature also encouraged a humanitarian orientation. Whereas other nationalities might become submerged in the modern world by the authoritarian state, thereby losing their "task for humanity," the Jewish Volk was free from the clutches of such a state. For this reason Landauer regarded political Zionism as a threat to the integrity of the Jewish identity. In 1913, in a speech before a Zionist socialist group in Berlin, a group with which Buber was closely associated, Landauer argued that the primary function Jews could serve in the Diaspora was to help in the construction of socialist communities apart from the state and political parties. Unlike most socialists, he claimed, Jews were particularly equipped for this task because they were less addicted to the cult of the state.[148]

This was more true of east European Jews than of the prosperous and far more assimilated Jews of central Europe. When, in 1916, many German Jews called for the drastic limitation of an influx of Polish Jews into the German Reich, Landauer came to the defense, once again, of the eastern Jews. He argued that closer contact between western and eastern Jews would be of great benefit to the former because they might learn to feel themselves strangers, as the Polish Jews did, to the modern system of states which was presently tearing Europe to shreds.[149]

Although Landauer's thought was without lasting influence upon one of his "nationalities," Germany, the same cannot be said of the other. Solomon Liptzin has pointed out that Landauer's panhumanist form of Zionism, his affirmation of the "desirability and even the necessity for the continued existence or the reconstitution of the Jews as a distinct people, tribe, or nation," justifying this survival of a unique group, however, in terms of "its dedicating itself to the service of humanity at large," [150] "profoundly affected the Jewish National Humanists of Central Europe. It infiltrated into the essays of his friend Martin Buber. It stimulated a re-examination of Zionist theory. It was modified and deepened, but not contradicted, in the works of Erich Kahler and Arnold Zweig." [151]

Besides these intellectuals and the Berlin group of Zionist socialists mentioned above, whose indebtedness to Landauer's internationalism was acknowledged after the war,[152] Landauer made a strong impression upon a circle of young Prague Jewish intellectuals which included Hans Kohn.[153] We have already noted, in addition, his impact upon the Hashomer Hatzair youth movement in Vienna. The fact that Landauer's völkisch romanticism could be readily applied by these various socialists and internationalists is another demonstration of the viability of left-wing forms of the völkisch heritage. Anti-Semitism, in either its "Aryan" or Jewish self-hatred form, was far from a necessary result of this tradition.

Although not an inevitable deduction from early romantic thought, racism was often grafted upon the völkisch heritage by the end of the nineteenth century. In the year 1898 there appeared Houston Stewart Chamberlain's *The Foundations of the Nineteenth Century*, a work that was to have a great impact in Germany, one in which völkisch mysticism was fused with the pseudo science of biological racism.[154] In his defense of Judaism, Landauer had to come to grips with this racist accretion to the German romantic heritage, the assertion that there are some groups of human beings who are inferior from birth by virtue of the blood that runs in their veins.

By 1913 this doctrine was already in evidence within the German youth movement, as we have seen. In his answer to the request to support the movement, Landauer clarified his opposition to racist thinking. "Others fight against opinions, plans, tendencies," he wrote, "but all of them acknowledge the possibility that whoever is a human being can be convinced by them; even the Socialists take for granted that an individual, though a member of the privileged classes, may be won over. For the anti-Semite, however, the Jew . . . is innately an obnoxious creature." [155] The accretion of deterministic racism to the völkisch concept was strongly resisted by Landauer because he clearly saw the dangers of replacing participation in the Volk in the sense of consciousness of one's roots with the conception of a biologically given and unalterably fixed racial participation. Like his rejection of xenophobic nationalism, Landauer's opposition to racial theories was carried out in the name of the universalist and humanist culture of the early romantics. Early in 1913 he wrote in *Der Sozialist*:

> What difference does it make, one asks, if you speak of race or *Volk?* . . . It wouldn't make any difference at all if we remained with this difference of rubrics. But the racial theorists of the day do not do so. Drawing from the species of animals the sign of fixed separation, they want us to concentrate on the races of man which are given for all time. . . . That a Volk has performed nothing up to now, however, will perform nothing in the historically visible future, does not prove that it never will perform anything. . . . These [racial] theories sow hatred, discord, and mistrust not only between different Völker but also between different members of the same fatherland. . . . There are no eternally separated races. . . . It is not true that the mixing of races leads to degeneration; the contrary is true. . . . Mankind, at its source, is one.[156]

Landauer's faithfulness to the idealist and voluntarist sources of romantic thought was at the base of his rejection of racism; unlike Chamberlain and much of the völkisch Right, Landauer continued to conceive of the nation and the Volk in terms of the awareness and consciousness of man's internal communal spirit—his "verbindender Geist"—not in terms of biological blood ties which were fixed and unalterable, a kind of rootedness in which consciousness was irrelevant. The past, Landauer wrote, is meaningful to us only if it is appropriated by our consciousness and is alive within us.[157] Redemption, moreover, was accessible to everyone: " 'verbindender Geist' . . . that which I know to be present in me, is present in all men." [158] It was an idealist socialism that Landauer fused with pre-Darwinian völkisch concepts.

Other features of Landauer's view of the Volk sharply distinguished it from the racism and imperialism of the völkisch Right. The rejection of deterministic racism meant that Landauer's qualified elitism was a far cry from the later *Herrenvolk*; if the liberation of the Volk and of humanity had to be started by an elite, it was not an elite whose ranks were open only to members of certain predetermined ethnic or racial groups, but one that was accessible to all men. Defining an elite in terms of democratic accessibility and not according to a hierarchy of either fixed social classes or races, Landauer's views ran counter to the profoundly antidemocratic and authoritarian currents on the völkisch Right. Although Lagarde, Langbehn, and Landauer all rejected liberal parliamentarism, Landauer did so in the name of direct democracy and local self-government; the danger of party democracy and parliamentary rule, Landauer held, was not only that they divided the Volk—here Langbehn would have agreed —but that they contributed to the atrophy of "the institutions of self-determination" and caused men to become unaccustomed to direct participation in the decisions that rule their lives.[159] Völkisch antiparliamentarism is not identifiable with antidemocratic sentiments if parliament is rejected, as Michels wrote of the Social Democratic Party, as an oligarchy masquerading as a democracy. In Landauer's view the nation should be ruled neither by parliaments nor by "superior" races, nor should it be structured along hierarchical lines; if participation in the Volk is conceived of in terms of individual consciousness of internal verbindender Geist, an awareness of which all men are capable, then all men are capable of governing themselves and should not delegate authority to party oligarchies.[160]

Landauer rejected, as we have seen, both the notion of rule by elites and the populist belief in the superior virtue of the poor. Yet his völkisch version of radical democratic thought bears certain important resemblances to populism. According to the sociologist Edward Shils's definition, Landauer would actually qualify as a populist: "Even where . . . the actual state of the lower classes is not esteemed," Shils writes of the populist tradition, "they are alleged to be by destiny fitted to become the salvationary nucleus of their whole society." [161] With such a definition in mind Isaiah Berlin has characterized Herder's views as essentially populist, comparing his democratic celebration of German folk culture with the nineteenth-century Russian Narodniks.[162] There is a sense, moreover, in which the entire völkisch tradition in Germany shares this populist faith. In its right-wing interpretation, however—in Langbehn, for example—the belief in popular culture and the peasant-craftsman world is radically separated from any advocacy of democratic decision making; his envisioning of an elitist manipulation of the Volk makes it clear that the populist component has become largely rhetorical, as it was, of course, among the Nazis. For Landauer, however, it was different: the purpose of local autonomy and of the preservation of peasant communal traditions was to secure popular self-government at the grass-roots level.[163]

In a number of ways left-wing versions of völkisch thought in Germany were very similar to nineteenth-century Russian populist beliefs. Both Landauer and the Russian populists hoped for a cooperative, communitarian socialism that would derive from peasant communal traditions and would reject or bypass the allegedly necessary stage of urban, capitalist industrialism. A comparison of Landauer's socialist writings with the works of N. K. Mikhailovsky would show, in addition, a similar concern both for the development of the all-around capacities of the individual peasant—instead of a division of labor—and for cooperation among peasants.[164] The basic tenet of Russian populism, moreover, the idea of the direct transition to socialism through the peasant commune, contained something of Landauer's völkisch stress upon the uniqueness of national traditions. According to Angus Stewart there is an emphasis in all forms of populism upon the "'uniqueness,' identity, culture or current situation of the society which had produced the movement. Unlike the Slavophils, the Russian populists did not emphasize the uniqueness of the Russian character. But they did argue that the institutions of Russian rural society gave Russia the possibility of a special path to industrialization." [165] "Populism is a form of nationalism," Stewart writes, "the distinguishing feature of populistic nationalism being its equation of the 'nation' and 'the people.' " [166] For Landauer the word "Volk" had emphatically contained both these meanings, as it had for Herder. Radical democratic communitarianism was combined, for Landauer and the Russian populists, with a belief in the unique mission of their respective Völker.

Direct democracy, as opposed to parliamentary representation, is possible only on the local level. We have seen how Landauer directed his attention to the formation of rural village Gemeinden for the construction of his völkisch socialist ideal. In Landauer's view the world was constructed of microcosms and if the nation was humanity writ small, then the region or locality was the nation writ small. It was his contention that real commitment toward and love of humanity were impossible without a prior discriminate attachment to family, friends, and local community. Such notions had been in evidence among the early romantics—Möser had been deeply attached to his locality of Osnabrück—and an emphasis upon regional and local color and landscape had characterized the völkisch definition of the nation,[167] but for Landauer romantic regionalism was fused with a commitment to radical anarchist decentralization. Yet even the locality was an insufficiently powerful emotional tie upon which to build one's love of nation and humanity. If one's commitment to large social units was to be more than an empty formalism, it had to be rooted in smaller microcosms than the region or the town; it had to be based upon the family and the small circle of friends:

A definite sympathy is given toward family and friends; it is found also within the Gemeinde and the region; if this is not true . . . then there are only coldness and cant. . . . Modern men who want to lead their lives without the exclusiveness and seclusion of love and family . . . and without the justice of Gemeinde and societal institutions are comically degenerated mammals. . . . My house, my town! My house, my farm and garden, my wife and my children —my world! On this feeling, on this exclusive solidarity, this voluntary union, this small and natural community, all larger organisms arise, at first the Gemeinde and the professional associations. These will then say to all others outside: leave us in peace; we are free and autonomous in what concerns us.[168]

In a manner anticipating Freud's conception in *Civilization and Its Discontents*, Landauer argued that all community life is based upon the sexual bond which is solidified in the creation of the family. With his characteristic
fusion of neoromantic "mythologizing" and nature worship, Landauer stressed that the "emotional cement" of all
community life must be found in a Wahn ("sexual love")
which is not artificial but is rooted in our natural selves:

> We have no religion and can therefore make no attempt at
> communism. Our socialism is founded on the individual; our
> Gemeinden should be based upon the family. Our communal
> spirit can find its inwardness, solidity, and passion from no
> other Wahn than the specifying and excluding natural Wahn
> of sexual love. . . . Love will then be carried over step by
> step from the family into the Gemeinde, the Volk, and
> humanity.[169]

Only the emotional life of the family and the active participation afforded by local community involvements
would ensure that one's commitment to nation and humanity was rooted directly in immediate experience and
not in mere theory. Family, community, nation, and humanity were social roots which, far from working against
one another, were allegedly interdependent, just as the
smallest unit, the individual, revealed the largest unit, the
universe, within his soul.

In response to the upsurge of chauvinist and imperialist
sentiments in Germany in the years after 1911, Landauer
had drawn upon his microcosmic view of the self and
applied it to the question of nationalism. The nation, he
held, is but a unique reflection of humanity; its task is not
to dominate other nations but to serve the humanity in
which all are rooted. In his literary criticism Landauer

applied this faith. The years of his concern with the national question were also those in which he produced most of his literary studies. To complete the discussion of Landauer's work in these years, we need to examine his humanitarian poets of the Volk.

## The Literature of the Volk

Landauer's aesthetic philosophy in his mature years was a direct consequence of his social thought. If our age of "decay" is characterized by "stupid force" and "infamous isolation," [170] then the purpose of the artist must be to help awaken the masses to a consciousness of their völkisch roots[171] and to create the mythos for the development of a cultural nation. As Landauer stated in *Ein Weg deutschen Geistes*, written in 1915:

> We will understand art if we first grasp its function with regard to humanity. . . . But the Völker no longer know what their poets should perform for them, no longer know that they, the Völker, are called to realize materially, in the form of living men and conditions, what the poets have awakened spiritually in their presentiments, visions, loves, longings, and desires. Men of our time do not know that the mythos stems from the poet. . . . Have not all nations originated from the spiritual bonds, spiritual power, and mythos of the poet or the goal envisioned by a prophet, from communal veneration and communal work? [172]

Once the prophetic vision of the poet has materialized in the creation of a new Volk, then art will no longer be the pitiful "longing of the rejected" but the "expression of the community." [173] In the face of his own isolation, Landauer asserted that the relationship between the artist and his public is one of mutual dependence and not antagonism. The poet and the Volk need each other: the latter needs the former to help awaken its dormant spirituality and capacity for self-determination, and the former needs the latter as the communal environment that will destroy his isolation.[174]

Landauer's völkisch and mystical philosophy formed the basis of most of his literary judgments. Since the decadents, such as Walter Calé and Erwin Kirchner, two leading poets of the early twentieth century, were victims of modern isolation and artistic alienation, their lives might well end, as Calé's did, in suicide.[175] Concern for the alienation of many young and sensitive individuals in his own time was voiced by Landauer in an article he wrote in 1911 on the wave of youthful suicides in Germany. Because of the atrophy of community participation in Germany, Landauer argued, numerous young individuals, many of them artists, become intensely withdrawn and despondent; in order to offset this strong tendency toward isolation in modern society, young persons and artists must be able to "participate in the realities of public life." [176]

Art, Landauer contended, offered a prophylactic against isolation. If an organic Volk does not now exist and art is merely the "creation of lonely natures" in the atomized world of the present, if it is prophetic art, an art that "experiences beforehand and forms a conception of what the coming beauty of the Volk will be," then the artist will at least be able to participate in the communal ideal he has envisioned.[177] If organic community lives only within our souls and not in the atomized present, then art will not be of great value if it is merely descriptive and naturalistic. Landauer had long before been unsatisfied with literary naturalism and in 1905 he criticized the Neue Freie Volksbühne for lately performing so many naturalistic plays.[178] Only if art is visionary and prophetic, only if, "in dream and picture, it makes possible the origin of new spiritual life and new world beauty," [179] will it serve the purposes of community. Scientific naturalism and the aestheticism of aristocratic decadence were both incapable of performing the function of meaningful artistic creation: the awakening of the masses to a deeper awareness of their roots in Volk and humanity and a stronger desire to carry out the actual building of a new organic community.[180] The poets and dramatists to whom Landauer was most attracted—significantly, he was little interested in most novels since the novel form had long been dominated by realists and naturalists—were all visionaries and prophets of a "new humanity." All of them shared Landauer's *Lieblingsgedanken:* the mystical notion that the universe, humanity, and the Volk are indwelling in the interior of the seemingly isolated individual. We have seen how important Eckhart and Tolstoi were to Landauer's intellectual development. They were not, however, the only prophets of Landauer's new humanity. Beginning in 1913 with his newly awakened concern for a humanity-oriented view of the Volk and the nation, Landauer's literary criticism focused upon poets and dramatists who had created a mythos for their Volk which sharply contrasted with the contemporary tenor of German nationalism. In response to the war hawks and the chauvinists of the day, Landauer called upon Whitman and Hölderlin, his favorite poets, and Georg Kaiser, his favorite modern dramatist, to lead the way toward a peaceful humanity.

Landauer's literary favorites were democratic mystics of one kind or another and reflect his left-wing völkisch position. Concerning Tolstoi, it seems unnecessary to dwell upon the similarity of the mystical romantic, antiurban, populist anarchist with the German anarchosocialist. If

Tolstoi, however, was the literary pathfinder for the Russian Volk, Whitman was the mystical poet of American völkisch democracy. In an essay on Whitman written in 1913, Landauer wrote:

> America is for Whitman the realm of the future, of the not yet finished, of the *Volksgemeinschaft* that is first being tested, first growing together. . . . So, for Whitman, . . . the Americans are an emerging new Volk, barbarian and beginning, and the new great belief, the new art, which must precede all great Völker, he wants to help create himself. His awareness of himself is much more a feeling of his Volk than of himself; one should not allow oneself to be mistaken about the mystical "Myself" of his verse [Landauer is referring here, of course, to Whitman's famous "Song of Myself"]; he has felt it clearly and said that he is only a first, a small beginning, an early precursor of an American Periclean age. . . . His democracy is a free Volk of active men, . . . each one with his clod of land, his handwork, his machine—a man for himself. Whitman fuses conservative and revolutionary spirit, individualism and socialism, as Proudhon does, a figure to whom he is bound spiritually. . . . Only a great Volk, he thinks, can have great poets; but first poetry must be there to form the great Volk. . . . The poet, therefore, which is Whitman's feeling of himself and his task, is a priest, a prophet, a creator.[181]

Although committed to Goethe's concept of world literature, Landauer's main attention had always been focused upon Germany, and it was the poet Hölderlin who was the great pathfinder of his own German Volk.[182] Hölderlin, like Landauer and like most of the other early German romantics, had been a cosmopolitan nationalist; but he was also a radical democrat and a mystical idealist. All that seems to have been missing from the Landauer synthesis was libertarian socialism, which might well have been present in Hölderlin's views if his conscious life had extended to the mid-nineteenth century. In 1913 Landauer published long selections from Hölderlin's letters of 1793, mainly concerning the purpose of art, especially poetry, in uniting mankind into a body of "thousands of limbs," not a homogeneous mass.[183] Peace, love, Volk, and humanity were already present, however, in the interior of the soul; for Landauer, Hölderlin's mystic view of the self rooted in humanity was the most appealing element in his poetry. Writing of Hölderlin in 1916, in the midst of the carnage of the war, Landauer emphasized Hölderlin's desire that Germany awake from its spiritual torpor and help bring about a spirit of peace and love among all mankind:

> In his odes Hölderlin is the advocate of nature, spirit, and Volk, all of which belong together for him, against the confused impulses of the present. . . . Because of the French Revolution, the call and the expectation had awakened in him, yet he suffered from the fact that in the miserable conditions of Germany the spirit and the Volk were suppressed, and he concerned himself with the questions: Are we to remain in the rear? Do we lack all desire for action, all creativity and initiative? . . . But the hope climbs again and again in him that in Germany a redemptive message will be brought to mankind, not by way of noise and weapons, but in stillness and through the spirit. . . . We need heroes of love, and so Hölderlin is a leading spirit for our future and our present. Love and peace, spirit and Volk, beauty and community—all these were combined for him and were of one piece. And his own beloved . . . was for him a symbol of general love, which he felt to be something present in us . . . but horribly suppressed, as something natural, as the very power of life itself, something that must permeate a beautiful, free, public life and put an end to struggle as much as to the spirit of servility.[184]

Hölderlin was a romantic Hellenophile who hoped that Germany would become a new Greece. The "full impact of Greece in her glory" would have been crushing to this poet "unless it were accompanied by the belief that it could be re-established." [185] This aspect of Hölderlin's life was not lost on Landauer. In his 1916 essay on Hölderlin, Landauer pointed directly to the poems "Germanien" and "An die Deutschen" as proof of Hölderlin's present-minded German orientation, his hope for a spiritual renewal of Germany through a recapturing of the Hellenic ethos.[186] But poetry was not quite adequate to the task of renewing the German Volk. The experience of poetry was not so compelling as that of drama, not so capable of arousing its audience to immediate action. If Hölderlin was Landauer's favorite German poet, he was still not so valuable in Landauer's eyes as the contemporary dramatist of völkisch renewal, Georg Kaiser.

In *Ein Weg deutschen Geistes*, "A Way of the German Spirit," Landauer lauded Kaiser as the fulfillment of the entire German dramatic tradition since Goethe. Kaiser was linked not so much with the author of *Faust* as with the author of *Iphigenia*, Goethe's great drama of humanitarian love. Basing his comments largely upon Kaiser's brilliant pacifist work, *Die Bürger von Calais*, written just before the outbreak of the war, Landauer wrote that Kaiser best expressed in his time the essential unity of mankind, the "invisible chains that bind each of us in spirit." He emphasized that Kaiser, as a great dramatist, does not only teach us, but impels us toward vital action to create a peaceful and unified humanity. If men are "unified in spirit" their way to humanity leads through their separate and distinct nationalities, and, for Landauer, Kaiser's *Bürger von Calais* provided a promising new mythos for the regeneration of the German Volk as a community of peace.[187] In opposition to the visible world of "stupid force" and "infamous isolation," Kaiser presented a vision born from within, a prophecy of community and peace against modern alienation and war. Like Whitman and Hölderlin, Kaiser based his art upon an awareness of man as a microcosm of Volk and humanity and not as he appeared in the external world, an isolated artist-intellectual living in the atomized urban metropolis.

If the function of art is to awaken the community consciousness of the Volk, then a dramatist like Kaiser is in the best position to realize that goal. Like Wagner before him, Landauer was drawn to the theater as an art form of communal experience, a medium, therefore, which was peculiarly capable of implementing his völkisch view of art. Landauer's first active connection with the theater had to do with the educational project of the Independent Socialists of 1892, the Neue Freie Volksbühne on whose "artistic committee" Landauer sat throughout much of the 1890s and again from 1910 through 1917.[188] In October 1918 Landauer was asked to become dramaturgist of the Düsseldorfer Schauspielhaus, one of the leading dramatic companies in Germany, and to edit its journal, *Masken*, but the revolution soon broke out and Landauer felt that he was needed more in Munich.[189] The director of the theater, Louise Dumont, shared Landauer's philosophy of art and drama and intended her house to be a great German national theater dedicated to the revitalization of German social and spiritual life. Socialist and völkisch currents were fused in her perspective, as in Landauer's, since she conceived of dramatic productions as a form of socialist mutual aid and communal work for the purpose of improving the spiritual qualities of the German Volk.[190]

Landauer's compelling interest in dramatic art led him during World War I to the work of William Shakespeare.

In 1916 Landauer gave an extensive series of lectures on Shakespeare to groups of wealthy middle-class women in Berlin.[191] These talks provided Landauer with needed funds; they were also a vehicle for expressing veiled social and political criticism as well as his views of the great English dramatist. After the posthumous publication of these lectures in 1920,[192] they were greeted with less than enthusiasm by most German Shakespeare scholars, who generally found them "unscholarly." [193] The lectures attracted a large reading public, however, and have been described by Arnold Zweig as the "best analysis of Shakespearean drama in the German language." [194]

Landauer's Shakespeare criticism, like his essays on Whitman, Kaiser, and Hölderlin, once again exhibited his heritage in the völkisch romantic tradition. While regarding his work on Shakespeare as a contribution to the "community," as a "Gemeinschaftssache," as he put it in a letter of 1917,[195] he conceived of Shakespeare himself as a tragic figure because his plays were written in isolation from any meaningful community; as Landauer read Shakespeare's plays, many of them, but especially *Measure for Measure*, *The Tempest*, *Julius Caesar*, and *Hamlet*, were investigations of the tragedy of personal isolation, of the inability of the sensitive individual to experience a rootedness in community, since the society around him no longer cohered and was the prey of personal ambitions. The tragedy of Brutus, for example, was that his republican desires could not be realized since he was "the representative of a Volk that no longer existed, a leader without an army." [196] The tragedy of Hamlet, Landauer asserted—projecting his own, very modern, concern for the "alienation of the intellectual" and his social and political isolation—was that of an extraordinarily sensitive and intelligent man who felt himself totally cut off from any participation in a human community marked by injustice and deceit. Hamlet's final murder of Claudius represented to Landauer the culmination of "the struggle of the intellectual against the world that had sought to crush and suffocate him." [197] No doubt a case can be made for this interpretation of Hamlet and Brutus, at least as an element of their situations; yet the centrality of the problem of modern isolation and the necessity of communitarian integration in Landauer's own views were such that he naturally made Shakespeare a man of völkisch concerns. If the great dramatist had not exhibited these concerns to Landauer, he would have lacked the value for the present which Landauer felt that he had.[198]

Landauer's Shakespeare lectures revealed more than his völkisch romanticism, however. Although he did not find in Shakespeare the mystical, microcosmic conception of the self which he had found in his other favorite writers, Landauer's central interpretation of Shakespeare was directly in line with his own idealist brand of philosophical anarchism. The central theme of Shakespeare's plays, according to Landauer, was the battle within the self of Geist and Trieb, of man's capacity for spiritual and ethical freedom and his continuing voluntary servitude born of his own meaner drives: addiction to a sexual impulse devoid of compassionate love, for example, as in the case of Othello, or, more often, to a power drive that makes a man a slave. In Landauer's interpretation, Shakespeare viewed human freedom as a quality of human life which men either chose or rejected. Following his own view of servitude and authoritarian power as an internal submission of men, not merely their external manipulation, Landauer held that Shakespeare's dramas reveal that man is his own slave, that he serves voluntarily:

. . . the gods and the demons that tease, plague, and chase you live within yourselves. Shakespeare has shown the subjection and the imprisonment of men all the more profoundly because he has shown us their freedom: because we shudderingly recognize with him that we are all our own jailers, our own servants, our own murderers, and because we see with him the entire gearing of our inner mechanism by which we make our hearts into our own torture chambers.[199]

In his analysis Landauer often dwelt on the ravages caused by a personal drive for power in such plays as *Macbeth*, *King John*, and *King Lear*.[200] Such an admission of an innate drive for power in man might be seen as inconsistent with his anarchist assumptions. We must take Landauer's philosophic idealism literally, however, and assume that for him anarchism would be born of man's spiritual, not his natural, self, as he had argued against Kropotkin's more positivistic views. The assumption seems to be borne out in a number of places in the Shakespeare lectures, moreover; the way from Trieb to Geist, from man's lower drives to his spiritual liberation, is seen as man's emergence from servitude to freedom, "from war to peace, from death to life." [201] For Landauer, man's freedom is born of his spiritual consciousness, not of his lower, natural self. In his view Shakespeare anticipated the early German romantics in his late plays which culminated in the figure of Prospero, the man whose freedom is a conscious creation of his spirit and a triumph of Geist over Trieb.[202]

Landauer's lectures on Shakespeare, as well as his other works of literary criticism, were a mirror of his current concerns and his romantic and anarchist philosophies. Whereas the studies of 1913–1916 on Whitman, Hölderlin, and Kaiser had focused upon their humanity-oriented cultural nationalism, in the Shakespeare work of 1916–1918

Landauer had returned to a related, but older, concern: the need for community integration felt by the isolated intellectual. It had been in isolation, once again, that Landauer opposed the war. By late 1917, however, as we have seen, there had developed a new interest in his ideas among the German reading public and, after the emergence of mass pacifist and antigovernment sentiment with the strike waves of early 1918, Landauer hoped that he would be listened to more closely in the future. Waiting alone for the end of the war and the collapse of the monarchy, in a small town in the Bavarian countryside, Landauer had reason to believe in 1918 that his future political activities would not be so isolated as they had been in the preceding decade.

Yet this decade of great intellectual accomplishment, of prolific literary, political, and social criticism, had been marked by the development of an antiurban and antiindustrial völkisch philosophy which would have little appeal to the urban working classes in the revolution ahead. The anarchosocialist aspect of Landauer's romanticism, the call for the replacement of centralized authority by decentralized, local control, was to find some resonance among the supporters of the *Räte*, or council, movement in 1918–19. Parts of Landauer's synthesis of völkisch romanticism and libertarian socialism, which we have examined in these last two chapters, were serviceable in the postwar revolution and some were not. Participation in the Bavarian Revolution of 1918–19 gave Landauer his final opportunity to implement his social philosophy.

# 6. Revolution in Bavaria

In the fluid revolutionary situation in Munich from November 1918 to April 1919, Landauer at last seemed to find a significant movement and a power center within which he could work: the workers', peasants', and soldiers' Räte. It was through the Räte movement that Landauer would attempt to realize his plans for a federalized Germany based on local, grass-roots democracy and not on centralized parliamentary control. In Germany's postwar revolutions, however, parliamentarism was to carry the day, in Berlin as well as in Munich, and even a majority within the Räte movement—outside the radical elements of the USPD, the KPD, and independent socialists such as Landauer—opted for this development.

In the course of the revolution Landauer was to find that the social base of his politics was indeed far narrower than the massive working classes in whom he had, for the first time since the 1890s, placed his hope; in conformity with his intellectual and political development since the turn of the century, Landauer's real ambience was to remain the world of the marginal, middle-class artist and intellectual, a world centered in Munich in Schwabing, the bohemian section of the city. His völkisch socialism, in particular, could have had little appeal for the industrial working classes of Munich; and the peasants, whom he had celebrated in his prewar social theory, were in Catholic Bavaria particularly unresponsive to socialism of any kind. The man who has so often been seen as one of the central figures in the Bavarian Revolution of 1918–19 was in fact almost as isolated as he had always been politically. Although his eloquence commanded much attention at meetings and demonstrations and in the press, in the end Landauer's participation in the Bavarian Revolution turned out to be both tragic and futile.

## Landauer and Munich's November: A Democracy of Councils?

In the spring and summer of 1918 Landauer's health and disposition had changed little from the days following Hedwig's death in February. Unable to work, he referred to himself as a "wreck" and predicted that he might soon break down completely.[1] By October, however, with the imminence of German military collapse and the return of peace, as well as the increase of his appeal in Germany (as evidenced by the rapid rise in sales of his books, especially *Aufruf zum Sozialismus*), Landauer began to be more confident about the future and the role he might profitably play in it.[2] Before the collapse of the Wittelsbach and Hohenzollern monarchies and the outbreak of revolution early in November, Landauer planned to go to Düsseldorf and become the dramaturgist of the renowned theater company in that city and edit its theatrical journal.[3] The political events of early November in Germany changed his plans.

Until recently most historians have written of the events of November 1918 in Germany as more of a collapse than a revolution. The assumption has been that parliamentary government had already been established in Germany by late October and that it was only war weariness and the fact that constitutional changes had not been made explicit to soldiers, workers, and peasants which set off the sailors' revolt in Kiel and the outbursts in Berlin and Munich.[4]

There is considerable documentary evidence, however, that the Kiel mutiny resulted from the fact that the naval command "deliberately evaded government control" in late October and pursued its own plans for launching a new major battle. One revisionist, Reinhard Rürup, has commented that such a "violation of parliamentary rule leads one to ask how far parliamentary rule had in fact been established. . . . It seems very doubtful," he continues, "that evolutionary methods alone could have enabled the democratic forces to conquer." Based upon such considerations, as well as the fact that the revolutionary movement had a political program and was not merely a call for peace, historians are beginning to speak of a real revolution in November 1918. Rürup writes:

> True it was a movement born of misery and exhaustion, and the overthrow of the monarchy was in itself not a creative act. But that was not all that happened. The revolutionary mass movement which developed in early November pursued aims which went beyond a revolt against the symptoms of mismanagement. The revolution had a program: . . . it strove for an abolition of the authoritarian state and for a truly democratic transformation of political, social and economic conditions.[5]

While it is not necessary for our purposes to discuss all the details of the November revolution, we need to say something of the upheaval in Munich, in which Landauer was to be involved. Bavaria, the first German state to become a republic and the last in which revolutionary socialists were defeated, was a most unlikely place for a radical revolution, at least before 1918. In all Germany, Social Democracy was most moderate and reformist in that state. Primarily rural, small-town, and Roman Catholic, Bavaria had had almost no radical movement to speak of before 1918.[6]

Developments of the last two years of the war, however, brought about a leftward movement in Bavarian political sentiment, mainly toward the SPD but also toward the Independents. The deeply conservative Bavarian peasantry became profoundly angered by food regulations and by the absence of farmhands in the course of the war, while the lower middle class in the cities, suffering from rising prices, were driven into the arms of the Majority Socialists.[7] In such a situation leading pacifists like Professor Friedrich Wilhelm Förster were given a wide hearing.[8] In Munich itself, the rank and file of USPD and Spartacist organizations during the revolution were bolstered by the influx of thousands of class-conscious industrial workers in the course of the war; with the expansion of the Krupp munitions factories in the Munich suburb of Freimann, large numbers of workers came to the city from the Ruhr and Saxony.[9] The intellectual leadership of the radical revolution came from the city's old bohemian community, Schwabing, where "writers, painters, and draftsmen vied with one another in caricaturing and lampooning the state, the church, king and God, fatherland and family, officials and officers—everything, in short, that stood for authority and morality." [10] This center for artists and literati, where Landauer and Mühsam met with other idealists, anarchists, and assorted radicals during the revolution, attracted precisely the kind of disaffiliated, often Jewish, writers[11] who were particularly responsive to the independent and libertarian brand of socialism taught by Landauer.

Although the demand for immediate peace was widespread throughout Germany in early November 1918, matters came to a head especially quickly in Bavaria. The party associated with opposition to the war, the Independent Socialists, whose leader in Bavaria was the "ethical socialist" Kurt Eisner, gained a large following and became the "spearhead of the revolution." [12] With the Majority Socialists refusing to take power, Eisner and the Independents seized the initiative on November 8—three days before Scheidemann's declaration of a German republic in Berlin—and organized the Constituent Soldiers', Workers', and Peasants' Council which proclaimed the establishment of the Bavarian Democratic and Social Republic headed by Eisner, with a cabinet made up of Majority and Independent Socialists.[13] Eisner had earlier been an outstanding critic of Prussian militarism and a leader of Munich's working-class strikes against the war in January 1918.[14] Like Landauer, Eisner was a literary intellectual who was drawn to socialism primarily because of its ethical appeal.[15]

Because of the upsurge in early November of Bavarian particularism, fed by fears that the government in Berlin would not end the war, and even before Eisner's proclamation of November 8, Landauer placed his best hopes for a libertarian revolution in the southern German state.[16] By November 11, however, Bavaria seemed to Landauer to be only one example of a powerful wave of independent and autonomous federalist revolts against centralized political authority in Germany.[17] "All my life I have been a federalist," Landauer wrote on the 22d, just before leaving for Munich, "and the spontaneous movements of these days have shown me how strong the feeling of independence is in the individual regions." [18] Closely following events throughout Germany, Landauer felt that the revolts in Hamburg and Hannover, Karlsruhe and Darmstadt, as well as in many other localities, where workers' and soldiers' councils were quickly set up, might well bring about the dissolution of the centralized state in Germany, directed

from Berlin: ". . . everywhere the same thing is happening," he wrote at the end of the month—by which time he
should have been more cognizant of the centrality of
Berlin's revolution—"destruction of the old is occurring
through one's ignoring it, just as Etienne de La Boétie
proclaimed. . . . Germany is fortunately not France and
1918 is not 1789; we have no central city in which the
fate of the German Volk is being decided." [19]

At times Landauer's enthusiasm was almost unbounded.
On November 11, the day the armistice was signed and
the German Republic proclaimed, Landauer wrote: "I am
filled with greater and greater happiness—how well I know
what will occur now. Now I will be needed and perhaps
also be listened to." [20] Later in the month he wrote to Fritz
Mauthner: "The German Volk is victorious, the Reich
has fallen, and all at once it stands at the head of all Völker
in the struggle for justice and reason in man's public institutions." [21] There were numerous independent revolts, but
the most exemplary was the one in Munich[22] which Landauer was about to join.

Landauer was called to Munich directly by Eisner, who
on November 14 wrote Landauer a personal note: "Come
as soon as your health permits. What I want of you is that,
through forensic activity, you will cooperate in the reformation of spirits." [23] Because of an attack of the flu Landauer was unable to join Eisner for two weeks. After coming to Munich, however, Landauer did not so much work
with Eisner as attempt to steer him away from cooperation
with the Majority Socialists and from the plans for elections to the Bavarian Landtag.[24] As long as socialism was
described as an ethical "reformation of spirits," as long,
that is, as politics remained in the realm of general theory,
then Landauer and Eisner could work hand in hand. Eisner

knew, when he called Landauer to Munich, that Landauer shared with him a strong detestation of war and Prussian militarism and that he placed a similar emphasis upon the ethical aspects of socialism; both regarded socialism as a product of man's conscience and free will—Eisner had been a student of the Kantian philosopher Hermann Cohen —and not simply as an inevitable historical consequence of modern capitalist development.[25] When it came to more specific matters, notably Eisner's willingness to seek a compromise between the claims of parliamentary rule and those of the councils,[26] Landauer parted company with Eisner; although both were ethical socialists and idealist intellectuals, Landauer remained an anarchist and was categorically opposed to parliamentarism.

If he did not simply work with Eisner, then, where did Landauer stand in the Munich situation? Early in the revolution a group of fifty radicals, including many from Eisner's USPD but also a handful of anarchists, constituted themselves as the Revolutionary Workers' Council. Having evolved from the earliest workers' council formed on November 7, the RAR (Revolutionäre Arbeiterrat) intended, in the words of its leader, the anarchist Erich Mühsam, to "drive the revolution forward toward a socialism constructed on the foundation of the Räte idea." [27] Such a formulation of aims was rather vague, yet it was specific enough to indicate that the RAR was a minority group even within the context of the Räte movement. In his proclamation of a Bavarian republic on November 7, Eisner had promised that a constitutional national assembly would be elected as soon as possible and that his government would be marked by cooperation between the two socialist parties, without saying a word about plans for socializing the economy; in so doing he had spoken for the councils of workers, soldiers, and peasants which had elected him president on that day, the so-called Provisional National Council.[28] After its formation in the days following November 7, the RAR was the only organization that stood firmly for socialist democracy based upon the councils and opposed the plans for parliamentary elections. Given such a situation, Landauer naturally joined this group when he arrived in Munich late in November.[29] He and Mühsam were thereafter the two leading figures in the RAR, whose primary purpose was to prevent the abdication of the Räte movement to the authority of a Bavarian parliamentary assembly.

In the first month of its activity, the RAR, led by Landauer and Mühsam, made various unsuccessful attempts to realize its goal. In the first place it attempted to build a radical council movement by organizing shop councils (*Betriebsräte*) in Munich's industrial centers. These quickly formed Räte, however, were soon controlled by trade-union leaders who forced the RAR to agree that their 50 members would join 550 delegates from the shop councils in forming a Munich workers' council. "Within the system of the workers' councils in the city of Munich, then," one recent historian of the Bavarian Revolution has written, "the 'revolutionaries' were formally in a minority of eleven to one." [30] In the Provisional National Council, however, ostensibly the highest authority in the Bavarian state until the election of a national assembly, the RAR had disproportionate strength since it was outnumbered there only by five to one.[31] In this body, which met on December 9 and 10, shortly after Landauer's arrival in Munich, Landauer led RAR members in various denunciations of the SPD, especially of Erhard Auer, the minister of the interior in Eisner's coalition government.[32] At the same time Landauer offered concrete plans for drastic educational reform to the National Council, a central concern for ethical socialists such as Eisner and himself. The plan, which was never acted upon, contained recommendations concerning the abolition of compulsory participation in religious instruction, total freedom of political association for all students and *Dozenten*, and freedom of access for all individuals, regardless of political party, religion, or sex, to all *Hochschule*.[33]

Even with its "overrepresentation" in the National Council, the RAR had little power to steer the revolution in a more leftward direction. In a situation where the Majority Socialists and the trade unions commanded the allegiance of the mass of Munich's working classes, Landauer made his own personal attempts to strengthen the radical wing of the Räte movement. Besides leading the RAR in the National Council, Landauer attempted to gain the support of troops returning from the front in December 1918. Faced with the prospect of unemployment on their return, soldiers were addressed by Landauer in Munich's National Theater soon after their arrival at the railroad station: "You, who for years were compelled to sacrifice your lives in a senseless slaughter of the peoples," Landauer impassioned; "The hour of freedom has struck—now fight for yourselves." [34]

As a result of the failure of the RAR to make any significant headway in its struggle, Mühsam formed another organization on November 30, a loosely knit group called the Revolutionary Internationalists of Bavaria, or VRI (Vereinigung revolutionärer Internationalisten). The group, whose members shared a common admiration for the Russian Revolution, was devoid of any specific program besides the general desire for radical social transformation. Soon after its formation, it engaged in direct-action tactics, such as an attack on December 6 against the offices of the middle-class paper, *Der Bayerische Kurier*. Landauer, significantly enough, never joined this other venture of Mühsam's,[35] possibly because he anticipated its later course: in January the VRI was absorbed by the Spartacist group in Munich, which was then gathering strength within the radical movement, and Mühsam was drawn into direct cooperation with the Communist leader Max Levien.[36] Although Landauer and Mühsam had been friends since their initial meeting at the Neue Gemeinschaft in Berlin, eighteen years before,[37] their temperaments and conceptions of anarchism had always been very different. Landauer, Mühsam's senior by eight years, rejected Mühsam's attachment to Bakunin's anarchism—with its view that the destruction of the state would, of itself, constitute a great moral and social revolution—and had repeatedly warned Mühsam against the tendency to regard *all* existing customs, traditions, and institutions as needful of destruction.[38] As his manifesto of the VRI indicated, moreover, Mühsam was not a consistent anarchist in his stated objective to follow in Munich the model of the Bolshevik Revolution.[39] With such an objective it is little wonder that Mühsam was willing to cooperate with Leninists, whom Landauer detested as "militarists," [40] and that Landauer never joined the group.

Landauer's view of the Räte movement was rather different from that of the Communists with whom Mühsam would soon cooperate. He did not regard the struggle against parliamentarism, against the convening of the Bavarian Landtag, as a struggle for a "dictatorship of the proletariat" based upon the Räte. In letters he wrote in November and December 1918, in his speeches before the Bavarian Provisional National Council, and in an important article he wrote in November, "The United Republics of Germany and Their Constitution," Landauer carefully distinguished his own position from both SPD and bourgeois parliamentarism and the Communist conception of the Räte. In the exposition of his views Landauer demonstrated once again that his opposition to parliamentarism, far from being antidemocratic—like that of the German Right and the Bolsheviks—was aimed at the development of what he regarded as real democracy, the full and continuous participation of all members of the community in decision making. Landauer's Räte conception and his antiparliamentarism were based on a participatory democracy from below, coupled with a plan for the federalist decentralization of authority in Germany. In November he wrote to his cousin Hugo: ". . . the new democracy will be entirely different from the silly electioneering, which is only a resignation on the part of the people and a disgusting rule by the parties." [41] Instead of envisaging rule by the proletariat in place of parliamentary oligarchy, however, Landauer called for a broadening of the definition of a worker to include all "active" members of the community, with the "abolition of the proletariat" as a distinct class. "The concept of the worker must be widened," he wrote; "all technical, commercial, and other organized activities must be included. Not the dictatorship, but the *abolition of the proletariat* must be the slogan." [42]

For Landauer socialism was not a matter of historically favored social groups, especially not those groups whose life was defined by the urban factory, but involved the development of cooperation among all working members of the community. Before the December 9 meeting of the Bavarian Arbeiterräte, Landauer said: "It does not occur to us to want to perpetuate the proletariat, privation, deprivation of rights, and servitude. It does not occur to us to help the proletariat assume domination or a dictatorship; the sense of a democratic-socialist revolution can be accomplished only through the abolition of the proletariat for all time." [43] Although he had little hope of realizing this objective immediately—rational persuasion was not enough, he admitted, for the workers were too habituated to their jobs and would be convinced only after experiencing industrial ruin and the coming mass unemployment[44]—Landauer envisaged a possible return of large numbers of Munich proletarians to the land in the course of the revolution. Such a development might be accomplished, he wrote in November, if the various Räte of the Bavarian districts would grant land in their districts to industrial workers and returning soldiers.[45] In Landauer's view of the Räte movement, as in almost all his thought and activity after the turn of the century, anarchist socialism and völkisch antiurbanism combined.

Instead of a dictatorship of parliament or of the proletariat, of Scheidemann or of Liebknecht, Landauer called for a democracy of the entire working community based upon the decentralized Räte. For the libertarian romantic the Räte would not be organized along class lines or be directed from above, but would unite all active members of the community on a local level from which all authority would flow. In November 1918 Landauer worked out a means by which to apply his earlier social thought—federalist, communitarian, romantic, and anarchist—to the Räte movement of 1918–19:

> Every continuity with the old Reich must cease, otherwise we will have a Caesaro-proletarian dictatorship no matter whether it is called Scheidemann or Liebknecht. The National Assembly for the entire Reich ought to consist only of delegates of the autonomous republics, and these again

should have their special assemblies beforehand, whose delegates have come from the corporation. These are the workers', peasants', and soldiers' councils. The factory owner or
businessman who is organizationally active is a worker. The
stockholder, if he is otherwise nothing else, is nothing. For
that reason citizens' councils [*Bürgerräte*] and councils of
intellectual workers [*Räte geistiger Arbeiter*] are a useless
nuisance. [Two of the latter had already been formed, one
under Lujo Brentano, the economist, and the other under
Heinrich Mann, the novelist.] I equate the former conditions
of repression with direct (atomized) and secret election; for
freedom we need corporative (thus indirect) and open election, the continuing mutual agreement, the imperative man-
date, and the possibility of more immediate recall of delegates, whose function is not as people's representatives but
as deputies of a permanently meeting corporation.[46]

Landauer coupled his call for a radical democratic alternative to parliamentary rule with a plan for a federalist
reconstitution of Germany. In November he wrote a pamphlet on this subject, *The United Republics of Germany
and Their Constitution*, which may have been inspired by
his reading of the federalist thinker Konstantin Frantz during the war.[47] Describing the democratic base of a decentralized Germany in the Räte of each separate local community (Gemeinde), Landauer called for a federal Bund
of autonomous German republics, each to be controlled by
its constituent councils below.[48] Unlike Frantz, Landauer
was not a conservative federalist, but an anarchist who felt
that even federal states were in need of decentralized control from the local level. Consistent with his romantic social
theories, moreover, Landauer held that each autonomous
republic should be made up of an area that cohered historically and culturally; since it was not an organic unity, therefore, the state of Prussia should be dissolved into a number

of separate republics, one in west Germany—the Rhineland
—one in the north, and one in the eastern part of the country. If Prussia does not agree and refuses to give up her
earlier domination of the Reich, Landauer emphasized, she
should not be asked to join in the Bund. Only if each of the
republics that make up Prussia agrees to participate on an
equal footing with the other German republics—Landauer
included Austria in his Greater Germany scheme—would
she be included in the union.[49] Such was the libertarian,
federalist dream that Landauer imagined for Germany in
the wake of the seemingly decentralized revolts of early
November.[50]

Landauer's hopes for the decentralization of Germany
had little chance of success. Although Eisner had gained
some conservative and peasant support through his attacks
on Prussian hegemony in Germany and had severed diplomatic relations with Prussia by the end of the month,[51] his
motives for separatism had been very different from those
of conservative Bavarians, and secession was not likely to
occur during the revolution. Although the Bavarian Revolution of November seemed to Landauer to be the beginning of the dissolution of a centralized German state, "the
potentiality of an active separatism," according to Alan
Mitchell, "was not to become a significant factor during
the revolutionary period. The principal reason for this was
quite simply that traditional Bavarian particularism had also
been monarchist, and was therefore undercut in 1918 by the
very fact of the revolution. The threat of secession, therefore, was necessarily limited in November to a political
gambit of Eisner's personal diplomacy."[52]

Although some control over local affairs was allowed to
Bavaria and other German states in the Weimar Constitution, passed in 1919, Bismarck's work had not been undone;

if anything centralization was strengthened.[53] Landauer's federalist hopes of November stood almost no chance of realization. By December, moreover, parliamentarism was carrying the day and Landauer's fight for *Rätedemokratie* was imperiled. As we shall see, however, the final victory of parliamentarism—an accomplished fact in the Berlin Revolution after the suppression of the Spartacists in January— was deferred for a number of months by events that were peculiar to Munich.

## The Advance of Parliamentarism and the Response of the Radicals

The events of December soon dissipated the hopes of November. On December 5, after delaying a month, Eisner set January 12 as the date for elections to the Bavarian Landtag. Although the personal feelings of the President were very close to those of Landauer—in November Eisner had repeatedly spoken against ballot-box democracy and in favor of the council system—he had become convinced by December 5 that it was not only the bourgeois parties and the Right who favored parliamentary elections, and he decided to attempt a compromise between parliamentary and council rule.[54] In Berlin, however, events moved even more quickly. The National Congress of Councils meeting in Berlin (December 16–21), in which 60 percent of the delegates were supporters of the Majority Socialists, passed a resolution that delegated power to the provisional government of Ebert and Scheidemann until a parliamentary National Assembly could convene.[55] Immediately thereafter a radical sailors' revolt was suppressed and the three Independent Socialist ministers resigned from the government, leaving control in the hands of the Majority Socialists alone.[56] Instead of socialism and council democracy, the revolution had been reduced to the political program of the SPD: parliamentary government.

Because of his overinflated hopes of November, Landauer reacted bitterly to the events of the succeeding month. Asked by Eisner to edit the Munich organ of the USPD, Landauer refused on the ground that he would then be dependent on a ministry that stood against council democracy from below. "The calling of the Landtag," he wrote, "has produced bad blood among the revolutionaries, including myself." [57] Before the Provisional National Council, Landauer began to propose more radical measures than Eisner would accept in attempting to prevent the rightward swing of the revolution. At the end of December he called for the "liberation of the press" from all control by capitalist parties and individuals,[58] but he did not make clear how this was to be accomplished.

Spending Christmas with his and Eisner's children in Krumbach, Landauer became more and more despondent and bitter about the course of events. In one letter he expressed sharp disappointment with the revolution in connection with a personal premonition of death, a subject that had been on his mind since the loss of Hedwig earlier in the year: "I feel only as if I am on furlough in this world, with the children and the revolution, and for that reason I am at the same time both radical and peaceably quiet." [59] His earlier equilibrium and circumspection had begun to recede under the impact of personal and now political disasters. The older feeling of isolation was coupled with an only slightly exaggerated fear of numerous enemies. The day after Christmas he wrote: "I am with the children here— in a world of ugly enemies." [60] Two weeks before the proposed convening of the Landtag, in early February, Landauer had given up all sense of purpose in his work and expressed even darker sentiments than he had in December: "I can be happy only if I sink into the past and forget about life. What I do is only a kind of obligation, and from general and personal reasons I do it without hope." [61]

Two days before the elections to the Landtag were to take place, on January 10, Landauer wrote to Eisner and pleaded with him to prevent the meeting of the assembly. "Immediately after the election the counterrevolutionaries will be immoderately impetuous and offensive," he wrote, "and their cry will be: Down with Eisner! A Parliament of this kind *must* be broken up. If that does not happen, you will allow yourself to be pushed into parliamentary opposition (where you would stand almost alone). There our only help would be the social despair of the unemployed or tormented masses; and that would even be worse than an immediate coup against the misbegotten parliament." [62] Landauer was beginning to throw his own social theories overboard under the pressure of political urgency. The sense of desperation was heightened by persistent brooding over the personal tragedy of his wife's death. Besides the evidence of his letters, we have the testimony of his friend Martin Buber on this point. Describing Landauer during the early months of 1919, Buber wrote: ". . . he appeared dispirited and nearly exhausted—a year before his wife had succumbed to a fatal illness, and now he relived her death in his heart." [63]

In such a state of mind Landauer went through the motions of following Eisner's request that he run for a Landtag seat; he electioneered in Krumbach, not to be elected, but "to use the opportunity to say what is right to the voters." [64] Predictably enough he received only a handful of votes in this rural town. His showing, however, merely reflected that of all candidates associated with the Räte movement (most of whom were USPD leaders, as the Spartacists decided to boycott the elections). Eisner was soundly defeated and the other Independent cabinet ministers fared even worse.[65] In the elections of January 12, the SPD and the Bavarian People's Party dominated the voting.[66] From the point of view of Landauer and the other radicals, Munich's Thermidor seemed to be following that of Berlin.

After the elections Landauer bitterly criticized Eisner for compromising with the SPD. Eisner has "lost his way" in his earlier attempt to define a course between compromise and the Spartacists, Landauer commented, adding, "His participation for so long in the ranks of Social Democracy has taken its revenge."[67] Urging Eisner to resign, Landauer advised him to work solely within the Räte movement,[68] a course of action which Eisner soon adopted. Having failed to make his intention public, however, Eisner neglected to disabuse many persons outside the government of the mistaken suspicion that he planned a new revolution and would prevent the meeting of the Landtag, a suspicion that was to contribute to his assassination.[69]

Although a new revolution was feared by elements on the Right, Landauer had no such expectations. In January he wrote that the Right had nothing to worry about: their counterrevolution would triumph with the convening of the Landtag, which had been set for February 21. "One will have to count on other *völker*," Landauer wrote on January 29, "the Germans are too wretched."[70] Whereas in November he had spoken of the superiority of the German Revolution to the French one of 1789, since it seemed at the time that it might lead to a decentralization of the country, in early February he wrote: "To the Devil with the Germans! This isn't even up to 1848 and it's not possible to speak 1789 in the same breath."[71] The prospect for real social change had vanished: "The entire spirit of renewal," he wrote, "which would have led to self-determination, and the self-government of new institutions and voluntary associations, has evaporated." [72]

Soon after the elections to the Landtag, Landauer wrote an article, "The Overestimation of Voting," in which he clarified his opposition to the victory of ballot-box democracy in the revolution. Condemning the "counterrevolutionary victory of the militaristically led Social Democratic regime" in Berlin—through its massacre of the Spartacists, carried out with the cooperation of the old military—Landauer contended that the present government was merely a continuation of the prewar authoritarian regime. Landauer's antiauthoritarian critique, however, was based upon the conception of the state which he had held since the mid-1890s, a conception he developed after reflection upon SPD strength among the Berlin working classes; the tutelage of the masses was not merely based upon their coercion by SPD and Reich authorities, but rested upon the voluntary servitude of a docile and passive community. Now the fusion of the SPD and the capitalist, authoritarian state, long predicted by Landauer, had been accomplished, and it too rested upon the dependency and the voluntary submission of the Volk: "Up to the time of the revolution we had an authoritarian regime," Landauer wrote in January 1919, "and the Volk dumbly complied with it; now, after the revolution, we have an authoritarian regime and the majority of the Volk follows it with exultant acclaim. In all these years . . . it was a very doubtful honor to be a German; it is even more doubtful now." [73]

In line with the view of authority which he had developed fully in the years before the war, Landauer argued that there was still a chance to prevent SPD perpetuation of the authoritarian institutions of the monarchy: we should not attempt to overthrow the state directly, since its strength lies not merely in itself but in the recognition granted it by the masses, but we can still prevent the victory of the counterrevolutionary National Assembly by ignoring it and by building autonomous institutions on the local and regional level. In the context of 1919 Landauer assigned to the Räte the job of fulfilling the doctrine of Étienne de La Boétie. If a real revolution is to be accomplished, Landauer concluded, the German Räte movement must reverse the decision made by the *Rätekongress* of December 16–21 and begin building an alternative to centralized, parliamentary government. Since the present parliamentary parties are continuous with the war criminal parties of the past, Landauer claimed, the building of this alternative would alone place Germany on a better footing with the Entente.[74]

What could be done in Bavaria, however, to prevent the victory of the parliamentary counterrevolution in that state? From the very beginning the Munich Revolution had rested upon a narrower social base than the one in Berlin. Here the Center party was much more closely allied with Catholic forces which were unalterably opposed to a socialist transformation,[75] and the radicals of Munich were more an isolated group in primarily rural and small-town Bavaria than Berlin's radicals were with respect to northern Germany. It is hardly surprising that by January the Munich council movement had no real political weight in the Bavarian power structure; the same had occurred in Berlin where the prospects for radical change had been brighter.

What is surprising is that the council movement had any significance at all after the elections of January 12. One important reason for this had to be lost upon so passionate a decentralist and antiurban socialist as Landauer: if radicalism continued in the Bavarian Revolution, it was because it was of significance in its center, in Munich, where Bavaria's only marginal bohemian intellectual community and sizable industrial working-class population lived. In January and February, between the elections to the Landtag and its convening, there was considerable working-class discontent in Munich, which strengthened the hand of the radicals; "pressing problems of demobilization and reconversion, stagnation in key sectors such as construction, devaluation of the mark and spiraling unemployment," were to play their part in prolonging the life of the Räte movement.[76] Surprisingly enough, in Berlin, where the radical forces were stronger, the issue of parliamentary or Räte control was settled earlier and unmistakably in favor of the former; in Munich, where they were weaker, although strengthened by working-class discontent in January, the radicals were not squashed until a number of months later, and not until after actual council republics had been set up for a time in April. The solution to this paradox, which prolonged Landauer's importance and that of the Munich Räte movement beyond the elections of January 12, is carefully delineated by Alan Mitchell:

In the given circumstances . . . the stability of republican authority in Munich was much less threatened than in Berlin. Throughout most of Northern Germany there was a clear and present danger of further revolution. In Southern Germany, with the possible exception of Stuttgart, no such danger was apparent. Whether due to the absence of a vigorous radical tradition, to the rural structure of society, or just to the disinterest of Bolshevik agents in the less industrialized and presumably less "promising" areas of Germany, the Eisner regime enjoyed a temporary security which the Ebert government did not. Berlin passed almost immediately from the crisis of the November Revolution to a decision as to its character—with the outcome resting frankly on military authority. Unlike Ebert, the Bavarian Prime Minister had no secret telephone connection to *Reichswehr* headquarters as, for the time being, he had no need of one. There was another reason: Eisner was much less intent than Ebert on restricting the power of the revolutionary councils. . . . They had provided his route to power: he had first of all become a council leader and only then the Prime Minister of the Bavarian state . . . [a situation that] created a pattern of negotiation in Munich fundamentally different from that in Berlin.[77]

Although they did not directly attack, and were not squashed by, Eisner's government, the radicals bitterly criticized Eisner for compromising with the SPD on the matter of parliamentary elections and sought means to strengthen their movement in the wake of the January elections to the Landtag. At a meeting of workers' and soldiers' councils on January 15, Landauer called for the solidarity of all socialists opposing the convening of the Landtag, for union in the furtherance of the Räte movement. The desperation of the moment had overwhelmed Landauer so completely that he was now willing to include the Spartacists in such a united front.[78] In the Bavarian situation of January 1919, Landauer had concluded that the only chance for radical social change lay in a solidarity of all segments of the working class and intellectual community who were opposed to parliamentary oligarchy. When challenged by an SPD delegate to defend his opening to the Left, Landauer responded: ". . . there are many workers who have flown to the Spartacists as a butterfly to the light." [79]

The revolution in Bavaria was to cause Landauer to reverse some of his earlier political positions for a time; desperation and the feeling that he was only on "furlough in this world" were pushing him toward the kind of political associations he would never have made in the past. By the beginning of February the Communists (as the Spartacists were called after January) were making great inroads into the Munich workers' councils[80]—aided by the economic discontent of which I have spoken—and Landauer was now willing to have them join, but not lead, a common resistance to the Majority Socialists. After the February 7 arrest of Max Levien, a prominent Communist leader, by the government—against Eisner's wish—Landauer was one of the leaders of a protest demonstration that resulted in Levien's release. In explanation of his part in this protest Landauer asserted that he was not really concerned about Levien but about the fact that such an arrest, if it went unchallenged, would be repeated against more and more leaders of the Räte movement.[81]

With the same solidarity of all radical socialists in mind, Landauer was one of the leading advocates of a mass demonstration that took place on February 16 in the name of the continuation of the Räte system. The demonstration, which he urged Eisner to join, included USPD, KPD, anarchist, and even SPD supporters.[82] After the demonstration Landauer allowed himself to be encouraged by a turnout he estimated at 80,000, commenting that it would "not fail to make its impression." [83] Such an event was of great importance to Landauer and other radical leaders, such as Mühsam and Toller, since it served to demonstrate to them that there was mass support for a council system of government, although this support had not been noticeable in the January elections where the USPD had received only 3 percent of the vote.[84] The support, of course, was all in Munich.

The willingness to form a united front, for the first time in his political life, had provided Landauer in February with a short-lived sense of social support. In the days before the convening of the Landtag, Landauer had emerged from his earlier isolation and had become one of the leading figures of the radical movement. Desperation had made him abandon his lifelong insistence upon autonomy and independence. What he did not seem to understand, however, was that Communist strength in the industrial sectors of Munich was growing at a pace that would soon work against their cooperation with such petit-bourgeois intellectuals as himself. The basis of his opening to the Left had been a desire to secure the existence of the Räte movement in the face of the soon to be convened Landtag. If, however, he could not compete with Levien and Leviné for the support of Munich's industrial workers (which was, in fact, the case, given his refusal to see the Räte movement as the vehicle for a working-class seizure of power),[85] there was little chance that he would succeed in convincing the Communists to follow his conception of a Rätedemokratie. The isolation of the past had been only superficially erased. Landauer's solidarity with the estimated 80,000 demonstrators of February 16 was largely of a purely negative kind: common opposition to the destruction of the council movement.

At the same time, however, Landauer's powerful speeches at various workers' council meetings of February, in the period just before the expected convening of the Landtag on the 21st, often carried considerable weight.[86] Landauer was instrumental, for example, in attracting support from the Munich Workers' Council, which had an SPD and trade-union majority, for the February 16 demonstration in favor of the council system and its continued existence. At the February 12 sitting of the council, Landauer charged that the SPD minister of the interior, Erhard Auer, was planning a coup against Eisner and the other Independents in the government and was forming a bourgeois coalition that would put an end to the council system. After radical delegates prevented a defender of Auer from speaking, the SPD and trade-union delegates left the hall in protest and Landauer called upon a large group of radical shop stewards, who had been sitting in the gallery, to replace the departed council members. With its SPD majority missing, the Munich Workers' Council easily passed a resolution in favor of the February 16 demonstration.[87]

Such tactics were not necessary, however, at the sessions of the Bavarian Workers', Peasants', and Soldiers' Rätekongress which met during the entire week before February 21; since mid-January, as we have seen, large sections of Munich's working classes had become radicalized by worsening economic conditions and the failure of the Eisner government to bring about meaningful social reforms, and the Rätekongress provided expression for their discontent. In this forum Landauer's speeches against the SPD and ballot-box democracy and in favor of a direct democracy based upon the councils were greeted with stormy applause.[88] At the February 19 sitting of the congress, Landauer escalated his charges against Auer and other SPD ministers, claiming that they were planning a counterrevolutionary putsch against the Räte and the Independent Socialists, in league with a contingent of sailors.[89] Because of these fears Landauer had called on Eisner, in a speech after the February 16 demonstration, to cease all cooperation with the SPD and form an administration committed to break from the old military and bureaucracy; in place of SPD and bourgeois centralized bureaucracy, he emphasized, a socialist economy must be built which would be based upon district and local control.[90]

Such a conception of socialism was different from that of both right-wing socialists and Communists, and Landauer did not hesitate to make this clear to the Rätekongress. He did not merely attack the SPD and ballot-box democracy at the congress, but emphasized that his cooperation with the Communists against parliamentarism did not mean that he subscribed to their conception of the Räte: "There is no more pitiful revolution in world history than this one in Germany," he said in one speech; "it chooses ballot-box democracy which does not bring the clear will of the Volk to expression. But what we need is not a dictatorship of the proletariat as such, but an always visible, always working, democracy of all creative forces, forces that will together determine the life of the Volk." [91] Landauer was not about to abandon his commitment either to direct democracy or to anarchosocialism. In another speech he clearly distinguished the kind of libertarian socialism he favored from that of both SPD and KPD; in the account of the USPD paper, the *Neue Zeitung*, Landauer "warned against a bureaucratization of the distribution of the necessities of life. Socialism is not based upon our looking up to the father state," he said, "but upon our own initiative, the free exchange of goods carried out by working people." [92] Such speeches were, significantly, not greeted with thunderous applause; the followers of Landauer's positive social theories, as distinguished from his more generally appealing negative attacks on the SPD and parliamentarism, were few in number and were largely concentrated among the antiauthoritarian Schwabing intellectuals.[93]

Although his social theories carried little weight with the mass of workers in the Rätekongress, beyond his general commitment to a Räte system of rule, it was Landauer's motion that was finally adopted in the crucial debate of the last day of the congress. With the Landtag about to meet on the following day, the congress had to decide upon an immediate course of action. While an SPD delegate called for outright adjournment and total abdication of authority to the Landtag, and the KPD countered with a demand that the congress remain in session in spite of the Landtag, Landauer suggested a compromise that was finally adopted: ". . . the *Kongress* would adjourn temporarily, to meet again soon, and would in the meantime organize a series of public demonstrations in favor of the integration of the council system in the constitution." [94] In the end, Landauer stood against direct confrontation tactics and resigned himself to an attempt to salvage as much Räte authority as possible in the midst of the imminent regimen of counterrevolutionary parliamentarism. If, however, he was willing to compromise on February 20, the next day was to unleash all the pent-up bitterness and desperation that had been gathering since early December. After February 21 Landauer and Munich moved to the Left: Thermidor had been deferred by the assassination of Kurt Eisner.

### Thermidor Deferred: Eisner's Assassination and the Council Republics

After his speech to the final session of the Rätekongress on February 20, Landauer left for Krumbach, in the Swabian part of Bavaria, to spend the next day, February 21, with his children; it had been exactly one year before that Hedwig had died. After returning to Munich at the end of the sad day, Landauer was greeted with the news that his close friend Eisner had been murdered by a demented man who had earlier been rejected by the reactionary Thule Society, Count Arco-Valley.[95] Eisner was shot on the way to the Landtag building where he had intended to offer his resignation and go into peaceful opposition—a fact that was, unfortunately, little known among the populace of

Bavaria.[96] Along with most of Munich's population, Landauer was deeply shocked and horrified by Eisner's murder. For him, however, the tragedy was a great personal loss, especially as it came exactly one year after the death of his wife.[97] He conveyed this sense of personal loss publicly in the memorial address he delivered at Eisner's funeral on the 26th of February, in which he spoke of Eisner as "one like Jesus, like Huss, . . . who were executed by stupidity and greed," [98] and wrote privately: ". . . it is very difficult for me to go on with my work—and with my life." [99] After such an event existence was becoming more and more of a burden to Landauer.

After a delay of an hour, during which the shock of Eisner's assassination was absorbed, the Landtag opened its scheduled meeting with a speech by the SPD minister Erhard Auer. Before he could complete his first sentence, however, Auer was severely wounded by a bullet fired by a butcher named Alois Lindner, who had been maddened by the murder of his idol, Eisner, and believed that Auer was the initiator of the assassination. In panic the deputies immediately ran from the hall, after Lindner, in making his escape, killed two persons. The deputies did not return.[100]

After February 21 a power vacuum developed, but it was promptly filled by an immediately radicalized Räte movement. Eisner's assassination led very quickly, in Munich, to a mass flight of workers from the ranks of the SPD and into the camp of both the USPD and the KPD, a flight brought on by the workers' feeling that they had been "betrayed by their party leaders and that reaction was on the march." [101] Instead of being the day on which the revolution would have ended, the day on which the Landtag would have accepted Eisner's resignation and established its sole authority in Bavaria, February 21 saw the beginning

of a second revolution which was to lead to the radical
council republics of April:

> February 21 might well have marked the conclusion of the
> revolution in Bavaria except for the political stupidity and
> criminal action of Kurt Eisner's assassin. Had Eisner been
> permitted to carry out his intention to resign on February 21,
> a legally elected and constituted parliamentary government
> would have been inaugurated that day. . . . As one lawless
> act led directly to another, [however,] Bavaria was suddenly
> and literally returned to a state of lawlessness, and every
> question which might have been settled was at once re-
> opened. . . . Even in terms of its own motive Count Arco's
> deed was a failure. Instead of averting a second revolution,
> he initiated it.[102]

Even with the shift in working-class sentiment in Munich, the SPD and the right wing of the USPD still retained
a majority of delegates to the various Bavarian Räte. Although large sections of the Munich working class had been
radicalized by Eisner's assassination, as well as by unemployment, inflation, and scarcities, and each week saw the
return of more troops, adding to the number of aimless and
jobless in the city, this development was not immediately
expressed within the Räte movement as a whole.[103] Left-
wing Independent Socialists, Communists, and anarchists
were still only a minority within the Bavarian Räte, a fact
that was evident at the meetings of the Rätekongress which
assembled on February 25 to decide upon the future of the
revolution. On the fourth day of the congress Erich Mühsam's call for the immediate establishment of a Bavarian socialist *Räterepublik* was soundly rejected by a vote of 234
to 70, with Landauer voting against his friend's motion. In
explanation of his position Landauer said that the calling of
a Räterepublik would be premature, since he was "acquainted with the mistrust, the hate, and the ignorance of

the facts in the *Land* [Bavaria] against which one would proclaim the council republic at this time." [104] Instead of a Räterepublik, what was decided upon was a motion that Landauer also voted against: a cabinet would be formed and the Landtag reconvened in order to grant it special powers.[105] Outside the Landtag building where the Rätekongress was meeting, a crowd of angry workers had gathered who threatened to storm the bulding when they heard of the congress's decisions. Landauer appeared to present his reasons for opposing a Räterepublik at this time, but it took Mühsam and Levien to dissuade the unarmed crowd from disrupting the congress.[106] Such a demonstration of Munich's workers against the majority of the delegates to the congress convinced many radicals—especially Mühsam, but possibly also Landauer—that the congress was not giving expression to the radical sentiments held by a majority of the masses of Munich.[107]

Early in March the Rätekongress appointed a unity commission which reported to it on March 7. The commission proposed a cabinet composed of SPD and USPD members, to be headed by the former SPD minister of culture under Eisner, Johannes Hoffman. It recommended that the Landtag be called into session to approve the cabinet, but then it was to recess and allow the new government to rule provisionally by executive decree. The central point of the commission's report, however, was its recommendation that the councils continue to exist only in an advisory capacity, with the power merely of being able to demand a referendum on any action taken by the Landtag in the future. With the congress's adoption of the commission report on the following day, Landauer and the radicals had been defeated: the Landtag would be reconvened on March 17 to approve the SPD-led cabinet.[108] Given the turbulent atmosphere in Munich, however—there was frequent street fighting now between security guards and workers—the Hoffman government was advised by Berlin to withdraw to Nuremberg in northern Bavaria.[109] After the murder of Eisner, Munich was a polarized city on the verge of civil war. To the consternation of the radicals, however, the Rätekongress had adopted the program of the Majority Socialists and planned to abdicate its authority to the Landtag; it had come out against the workers in the streets. The radicals' disgust was best expressed by Gustav Landauer. After three persons had been killed when armed security guards broke up a crowd of demonstrators on Munich's Theresienwiese—an event received by SPD delegates in the congress with relief—Landauer stood up and said: "In the whole of natural history I know of no more revolting creature than the Social Democratic Party." [110]

Before the final vote was taken in the congress on the commission's report, Landauer made a plea for the adoption of his own conception of democracy, one based upon the Räte themselves and not upon centralized cabinets and parliamentary rule. He repeated his plan in a letter he wrote later in the month. Although his plan was rejected by the congress, it is of interest as an example of Landauer's application of his social views to the Bavarian Revolution. Once again he rejected both parliamentarism and the dictatorship of the proletariat as political solutions for the revolution. The Räte, he insisted, must not resemble parliamentary bodies, as the unity commission had in effect proposed; instead of being central bodies elected by workers and peasants, as the commission had suggested, Landauer proposed that the Räte be agents for the development of real communities, within both rural and urban areas, and that they provide a focus for the full and ongoing participation of all community members in the political life of their localities.

Since the economy was so organized that members of various professions were not "organic parts of the Volk," however, but rather isolated atoms that participated in the social antagonisms and disruptiveness of capitalism, it would be necessary for Rätedemokratie to develop in conjunction with the transformation of the economy to a socialism rooted in the Gemeinde and the urban neighborhood.[111] Real democracy, Landauer argued, continuing the pattern of his prewar social thought, would evolve only through the development of organic and decentralized community life. Such community life, he emphasized, would be much more difficult to develop in large cities where individuals were both more isolated and more controlled by centralized administrations; but even there Rätedemokratie might be able to evolve. By March 1919 Landauer was willing to make a partial compromise with the urban present and was no longer calling for massive depopulation of the large cities. Through his exposure to a radicalized urban proletariat in postwar Munich, he was now willing to formulate a conception of communitarian and völkisch anarchism which would, no doubt, still be rooted in small-town and rural life but would include the attempts to realize an integrated, local community life within decentralized urban neighborhoods.[112]

Contained in Landauer's suggestion were many aspects of his völkisch anarchosocialism: the resistance to class struggle in the name of the organic community of all working people from all social classes, the Volk, as a whole; the conviction that this community would exist only by being developed first on local and district levels, and through the autonomy and decentralization of these small units. What was new, however, was Landauer's willingness to begin thinking about the possible applicability of völkisch anarchism to urban society. Granting that the difficulties were greater in a mass metropolis, Landauer had been sufficiently impressed by the radical industrial workers of postwar revolutionary Munich to revise his earlier extreme antiurbanism and to begin formulating a conception of neighborhood socialism in the midst of the modern city. Significantly, of course, the way to urban Rätedemokratie was through the leadership of devoted intellectuals who would awaken the community spirit of the urban district and lead in the development of local socialist democracy through the decentralized Räte; to the end, Landauer remained a libertarian who assigned a rather significant role to intellectuals, not as rulers, but as midwives in the rebirth of the community consciousness that lay hidden in all men. All the same, Landauer had begun to revise some aspects of his antiurban social outlook. It was only his murder in May 1919 that prevented the development of this more pragmatic anarchist approach to modern society.[113]

Although somewhat more realistic than his earlier Räte conception of November and December, in which he thought of the Räte as vehicles for deurbanization as well as decentralization, Landauer's proposal of March 7 to the Rätekongress was rejected and the motion for the Hoffman government was passed. On March 17 the Hoffman government came to power, but remained in Nuremberg in order to avoid a direct confrontation with the increasingly radical Munich bohemian and working-class communities. Because of the radicalization of public sentiment in much of Munich, Landauer did not give up all hope after March 17. He wrote soon after: "Outwardly we have arrived at the intermezzo of reaction in Bavaria, which is called the Social

Democratic Ministerium, but I don't believe it will last." [114] Elsewhere he commented: "So long as a little spark of hope still glows, I will not give up my work in public life, which will lay a basis for life in a truer community." [115] The end of the month provided a few of these sparks. In response to pressure from the USPD and other more radical elements in Munich, the Hoffman government showed some signs of approaching the social demands of the Left by appointing a socialist economist, Otto Neurath, to draw up plans to "prepare and realize socialism." Before Neurath's plans were announced, Landauer wrote: "We have built such a fire behind the government that it is now seriously dealing with socialism. We want to see how it goes." [116] In the end, however, Neurath's plan to use a part of Bavaria for a three-year experiment in socialism was never put into effect.[117]

Landauer knew that time was running out on prospects for any socialist transformation in Germany. Although in March Munich's workers became more and more discontented with the inadequacies of previous revolutionary accomplishments, Landauer noted that the various SPD governments were increasingly entrenched in power throughout Germany, and that the Entente was now ready to aid them in the shoring up of the capitalist economy after the ravages of the war. He wrote in late March:

. . . there is not much time to lose; the danger that capitalism with the help of the Entente governments and the Entente capitalists will resurrect itself is very great. Above all, that is the reason that the rebellious mood in the mass of industrial workers and the unemployed must now be encouraged; . . . capitalism should not function again. Both in the actual state of things and in the mind it must be stamped out. . . . I still have a mild hope for Bavaria, that the councils, which are forced to more positive work, will be permitted to do this work before it is too late.[118]

On the last day of March Landauer spoke to a meeting of the Revolutionary Workers' Council on the subject, "The Revolution and the Realization of Socialism," and cited the danger to socialist construction present in the reliance of the masses on the German government to protect Germany from Bolshevism.[119] On the same day, however, renewed demands were heard in Munich for the calling of a Räterepublik after news had been received that such a government had been established in Hungary under Béla Kun, and that further revolution was under way in Saxony.[120]

With the Hoffman government in exile in northern Bavaria, a Räterepublik was proclaimed in Munich on April 7, 1919. Although in contemporary newspaper accounts and in many textbooks since, Landauer has been cited as one of the leading figures behind the proclamation, or even as the man who was most responsible for it,[121] this contention was denied by Landauer and recent research has substantiated his denial. It was not Landauer or any of the other radicals who took the initiative in calling a Räterepublik in early April. Recent accounts of the Bavarian Revolution have clarified the long-confused matter; they make it clear that the Räterepublik was first urged upon the radicals by the Social Democratic minister of military affairs in the Hoffman government, Ernst Schneppenhorst. Without apparently clearing the matter with the other members of the Hoffman cabinet, Schneppenhorst met with all the leading Munich radicals in the early morning of April 5 and insisted that a Räterepublik be immediately proclaimed, a government that would include all socialist parties from the SPD to the KPD. Why Schneppenhorst should have committed his party to a policy they had long opposed is a difficult question to answer, though recent historians have offered a variety of speculations as to his motives. The one proposed by Alan Mitchell seems most likely: "By drawing the KPD into a coalition regime, Schneppenhorst hoped to commit its leaders to official responsibility for their words and deeds, which could then be—somehow or other—vigorously opposed. He could thereby achieve two objectives at once: keep the SPD in a position of authority and control the Communist threat. It was a dangerous gamble and, as it proved, a mistaken one." [122]

At first Landauer took Schneppenhorst's action as a sincere call for proletarian unity encouraged by the show of socialist solidarity in Béla Kun's Hungary.[123] By the evening of April 5, however, two developments occurred which brought him to suspect that the calling of a Räterepublik was a mere "machination of the Bavarian SPD." [124] First Schneppenhorst changed his mind and asked that the proclamation of a Räterepublik be delayed for two days so that he could go to Nuremberg and rally support for it in the north of Bavaria and enlist troops to protect it from counterrevolutionary regiments of the Bavarian army corps.[125] By the end of the day, however, Schneppenhorst's maneuvering for a popular front Räterepublik had been defeated, for the KPD and the SPD each refused to participate in any coalition with the other. With suspicion of the SPD stronger than ever in Landauer's mind and in the minds of the other Munich anarchists and radical Independent Socialists, a Räterepublik was finally proclaimed on the morning of April 7; it contained neither Majority Socialists nor Communists.[126] It had proved too late to undo what Schneppenhorst had done.[127]

Appointed commissioner for "Enlightenment and Public Instruction" in what has been called the "happy, irresponsible government of the Coffee House Anarchists," [128] Landauer was deeply aware of the tenuousness of the Räterepublik's position and realistic about its chances for extended survival. On April 7, the day of the proclamation of the new government, Landauer wrote privately: "If we are allowed a few weeks' time, then I hope to be able to accomplish something; it is very possible, however, that it will last only a few days and then seem as if it had been a dream." [129] Landauer was aware, moreover, that by participating in a government in competition with the far more powerful Hoffman regime in northern Bavaria, which could readily enlist the Bavarian garrisons of the Reichswehr and the reactionary Free Corps army against it, he was inviting his own murder. Still despondent over the death of Hedwig and the assassination of his friend Kurt Eisner, Landauer seems to have been willing to risk this likely eventuality. In a public speech of April 12 he said: "Though it is possible that our lives may be short, I have the desire, and this you share with me, that we leave behind lasting effects in Bavaria . . . so that we may hope, when authoritarianism returns, that perspicacious circles will say that we did not make a bad beginning during the Räterepublik and that it would not have been a bad thing if we had been permitted to continue our work. This is in case we collapse." [130]

How could an anarchist justify his entrance into a "government" of any kind, even one that had a number of other anarchists in it? One possible answer to this question is that through personal tragedies and severe disappointment with the course of the revolution, of which he had expected too much in November, Landauer had become a very impatient man by April 1919 and was ready to abandon his earlier less apocalyptic approach to the building of socialism.[131] He did not regard the Räterepublik, however, as a government in the authoritarian sense that he understood that term; it was Landauer who insisted to the other leaders of the Räterepublik—Ernst Toller, the chairman of the Central Committee; Sylvio Gesell, the Proudhonian finance minister; and Erich Mühsam, who did not accept an official post[132]—that all decrees issued by the regime be marked "provisional" and go into effect only when approved by the Räte themselves.[133] Although impatient and frustrated, Landauer was by no means ready to try to introduce an anarchosocialist society by dictatorial decree from above.

If Landauer was aware of the imminence of counterrevolution while he was participating in the Räterepublik, one question still remains: How was a Räterepublik possible at all in the spring of 1919 in Bavaria? In a sense, of course, a Bavarian Räterepublik did not exist, since the Hoffman government still commanded the loyalty of northern Bavaria and of most of the Bavarian countryside. The Bavarian Räterepublik could claim precedence over the Bamberg and Nuremberg government of Hoffman only in the small triangle formed by Augsburg, Rosenheim, and Garmisch; in fact, it was little more than a Munich Räterepublik.[134] Yet the fact remains that the Hoffman administration had collapsed in Munich and the surrounding area. Factors contributing to this collapse—besides, of course, the concerted activities of a devoted radical minority in Munich—included the worsening situation of the economy in the industrial sectors of the city, which increased working-class support for the radicals; the inadequacy of security preparations; and the lack of real support for the Hoffman government by the largest political party in Bavaria, the Bavarian People's Party, which had been alienated by the failure of the SPD to oppose the centralist bias of the Weimar Constitution. Munich, however, was not the only center of revolutionary activity in April. Outside Bavaria, strikes in the Ruhr, riots in Frankfurt, and martial law in

Stuttgart provided Munich with models of radical resistance to SPD and parliamentary authority.[135]

As a group of ethically and aesthetically oriented socialist intellectuals, the leaders of the Räterepublik concerned themselves far more with reforming Munich's cultural and educational institutions than they did with improving the economic situation or building an effective administrative apparatus for the implementation of their goals. Although there were pronouncements relating to the nationalization of banks and attempts, on paper, to alleviate the housing and food shortages, the Central Council of the Räterepublik was "more intent on socializing the university and the theater than the economy." [136] Given this orientation, Landauer occupied a central post as commissioner of enlightenment and public instruction.

The most significant action taken by the Räterepublik was within Landauer's department. On the day of the proclamation of the new regime, Landauer granted full power to a group of radical students and *Privatdozenten* at the university, a group fashionably entitled the "Revolutionary University Council," to bring about drastic changes in the curriculum and governance of the University of Munich; in order to give the council a broad base of support, however, Landauer convinced it to work in conjunction with a new "Shop Council of the Working Community of the University" to comprise four students, two professors, and one official and to be elected by the student body and the *Dozenten*.[137] To enable the students and faculty fully to discuss and immediately to implement the envisioned educational reforms, Landauer suspended all classes on April 7 and called for their resumption during the summer semester on a new reformed basis. Although never put into effect, as Landauer's tenure in office lasted only one week, the reforms planned by the Revolutionary University Council would have brought sweeping changes: they would have opened the university to more students from the working classes; they would have begun the integration of scientific and philosophical faculties; and, most important, they would have brought about a radical revision of university governance by drastically increasing student and Dozenten participation in educational and administrative decision making, thus fashioning the university into a libertarian cooperative society of Dozenten and students. It was to this program, not surprisingly, that the anarchist Landauer gave his full consent.[138]

As commissioner of public instruction Landauer drew up his own educational reform program, which was also never put into effect, a program he was later asked to submit to the Communist Räterepublik that succeeded his own regime. Although Landauer was encouraged by a Communist admirer by the name of Fidelis to send his program to Leviné, the Communist regime rejected his suggestions.[139] The program was Landauer's most detailed proposal in the educational field and is, therefore, of value as an example of his attempts to implement concretely his social theories.

Since Landauer held that all men are potentially capable of autonomously determining their own lives, but that their present dependence upon authority and docile passivity made them mere subjects under the control of others, his educational program stressed the development of intellectual and ethical autonomy and not merely vocational training in skills. Whereas the authoritarian school system of the past had taught children and adolescents to think less and obey authority more, the new system was to help awaken the intellect of the child and encourage his self-reliance. Children would be enrolled in school when they reached the age of seven, later than under the prevailing system, and would all be given both manual and intellectual instruction; soon after, the desires and abilities of each individual child would be the determining factor in deciding in which direction his education would go.[140] For the pre-gymnasium level of education, Landauer proposed the establishment of powerful *Elternräte*, or parent-teacher associations, which would facilitate the cooperation of each school with the local community of which it was a part.[141] As to curriculum and reading material, Landauer told the American writer Ben Hecht, who visited him in his office during the first days of the Räterepublik, that he hoped to make Walt Whitman the cornerstone of his educational system: ". . . every Bavarian child at the age of ten is going to know Walt Whitman by heart," Landauer said.[142]

While on the one hand Landauer insisted upon a vast increase in student power within the structure of higher education, calling for the development of numerous revolutionary student senates to play a vital role in the governance of each university, he also concerned himself with the redevelopment of community cultural life to replace the frustrating isolation of the contemporary artist-intellectual. One means by which to encourage a public-spirited art, one that would give expression to the aspirations of the Volk, was to have frequent commissions granted to young artists by an artistic academy made up of all practicing writers and artists; this academy, in turn, would set down guidelines for these commissions in cooperation with other democratic councils of the Volk.[143] As commissioner for enlightenment and public instruction, Landauer hoped to make a beginning in the construction of both a communitarian and an anarchosocialist society.

Besides work on educational and cultural reform, Landauer made efforts during the life of the Räterepublik to prevent the use of force in the realization of the aims of the regime. Resisting the call for a wholesale imitation of Bolshevik practice, a call to which Mühsam often responded, Landauer insisted in his cultural program, for example, that the Bavarian people could not be freed from the reactionary clutches of the Catholic church by an immediate nationalization of church possessions, but that the desired result could be achieved only by exposing the Bavarian Volk to a community life that would make the Church "superfluous." For Landauer neither the state, capitalism, nor the Church could be destroyed by direct attack; all of them would wither away only after the development of a real anarchosocialist community had begun to replace them. As the community increasingly satisfied the spiritual aspirations of the population, the Church would lose many of its members, and its property and power could then be gradually limited.[144] In this connection Landauer took action to prevent the Räterepublik from forcing the Catholic *Bayerische Kurier* to publish articles denouncing religion.[145] It was not only with regard to religious issues that Landauer resisted authoritarian measures. Although participating in a joint statement condemning attempts by the Munich middle classes to launch strikes against the Räterepublik or to engage in any other counterrevolutionary actions,[146] Landauer worked with Ernst Toller to prevent the use of the death sentence against anyone, including the active enemies of the regime.[147]

The German public, however, was not informed of Landauer's humanitarian approach. Instead, while he opposed the resort to authoritarian tactics against the Right, Landauer was often the focus of many right-wing attacks on the Räterepublik. Early in April numerous newspapers reported that Landauer had already put into practice the total communization of the women of Munich, that he was planning a reign of terror against the middle and upper classes, and that he was living in sin with the widow of Eisner on state funds in various Bavarian castles.[148] As has been pointed out in a recent study of the revolution, most middle-class diaries and memoirs of Munich in 1918–19 exhibit a far deeper hatred and a far more pervasive fear of the Schwabing bohemians than of the industrial working classes.[149] It was not unusual for Landauer to be attacked as an egomaniac or a psychopath by conservatives.[150] Of more direct, tragic significance for Landauer's fate, however, was the fact that such slanderous attacks on him were continually fed to the growing numbers of Thuringian Free Corps troops by the right-wing extremist Thule Society. For these two organizations, from which the Nazis were to recruit many of their first members in the early 1920s, Landauer was the "evil genius" behind the revolutionary movements in Munich.[151]

Although such propaganda continued to be circulated until early May, Landauer played no role whatsoever in the events of Munich, either as an evil genius or a humanitarian idealist, after Palm Sunday, April 13. After the "Coffee House" Räterepublik had been in existence for only one week, a Munich garrison loyal to the Bamberg government of Hoffman staged an attempted coup d'etat against the regime on April 13 which led to its replacement by a Communist Räterepublik. Of all the groups on the Left, it was only the Communists who were able to command any military force to protect the existence of Räte government. After the coup had been defeated, the workers' councils, thinking mistakenly that all the leaders of the first Räterepublik had been captured and taken away by the insur-

gent troops, replaced the Landauer-Toller regime with a
new fifteen-member action committee, made up mostly of
Communists, which soon elected Leviné as its chairman. An
attempted counterrevolution had delivered power into the
hands of the Communists and on April 14 a new, "truly
proletarian," Räterepublik was proclaimed in Munich.[152]

One day before the attempted coup, Landauer had appealed to the Hoffman government not to intervene vio-
lently in Munich: "If we are not disturbed in our work, by
that I mean through violence, then the power of the spirit
will go from brain and heart into the hands, and out of the
hands into the arrangements of the external world." [153] Intervention was attempted, however, and, like Rosa Luxemburg before him, Landauer was not ready to abandon the
working-class ship as it threatened to sink, even if he did
not agree with all those who were now its captains. After
the Communist Räterepublik was proclaimed on April 14,
Landauer offered his assistance to the new regime in order
to help build a united front against counterrevolution. In a
public statement he declared: "Through the active intervention of the Munich proletariat, the Räterepublik has
been saved from the impudent putsch attempt of the counterrevolutionaries. I recognize and greet the reorganization
that has taken place. The old central committee no longer
exists. I place my strength at the disposal of the Action
Committee, to be used as needed." [154]

Yet Landauer's offer of support was given only halfheart-
edly. Although anxious to prevent the immediate destruction of the revolution, Landauer would never agree to the
use of terror tactics in the building of socialism. With the
rejection of his offer of cooperation by the Communists,
who suspected his pacifist tendencies, and Leviné's first
threats of antibourgeois terrorism (which were never, in

fact, carried out), Landauer wrote to the Action Committee that the "rejection of cooperation . . . [was] mutual." After the Action Committee had begun to plan revolutionary measures patterned on Bolshevik Russia, including the disarming and expropriation of the middle classes, and had issued repeated threats of terror against all enemies of the regime, Landauer wrote to the Communist leaders on April 16:

> For the sake of liberation and the beautiful life of man I placed myself at the further disposal of the Räterepublik. . . . You have not accepted my services. Meanwhile I have seen how you work, have become acquainted with the manner in which you propose to bring enlightenment, how you carry out the struggle. I have seen how, in opposition to what you call the *Scheinräterepublik* [the Communist term, then and now, for the first Räterepublik of Landauer, Toller, and Gesell], your reality appears. My concept of the struggle, whose goal is to create conditions that will permit every man to share in the goods and culture of the earth, is somewhat different from yours. I therefore assert what was formerly no secret; the rejection of cooperation is mutual. . . . I shall keep this communication strictly private; it is not my intention to destroy in the least the hard work of the defense which you have undertaken. But I deplore most painfully that only the least portion of my work, a work of warmth and elevation, of culture and regeneration, is now preserved.[155]

Landauer had finally withdrawn from the turbulent Munich Revolution. After his letter to the Communist Action Committee, he joined Kurt Eisner's widow, Else, in the Munich suburb of Gross-Hadern and took up his literary activities again. With the final capture of Munich on May 1, however, by White troops sent by the SPD minister in Berlin, Gustav Noske, Landauer was not allowed to return to private life.[156] The slanderous lies against him spread by the press and such groups as the Thule Society now reaped their harvest: on May 2, Landauer was brutally beaten to death as a leader of the Communists.

## Thermidor with a Vengeance: Landauer's Failure and Martyrdom

Why did Landauer fail in 1918–19? One obvious answer is that he lacked experience as a political leader, was primarily a socially concerned intellectual with no taste for political maneuvering, and, as an anarchist, was temperamentally and ideologically opposed to strong efforts to organize effective revolutionary cadres. From early January on, it was quite obvious that Landauer could not compete with the Communists for the loyalty of the increasingly radical Munich working classes. Unlike Eisner or Leviné, for example, Landauer had no organizational structure or effective party upon which to base his political actions, although he was able at certain times to exercise considerable influence as an independent voice on the Räte movement. His previous sociological commitments, moreover, had militated against his study of urban social and political problems and brought him to the proletarian cause as a newcomer who had just revised his prewar disgust at their lack of militancy. The peasantry, moreover, the social group that Landauer had long regarded as the nucleus for the creation of an anarchist community, was one of the main social sources of reaction in Bavaria and consistently resisted any authority the Räterepublik had in the rural areas surrounding Munich.[157] To be at all effective in the modern world, Landauer would have had to revise his social theories far more than he had had the opportunity to do in the limited time of the revolution.[158]

Yet it was not only Landauer who failed, but the entire

movement for any kind of Räte reorganization of Bavaria. Even if he had been a far more effective political leader, had long studied the application of libertarian socialism to the life of the urban working classes, and had been able to move the Bavarian Räte movement in the direction of decentralized Rätedemokratie based upon the factory and the urban neighborhood, he still would not have succeeded in Munich in 1918–19. After the victory of SPD parliamentarism and the abdication of all authority by the German Räte movement in Berlin in December and January, the long-term transformation of Bavaria into any kind of council republic was virtually impossible. As Alan Mitchell has written:

> The decisive moment of the revolution in Germany had in fact already occurred during the second week of January, 1919 when the Spartacist insurrection in Berlin was crushed beyond redemption; . . . there was open talk of a Bavarian Soviet Republic among men who seriously aspired to power. For some it was a goal; for others, a last resort. For all of them it was a delusion. So long as the Berlin government survived and had the Free Corps at its command, the sovietization of Bavaria was a mirage. . . . The events which seemed climactic to many Bavarians (the events from Eisner's assassination to the Communist *Räterepublik*) were therefore only an ugly aftereffect of the German Revolution.[159]

In late April 1919 the Communist Räterepublik recruited its own Red Army and braced itself for the imminent invasion of Munich by Reichswehr and Free Corps troops sent by the SPD minister Gustav Noske. Whereas earlier the Communist regime had not engaged in any of the terroristic practices it often threatened, as White troops began to encircle the city in the last days of April the Red Army executed ten prisoners, six of them members of the Thule Society. Such an act, of course, only invited massive and indiscriminate retaliation by the stronger White troops, already anxious to wipe out all participants in Munich's radical revolution.[160] As Thermidor threatened to conquer with a vengeance, Landauer's friends pleaded with him to leave Bavaria immediately, since it was unlikely that his life would be spared by the bloodthirsty White troops. At first he refused to leave, then agreed to flee to Switzerland, but then once again decided to stay. On May 1 he was arrested in Eisner's study in Gross-Hagern, the Munich suburb. Only the intervention of a neighbor prevented his immediate assassination by the White troops. After being told that Landauer had not belonged to the Communist Räterepublik and was an opponent of the Communists, the lieutenant in charge promised him a trial and put him in jail in the town of Starnberg. The next morning, however, May 2, he was transported to Stadelheim prison near Munich. An eyewitness in Stadelheim later described to Ernst Toller what was done to Landauer:

Amid shouts of "Landauer! Landauer!" an escort of Bavarian and Württemberger Infantry brought him out into the passage outside the door of the examination room. An officer struck him in the face, the men shouted: "Dirty Bolshie! Let's finish him off!" and a rain of blows from rifle-butts drove him out into the yard. He said to the soldiers round him: "I've not betrayed you. You don't know yourselves how terribly you've been betrayed." Freiherr von Gagern went up to him with a heavy truncheon until he sank in a heap on the ground. He struggled up again and tried to speak, but one of them shot him through the head. He was still breathing, and the fellow said: "That blasted carrion has nine lives; he can't even die like a gentleman." Then a sergeant in the life guards shouted out: "Pull off his coat!" They pulled it off, and laid him on his stomach; "Stand back there and we'll finish him off properly!" one of them called and shot him in the back. Landauer still moved convulsively, so they trampled on him till he was dead; then stripped the body and threw it into the wash-house.[161]

According to other accounts, Landauer said something about "this damned militarism!" as he was being shoved into the yard of the prison. After receiving additional blows on the head for that remark, he "declared that he included the militarism of the Red Army." Another witness told Toller that Landauer's last words to his murderers were: "Kill me then! To think that you are human!" [162]

In the Weimar Republic, which had failed to overhaul the old imperial judicial and administrative systems, acts of violence committed by those on the political Right were rarely punished and, in the few cases where they were, the sentences were extremely light. Because of their fears of the Spartacists and other elements to their left, the SPD had cemented an alliance with the old imperial army and bureaucracy to defend the parliamentary republic; such an alliance, however, made the new government a "republic without republicans," since the Majority Socialists did little to displace reactionary personnel within the administrative, military, and judicial systems.[163] Accommodation to right-wing forces—who stood against the republic but were willing to use it to preserve their power in Germany—began as early as Ebert's famous call to General Groener in November 1918 and continued throughout the Revolution of 1918–19 and into the twenties. In Bavaria, in May 1919, this accommodation took the form of a refusal to bring the White reaction to task for its indiscriminate and arbitrary terror in the aftermath of the Munich Revolution. Besides the multitude of workers who were slaughtered in the fighting of late April and early May, the White troops executed 154 individuals, without trial, who had not participated in any way in the military defense of the Räterepublik. After this bloodbath the SPD minister of defense in Berlin, Gustav Noske, sent a letter to the commander of the White army congratulating him for the "discreet and wholly successful way in which you have conducted your operations in Munich." Very few of the White troops were ever brought to trial for their arbitrary murder of 154 persons.[164] The punishment later accorded to two of Gustav Landauer's assassins, in fact, was unusually stiff: the man who shot Landauer through the head was acquitted of any charge of murder because he had merely been "following orders," although the officer who allegedly gave the orders was never found; another who was "obeying orders" was given five weeks in jail, not for murdering Landauer, but for stealing his watch; and Freiherr von Gagern, the officer who beat Landauer with his truncheon, was fined 500 marks.[165]

The question remains, however: Why did Landauer remain in the Munich area and leave himself open to such brutality? When escape was still possible why did he choose not to flee and thus endanger his own life? In answering this question it is difficult to avoid the impression that Landauer saw little reason to go on living at the end of April 1919. Although he vacillated, and at one point agreed to follow his friends' plans for escape to Switzerland, Landauer had reached a point where personal and political tragedy could no longer be endured. As we have seen, Landauer was often driven to despondency in the course of the revolution, largely because he had not recovered from the death of his wife, but especially after the murder of Eisner exactly one year after Hedwig's end. Early in March he had written: "It is very difficult for me to go on with my work—and with my life." [166] After Eisner's assassination Landauer developed sufficient resources to enter the radicalized Räte movement again and become a leading figure in the first

Räterepublik of April. Yet he was not his usual self in these months. A number of friends have provided evidence that Landauer had lost his earlier equilibrium and emotional stability in the last months of the revolution, was far more impatient and intolerant than he had ever been in his life, and was driven by a frenzy to realize at least a morsel of his social program in the Räterepublik of April.[167] As Martin Buber has written, Landauer "appeared dispirited and nearly exhausted" during the revolution; "a year before his wife had succumbed to a fatal illness, and now he relived her death in his heart." [168] According to Stefan Grossman and Fritz Mauthner, both of whom had known Landauer since his days in Berlin in the 1890s, Landauer was driven in the last months of the revolution by a will for self-sacrifice, and Grossman goes so far as to say that Landauer's murder by the White guards was, to a large extent, not only a sacrifice for the cause of social liberation, but a suicide.[169]

The libertarian and pacifist radical, the philosopher of anarchosocialism and völkisch romanticism, had fallen in Germany's stillborn revolution of 1918-1919. Like her earlier revolutions, this one was largely dominated by decisions and action from above—Ludendorff's abdication of authority to the Reichstag in October, Ebert's alliance with the military cemented in November, and so on—the form of political activity Landauer had always regarded as authoritarian. With the decision of the German Räte movement in Berlin to give way to parliamentary authority, all Landauer's attempts to realize a new Germany based upon federalized and direct political control from below, upon a democracy of the Räte, were in vain. Although he did not comment adequately on the matter and too readily assumed that Bavaria might be able to develop its own political forms without interference from Berlin, Landauer might have cited the Räte decision in Berlin in December as another example of voluntary servitude by the masses, the submission from below which facilitated manipulation from above. Events in Munich, especially the assassination of Eisner, had worked against an early voluntary submission to parliamentarism; yet Thermidor was not long in arriving there either and, when it came, it was even more authoritarian than it had been in Berlin. Deferred by a few more months of seemingly radical revolution, Thermidor came with special vengeance in the later home of the early Nazi movement.

After Landauer was brutally beaten and murdered by the White troops dispatched by Noske, his body was taken to a mass grave from which his daughter, Charlotte, obtained its release on May 19. It was not until May 1923 that Landauer's urn was interred in Munich's Waldfriedhof. When the Nazis came to power in 1933 they removed the urn from the cemetery and sent it to the Jewish community in Munich. They also destroyed a monument that had been erected as a tribute to Landauer in 1925 by the Anarchist-Syndicalist Union of Munich, a monument to which Georg Kaiser had given all his savings.[170] On it there had been inscribed a statement from Landauer's *Aufruf zum Sozialismus*. The epitaph read:

1870            Gustav Landauer            1919

Now is the time to bring forth a martyr of a different kind, not heroic, but a quiet, unpretentious martyr who will provide an example for the proper life.[171]

The inscription was a tribute to Landauer's ethical approach to socialism, one that implied, as Arnold Zweig once wrote, that Landauer's political weaknesses "betrayed more humanity than the virtues of those who are successful." [172]

# Conclusion

Landauer's murder in the aftermath of the Bavarian Revolution marks the end of this study. In it I have focused on his absorption of a variety of philosophic traditions and political ideologies, among which the most important were mystical idealism and vitalism, libertarian anarchosocialism, and völkisch romanticism. It has been my purpose to demonstrate that his importance for the intellectual historian of modern Germany was not so much the originality of his ideas, but, rather, the very fact of his synthesis of a pacifist, humanitarian, and profoundly democratic version of anarchistsocialism with the outlook of völkisch romanticism.

Landauer's völkisch socialism should provide an antidote to the tendency of intellectual historians to view romanticism and socialism teleologically, in terms of the triumph of the Hitlerite version of völkisch ideology and the Stalinist distortion of socialism. In studying völkisch romanticism, especially, one should not neglect the radical democratic descendants of Herder in the early twentieth century. The domination of racist and imperialist interpretations of the ideology in the political arena should be treated as a development conditioned more by Germany's social and political growth than as a seemingly inevitable result of romanticism itself. If the administrative, judicial, academic, and military classes in Germany were largely oriented toward a right-wing version of the German idealist and romantic heritage, the intellectual historian need not concentrate only on their parallels among the literati.

In a recent article Dr. Wolfgang Sauer has called for a

revision of our unbalanced and one-sided views of modern German thought and culture. Commenting on recent studies of völkisch ideology, Dr. Sauer writes:

> Parallel to the rise of the *völkisch* ideology, Germany experienced one of the greatest intellectual flowerings in its history during the first three decades of this century. In many cases it reached the level of the classical period around 1800, and it certainly surpassed it in breadth. [In a footnote Dr. Sauer continues:] It is indeed surprising to what extent a split in our knowledge of this period has developed. The general facts are known; in the sciences—Max Weber, Max Scheler, Mannheim, Troeltsch, Meinecke . . . ; in literature —Thomas and Heinrich Mann, Brecht, the Expressionists. . . . And yet in our conception of this period of German intellectual history the notion prevails that there were few but nationalists and racists in Germany. A well-balanced history of the Weimar Republic is, thus, still painfully needed for the study of modern Germany. The real question is, then, why this parallelism occurred and why the *völkisch* ideology eventually triumphed.[1]

While calling for a healthy release from the fixation of searching for protofascists, this statement does not offer a way out of the confusion about the role of völkisch romanticism in modern German life. Is it not true that a number of the figures mentioned above were in fact narrow nationalists and power worshipers, Weber and Meinecke, for example, and that, on the other hand, there were opponents of nationalist chauvinism and racism among the adherents of völkisch thought, as this study of Landauer has attempted to demonstrate? The real opposition was not so much between völkisch romantics and others, but between those who developed the racist doctrine and celebrated authoritarian imperial power and those who were oriented toward humanitarian and democratic goals. This opposition cannot always be associated with parliamentary or antiparliamentary sentiments, as the examples of Weber and Landauer demonstrate: Weber, the defender of Weimar parliamentarism, was, in fact, a man of very superficial democratic sentiments and a celebrant of the power of the German state;[2] Landauer, the opponent of centralized parliamentary government, was devoted to all nations and to the full participation of all men in the decision-making process, a criterion for democracy which, according to Landauer, was not met by parliaments. Instead of superficial divisions of "good" liberals and "evil, protofascist" romantics, we must examine the great complexity of romantic reactions against technological modernity and urban, rationalistic civilization, reactions that ranged in origin from Martin Buber and Gustav Landauer to Alfred Rosenberg and pervaded all circles of the literate middle classes in late nineteenth- and early twentieth-century Germany. On the other hand, intellectual historians might be well advised to view Nazi völkisch romanticism in the context of their very modern and antiromantic uses of depersonalizing bureaucracy and industrial rationality.

In the history of socialist ideas such a warning against unbalanced analysis is not quite so pressing. We have seen too many versions of the socialist heritage in our own time, from Israeli kibbutzim to west European social democracy to Stalinist authoritarianism, to warrant a similar exclusive concern for proto-Stalinist versions of socialism such as we have seen in the distorted accounts of the völkisch current. At the same time, however, the history of socialism has also been confused by teleological distortions: although "scientific" Marxism dominated the political history of socialism in central Europe after 1890, the same kind of dominance was much less obvious in socialist intellectual history, in which idealist and ethical socialists like Max Adler and Kurt Eisner, utopians like Franz Oppenheimer and Martin Buber, and anarchists like Landauer and Mühsam should be included along with more orthodox Marxists like Kautsky. With the new interest in the West in libertarian alternatives to bureaucratic socialism, and in a decentralist version of social democracy, it seems worthwhile to study socialist intellectual history since 1890 not only in terms of the opposition of revisionist and revolutionary Marxists, but also in terms of a continuing debate among socialist intellectuals on the merits of centralized authority and industrial modernization.

This study of Landauer's intellectual development has revealed some of the intellectual fluidity of the German cultural scene in the years 1900–1919. With the spread of neoromantic notions among the literate middle classes after the turn of the century, völkisch and/or communitarian perspectives were often combined with varieties of utopian and libertarian socialism. After he turned his back on the Berlin anarchist labor movement in 1898, Landauer participated in a variety of middle-class left-wing communitarian circles during the next two decades. These included the Moritz von Egidy Kreis, the Neue Gemeinschaft, and the Gartenstadt Gesellschaft in the years 1898–1903; Berlin Zionist socialists and his own Socialist Bund in the prewar years; the Aufbruchkreis of 1915 in which Landauer was in close contact with politically active expressionist writers as well as the socialist wing of the German youth movement; and the Düsseldorfer Schauspielhaus in 1918. In addition, a number of close friends or acquaintances of Landauer's in these years were intellectuals who developed some species of left-wing romantic social thought: the utopian socialists Franz Oppenheimer and Silvio Gesell; the anarchist Erich

Mühsam; the expressionists Ernst Toller and especially Georg Kaiser; and, most important, Martin Buber, whose libertarian völkisch outlook most closely resembled Landauer's. Of all these individuals and groups it is possible to say that the critique of modern urban civilization with which they were engaged was carried out in connection with the radical democratic ideals of 1789.

The transideological character of much of communitarian and völkisch thought was graphically displayed in the immediate postwar history of the youth movement. At the Freideutsche meeting at Jena in April 1919, the period of the Bavarian Räte regimes, it was only the Communist groups that defeated a common resolution in which "völkisch and socialist agreed upon the practical goals of socialization" and the term "Volksgemeinschaft" was used in connection with the "idea of a human kingdom of brotherhood and mutual aid." [3] In the period 1918–1921, according to a recent historian of the youth movement, Harry Pross, the words "Volk" and "Gemeinschaft," with their anti-industrial romantic connotations, were attractive to a variety of Wandervogel groups. For the middle-class socialists among them, he points out, it served to differentiate their own ethical and idealist views from Marxism.[4] In the *Freideutsche* literary journal *Junge Menschen*, which began publication in 1920, much of this same völkisch socialist orientation continued. Edited by the noted left-wing youth movement leaders Kund Ahlborn and Walter Hammer, this bimonthly publication had a readership of about 16,000 and was most influenced in its early years by the writings of Landauer, Toller, Kropotkin, and Herman Hesse.[5] It is significant that the journal attempted to win the youth movement to the support of the Weimar Republic in the name of the great romantic republicans of 1848.[6]

War and revolution had brought about a political polarization within the youth movement. After 1921, however, völkisch romantic perspectives were increasingly monopolized by the right-wing opponents of the Weimar Republic, and the left-wing Freideutsche went into decline.[7] Whatever the reasons for this development—and it cannot have been unrelated to growing animosity among the middle classes to the republic—it represented a split of romantic communitarian views from democratic and socialist ones. It is only in the period after 1920 that the völkisch constellation of ideas took on its exclusively racist and rabidly antidemocratic character in German public life.[8] Despite this fact, however, many members of the youth movement continued to prefer privately the Left and left-of-center parties of the republic.[9]

Because of the tendency of historians to focus upon protofascist versions of völkisch romanticism, they have overlooked the intermixture of communitarian, democratic, and socialist perspectives in early twentieth-century German culture. Behind the teleological distortion, however, there often lies the complacent assumption of the total adequacy, or at least the inevitability, of our form of urban industrial civilization.[10] With the contemporary search for new models of community life which might help to meet the crisis of metropolitan centers, we should be more hesitant to write off all romantic cultural criticism as protofascist or, at best, as unrealistic and antimodern. Are we so certain today that technological and urban expansion will solve most of our problems?

# Appendix

## THE TWELVE ARTICLES OF THE
## SOCIALIST BUND
### (June 14, 1908)

1. The basic form of socialist culture is the Bund of independent economic groups, exchanging goods with one another in justice.
2. This Socialist Bund treads the path that history assigns, in place of the state and the capitalist economy.
3. The Socialist Bund accepts the word "republic" in its original sense as the goal of its endeavors: the affairs of the commonweal.
4. The Socialist Bund declares anarchy in its original sense as the goal of its endeavors: order through voluntary union.
5. The Socialist Bund embraces all workingmen who want the social order of the Socialist Bund. Its task is neither proletarian politics nor class struggle, both of which are necessary accessories of capitalism and the authoritarian state, but the struggle and organization for socialism.
6. The real activities of the Socialist Bund can begin once the organization has been joined by large sections of the masses. Until then its task is propaganda and organizing.
7. The members of the Socialist Bund want to place their work in the service of their consumption.
8. They shall unite their consumption in order to exchange the products of their labor with the aid of their bank of exchange.
9. They shall send out pioneers who, in domestic settlements of the Socialist Bund, shall produce everything they need, including the products of the earth.
10. Culture does not rest upon some form of technology or upon the satisfaction of needs, but upon the spirit of justice.
11. The settlements should be models of justice and of joyous

labor; not a means to reach these goals. The goal is only to be reached if the ground and earth come into the hands of socialists by means other than purchase.

12. The Socialist Bund strives for justice and, with that, for the power to abolish private property in land and soil through great fundamental measures; it seeks to give all Volk comrades the possibility of living in culture and joy through a union of industry and agriculture in independent economic exchange communities on the basis of justice.

# Notes

[Throughout the notes, Gustav Landauer's name is abbreviated as GL in references to his writings.]

## INTRODUCTION

1 Two fine recent works on Luxemburg and Eisner are J. P. Nettl, *Rosa Luxemburg* (London: Oxford University Press, 1966), and Alan Mitchell, *Revolution in Bavaria, 1918–19: Kurt Eisner and the Bavarian Soviet Republic* (Princeton, 1965).

2 Following are the major studies on Landauer which have appeared since 1960: Sterling Fishman, "Prophets, Poets and Priests: A Study of the Men and Ideas That Made the Munich Revolution of 1918–19" (Ph.D. dissertation, University of Wisconsin, 1960); Thomas Esper, "The Anarchism of Gustav Landauer" (M.A. thesis, University of Chicago, 1961); Heinz-Joachim Heydorn, foreword to GL, *Aufruf zum Sozialismus*, 3d ed. (Frankfurt a. M., 1967), pp. 5–46; Wolf Kalz, *Gustav Landauer: Kultur Sozialist und Anarchist* (Meisenheim am Glau, 1967); and Charles Maurer, *Call to Revolution: The Mystical Anarchism of Gustav Landauer* (Detroit, 1971).

3 Günther Bartsch, "Gustav Landauer: Der Edelanarchist," *Geist und Tat* (April–June 1969), pp. 127–128.

4 A recent historian of the völkisch tradition, George L. Mosse, who (in *The Crisis of German Ideology: The Intellectual Origins of the Third Reich* [New York, 1964]) had assimilated almost the entire spectrum of romantic social thought to the origins of Nazism, has begun to retreat, in part, from his own argument. In his article ("The Influence of the *Völkisch* Idea on German Jewry," in *Germans and Jews: The Right, the Left and the Search for a "Third Force" in Pre-Nazi Germany* [New York, 1970]) there are disclaimers of the simple causal connections between the völkisch tradition and Nazism which underlay his earlier work.

5 Eduard von Bendemann, "Erinnerung an Gustav Landauer," *Masken,* XIV (May 1919), 308.

6 Rudolf Rocker, *The London Years* (London, 1956), p. 90.

– 351 –

7 See Julius Bab, *Gustav Landauer: Gedächtnisrede*, 2d ed. (Nürnberg, 1924), pp. 18–21; Fritz Mauthner, "Zum Gedächtnis," *Masken*, XIV (May 1919), 300–304; Martin Buber, "Landauer und die Revolution," *Masken*, XIV (May 1919), 282–291; Ernst Niekisch, *Gewagtes Leben: Begegnungen und Begebnisse* (Köln and Berlin, n.d.), pp. 78–79; Margaret Susman, "Gustav Landauers Briefe," *Der Morgen*, V (1929); Ludwig Berndl, "Gustav Landauers Briefe an Ludwig Berndl (Einleitung)," manuscript in Gustav Landauer Archives, International Institute of Social History, Amsterdam (hereafter cited as GL Archiv), fol. A.2; Hans Blüher, *Werke und Tage* (München, 1953), p. 376.
8 Niekisch, *Gewagtes Leben*, p. 78; Bab, *Gedächtnisrede*, p. 18.
9 Niekisch, *Gewagtes Leben*, p. 78.
10 Frederik van Eeden, "Tagebuchblätter aus der Zeit in Potsdam 1914," GL Archiv, fol. Z.
11 GL, *Sein Lebensgang in Briefen*, ed. Martin Buber, 2 vols. (Frankfurt a. M., 1929).
12 Quoted in Paul Breines, "The Jew as Revolutionary: The Case of Gustav Landauer," *Leo Baeck Yearbook*, XII (1967), 75.
13 See n. 7.
14 Letter dated Sept. 23, 1907, GL Archiv, fol. M.
15 Isidore Epstein, *Judaism: A Historical Presentation* (Baltimore: Penguin Books, 1959), pp. 55–64.
16 Bab, *Gedächtnisrede*, p. 11.
17 *Selected Poems of Bertolt Brecht*, trans. H. R. Hays (New York: Grove Press, 1959), pp. 173–177.
18 GL, *Sein Lebensgang*.
19 GL Archiv, fol. X.
20 GL, *Rechenschaft*, 1st ed. (Berlin, 1919); *Der Werdende Mensch: Aufsätze über Leben und Schriftum*, ed. Martin Buber (Potsdam, 1921); and *Beginnen: Aufsätze über Sozialismus*, ed. Martin Buber (Köln, 1924).
21 Letter dated April 29, 1891, GL Archiv, fol. X.2.

## 1. THE MAKING OF AN ANARCHIST

1 "Manuskript Kronstein über Landauer (Einleitung)," Anhang 4 in Gustav Landauer Archives, International Institute of Social History, Amsterdam (hereafter cited as GL Archiv); letter dated April 24, 1892, GL Archiv, fol. X.3.
2 GL, "Tagebuch, 1884–5," GL Archiv, fol. X.1.

3 Theodor Heuss, "Gustav Landauers politischer Nachlass," *Literarische Echo*, XXI (1919), 1097.
4 Denis W. Brogan, *Proudhon* (London, 1934), pp. 1–11.
5 J. H. Clapham, *The Economic Development of France and Germany, 1815–1914*, 4th ed. (London, 1936), p. 41; Hildegard Hoffman, *Landwirtschaft und Industrie in Württemberg insbesondere im Industriegebiet der schwäbischen Alb* (Berlin, 1935), p. 20.
6 Hoffmann, *Landwirtschaft und Industrie*, p. 64.
7 See, for example, the letter dated April 24, 1892, GL Archiv, fol. X.3.
8 GL, "Brot," *Der Sozialist*, June 1, 1911. See also Landauer's reflections on returning to Berlin after a summer in the south German mountains ("Rückkehr in die Grossstadt," *Der Sozialist*, Sept. 15, 1912).
9 *Karlsruher Addressbuch für 1875* (Karlsruhe: A. Sielefeld Verlag, 1875), p. 34.
10 GL, *Sein Lebensgang in Briefen*, ed. Martin Buber, 2 vols. (Frankfurt a. M., 1929), II, 253 (hereafter cited as *Briefe*).
11 Peter G. J. Pulzer, *The Rise of Political Anti-Semitism in Germany and Austria* (New York, 1964), pp. 8–9; Ismar Elbogen, *Die Geschichte der Juden in Deutschland* (Frankfurt a. M., 1966), pp. 229, 242.
12 H. G. Adler, *Die Juden in Deutschland: Von der Aufklärung bis zum Nationalsozialismus* (München, 1960), p. 81.
13 Karlsruhe Realgymnasium report cards, GL Archiv, fol. C.1.
14 GL, "Tagebuch, 1884–5," GL Archiv, fol. D.1, p. 1.
15 *Ibid.*, p. 7.
16 GL, *Rechenschaft*, 1st ed. (Berlin, 1919), pp. 145–146.
17 "Tagebuch, 1884–5."
18 "Bayreuth," *Der Sozialist*, Aug. 15, 1912.
19 *Rechenschaft*, p. 146.
20 *Ibid.*, pp. 146–147.
21 Letter dated April 16, 1889, GL Archiv, fol. X.1.
22 George L. Mosse, *The Crisis of German Ideology: The Intellectual Origins of The Third Reich* (New York, 1964), p. 154.
23 *Ibid.*
24 *Ibid.*, p. 152.
25 Fritz Stern, *The Politics of Cultural Despair: A Study in the Rise of the Germanic Ideology* (New York, 1965), p. 10.
26 Franz Schnabel, *Deutsche Geschichte im neunzehnten Jahrhundert*, 4 vols., 2d ed. (Freiburg im Breisgau, 1948–1951), II, 226.

[27] Leonard Krieger, *The German Idea of Freedom: History of a Political Tradition* (Boston, 1957), pp. 318–322.

[28] Hans Kohn, *The Mind of Germany: The Education of a Nation* (New York, 1960), p. 136.

[29] Krieger, *German Idea of Freedom*, pp. 450–452.

[30] *Bismarck-Gymnasium Karlsruhe Festschrift: Jahresbericht 1960/61* (Karlsruhe, 1961), p. 165.

[31] *Ibid.*, p. 172.

[32] "Tagebuch, 1884–5," p. 5.

[33] *Rechenschaft*, p. 144.

[34] *Ibid.*

[35] *Ibid.*, p. 146.

[36] Letter dated Feb. 20, 1889, GL Archiv, fol. X.1.

[37] Letter dated April 18, 1899, GL Archiv, fol. X.1.

[38] Letters dated Jan. 12, 1891, and March 16, 1908, GL Archiv, fols. X.1 and H, respectively.

[39] Jethro Bithell, *Modern German Literature, 1880–1950*, 3d ed. (London, 1959), p. 4.

[40] See letter dated March 5, 1890, GL Archiv, fol. X.1.

[41] *Rechenschaft*, p. 146.

[42] Arnold Hauser, *The Social History of Art*, IV (New York, 1958), 215. See also Gerhard Masur, *Prophets of Yesterday: Studies in European Culture, 1890–1914* (New York, 1961), p. 237.

[43] University records, GL Archiv, fol. C.1.

[44] Letter dated March 19, 1890, GL Archiv, fol. X.1.

[45] Julius Bab, *Wien und Berlin* (Berlin, 1918), pp. 259–260.

[46] GL, "Über epische und dramatische Dichtung," *Deutschland*, Jan. 4, 11, 1890.

[47] See letter dated May 1890, GL Archiv, fol. X.1.

[48] Bithell, *Modern German Literature*, p. 13.

[49] See, for example, the letters dated Jan. 22 and Feb. 13, 1891, GL Archiv, fol. X.2, and the article "Die Religiöse Jugenderziehung," *Freie Bühne*, Feb. 11, 1891.

[50] The influence of Nietzsche's philosophy is indirectly noted in GL's autobiographical article of 1913, "Vor funfundzwanzig Jahren," in *Rechenschaft*, pp. 146–147.

[51] Friedrich Nietzsche, *The Birth of Tragedy*, trans. Clifton Fadiman, in *The Philosophy of Nietzsche* (New York, 1954), p. 985.

[52] Letter dated Feb. 13, 1891, GL Archiv, fol. X.2.

[53] Letter dated Nov. 8, 1890, GL Archiv, fol. X.1.

[54] GL, "Religiöse Jugenderziehung."

55 Letter dated May 30, 1891, GL Archiv, fol. X.2.
56 In *Freie Bühne*, Feb. 11, 1891.
57 *Ibid.*
58 Letter dated Jan. 22, 1891, GL Archiv, fol. X.2.
59 *Rechenschaft*, p. 147.
60 Cf. Oscar Levy, ed., *The Complete Works of Friedrich Nietzsche* (London: T. N. Foulis, 1911), VI, 327.
61 Letter dated Feb. 13, 1891, GL Archiv, fol. X.2.
62 "Tagebuch, 1884–5," GL Archiv, fol. D.1, p. 9.
63 GL, "Religiöse Jugenderziehung."
64 Letter dated Nov. 7, 1890, GL Archiv, fol. X.1.
65 Arthur Rosenberg, *Imperial Germany: The Birth of the German Republic, 1871–1918* (Boston, 1964), p. 36.
66 *Ibid.*, p. 37.
67 Koppel S. Pinson, *Modern Germany: Its History and Civilization* (New York, 1954), pp. 281–282.
68 Richard Dietrich, "Berlins Weg zur Industrie- und Handelstadt," in *Berlin: Neun Kapitel seiner Geschichte* (Berlin, 1960), pp. 169–170, 191–192.
69 Eduard Bernstein, *Die Geschichte der Berliner Arbeiterbewegung: Ein Kapitel der Geschichte der deutschen Sozialdemokratie*, III (Berlin, 1910), 61–62.
70 Hans Rosenberg, "The Political and Social Consequences of the Great Depression in Central Europe, 1873–1896," *Economic History Review*, XIII (1943), 58–73.
71 Carl E. Schorske, *German Social Democracy, 1905–1917: The Development of the Great Schism* (Cambridge, Mass., 1955), p. 3.
72 George Lichtheim, *Marxism: An Historical and Critical Study* (New York, 1961), p. 261.
73 Bernstein, *Geschichte der Berliner Arbeiterbewegung*, III, 182.
74 Dietrich, "Berlin's Weg zur Industrie- und Handelstadt," p. 187.
75 Mario Kammer, *Berlin im Wandel des Jahrhunderts: Eine Kulturgeschichte der deutsche Hauptstadt* (Berlin, 1956), p. 211.
76 Bithell, *Modern German Literature*, p. 75.
77 *Ibid.*, p. 25.
78 Siegfried Nestriepke, *Geschichte der Volksbühne Berlin* (Berlin, 1930), I, 9–12
79 Julius Bab, *Wesen und Weg der Berliner Volksbühnenbewegung* (Berlin, 1919), p. 6.
80 "Manuskript Kronstein über Landauer (Einleitung)," GL Archiv, Anhang 4, p. 2.

81 Letter dated April 29, 1891, GL Archiv, fol. X.2.
82 Letter dated Nov. 4, 1891, GL Archiv, fol. X.2.
83 Agustin Souchy, *Landauer, el filósofo de la revolucion*, trans. from Swedish by D. A. de Santillan (Buenos Aires, 1934), pp. 19–20.
84 Letter dated July 26, 1892, GL Archiv, fol. I.
85 Letter dated Dec. 23, 1891, GL Archiv, fol. X.2.
86 Bruno Wille, *Aus Traum und Kampf: Mein 60 Jähriges Leben* (Berlin, 1920), p. 29.
87 *Ibid.*, pp. 32–33; Franz Oppenheimer, *Erlebtes, Erstrebtes, Erreichtes* (Berlin, 1931), pp. 123–126.
88 University records, GL Archiv, fol. C.1.
89 Wille, *Aus Traum und Kampf*, p. 14.
90 See the official Social Democratic Party paper, *Vorwärts*, Dec. 30, 1891.
91 Schorske, *German Social Democracy*, p. 98.
92 *Vorwärts*, Dec. 30, 1891.
93 GL, "II. Entwurf zu einer Kundgebung Berliner Sozialistischen Studenten an der Brüssler Studenten-Kongress 1891," GL Archiv, fol. BB.4, p. 1.
94 *Ibid.*, p. 6.
95 *Ibid.*, pp. 5–6.
96 *Vorwärts*, Dec. 30, 1891.
97 See the discussion of the ethical-idealist orientation of many bourgeois intellectuals who turned to socialism in the late nineteenth century in Robert Michels, *Political Parties: A Sociological Study of the Oligarchical Tendencies of Modern Democracy* (New York, 1962), pp. 240–242.
98 Letter dated Jan. 25, 1892, GL Archiv, fol. X.2.
99 GL, "Die Zukunft und die Kunst," *Neue Zeit*, X (1892), 532–534.
100 GL, "Gerhard Hauptmann," *Neue Zeit*, X (1892), 615.
101 Letter dated May 28, 1892, GL Archiv, fol. X.2.
102 For an alternative interpretation of *Der Todesprediger*, one concerned largely with Landauer's views on sensuality and love as expressed in the novel, see Charles Maurer, *Call to Revolution: The Mystical Anarchism of Gustav Landauer* (Detroit, 1971), pp. 32–34, and Maurer's more detailed treatment in "Gustav Landauer: A Study of His Life and Work" (Ph.D. dissertation, Northwestern University, 1965), pp. 134–138. Not having read Landauer's letters from this period (his research is solely confined to published materials), Maurer was not aware of the im-

pact of Nietzsche's writings and socialist associations upon Landauer in the years 1890–1892 when he was working on the novel.

[103] GL, *Der Todesprediger*, 3d ed. (Köln, 1923), p. 17.

[104] *Ibid.*, pp. 56–59.

[105] *Ibid.*, p. 66.

[106] *Ibid.*, p. 123.

[107] GL, *Aufruf zum Sozialismus*, 2d ed. (Berlin, 1919), p. 61.

[108] *Ibid.*, p. 5.

[109] GL, "Der Londoner Kongress und die Anarchie," *Der Sozialist*, Aug. 15, 1896.

[110] GL, *An den Züricher Kongress: Bericht über die deutsche Arbeiterbewegung* (Berlin, 1893), pp. 7–8.

[111] GL, "Der Fall Liebknecht," *Der Sozialist*, Aug. 29, 1896.

[112] Harry J. Marks, "Movements of Reform and Revolution in Germany, 1890–1903" (Ph.D. dissertation, Harvard University, 1937), pp. 11–12.

[113] Schorske, *German Social Democracy*, p. 7.

[114] Franz Mehring, *Geschichte der deutsche Sozialdemokratie* (Berlin, 1960), II, 676

[115] Vernon Lidtke, *The Outlawed Party: German Social Democracy, 1878–1890* (Princeton, 1966), pp. 244–247.

[116] Otto von Leixner, *1888 bis 1891: Soziale Briefe aus Berlin* (Berlin, 1891), p. 345.

[117] Lidtke, *Outlawed Party*, p. 305.

[118] *Ibid.*, p. 307.

[119] Marks, "Movements of Reform and Revolution," p. 90.

[120] Lidtke, *Outlawed Party*, p. 310.

[121] Carl Landauer, *European Socialism: A History of Ideas and Movements from the Industrial Revolution to Hitler's Seizure of Power*, 2 vols. (Berkeley and Los Angeles, 1959), I, 297.

[122] *Ibid.*, pp. 86–87.

[123] Bernstein, *Geschichte der Berliner Arbeiterbewegung*, III, 128.

[124] Carl Landauer, *European Socialism*, I, 296.

[125] GL, *An den Züricher Kongress*, pp. 6–8.

[126] Rudolf Rocker, "Die Jugend eines Rebellen," typescript, Rocker memoirs, International Institute of Social History, Amsterdam, I, 364–365.

[127] "Unser Zweck," *Der Sozialist*, Nov. 15, 1891.

[128] *Ibid.*

[129] See, for example, the article "Zur Taktik des Proletariats," *Der Sozialist*, April 10, 1892, and the series of pieces by Kropotkin begun on June 26 with "Die Politischen Rechte."

[130] Letter dated Oct. 15, 1892, GL Archiv, fol. X.2.

[131] GL, "Referat über Eugen Dühring's 'Kursus der National- und Sozialoekonomie,' " *Der Sozialist*, Aug. 27, 1892.

[132] Lichtheim, *Marxism*, p. 224.

[133] Cf. Benedikt Friedländer, "Gegen den Staatssozialismus," *Der Sozialist*, Nov. 15, 1891; "Die Unhaltbarkeit des Kommunismus," *Der Sozialist*, June 12, 1892; and his untitled article in *Der Sozialist*, Jan. 24, 1892.

[134] GL, "Referat über Dühring's 'Kursus.' "

[135] Lichtheim, *Marxism*, pp. 237–238.

[136] GL, "Dühringianer und Marxisten," *Der Sozialist*, Oct. 22, 1892. Landauer's critique of Marxism is discussed at greater length in chapter 4. That he should have been influenced in his views of Marx by the official SPD version of the 1890s is not surprising. Both views, however, were a gross oversimplification. For an excellent recent discussion of Marx's historical outlook, in which materialism is clearly distinguished from crude economic determinism, see Schlomo Avineri, *The Social and Political Thought of Karl Marx* (London: Cambridge University Press, 1968).

[137] GL, "Dühringianer and Marxisten."

[138] Peter Gay, *The Dilemma of Democratic Socialism: Eduard Bernstein's Challenge to Marx* (New York, 1962), pp. 100–101.

[139] GL, "Referat über Dühring's 'Kursus.' "

[140] GL, "Dühringianer und Marxisten."

[141] *Ibid.* Marx had written much the same in the *Economic and Philosophical Manuscripts of 1844* (the first American edition of which is in *Marx's Concept of Man*, ed. Erich Fromm [New York, 1961]), but Landauer could not have known this, since the manuscripts were not discovered until the 1930s.

[142] Cf. Eugen Dühring, *Kursus der National- und Sozialökonomie* (Berlin, 1873), secs. 2–8.

[143] See Friedländer, "Gegen den Staatssozialismus."

[144] GL, "Dühringianer und Marxisten."

[145] *Ibid.* The passage is from Dühring's *Kursus*, p. 23.

[146] Bernstein, *Geschichte der Berliner Arbeiterbewegung*, III, 394–396; Nestriepke, *Geschichte der Volksbühne Berlin*, I, 69.

[147] Max Nettlau, "Anarchisten und Sozialrevolutionäre, 1886–1914," Nettlau Archives, International Institute of Social History, Amsterdam, fol. "1895–1914 I," p. 139.

[148] Bab, *Wesen und Weg der Berliner Volksbühnenbewegung*, p. 7.

[149] Nestriepke, *Geschichte der Volksbühne Berlin*, I, 66; "Manu-

skript Kronstein über Landauer (Einleitung)," GL Archiv, Anhang 4, pp. 2-3.

150 Letter dated Nov. 8, 1892, GL Archiv, fol. X.2.

151 Letter of Max Kronstein dated March 4, 1928, GL Archiv, Anhang 5.

152 Letter of Landauer dated Nov. 11, 1890, GL Archiv, fol. H.

153 Letter dated April 16, 1895, GL Archiv, fol. X.

154 *Ibid.*

155 See Harry Pross, *Jugend-Eros-Politik: Die Geschichte der deutschen Jugendverbände* (München, 1964), pp. 36-37.

156 Letter dated May 18, 1892, GL Archiv, fol. I.

157 Letter dated Dec. 16, 1892, GL Archiv, fol. X. See also a letter of April 23, 1894, to his wife, fol. G.2.

158 Letter dated May 30, 1899, to his father, GL Archiv, fol. H.

159 Nettlau, "Anarchisten und Sozialrevolutionäre, 1886-1914," fol. "1895-1914 I," p. 164.

160 *Ibid.*

161 *Ibid.*; letter of Max Kronstein dated March 4, 1928, GL Archiv, Anhang 5.

162 *Der Sozialist* issues of January through April, 1893.

163 *Der Sozialist*, March 4, 1893.

164 GL, "Wie nennen wir uns?" *Der Sozialist*, April 1, 1893.

165 See Dühring, *Kursus*, pp. 265-271.

166 GL, "Zur frage: Wie nennen wir uns?" *Der Sozialist*, April 8, 1893.

167 E. V. Zenker, *Anarchism: A Criticism and History of the Anarchist Theory* (London, 1898), p. 176; Nettlau, "Anarchisten und Sozialrevolutionäre, 1886-1914," fol. "1895-1914 I," p. 146.

168 Unfortunately I have been unable to find biographical information on Friedländer, except for the interesting comments in Hans Blüher's memoirs, *Werke und Tage* (München, 1953), pp. 235-236, 345. Friedländer seems to have exercised some influence on Blüher's own interpretation of the German youth movement as a community held together by male libidinal ties. Blüher was an associate of Landauer's during World War I (see chap. 5).

169 Benedikt Friedländer, *Der freiheitliche Sozialismus im Gegensatz zum Staatsknechtum der Marxisten* (Berlin, 1892), pp. 51, 58-59.

170 *Ibid.*, p. v.

171 Irving L. Horowitz, ed., *The Anarchists* (New York, 1964), pp. 583-584.

172 Michels, *Political Parties*, p. 335. On page 325 Michels reveals his debt to anarchist theory: "Anarchists were the first to insist

upon the hierarchical and oligarchical consequences of party organization. Their view of the defects of organization is much clearer than that of socialists and even that of syndicalists."

[173] GL, "Zur frage: Wie nennen wir uns?"

[174] GL, "Manchesterfreiheit-Staatshülfe-Anarchie," *Der Sozialist*, June 24, 1893.

[175] GL, "Die Sozialdemokratische Wahlagitation," *Der Sozialist*, June 10, 1893.

[176] Nettlau, "Anarchisten und Sozialrevolutionäre, 1886–1914," fol. "1895–1914 I," p. 140.

[177] *Ibid.*, p. 164.

[178] *Ibid.*, p. 140.

[179] *Ibid.*; Rocker, "Die Jugend eines Rebellen," p. 444.

[180] Rocker, "Die Jugend eines Rebellen," p. 444. Nettlau argues in much the same vein (see "Anarchisten und Sozialrevolutionäre, 1886–1914," fol. "1895–1914 I," p. 164).

[181] Marks, "Movements for Reform and Revolution," p. 52.

## 2. CHANGING PERSPECTIVES

[1] Pierre Joseph Proudhon, *What Is Property?* trans. Benjamin Tucker (New York, 1890), p. 277.

[2] George Woodcock, *Anarchism: A History of Libertarian Ideas and Movements* (New York, 1962), p. 13.

[3] It is not necessary for the purposes of this study to discuss the entire history of European anarchism. The most comprehensive works on the subject are those of the libertarian scholar Max Nettlau. The following three published works by Nettlau cover the period to 1886: *Der Vorfrühling der Anarchie: Ihre Historische Entwicklung von den Anfängen bis zum Jahre 1864* (Berlin, 1925); *Der Anarchismus von Proudhon zu Kropotkin: Seine historische Entwicklung in den Jahren 1859–1880* (Berlin, 1927); *Anarchisten und Sozialrevolutionäre: Die historische Entwicklung des Anarchismus in den Jahren 1880–1886* (Berlin, 1931). For the period after 1886, the International Institute of Social History, Amsterdam, has a huge manuscript left by Nettlau, "Anarchisten und Sozialrevolutionäre, 1886–1914," which he wrote in 1931 and 1932. The most reliable work in English is Woodcock, *Anarchism*. For a recent excellent discussion of anarchist theory see Daniel Guerin, *Anarchism* (New York: Monthly Review Press, 1970).

[4] Woodcock, *Anarchism*, pp. 429–430.

5 Vernon Lidtke, *The Outlawed Party: German Social Democracy, 1878–1890* (Princeton, 1966), pp. 106–128.

6 Nettlau, "Anarchisten und Sozialrevolutionäre, 1886–1914," fol. "1895–1914 I," p. 130.

7 George Adler, "Anarchismus," *Handwörterbuch der Staatswissenschaft*, 2d ed. (1909), I, 462–463.

8 Woodcock, *Anarchism*, p. 27.

9 Adam Ulam, *The Unfinished Revolution: An Essay on the Sources of Influence of Marxism and Communism* (New York, 1960), p. 162

10 Woodcock, *Anarchism*, p. 27.

11 Irving L. Horowitz, ed., *The Anarchists* (New York, 1964), p. 37.

12 *Ibid.*, pp. 20, 27.

13 Hans Beyer, *Von der November Revolution zur Räterepublik in München* (Berlin, 1957), p. 24.

14 Robert Michels, *Political Parties: A Sociological Study of the Oligarchical Tendencies of Modern Democracy* (New York, 1962), pp. 246–247.

15 *Ibid.*, p. 247.

16 *Ibid.*; Erich Rosenthal, "Trends of the Jewish Population in Germany, 1910–1939," *Jewish Social Studies*, VI (July 1944), 255–256; Ismar Elbogen, *Die Geschichte der Juden in Deutschland* (Frankfurt a. M., 1966), p. 251.

17 Cf. Hannah Arendt, "The Jew as Pariah: A Hidden Tradition," *Jewish Social Studies*, VI (April 1944), 99–122; Sterling Fishman, "Prophets, Poets and Priests: A Study of the Men and Ideas That Made The Munich Revolution of 1918–19" (Ph.D. dissertation, University of Wisconsin, 1960), p. 319; Peter G. J. Pulzer, *The Rise of Political Anti-Semitism in Germany and Austria* (New York, 1964), pp. 261–262.

18 Jacob Toury, *Die politischen Orientierungen der Juden in Deutschland von Jena bis Weimar* (Tübingen, 1966), pp. 237–238.

19 Many other idealist writers, often Jewish, reacted in the same manner as Landauer. As examples, from both the beginning and the end of Landauer's political career, the following may be noted: Berlin's Friedrichshagen bohemian community siding with the Independents against the SPD in 1891–92 and, in 1918–19, the vast majority of the expressionists siding with, or joining, either the USPD or anarchist circles (see Jürgen Rühle, *Literatur and Revolution* (Berlin, 1960), pp. 131–132). In the

Munich Revolution of 1918–19 all the leading USPD and anarchist figures were Jewish idealist intellectuals: Kurt Eisner, Ernst Toller, Ernst Mühsam, and Landauer (see Fishman, "Prophets, Poets and Priests," pp. 317–319).

20 GL, "Land-Agitation," *Der Sozialist,* June 24, 1893.

21 GL, "Gewerkschaftskampf," *Der Sozialist,* June 24, 1893.

22 Carl Landauer, *European Socialism: A History of Ideas and Movements from The Industrial Revolution to Hitler's Seizure of Power,* 2 vols. (Berkeley and Los Angeles, 1959), I, 311.

23 Val R. Lorwin, *The French Labor Movement* (Cambridge, Mass., 1954), pp. 36–37.

24 GL, "Die sozialdemokratische Wahlagitation," *Der Sozialist,* June 10, 1893.

25 Letter dated July 18, 1893, in Gustav Landauer Archives, International Institute of Social History, Amsterdam (hereafter cited as GL Archiv), fol. X.4.

26 GL, *An den Züricher Kongress: Bericht über die deutsche Arbeiterbewegung* (Berlin, 1893), p. 5.

27 *Ibid.,* pp. 7–8.

28 Hermann Greulich, ed., *Protokoll des International Sozialistischen Arbeiterkongress in der Tonhalle Zürich von 6. bis 12. August 1893* (Zürich, 1894), pp. 5–6; see also J. Langhard, *Die Anarchistische Bewegung in der Schweiz* (Bern, 1909), pp. 320–326.

29 James Joll, *The Second International, 1889–1914* (New York, 1966), p. 71.

30 GL, "Züricher Kongress," *Der Sozialist,* Aug. 26, 1893.

31 "Die Vorgänge in Zürich," *Der Sozialist,* Aug. 19, 1893.

32 Woodcock, *Anarchism,* pp. 262–263.

33 Langhard, *Anarchistische Bewegung in der Schweiz,* pp. 324–326; see also "Internationaler Kongress der revolutionären Sozialisten und Anarchisten in Zürich im Plattengarten," *Der Sozialist,* Aug. 26, 1893.

34 Joll, *Second International,* p. 60.

35 *Ibid.,* pp. 56–57.

36 Adler, "Anarchismus," p. 463.

37 "Unsere Bewegung," *Der Sozialist,* Oct. 22, Nov. 4, Dec. 30, 1893. See also GL, *Sein Lebensgang in Briefen,* ed. Martin Buber, 2 vols. (Frankfurt a. M., 1929), I, 3 (hereafter cited as *Briefe*). The trial reports are in GL Archiv, fol. C.2.

38 Rudolf Rocker, "Die Jugend eines Rebellen," typescript, Rocker

memoirs, International Institute of Social History, Amsterdam, I, 366.

[39] A list giving the names of those arrested and the charges against them is published in the supplement to the March 24, 1894, issue of *Der Sozialist.*

[40] "Anarchismus und Attentat," *Der Sozialist,* June 9, 1894; "Anarchismus und Gewalt," *Der Sozialist,* Aug. 4, 1894.

[41] GL, "Aus meinem Gefängnis-Tagebuch," *Sozialistische Akademiker,* I (1895), nos. 13–18.

[42] *Ibid.,* pp. 319–320.

[43] *Ibid.,* pp. 258–259.

[44] GL, *Arnold Himmelheber,* in *Macht und Mächte* (Berlin, 1903), p. 76. See also Charles Maurer, *Call to Revolution: The Mystical Anarchism of Gustav Landauer* (Detroit, 1971), pp. 53–54.

[45] Gerhard A. Ritter, *Die Arbeiterbewegung im Wilhelminischen Reich, 1890–1900* (Berlin, 1959), pp. 113–115.

[46] Carl E. Schorske, *German Social Democracy, 1905–1917: The Development of the Great Schism* (Cambridge, Mass., 1955), p. 11.

[47] GL, "Der Anarchismus in Deutschland," *Die Zukunft,* Jan. 5, 1895, p. 29.

[48] *Ibid.,* p. 30.

[49] *Ibid.,* pp. 33–34.

[50] *Ibid.,* p. 32.

[51] *Ibid.,* pp. 29–30.

[52] Letter dated Sept. 22, 1893, GL Archiv, fol. X.6.

[53] Letter dated Dec. 4, 1894, GL Archiv, fol. X.4.

[54] GL, "Alles oder Nichts!" *Der Sozialist,* Oct. 12, 1895.

[55] See Herbert Marcuse, *Reason and Revolution: Hegel and the Rise of Social Theory* (Boston, 1960), pp. 18–22.

[56] Immanuel Kant, "What Is Enlightenment?" in *The Philosophy of Kant: Immanuel Kant's Moral and Political Writings,* ed. and trans. Carl J. Friedrich (New York: The Modern Library, 1949), p. 132.

[57] Cf. *Briefe,* I, 1.

[58] Rocker, "Die Jugend eines Rebellen," I, 366–367; see also Stefan Grossman, "Gustav Landauer," *Das Tagebuch,* May 4, 1929, p. 732.

[59] Letter dated March 29, 1895, GL Archiv, fol. X.4. On the rejection of his application see *Briefe,* I, 1, and "Abschrift Brief Kronstein an Professor (inkomplett)—1929," GL Archiv, Anhang 5.

⁶⁰ *Briefe*, I, 3 (letter dated May 5, 1895).
⁶¹ See, for example, letter dated April 16, 1895, GL Archiv, fol. X.4.
⁶² *Briefe*, I, 3n.
⁶³ Carl Landauer, *European Socialism*, I, 315.
⁶⁴ GL, "Sozialismus und Genossenschaft," *Der Sozialist*, Oct. 13, 1910.
⁶⁵ Wilhelm Weise, "Wie die Arbeiter-Konsumgenossenschaft 'Befreiung' entstand," *Der Genossenschafts-Pionier*, Dec. 15, 1896.
⁶⁶ Adolf Marreck, "Eine Konsumgenossenschaft in Berlin," *Sozialistische Monatshefte*, IV (1898), 179.
⁶⁷ GL, "Sozialismus und Genossenschaft."
⁶⁸ GL, *Ein Weg zur Befreiung der Arbeiterklasse* (Berlin, 1895), p. 4.
⁶⁹ *Ibid.* The Marxian argument—that the task of creating socialism after a revolution involves merely the completion of the historical process of socialization carried out within the "bosom" of capitalism and therefore does not require any attempt to create socialism "out of nothing"—was not dealt with in this pamphlet. Landauer's most comprehensive and sophisticated critique of Marxian thought, his *Aufruf zum Sozialismus*, first published in 1911, deals with this point of contention at some length.
⁷⁰ GL, *Ein Weg zur Befreiung*, pp. 9–10.
⁷¹ GL, "Arbeiter aller Länder, vereinigt such!" *Der Sozialist*, Sept. 28, 1895.
⁷² *Ein Weg zur Befreiung*, p. 11.
⁷³ *Ibid.*, p. 18.
⁷⁴ *Ibid.*, p. 25.
⁷⁵ *Ibid.*, pp. 21–25.
⁷⁶ Marreck, "Eine Konsumgenossenschaft in Berlin," pp. 179–180.
⁷⁷ See, for example, the speech of Liebknecht at the SPD Congress at Gotha in 1896, in which the Berlin anarchist cooperative movement was attacked as a "reactionary bourgeois" endeavor (Wilhelm Schröder, ed., *Handbuch der Sozialdemokratischen Parteitage von 1863 bis 1909* [München, 1910], p. 34).
⁷⁸ GL, "Der Pionier," *Der Sozialist*, Oct. 10, 1913.
⁷⁹ Carl Landauer, *European Socialism*, I, 315.
⁸⁰ GL, "Die Wiedergeburt des 'Sozialist,'" *Der Sozialist*, Aug. 17, 1895.
⁸¹ George L. Mosse, *The Crisis of German Ideology: The Intellectual Origins of the Third Reich* (New York, 1964), p. 46.
⁸² Nettlau, "Anarchisten und Sozialrevolutionäre, 1886–1914," fol. "1895–1914 I," p. 159.

83 GL, "M. von Egidy und der 'Sozialistische Akademiker,' " *Sozialistische Akademiker*, II (1896), 186–187.

84 H. S. Hughes, *Consciousness and Society: The Reconstruction of European Social Thought, 1890–1930* (New York, 1961), p. 190.

85 Carl Landauer, *European Socialism*, I, 306–307.

86 Hughes, *Consciousness and Society*, p. 186.

87 *Ibid.*, pp. 195–198.

88 Marcuse, *Reason and Revolution*, p. 18.

89 GL, "Die unmoralische Weltordnung," *Der Sozialist*, Aug. 24, 1895.

90 GL, "Aus der Zeit," *Der Sozialist*, Aug. 17, 1895.

91 The articles, "Zur Entwicklungsgeschichte des Individuums," *Der Sozialist*, Nov. 16, 30, 1895, Jan. 11, Feb. 1, 8, 1896, were signed "ab"; we know they were written by Landauer, however, both from a letter he wrote concerning the articles on Feb. 11, 1896, preserved among the unpublished letters in "Jugendband," GL Archiv, fol. X.5, and from a note by Max Kronstein in folio CC of the Landauer Archives.

92 GL, "Zur Entwicklungsgeschichte des Individuums," I, *Der Sozialist*, Nov. 2, 1895.

93 "Zur Entwicklungsgeschichte," II, *Der Sozialist*, Nov. 16, 1895.

94 "Zur Entwicklungsgeschichte," III, *Der Sozialist*, Nov. 30, 1895.

95 Letter dated Feb. 11, 1896, GL Archiv, fol. X.5.

96 "Zur Entwicklungsgeschichte," I, *Der Sozialist*, Nov. 2, 1895.

97 GL, *Skepsis und Mystik: Versuche im Anschluss an Mauthners Sprachkritik*, 2d ed. (Köln, 1923), pp. 7–8. In his doctoral thesis on Landauer, Charles Maurer contended that the language criticism of Landauer's friend Fritz Mauthner, investigations with which Landauer became familiar through his work in 1899–1900 on the manuscript for Mauthner's mammoth study *Beiträge zu einer Kritik der Sprache* (Vols. I and II [Stuttgart, 1901]; Vol. III [Stuttgart and Berlin, 1902]), was "unquestionably the most decisive intellectual experience of Landauer's life" and that Landauer's philosophical position was a product of this contact with Mauthner's work ("Gustav Landauer: A Study of His Life and Work" [Ph.D. dissertation, Northwestern University, 1965], p. 51). In the recently published version of his work, *Call to Revolution* (see pp. 58, 92), Maurer has not altered this thesis. Having arrived at this conclusion Maurer analyzes Landauer's works after 1900, particularly *Skepsis und Mystik* and *Die Revolution*, almost exclusively in terms of Mauthner's language critique and

Landauer's response to it (see *Call to Revolution*, esp. chaps. 3, 4). Maurer did not read *Der Sozialist* of the 1890s or the unpublished letters in GL Archiv. He has therefore not seen the series of articles, "Zur Entwicklungsgeschichte des Individuums," written in late 1895 and early 1896 as a solution to a problem of social and political ideology, which contain in embryonic but unmistakable form the kernel ideas of Landauer's later philosophy, after 1899. Maurer also has not seen a letter of Feb. 11, 1896 (GL Archiv, fol. X.5), in which Landauer, responding to Mauthner's statement that the articles "Zur Entwicklungsgeschichte" sounded in certain ways like the ideas he himself was developing, told Mauthner concerning the articles: "From reasons that have solely to do with the anarchist movement I decided to write a series of polemical articles to which I give the pretentious title, 'Toward a Developmental History of the Individual.' I used the opportunity here to suggest some *year-old* ideas for the explanation of which I had not previously found the time—notably my ideas. I can show you notes about 'The Individual and the Community' in old notebooks. . . . In Sorau [the prison where Landauer stayed from late 1893 to the fall of 1894] I studied a *Kritik der Schopenhauer'schen Philosophie*. My excerpts from Schopenhauer and my own remarks written in Sorau stand as proof that what I have written in these articles are my own thoughts, from beginning to end." Landauer concluded the letter by saying that since he had now become aware that Mauthner's ideas ran in some ways parallel to his own, and since he was sure that Mauthner's formulation would be sharper and clearer, he had no intention of preempting Mauthner's work; the only persons who would know of Landauer's ideas would be the limited circle of readers of *Der Sozialist*.

The letter and the 1895–96 articles fit poorly with Maurer's thesis. They suggest that Landauer's philosophy after 1896—woven of völkisch, libertarian, and mystical elements—developed in reaction to his social and political experiences and was not merely a deduction from Mauthner's language studies. The formative years of the 1890s, as I attempt to show in this chapter, were of particular importance in this connection.

[98] "Zur Entwicklungsgeschichte," V, *Der Sozialist*, Feb. 8, 1896.
[99] Robert W. Lougee, "German Romanticism and Political Thought," in *The European Past*, ed. Shepard Clough, Peter Gay, and Charles K. Warner (New York, 1964), II, 93–94.

100 Peter Gay, *The Dilemma of Democratic Socialism: Eduard Bernstein's Challenge to Marx* (New York, 1962), p. 125.

101 Eduard Bernstein, *Die Geschichte der Berliner Arbeiterbewegung: Ein Kapitel der Geschichte der deutschen Sozialdemokratie* (Berlin, 1910), III, 298.

102 *Ibid.*, pp. 290–296.

103 *Ibid.*, pp. 294–302.

104 *Ibid.*, pp. 308–309.

105 *Ibid.*, p. 311.

106 *Ethische Kultur*, March 7, April 4, 1896, in GL Archiv, fol. X.5.

107 See letter dated Feb. 11, 1896, GL Archiv, fol. X.5.

108 *Ethische Kultur*, April 18, 1896, in GL Archiv, fol. X.5.

109 Unsigned article, "Das Ende des Konfektionsschneiderstreiks," *Der Sozialist*, May 2, 1896.

110 Some of the ideas in this paragraph were suggested to me by the labor economist and historian of socialism, Carl Landauer, who interviewed Gustav Landauer some time before his death in 1919. In their discussion the participation of Gustav Landauer in the Berlin needle-trade strike of 1896 was touched upon, and Carl Landauer gained some of the impressions repeated in the analysis above. Mention of Landauer's activity among needle-trade workers is made in Carl Landauer's *European Socialism*, I, 1154.

111 Joll, *Second International*, p. 74.

112 Woodcock, *Anarchism*, p. 263.

113 GL, *Social Democracy in Germany* (London, 1896), p. 2.

114 Woodcock, *Anarchism*, p. 263.

115 *Verhandlungen und Beschlüsse des International Sozialistische Arbeiter und Gewerkschaftskongress zu London 1896* (Berlin, 1896), p. 8.

116 GL, "Der Londoner Congress und die Anarchie," *Der Sozialist*, Aug. 22, 1896.

117 Woodcock, *Anarchism*, p. 264.

118 Rudolf Rocker, *The London Years* (London, 1956), pp. 89–90.

119 Karl Marx, *The Communist Manifesto* (New York, 1955), pp. 14–17.

120 Woodcock, *Anarchism*, p. 16.

121 Rudolf Rocker, "In Sturm und Drang," Rocker Archives, I, 63–64.

122 "Landauers Stellungnahme zur Agrarfrage in den anarchistische-sozialistiche Versammlung im London (St. Martin's Hall) am

30. Juli 1896," copy of Landauer's speech preserved in GL Archiv, fol. X.5.

[123] Rocker, "In Sturm und Drang," I, 67.

[124] Arbeiter-Bildungs-Verein Unabhängigen Sozialisten von Langbielau, "Zur Diskussion über den 'Sozialist,'" Der Sozialist, July 22, 1893.

[125] Rocker, London Years, p. 91.

[126] Nettlau, "Anarchisten und Sozialrevolutionäre, 1886–1914," fol. "1895–1914 I," p. 171.

[127] Rocker, London Years, p. 91. The conflict, with Landauer's resultant loss of support, is also described in Stefan Grossman's autobiography, Ich war begeistert: Eine Lebensgeschichte (Berlin, 1931), pp. 66–67.

[128] GL, "Reiseberichte," Der Sozialist, Oct. 23, Nov. 27, 1897.

[129] Albert Weidner, "Gustav Landauers Kampf mit Polizei, Justiz und Partei," Die Weltbühne XXVI (1930), 533–536.

[130] GL, "Vortragscyklus zur Geschichte der deutsche Literatur," Der Sozialist, Feb. 26, 1898.

## 3. THE CONSOLATION OF MYSTICISM

[1] GL, "Durch Absonderung zur Gemeinschaft," in Heinrich Hart and Julius Hart, eds., Das Reich der Erfüllung: Flugschriften zur Begründung einer neuen Weltanschauung (Leipzig, 1901), pp. 46–48.

[2] GL, Skepsis und Mystik: Versuche im Anschluss an Mauthners Sprachkritik, 2d ed. (Köln, 1923), pp. 7–9. The work was first published in 1903.

[3] GL, "Wesen und Aussichten des Revolutionarismus," Die Welt am Montag, May 10, 1899.

[4] GL, "Die Krise in der revolutionären Bewegung," Der Sozialist, June 4, 1898.

[5] GL, Sein Lebensgang in Briefen, ed. Martin Buber, 2 vols. (Frankfurt a. M., 1929), I, 11–12n (hereafter cited as Briefe).

[6] Letter dated Oct. 5, 1898, in Gustav Landauer Archives, International Institute of Social History, Amsterdam (hereafter cited as GL Archiv). fol. X.

[7] See Briefe, I, 16–17.

[8] Ibid., p. 17.

[9] Ibid., p. 37.

[10] Charles Maurer, "Gustav Landauer: A Study of His Life and Work" (Ph.D. dissertation, Northwestern University, 1965), pp. 18–21.

[11] Stefan Grossman, "Gustav Landauer," *Das Tagebuch*, May 4, 1929, pp. 733–735.

[12] *Briefe*, I, 51.

[13] GL, *Lebendig tot*, in *Macht und Mächte* (Berlin, 1903), p. 124.

[14] *Briefe*, I, 12.

[15] *Ibid.*, pp. 40–42.

[16] *Meister Eckharts Mystische Schriften*, trans. GL (Berlin, 1903), p. 246.

[17] *Meister Eckhart: A Modern Translation*, trans. with introduction by Raymond Bernard Blakney (New York, 1941), p. xiii.

[18] *Meister Eckharts Mystische Schriften*, p. 25 (English translation from *Meister Eckhart: A Modern Translation*, p. 105).

[19] *Ibid.*, pp. 18–19.

[20] *Briefe*, I, 59–60.

[21] *Ibid.*, p. 446 (letter dated Sept. 20, 1913).

[22] This is attested by Hans Blüher (*Werke und Tage* [München, 1953], p. 381), the first historian of the German youth movement, who knew Landauer in his later years.

[23] George L. Mosse, *The Crisis of German Ideology: The Intellectual Origins of the Third Reich* (New York, 1964), pp. 52–59.

[24] *Ibid.*, pp. 41–42.

[25] Fritz Stern, *The Politics of Cultural Despair: A Study in the Rise of the Germanic Ideology* (New York, 1965), pp. 138–140.

[26] A more extended comparison of Landauer with Langbehn and right-wing völkisch thought is made in chapter 5.

[27] GL, "Walt Whitman," *Der Sozialist*, Dec. 25, 1913.

[28] *Meister Eckharts Mystische Schriften*, pp. 50–51 (English translation from *Meister Eckhart: A Modern Translation*, pp. 209–210).

[29] Max Nettlau, "Anarchisten und Sozialrevolutinäre, 1886–1914," Nettlau Archives, International Institute of Social History, Amsterdam, fol. "1895–1914 I," p. 157.

[30] For example, Eugen Heinrich Schmitt, "Leo Tolstoj und der Anarchismus," *Der Sozialist* (1898), p. 191.

[31] GL, "Anarchische Gedanken über den Anarchismus," *Die Zukunft*, Oct. 26, 1901.

[32] GL, "Peter Kropotkin," in *Der Werdende Mensch: Aufsätze über Leben und Schriftum*, ed. Martin Buber (Potsdam, 1921), pp. 228–229.

[33] GL, "Anarchische Gedanken über den Anarchismus."

[34] Hans Kohn, *Martin Buber: Sein Werk und seine Zeit*, 2d ed. (Köln, 1961), p. 201.

35 GL, "Anarchische Gedanken über den Anarchismus."
36 GL, "Im Kampf um die Weltanschauung: Stimmungen zu M. von Egidy's Tod," *Der Sozialist,* IX (Jan. 1899), no. 2.
37 *Briefe,* I, 54.
38 Selections from von Egidy's journal *Versöhnung* printed in *Der Sozialist,* IX (Jan. 1899), no. 2.
39 *Ibid.*
40 GL, "Sozialismus und Genossenschaft," *Der Sozialist,* Oct. 13, 1910.
41 See "Aus der Zeit: M. von Egidy," *Der Sozialist,* May 2, 1896.
42 Mosse, *Crisis of German Ideology,* pp. 47–49.
43 *Ibid.,* pp. 111, 122, 160.
44 *Der Sozialist,* IX (1899), no. 2.
45 Nettlau, "Anarchisten und Sozialrevolutionäre, 1886–1914," fol. "1895–1914 I," pp. 174–175.
46 *Briefe,* I, 54.
47 GL, "Die neue Welterkenntnis," *Die Kultur,* I (1902), 616–617.
48 See *Briefe,* I, 82.
49 Erich Mühsam, *Unpolitische Erinnerungen* (Berlin, 1961), pp. 43–44.
50 *Briefe,* I, 59–60.
51 Stern, *Politics of Cultural Despair,* pp. 223–224.
52 In his study of the movement, *Young Germany* (New York, 1962), Walter Laqueur writes (p. 4): "Politically, this rejection of society and its values could lead to either left- or right-wing . . . solutions. The German youth movement was an unpolitical form of opposition to a civilization that had little to offer the young generation." Laqueur notes that in 1919 ex-members voted either right-wing nationalist or USPD.
53 Stern, *Politics of Cultural Despair,* pp. 223–224.
54 Kohn, *Martin Buber,* p. 29.
55 Carl Landauer, *European Socialism: A History of Ideas and Movements from the Industrial Revolution to Hitler's Seizure of Power,* 2 vols. (Berkeley and Los Angeles, 1959), I, 379–382.
56 Kohn, *Martin Buber,* pp. 29–30.
57 Buber's profound and thorough grasp of Landauer's thought is demonstrated in the chapter on Landauer in his *Paths in Utopia,* trans. R. F. C. Hull, 2d ed. (Boston, 1960), pp. 46–57.
58 Mühsam, *Unpolitische Erinnerungen,* p. 44.
59 *Ibid.,* p. 35.
60 *Briefe,* I, 91 (dated June 14, 1901), 101 (dated Nov. 28, 1901).
61 *Ibid.,* pp. vi–vii.

[62] See Mosse, *Crisis of German Ideology*, chaps. 8, 10.

[63] GL, "Anarchische Gedanken über den Anarchismus."

[64] Max Nettlau, "La Vida de Gustav Landauer segun su Correspondencia," in *Incitation al Socialismo*, trans. Diego A. de Santillan (Buenos Aires, 1947), p. 236.

[65] Stefan Grossman, *Ich war begeistert: Eine Lebensgeschichte* (Berlin, 1931), p. 66.

[66] R. Hulsen, "Deutsche Gartenstadt Gesellschaft," *Genossenschafts-Pionier* (Berlin), May 16, 1903, p. 74. Landauer mentions the organization in his preface to the translation of Peter Kropotkin, *Landwirtschaft, Industrie, und "Handwerk,"* 2d ed. (Berlin, 1910), p. 2.

[67] Nettlau, "La Vida de Gustav Landauer," pp. 227–228.

[68] These men are all listed as members of the board of organization in its first pamphlet, *Gartenstädte: Erste Flugblatt der Gartenstadt Gesellschaft* (Berlin, 1903).

[69] "The Garden City Movement," *Encyclopedia of Social Reform* (1908 ed.), p. 532.

[70] *Gartenstädte.*

[71] Nettlau, "La Vida de Gustav Landauer," pp. 227–228.

[72] *Ibid.*

[73] See *Briefe*, I, 107–110.

[74] Nettlau, "La Vida de Gustav Landauer," pp. 233–234.

[75] *Briefe*, I, 101 (letter dated Nov. 28, 1901).

[76] Rudolf Rocker, *The London Years* (London, 1956), p. 90.

[77] *Briefe*, I, 106.

[78] In 1903 and 1904 Landauer's translations of Eckhart, Oscar Wilde, and Kropotkin appeared, including the latter's *Fields, Factories and Workshops* and *Mutual Aid* (see bibliography).

[79] *Briefe*, I, 128.

[80] GL, *Aufruf zum Sozialismus*, 2d ed. (Berlin, 1919), p. 13. The work was first published in 1911 in the Verlag des Sozialistischen Bundes.

[81] *Ibid.*, p. 145.

[82] See chap. 2, section entitled "Idealist, Romantic, and Völkisch Perspectives."

[83] "Zur Entwicklungsgeschichte des Individuums," I, *Der Sozialist*, Nov. 2, 1895.

[84] *Briefe*, I, 76.

[85] Kohn, *Martin Buber*, pp. 59–61.

[86] *Briefe*, I, 286.

[87] Mauthner was born in Bohemia in November 1849 and died four

years after Landauer, in 1923. He was a longtime theater critic on the *Berliner Tageblatt* and became, in his thirties, a fairly successful historical novelist. After 1890 he devoted the rest of his life to his critical investigation of language. (*Der Grosse Brockhaus* [Leipzig, 1932], XII, 278–279.)

88 Fritz Mauthner, *Beiträge zu einer Kritik der Sprache*, 3 vols. (I and II [Stuttgart, 1901]; III [Stuttgart and Berlin, 1902]), I, 176. A comprehensive exposition of Mauthner's views may be found in Charles Maurer, "Gustav Landauer: A Study of His Life and Work," pp. 52–61, and a shortened version of the same in Maurer's *Call to Revolution: The Mystical Anarchism of Gustav Landauer* (Detroit, 1971), pp. 58–64. See also Gershon Weiler, "On Fritz Mauthner's Critique of Language," *Mind*, LXVI (1958), 80–87.

89 Gershon Weiler, "Fritz Mauthner as an Historian," *History and Theory*, IV, no. 1 (1964), 59.

90 *Beiträge zu einer Kritik der Sprache*, III, 293.

91 *Ibid.*, I, 662–663.

92 *Ibid.*, p. 661.

93 *Ibid.*, pp. 30–31.

94 GL, "Zur Entwicklungsgeschichte des Individuums," V, *Der Sozialist*, Feb. 8, 1896.

95 Julius Bab, *Gustav Landauer: Gedächtnisrede*, 2d ed. (Nürnberg, 1924), p. 12.

96 GL, *Der Werdende Mensch: Aufsätze über Leben und Schriftum*, ed. Martin Buber (Potsdam, 1921), p. 103.

97 Cf. Sidney Hook, *From Hegel to Marx: Studies in the Intellectual Development of Karl Marx* (Ann Arbor, 1962), pp. 248–251, on the religious criticisms of the Left Hegelians, in which man's self-alienation is seen as his "unconscious projection of human nature in objects of worship," and on the relation of self-alienation to Marx's social theory.

98 This view of Landauer's use of Mauthner's skepticism was taken by Martin Buber in the earliest article on *Skepsis und Mystik*, "Gustav Landauer," *Die Zeit*, June 11, 1904, and by Hans Kohn, "Gustav Landauer," *Selbstwehr: Judisches Volksblatt*, May 16, 1924.

99 *Briefe*, I, 80 (letter dated Sept. 28, 1900).

100 *Ibid.*, p. 450.

101 Blüher, *Werke und Tage*, p. 381.

102 Bab, *Gustav Landauer: Gedächtnisrede*, p. 10.

103 *Skepsis und Mystik*, pp. 2–3.

[104] *Briefe*, I, 119 (letter dated June 16, 1903, and addressed to Julius Bab).

[105] *Skepsis und Mystik*, pp. 7–8.

[106] *Ibid.*, pp. 9–10.

[107] *Ibid.*, pp. 13, 18.

[108] *Ibid.*, p. 15.

[109] *Briefe*, I, 300–301.

[110] *Skepsis und Mystik*, p. 14.

[111] *Briefe*, I, 107–108.

[112] *Skepsis und Mystik*, p. 55.

[113] *Ibid.*, pp. 52–54.

[114] *Meister Eckharts Mystische Schriften*, p. 13.

[115] *Aufruf zum Sozialismus*, p. 120.

[116] H. S. Hughes, *Consciousness and Society: The Reconstruction of European Social Thought, 1890–1930* (New York, 1961), p. 198.

[117] See Mosse, *Crisis of German Ideology*, chap. 5.

[118] See *Meister Eckharts Mystische Schriften*, p. 97.

[119] *Skepsis und Mystik*, p. 16.

[120] *Ibid.*, p. 13.

[121] *Ibid.*, pp. 15, 17.

[122] GL, *Ein Weg deutschen Geistes* (München, 1916), pp. 4–5.

[123] Mauthner, *Beiträge zu einer Kritik der Sprache*, II, 453.

[124] *Skepsis und Mystik*, pp. 44–45.

[125] *Ibid.*, p. 49.

[126] *Ibid.*, p. 73.

[127] *Ibid.*, p. 18.

[128] See, for example, Landauer's comments early in 1910 in *Briefe*, I, 283–284, as well as other instances of frustration over his isolation in *Briefe*, I, 314; II, 195, 225, 367. The point is emphasized by Nettlau ("Anarchisten und Sozialrevolutionäre, 1886–1914," fol. "1895–1914 I," p. 176) and Kohn (*Martin Buber*, p. 349).

[129] *Aufruf zum Sozialismus*, p. 145.

[130] In *The Politics of Cultural Despair* (p. 233), for example, Fritz Stern emphasizes the importance of the feeling of isolation both for Langbehn's thought, as we have seen, and for that of Moeller van den Bruck.

## 4. THE ROMANTIC AS SOCIALIST

[1] Published as part of the series "Die Gesellschaft," edited by Martin Buber (Frankfurt a. M., 1908).

[2] First published in *Die Zukunft*, Jan. 16, 1907; reprinted in the

posthumously published collection of articles, *Beginnen: Aufsätze über Sozialismus*, ed. Martin Buber (Köln, 1924), pp. 3-19.

[3] See Landauer's strictures on Mühsam's tendency toward Bakuninist anarchism in *Sein Lebensgang in Briefen*, ed. Martin Buber, 2 vols. (Frankfurt a. M., 1929), I, 166-167 (hereafter cited as *Briefe*).

[4] See *Briefe*, I, 210, 218, 342, 411, 413-415.

[5] See *Briefe an Auguste Hauschner*, ed. Martin Beradt and Lotte Bloch-Zavkel (Berlin, 1929), p. 251.

[6] See "Gustav Landauer Briefe an Ludwig Berndl," manuscript with notes by Berndl in Gustav Landauer Archives, International Institute of Social History, Amsterdam (hereafter cited as GL Archiv).

[7] *Briefe*, I, 131, 135-137.

[8] *Ibid.*, p. 182.

[9] *Ibid.*, p. 218.

[10] See *ibid.*, pp. 418-419.

[11] *Ibid.*, p. 91.

[12] See, for example, letter dated March 28, 1911, in "Constantin Brunner Briefe an Gustav Landauer," GL Archiv, fol. Q; see also *Briefe*, I, 151, 166-167, 284.

[13] *Briefe*, I, 425.

[14] Charles Maurer, *Call to Revolution: The Mystical Anarchism of Gustav Landauer* (Detroit, 1971), pp. 52, 76.

[15] Oscar Wilde, *Der Sozialismus und die Seele des Menschen*, trans. Hedwig Lachmann and GL (Berlin, 1904); Peter Kropotkin, *Gegenseitige Hilfe in der Entwicklung*, trans. GL (Leipzig, 1904).

[16] *Briefe*, I, 153.

[17] *Die Revolution*, pp. 30-32, 47.

[18] Peter Kropotkin, *Mutual Aid: A Factor in Evolution* (Boston, 1955), p. 57.

[19] GL, foreword to Kropotkin, *Gegenseitige Hilfe in der Entwicklung*, p. h.

[20] *Die Revolution*, p. 57.

[21] Kropotkin, *Mutual Aid*, p. 200.

[22] *Ibid.*, p. 181.

[23] *Ibid.*, p. 197.

[24] *Ibid.*, pp. 216-227.

[25] *Ibid.*, chapts. 7, 8.

[26] *Ibid.*, p. 292.

[27] Constantin Brunner, *Die Lehre von den Geistigen und vom Volke*, 3d ed., 2 vols. (Stuttgart, 1962), I, 13–23.

[28] *Ibid.*, pp. 244–255.

[29] GL, "Die Lehre von den Gestigen und vom Volke: Ein Gespräch zwischen einem Gebildeten und einem Lernenden," *Die Zukunft*, Jan. 16, 1909; reprinted in the posthumously published collection of articles, *Der Werdende Mensch: Aufsätz über Leben und Schriftum*, ed. Martin Buber (Potsdam, 1921), pp. 231–243.

[30] *Der Werdende Mensch*, p. 237.

[31] Brunner, *Die Lehre*, I, 449–452.

[32] *Ibid.*, pp. 450, 453.

[33] *Briefe*, I, 136–137.

[34] *Die Revolution*, pp. 8–9.

[35] *Ibid.*, pp. 12–13.

[36] *Ibid.*, p. 25.

[37] *Briefe*, I, 172.

[38] *Die Revolution*, pp. 25–26.

[39] In *Ideology and Utopia: An Introduction to the Sociology of Knowledge*, trans. Louis Wirth and Edward Shils (New York, 1958), Karl Mannheim wrote (p. 197) that "Landauer . . . regards the existing order as one undifferentiated whole . . . and . . . according esteem only to revolution and utopia, sees in every topia (the present existing order) evil itself." Mannheim went on to argue that Landauer's anarchism involved a condemnation of "all" aspects of existing reality and hence made his outlook fundamentally unhistorical, since "the possibility of noting any kind of evolutionary trend in the realm of the historical and institutional is obscured." Mannheim is unaware, however, that Landauer's topia-utopia dichotomy was presented as an object lesson against allegedly scientific historiography and that Landauer abandoned this approach after the first twenty pages of *Die Revolution*. What is more, by failing to read past these first twenty pages, Mannheim misses the crucial fact that Landauer identified the sharp "downward" trend of modern history as one long "revolution," hardly consistent for one who supposedly accorded "esteem only to revolution." For a thorough examination of Landauer's play at positivistic historiography in *Die Revolution*, a discussion that specifically refutes Mannheim's misreading, see Thomas Esper, "The Anarchism of Gustav Landauer" (M.A. thesis, University of Chicago, 1961), pp. 38–50.

40 *Die Revolution*, p. 32.
41 *Ibid.*
42 See Albert Kranold, *Zwang und Freiheit im Sozializmus* (Jena, 1925), pp. 82–85, for a criticism of Landauer's idealization of the Middle Ages. Kranold argues that instead of individualistic egoism, which for Landauer was characteristic of the modern era, the Middle Ages exhibited unlimited "group egoism."
43 *Die Revolution*, pp. 40–44.
44 *Ibid.*, pp. 44–48. This was a common complaint of romantic medievalists such as John Ruskin and Richard Wagner.
45 *Der Werdende Mensch*, pp. 36–37. The passage is from an article Landauer wrote in 1911.
46 *Die Revolution*, p. 52.
47 *Ibid.*, pp. 52–53.
48 *Aufruf zum Sozialismus*, 2d ed. (Berlin, 1919), pp. 4–5, 10.
49 *Die Revolution*, pp. 53–54.
50 *Ibid.*
51 See Johan Huizinga, *The Waning of the Middle Ages* (New York: Doubleday, 1956), pp. 150–151 and chap. 16.
52 *Die Revolution*, p. 60.
53 Hajo Holborn, *A History of Modern Germany, 1648–1840* (New York, 1965), pp. 350–351.
54 *Die Revolution*, p. 62.
55 *Ibid.*, p. 64.
56 *Der Werdende Mensch*, pp. 36–37.
57 *Die Revolution*, p. 101.
58 *Ibid.*, pp. 71–74.
59 *Ibid.*, pp. 69–70.
60 *Ibid.*, pp. 101–104.
61 *Ibid.*, pp. 113–115.
62 GL, "Volk und Land: Dreissig Sozialistischen Thesen," in *Beginnen*, p. 9.
63 *Ibid.*, pp. 14–19.
64 *Ibid.*, p. 11.
65 *Ibid.*, pp. 14, 18.
66 See appendix.
67 *Briefe*, I, 197–198; Max Nettlau, "Anarchisten und Sozialrevolutionäre, 1886–1914," Nettlau Archives, International Institute of Social History, Amsterdam, fol. "1895–1914 I," p. 176.
68 *Briefe*, I, 197.
69 *Ibid.*, pp. 202–203.
70 *Ibid.*, p. 216.

71 *Ibid.*, pp. 200–202, 204–209.

72 *Ibid.*, p. 236.

73 Nettlau, "Anarchisten und Sozialrevolutionäre, 1886–1914," fol. "1895–1914 I," p. 181.

74 Hans Blüher, *Werke und Tage* (München, 1953), p. 380; "Manuskript von Ludwig Berndl," GL Archiv, fol. A.1, p. vi.

75 *Briefe*, I, 339.

76 *Ibid.*, p. 247.

77 *Ibid.*, pp. 265–266.

78 Franz Jung, *Der Weg nach unten: Aufzeichnungen aus einer Grossen Zeit* (Berlin, 1961), pp. 77–82.

79 "Der Sozialistische Bund und das deutsche Reichsvereinsgesetz," *Der Sozialist*, April 15, 1909.

80 *Beginnen*, p. 18.

81 GL, "Was Will der Sozialistische Bund?" in *Beginnen*, pp. 91–92.

82 *Briefe*, I, 198–199. With regard to the Parisian "sections" of 1789, Landauer translated Kropotkin's article on that subject, "Distrikte und Sektionen in Paris 1789," *Der Sozialist*, April 1, 1909; the article was from Landauer's translation of the whole of Kropotkin's work on the French Revolution (Peter Kropotkin, *Die französische Revolution, 1789–1793* [Leipzig, 1909]).

83 The lack of real federation, in addition to centralization, was made clear in the April 1909 article cited above, "Der Sozialistische Bund und das deutsche Reichsvereingesetz."

84 Max Nettlau, "La Vida de Gustav Landauer segun su Correspondencia," in *Incitacion al Socialismo*, trans. Diego A. de Santillan (Buenos Aires, 1947), p. 229.

85 Nettlau, "Anarchisten und Sozialrevolutionäre, 1886–1914," fol. "1895–1914 I," p. 179.

86 Lecture announcements from 1910–11, GL Archiv, fol. B.

87 Blüher, *Werke und Tage*, p. 380.

88 *Briefe*, I, 252.

89 *Ibid.*, p. 259.

90 *Der Sozialist*, Sept. 1, 1909. Landauer discusses the collapse of any anarchist movement in Rhineland-Westphalia in a letter of April 2, 1910, to a fellow anarchist, Hugo Warnstedt (*Briefe*, I, 311).

91 Erich Mühsam, "Neue Freunde," *Der Sozialist*, Aug. 1, 1909. See also Mühsam's *Von Eisner bis Levine: Persönlicher Rechenschaftsbericht* (Berlin, 1929), p. 10.

92 Georg Franz, "Munich: Birthplace and Center of the National

Socialist German Workers' Party," *Journal of Modern History,* XXIV (1957), 321.

93 *Der Sozialist,* Jan. 15, 1910.

94 *Briefe,* I, 287n. Landauer may have become interested in libertarian schools after hearing of the educational work of the noted Spanish anarchist Francesco Ferrer, who had been executed in 1909. In the January 15, 1910, issue of *Der Sozialist,* the issue cited above, Landauer discussed a Berlin demonstration in protest against Ferrer's murder by the Spanish authorities (see "Die Gespenster").

95 Nettlau, "Anarchisten und Sozialrevolutionäre, 1886–1914," fol. "1895–1914 I," pp. 179–180.

96 *Briefe,* I, 222–223.

97 See George L. Mosse, *The Crisis of German Ideology: The Intellectual Origins of the Third Reich* (New York, 1965), pp. 108–125.

98 Unlike the Germanic utopias of the period the Bund was avowedly anarchist and socialist; it rejected the ideological elitism of the existing völkisch colonies, yet they both shared a common antipathy to Marxism and capitalism, to the world of "rootless" urban industrialism. This similarity, in fact, was enough to bring about at least one instance of cooperation between the Bund and the leading Germanic utopia, Eden. One group of the Bund, located in Oranienburg near Berlin, set up its Siedlung fund with the Eden colony. (Cf. *Der Sozialist,* Sept. 1, 1909; on Eden, see Mosse, *Crisis of German Ideology,* pp. 111–112, 121.) Eden had itself begun in the 1890s as a land reform project of the utopian socialist Hertzka, a thinker who had exercised some impact in Landauer's Berlin anarchist milieu in those years. Its director for twenty-five years, Otto Jackisch, was a close friend of Franz Oppenheimer, the most important utopian socialist thinker in Germany in the early twentieth century. (See Franz Oppenheimer, *Erlebtes, Erstrebtes, Erreichtes* [Berlin, 1931], pp. 159–162.)

99 Albert Weidner, *Aus den Tiefen der Berliner Arbeiterbewegung* (Berlin, n.d. [1905?]), p. 72.

100 Landauer letter to *Der Freie Arbeiter,* printed in its May 15, 1909, issue. See also *Briefe,* I, 254.

101 Fritz Flierl, "Kurze Notizen vom Kongress deutschen Anarchisten," *Der Sozialist,* June 1, 1910. See also Landauer's article "Die Politische Polizei," *Der Sozialist,* June 1, 1910, and his letter of June 10 (*Briefe,* I, 259).

[102] "An die Genossen!" *Der Freie Arbeiter*, May 15, 1909.

[103] "Wie Kann der Sozialismus kommen?" III, *Der Anarchist* (Leipzig), May 25, 1912.

[104] Pierre Ramus, "Ein Brief über den Sozialistischen Bund und gegen Landauer als Sozialist," *Jahrbuch der freien Generation: Volkskalender und Dokuments der Weltanschauung des Anarchismus-Sozialismus*, III (1912), 115–125.

[105] Oskar Maria Graf, *Prisoners All*, trans. Margaret Green (New York, 1928), pp. 58–59.

[106] GL, "Individualismus," *Der Sozialist*, July 15, 1911.

[107] GL, *Aufruf zum Sozialismus*, p. 5.

[108] For an analysis of other confrontations with Marxism among leading social thinkers of the day (Pareto, Croce, Gramsci, Sorel, and Durkheim), see H. S. Hughes, *Consciousness and Society: The Reconstruction of European Social Thought, 1890–1930* (New York, 1961), chap. 3.

[109] *Aufruf zum Sozialismus*, pp. 28–30.

[110] See *Briefe*, II, 168 (letter dated Nov. 4, 1916).

[111] See, for example, Engels's attack upon "vulgar" Marxist writings of the early 1890s in *Marx and Engels: Basic Writings on Politics and Philosophy*, ed. Lewis Feuer (New York, 1959), pp. 395–412.

[112] *Beginnen*, pp. 159–160.

[113] George Lichtheim, *Marxism: An Historical and Critical Study* (New York, 1961), pp. 244, 247. See also the excellent discussion in Shlomo Avineri, *The Social and Political Thought of Karl Marx* (London: Cambridge University Press, 1968), pp. 65–77.

[114] *Aufruf zum Sozialismus*, p. 62.

[115] Peter Gay, *The Dilemma of Democratic Socialism: Eduard Bernstein's Challenge to Marx* (New York, 1962), p. 195.

[116] Gustav Landauer, "Vom Wege des Sozialismus," *Der Sozialist*, July 1909, reprinted in *Beginnen*, p. 49.

[117] *Aufruf zum Sozialismus*, p. 69.

[118] *Ibid.*, p. 70.

[119] *Ibid.*, pp. 64, 67, 69.

[120] *Ibid.*, pp. 40–42, 47.

[121] Carl E. Schorske, *German Social Democracy, 1915–1917: The Development of the Great Schism* (Cambridge, Mass., 1955), chaps. 4, 5.

[122] See Denis Brogan, *The Development of Modern France* (London, 1940), pp. 419–431; and Élie Halévy, *A History of the English People in the Nineteenth Century*, 2d ed. (New York, 1961), Vol. VI, *The Rule of Democracy, 1905–1914*, pp. 441–486.

[123] Schorske, *German Social Democracy*, chap. 2.
[124] *Aufruf zum Sozialismus*, pp. 63, 77, 95.
[125] *Ibid.*, p. 93.
[126] *Ibid.*, pp. 48–52, 56.
[127] *Beginnen*, pp. 129–130.
[128] *Der Sozialist*, Nov. 11, 1911; reprinted in the posthumously published collection of articles, *Rechenschaft*, 1st ed. (Berlin, 1919), p. 68.
[129] *Rechenschaft*, p. 65.
[130] *Ibid.*, p. 70.
[131] *Ibid.*, p. 61.
[132] *Der Werdende Mensch*, p. 120.
[133] For a contemporary Marxist critique of Landauer's socialism, see Hans Beyer, *Von der November Revolution zur Räterepublik in München* (Berlin, 1957), pp. xiii–xiv.
[134] *Beginnen*, p. 111.
[135] *Aufruf zum Sozialismus*, p. 61. The translation is from Martin Buber, *Paths in Utopia*, trans. R. F. C. Hull, 2d ed. (Boston, 1960), pp. 46–47.
[136] See the analysis of Marx's thought in Marcuse, *Reason and Revolution: Hegel and the Rise of Social Theory* (Boston, 1960), pp. 273–323.
[137] *Beginnen*, pp. 55–58, 60–61; *Der Werdende Mensch*, pp. 86–87.
[138] See *Beginnen*, pp. 58, 171–172. For Marx's view see, especially, "The Economic and Philosophical Manuscripts of 1844," in *Marx's Concept of Man*, ed. Erich Fromm (New York, 1961), pp. 98, 102. Landauer, as noted above, could not have known this work of Marx's since it was not discovered until the 1930s.
[139] This distinction is central to the comparative analysis of the thought of Landauer, Buber, and Marx in Hans Kohn's *Martin Buber: Sein Werk und seine Zeit*, 2d ed. (Köln, 1961), pp. 195–201.
[140] *Aufruf zum Sozialismus*, p. 11.
[141] *Briefe*, I, 283.
[142] See George Woodcock, *Pierre-Joseph Proudhon* (New York, 1956), pp. 76–77, 204.
[143] See Peter Kropotkin, "Anarchist Communism: Its Basis and Principles," *Kropotkin's Revolutionary Pamphlets*, ed. Roger N. Baldwin (New York, 1927), pp. 47–192.
[144] In the preface to his translation of Kropotkin's *Mutual Aid* Landauer wrote, in 1904: "For my part . . . Kropotkin's material should be allowed to wander out into the immeasurable universe

and bore into the abysses of our inner experience, and the question should be asked: Is not all being a solidarity that is separated out into individuated parts through the force of our limiting and separating sense perceptions?" (foreword to *Gegenseitige Hilfe in der Entwicklung*).

145 *Der Sozialist*, Jan. 1, 1910.

146 Cf. *Aufruf zum Sozialismus*, p. 108. Landauer translated much of this material in *Der Sozialist*.

147 For a thorough discussion of Proudhon's ideas on mutual credit and banking, see Charles A. Dana, "Proudhon and His Bank of the People," in Pierre Joseph Proudhon, *Proudhon's Solution to the Social Problem*, ed. Henry Cohen (New York, 1927), pp. 15-31.

148 Denis Brogan, *Proudhon* (London, 1934), p. 52.

149 Mosse, *Crisis of German Ideology*, pp. 110-111, 120.

150 See the attack on capitalist and communized property in Pierre Joseph Proudhon, *What Is Property?* trans. Benjamin Tucker (New York, 1890), pp. 259-280. On völkisch anticapitalism and anticommunism see Mosse, *Crisis of German Ideology*, pp. 108-125.

151 *Beginnen*, p. 23.

152 Brogan, *Proudhon*, pp. 49-50.

153 *Aufruf zum Sozialismus*, p. 104.

154 Gustav Landauer, "Der Erste Mai," *Der Sozialist*, May 1, 1909.

155 *Aufruf zum Sozialismus*, pp. 141, 150.

156 *Ibid.*, pp. 142-143.

157 On Proudhon's peasant romanticism see Woodcock, *Pierre-Joseph Proudhon*, pp. 270-272.

158 Cf. *Briefe*, I, 169, 200-203, 313-320, etc.

159 *Beginnen*, pp. 106-108.

160 *Aufruf zum Sozialismus*, pp. 140-142.

161 *Ibid.*, p. 145. Martin Buber quotes this passage in support of his view of Landauer's sensitivity to historical traditions (*Paths in Utopia*, p. 50). It serves to disprove the contention made by Karl Mannheim (*Ideology and Utopia*, pp. 197-198) that "G. Landauer . . . regards the existing order as one undifferentiated whole, and . . . , by according esteem only to revolution and utopia, sees in every topia (the present existing order) evil itself. . . . By laying the evaluative emphasis on utopia and revolution, the possibility of noting any kind of evolutionary trend in the realm of the historical and institutional is obscured." Mannheim (p. 225) refers to Landauer as a representative of the

"chiliastic mentality" in that he does not know of a "road that leads to a goal or a process of development." Although in relation to Marxian socialism, Landauer's work contains far less evolutionary, historical analysis, Landauer did, in fact, hope to build upon certain potentially effective organs of decentralized communal life which existed in the historical present, i.e., the cooperative movement, rural communal institutions, and, in the revolution of 1918–19, the workers', soldiers', and peasants' councils.

162 *Aufruf zum Sozialismus*, p. 100.

163 Peter Kropotkin, *Fields, Factories and Workshops* (New York, 1907), p. 5.

164 *Beginnen*, pp. 70–72.

165 See Kropotkin, *Fields, Factories and Workshops*, esp. chaps. 4, 6, and pp. 213–215. On this aspect of Kropotkin's study see George Woodcock and Ivan Avakumovic, *The Anarchist Prince: A Biographical Study of Peter Kropotkin* (London, 1950), pp. 25–30, 318–319.

166 *Aufruf zum Sozialismus*, p. 132.

167 GL, "Preussen," *Diskussion: Eine Monatschrift für aktuelle Kulturfragen* (1910), no. 2, pp. 66–70.

168 *Rechenschaft*, p. 195.

169 Woodcock, *Anarchist Prince*, p. 315.

170 See Proudhon, *What Is Property?* pp. 259–262.

171 *Aufruf zum Sozialismus*, pp. 135–136.

172 *Der Werdende Mensch*, p. 33.

173 GL, "Tuckers Eröffnung," *Der Sozialist*, May 15, 1911.

174 Buber, *Paths in Utopia*, p. 44.

175 See Peter Kropotkin, "Anarchism," *Encyclopaedia Britannica*, 11th ed., I, 914; and his "Modern Science and Anarchism," in *Kropotkin's Revolutionary Pamphlets*, p. 181. For Proudhon see *What Is Property?* pp. 276–277.

176 Buber, *Paths in Utopia*, pp. 44–46.

177 GL, "Die Zwei Seiten," *Der Sozialist*, June 1909; reprinted in *Beginnen*, p. 128.

178 GL, "Die französische Syndikalisten," *Der Sozialist*, June 1, 1909.

179 See GL's articles, "Tuckers Eröffnung" and "Individualismus."

180 *Briefe*, II, 122–123.

181 *Die Revolution*, pp. 86–90. Landauer translated Étienne de La Boétie's "On Voluntary Servitude" for the readers of *Der Sozialist*; the work appeared over a series of months starting in the issue of Sept. 1, 1910.

182 This view is one of the essential leitmotifs of all Landauer's
writings after 1907; for its expression see, for example, the pamphlet entitled *Der Sozialist*, dated December 1908, announcing
the reappearance of the newspaper; *Aufruf zum Sozialismus*, p.
19; *Die Revolution*, p. 114; *Beginnen*, pp. 103–104; "Der Schlendrian," *Der Sozialist*, Sept. 15, 1910; "März 1910," *Der Sozialist*,
March 15, 1910. In the secondary literature, besides the excellent
chapter on Landauer in Buber's *Paths in Utopia*, pp. 46–57, see
Thomas Esper, "The Anarchism of Gustav Landauer" (M.A.
thesis, University of Chicago, 1961), pp. 28–29.

183 GL, "Schwache Stattsmänner, Schwacheres Volk!" *Der Sozialist*, June, 1910; reprinted in *Beginnen*, pp. 52–53.

184 GL, "Von Micheln und Antimicheln," *Der Sozialist*, Aug. 6,
1898. See also GL's article, "Der gallische Hahn und der
deutsche Esel," *Der Sozialist*, Aug. 13, 1898.

185 In *Briefe*, I, 337, Landauer compares Tolstoi with what he called
Eckhart's "panpsychism"; in *Werdende Mensch*, p. 202, he refers
to La Boétie as a great "predecessor" of Tolstoi's pacifist theories.

186 *Werdende Mensch*, pp. 228–229; see also the comparison of Tolstoi and Kropotkin in Woodcock and Avakumovic, *Anarchist
Prince*, p. 351.

187 *Werdende Mensch*, p. 202.

188 GL, "Brot," *Der Sozialist*, June 1, 1911.

189 *Briefe*, I, 377.

190 *Beginnen*, pp. 45–46.

191 See *Aufruf zum Sozialismus*, p. 145; *Briefe*, I, 377.

192 *Briefe*, I, 365–366 (letter dated June 7, 1911). Landauer continually spoke of the necessity of an immediate beginning of socialist construction in the years 1908–1911. Besides the quotations
given above, see *Beginnen*, pp. 131, 146, 150; *Briefe*, I, 273;
*Rechenschaft*, p. 57.

193 Julius Bab, *Gustav Landauer: Gedächtnisrede*, 2d ed. (Nürnberg, 1924), p. 12.

194 *Beginnen*, pp. 101–102.

195 *Ibid.*, pp. 133–135.

196 *Ibid.*, pp. 93–94, 102–103.

## 5. THE SOCIALIST AS ROMANTIC

1 Arthur Rosenberg, *Imperial Germany: The Birth of the German
Republic, 1871–1918* (Boston, 1964), pp. 61–64.

2 GL, "Parlamentskritik," *Das Blaubuch*, May 30, 1907.

3 Carl E. Schorske, *German Social Democracy, 1905–1917: The De-*

*velopment of the Great Schism* (Cambridge, Mass., 1955), p. 197.

[4] Fritz Fischer, *Germany's Aims in the First World War* (London, 1967), p. 25.

[6] E. Malcolm Carroll, *Germany and the Great Powers, 1866-1914: A Study in Public Opinion and Foreign Policy* (New York, 1938), p. 709. For an analysis of the German press during and after the Agadir crisis, see *ibid.*, pp. 643-699.

[6] Fischer, *Germany's Aim*, p. 25.

[7] *Ibid.*, pp. 25-26.

[8] *Ibid.*, p. 34.

[9] Schorske, *German Social Democracy*, p. 220.

[10] GL, *Rechenschaft* (Berlin, 1919), pp. 19-20.

[11] *Ibid.*, pp. 139-140.

[12] *Ibid.*, p. 37.

[13] *Ibid.*, p. 134.

[14] *Ibid.*, p. 21.

[15] *Ibid.*

[16] *Ibid.*, p. 29.

[17] *Ibid.*, pp. 88-90.

[18] *Ibid.*, p. 88.

[19] Schorske, *German Social Democracy*, p. 85. See also James Joll, *The Second International, 1889-1914* (New York, 1966), pp. 133-143.

[20] *Rechenschaft*, pp. 117, 120.

[21] *Ibid.*, pp. 70-71.

[22] *Ibid.*, pp. 134-135.

[23] See Joll, *Second International*, pp. 133-143.

[24] *Rechenschaft*, pp. 41-45, 54-55.

[25] *Ibid.*, p. 59.

[26] Hermann Giesau, "Erinnerungen an Gustav Landauer," *Besinnung und Aufbruch*, June 1, 1929, p. 10.

[27] *Der Sozialist*, March 1, 1912.

[28] Koppel S. Pinson, *Modern Germany: Its History and Civilization* (New York, 1954), pp. 313-316.

[29] *Ibid.*, pp. 313-314, 333.

[30] Friedrich Meinecke, *The German Catastrophe* (Boston, 1963), p. 25.

[31] Fritz Stern, *The Politics of Cultural Despair: A Study in the Rise of the Germanic Ideology* (New York, 1965), p. 258.

[32] Leon W. Fuller, "The War of 1914 as Interpreted by German Intellectuals," *Journal of Modern History*, XIV (June 1942),

145–160. Fuller examines the enthusiasm for World War I among a whole galaxy of leading scholars and writers, including, for example, Max Scheler, Otto von Gierke, Wilhelm Wundt, Friedrich Meinecke, Ernst Haeckel, etc.

33 Hans Kohn, *Martin Buber: Sein Werk und seine Zeit*, 2d ed. (Köln, 1961), p. 142.

34 *Rechenschaft*, p. 159.

35 *Ibid.*, pp. 114–115.

36 George Woodcock and Ivan Avakumovic, *The Anarchist Prince: A Biographical Study of Peter Kropotkin* (London, 1950), pp. 289–290.

37 GL, *Sein Lebensgang in Briefen*, ed. Martin Buber, 2 vols. (Frankfurt a. M., 1929), II, 11 (hereafter cited as *Briefe*).

38 See *Rechenschaft*, pp. 150–151; *Der Sozialist*, Jan. 15, 1915.

39 *Briefe*, II, 69.

40 *Ibid.*, pp. 1, 36 (letters dated Aug. 18, 1914, and March 31, 1915).

41 *Ibid.*, p. 10.

42 Johann Gottfried Herder, "Vom Wirken der Völker auf einander," *Der Sozialist*, Nov. 10, 1914.

43 The article "Zum Gedächtnis," which appeared in *Der Sozialist* on October 20, 1914, was reprinted in *Rechenschaft*, pp. 184–187.

44 "Ein Franzose, Romain Rolland and Die Geistigen aller Nationen," *Der Sozialist*, Dec. 1914.

45 See *Briefe*, II, 8, 96n.

46 Heinz-Joachim Heydorn, foreword to GL, *Aufruf zum Sozialismus*, 3d ed. (Frankfurt a. M., 1967), p. 14.

47 *Briefe*, II, 1–2n.

48 Frederik van Eeden, "Tagebuchblätter aus der Zeit in Potsdam 1914," typescript, Gustav Landauer Archives, International Institute of Social History, Amsterdam, fol. Z (hereafter cited as GL Archiv).

49 *Briefe*, II, 1–2n; Frederik van Eeden, "An die Freunde des Forte-Kreises," Sept. 19, 1914, GL Archiv, fol. Z; letter from Rang to Henri Borel, Sept. 26, 1914, GL Archiv, fol. Z.

50 *Briefe*, II, 4–5.

51 Letter dated Oct. 28, 1914, GL Archiv, fol. Z.

52 *Briefe*, II, 72–81.

53 See Fritz Mauthner's eulogy to Landauer after his assassination: "Zum Gedächtnis," *Masken*, XIV (May 1919), 300–304.

54 Reprinted in Martin Buber, *Vom Geist des Judentums* (Leipzig, 1916), pp. 9–48.

55 Letter dated May 12, 1916, GL Archiv, fol. R.

56 Buber's letter is quoted in Landauer's June 2, 1916, letter, GL Archiv, fol. R.

57 *Ibid.*

58 *Briefe*, II, 142–146.

59 *Ibid.*, pp. 142–143.

60 Charles Maurer, *Call to Revolution: The Mystical Anarchism of Gustav Landauer* (Detroit, 1971), pp. 133–134.

61 See *Briefe*, II, 101–102.

62 See section entitled "The Literature of the Volk," in this chapter.

63 *Briefe*, II, 159n; Pinson, *Modern Germany*, p. 316.

64 See George L. Mosse, *The Crisis of German Ideology: The Intellectual Origins of the Third Reich* (New York, 1964), pp. 52–63.

65 Hans Blüher, *Werke und Tage* (München, 1953), pp. 376, 393; Maurer, *Call to Revolution*, pp. 34–35.

66 Walter Laqueur, *Young Germany* (New York, 1962), p. 100.

67 Heinrich Jantzen, *Jugendkulter und Jugendbewegung: Studie zur Stellung und Bedeutung Gustav Wynekens innerhalb der Jugendbewegung* (Frankfurt a. M., 1963), p. 14; Mosse, *Crisis of German Ideology*, pp. 162–166.

68 Harry Pross, *Jugend-Eros-Politik: Die Geschichte der deutschen Jugendverbände* (München, 1964), pp. 155–159.

69 Jantzen, *Jugendkulter und Jugendbewegung*, p. 20.

70 Pross, *Jugend-Eros-Politik*, pp. 134–137, 513.

71 Charles Maurer, "Gustav Landauer: A Study of His Life and Work" (Ph.D. dissertation, Northwestern University, 1965), p. 35.

72 Laqueur, *Young Germany*, pp. 100–103.

73 Letter from Landauer to Hugo Warnstedt, Nov. 15, 1915, GL Archiv, fol. W.

74 GL, "Von Sozialismus und der Siedlung," and "Zum Problem der Nation," *Der Aufbruch: Monatsblätter aus der Jugendbewegung* (Jena: Diedrichs Verlag, 1915), I, Heft 4, nos. 2, 3. The two articles were published posthumously in *Beginnen: Aufsätze über Sozialismus* (Köln, 1924), and *Der Werdende Mensch: Aufsätze über Leben und Schriftum* (Potsdam, 1921), respectively.

75 See all four issues of *Der Aufbruch*, July–Oct. 1915.

76 *Briefe*, II, 100, 125–126n.

77 *Ibid.*, pp. 114, 224, 298; letter from Landauer to Ernst Joël, June 6, 1916, GL Archiv, fol. S.

78 *Briefe*, II, 100.

79 See George L. Mosse, "The Influence of the *Völkisch* Idea on German Jewry," in *Germans and Jews: The Right, the Left and the Search for a "Third Force" in Pre-Nazi Germany* (New York, 1970); Howard Becker, *German Youth: Bond or Free?* (London, 1946), p. 107; Ernst Holzer, "Jüdische Jugendbewegung; Ein Rückblick," *Der Morgen*, 4, no. 3 (1928), 279–288.

80 Elkana Margalit, "The Social and Intellectual Origins of the Hashomer Hatzair Youth Movement, 1913–20," *Journal of Contemporary History*, 4 (April 1969), 25–46.

81 Walter H. Sokel, *The Writer in Extremis: Expressionism in Twentieth-Century German Literature* (Stanford, 1959), pp. 137, 162–163.

82 Kurt Hiller, *Köpfe und Tröpfe: Profile aus einem Vierteljahrhundert* (Hamburg, 1950), p. 321.

83 Letter from Landauer to Rubiner, July 18, 1917, GL Archiv, fol. N.b.

84 *Kameraden der Menschheit*, ed. Ludwig Rubiner (Potsdam: G. Kiepenheuer, 1919).

85 Ernst Toller, *I Was a German* (New York, 1934), p. 131; letter from Toller to Landauer, Dec. 6, 1917, GL Archiv, fol. O.f.

86 Letter dated March 1, 1916, GL Archiv, fol. M.

87 Kaiser letters dated Dec. 1, 1917, GL Archiv, fol. O.f. and June 28, 1918, *ibid.*, fol. P.

88 Letter to Leo Kestenberg, April 22, 1918, GL Archiv, fol. T.

89 *Briefe*, II, 342.

90 Letter dated May 6, 1918, GL Archiv, fol. P.

91 *Rechenschaft*, pp. 200–203.

92 *Briefe*, II, 174–176.

93 *Ibid.*, p. 336; Ludwig Berndl manuscript on Landauer, GL Archiv, fol. A.1, pp. xii–xiii. See also Landauer's comments on the Bolsheviks in the introduction to the second edition of *Aufruf zum Sozialismus*, written in January 1919.

94 Rosenberg, *Imperial Germany*, pp. 158, 177.

95 *Ibid.*, p. 207.

96 *Briefe*, II, 201.

97 *Ibid.*, pp. 210–211.

98 Blüher, *Werke und Tage*, p. 397. See also the moving description by Landauer's daughter, Gudula, of her life with her father after Hedwig's death: "Gustav Landauer und Hedwig Lachmann," *Berliner Tageblatt*, Aug. 22, 1926. Landauer had a description he

had written of Hedwig's last days printed and mailed to a number of friends; a copy of the piece, entitled "Wie Hedwig Lachmann starb," is in GL Archiv, fol. H.

99 Toller, *I Was a German*, p. 131.

100 *Briefe*, I, 425.

101 "Philister über du, Hauptmann!" *Der Sozialist*, July 1, 1913, and *Der Werdende Mensch*, p. 107.

102 *Briefe*, I, 446.

103 Paul Kluckhohn, *Das Ideengut der deutschen Romantik*, 3d ed. (Tübingen, 1953), pp. 101–102; *Nationalism: A Report by a Study Group of Members of the Royal Institute of International Affairs*, 2d ed. (London, 1963), pp. xviii–xix.

104 Kluckhohn, *Ideengut der deutschen Romantik*, p. 104.

105 K. R. Minogue, *Nationalism* (London, 1967), p. 57.

106 Kluckhohn, *Ideengut der deutschen Romantik*, p. 124.

107 Isaiah Berlin, "Herder and the Enlightenment," in *Aspects of the Eighteenth Century*, ed. Earl R. Wasserman (Baltimore, 1965), p. 77.

108 See Mosse, *Crisis of German Ideology*, pp. 6, 61.

109 Friedrich Meinecke, *Weltbürgertum und Nationalstaat*, 3d ed. (München, 1915), pp. 69, 201, 320.

110 In *Politics of Cultural Despair* (p. 341), Fritz Stern emphasizes how his right-wing völkisch subjects, Lagarde, Langbehn, and Moeller van den Bruck, borrowed only selectively from the romantic heritage and entirely neglected the humanism and cosmopolitanism of the early romantics.

111 See Mosse, *Crisis of German Ideology*, pp. 88–107.

112 Mosse, "The Influence of the Völkisch Idea on German Jewry."

113 *Der Sozialist*, Sept. 1, 1914. In an article of June 1, 1911, Johannes Nohl compared Landauer's ideas with those of Fichte's *Reden* for the readers of *Der Sozialist*: "Fichtes Reden an die deutsche Nation und Landauers *Aufruf zum Sozialismus*."

114 Herder, "Vom Wirken der Völker auf einander."

115 See Arthur O. Lovejoy, *The Great Chain of Being* (Cambridge, Mass., 1936), pp. 292–294.

116 *Briefe*, II, 1.

117 *Ibid.*, p. 36.

118 *Der Sozialist*, Sept. 1, 1914.

119 *Briefe*, I, 451. For other expressions of Landauer's humanity-oriented völkisch nationalism, see *Briefe*, II, 57; *Werdende Mensch*, pp. 112–113; and especially the article, "Von der tierischen Grundlage," *Weltbühne*, July 4, 1918.

120 *Der Werdende Mensch*, p. 110.

121 In *Martin Buber* (p. 310), Hans Kohn links Landauer's view of the importance of the "myth" for the development of the Volk with the twenty-third chapter of Nietzsche's *Birth of Tragedy*, which was written under the spell of the völkisch romantic Richard Wagner. Landauer, however, never mentioned this particular work of Nietzsche's in his writings.

122 *Rechenschaft*, pp. 103–104.

123 See *Werdende Mensch*, p. 115; *Briefe*, I, 207–208. The parallel here between this expression of Landauer's "revolutionary conservatism" and that of the important völkisch thinker Moeller van den Bruck is particularly striking (see E. O. Lorimer, *Germany's Third Empire* [London: G. Allen and Unwin, 1934], pp. 193, 215). Klemens von Klemperer has argued that twentieth-century German revolutionary conservatism was derived largely from the intellectual mood of Nietzschean voluntarism, a philosophic component in the thought of both Moeller van den Bruck and Gustav Landauer, as well as, of course, the entire neoromantic generation in early twentieth-century Germany (see Klemens von Klemperer, *Germany's New Conservatism* [Princeton, 1957], pp. 36–40). The concept of the *Aufbruch*, which was central to Moeller's political thought, was an attempt to fuse Herder and Nietzsche by arguing that the Volk we create had long been evolving of itself.

124 *Werdende Mensch*, pp. 32–33.

125 *Die Revolution* (Frankfurt a. M., 1908), p. 38.

126 *Ibid.*, p. 24. For a discussion of the neoromantic conception of mythos (in the thought of Bergson as well as of the Germans, Joël, Simmel, and Buber) see Kohn, *Martin Buber*, pp. 62–67.

127 See Mosse, *Crisis of German Ideology*, p. 36; Stern, *Politics of Cultural Despair*, pp. 58–59; and Landauer's introductory remarks to Paul de Lagarde, "Deutschland nach dem Kriege: Auszüge aus Paul de Lagarde's 'Deutschen Schriften,'" *Der Sozialist*, Oct. 10, 1914.

128 On the widespread opposition in Germany to "divisive" parliamentarism, see Ernst Fraenkel, "Historical Obstacles to Parliamentary Government in Germany," in *The Path to Dictatorship, 1918–1933: Ten Essays by German Scholars*, trans. John Conway (New York, 1966), p. 29.

129 See *Aufruf zum Sozialismus*, pp. 22–23, and "Parlamentskritik," *Das Blaubuch*, May 30, 1907.

130 *Werdende Mensch*, p. 107.

131 *Briefe*, I, 425.

132 *Ibid.*, p. 430.

133 Martin Buber, "Landauer und die Revolution," *Masken*, XIV (May 1919), 282–291; Alfred Werner, "Saintly Revolutionary," *Jewish Quarterly* (Summer 1959), p. 11; Julius Bab, *Gustav Landauer: Gedächtnisrede*, 2d ed. (Nürnberg, 1924), p. 11; Paul Breines, "The Jew as Revolutionary: The Case of Gustav Landauer," *Leo Baeck Yearbook*, XII (1967), 75. Richard Detlev Loewenberg compares Landauer's view of the state with the Old Testament prophet Samuel ("Gustav Landauer zum Gedächtnis," *Der Morgen* [Dec. 1928], pp. 462–472). Landauer himself wrote to Hans Blüher in February 1916 of the great importance of the prophetic books of the Old Testament for all Jews (see *Briefe*, II, 130).

134 Heydorn, foreword to GL, *Aufruf zum Sozialismus*, p. 23.

135 This point contradicts the view stated recently by Breines and Heydorn in the articles cited in notes 133 and 134 that Landauer's view of Judaism is of central importance to all his thought. Their evidence for this claim is taken almost entirely from the years 1913–1916, when the question was of importance for Landauer. Before that time, and especially before 1908, Landauer wrote almost nothing about matters pertaining to Judaism; he showed little concern, for example, for the anti-Semitic aspects of the Dreyfus affair (see *Briefe*, I, 37, and "Die Dichter als Ankläger," *Der Sozialist*, Feb. 5, 1898).

136 *Briefe*, I, 210, 218, 411–415.

137 *Ibid.*

138 *Werdende Mensch*, p. 244.

139 *Ibid.*, pp. 244–259. For a careful comparison of Buber's work on the Chasidim and Landauer's mystical views, see Ernst Simon, "Der Werdende Mensch und der Werdende Jude," *Der Jude*, VI (1921–22), 457–475. Simon claims that Landauer's social philosophy of community "between man and man" is particularly in line with Chasidic tradition, as in the Baal-Schem legend and the "Grossen Maggid."

140 Reprinted in *Werdende Mensch*, pp. 129–134.

141 *Briefe*, I, 448.

142 *Werdende Mensch*, p. 245.

143 Julius Bab, "Assimilation," *Die Freistatt: Alljüdische Revue*, I (1913–14), 171–176; GL, "Dur Poesie der Juden," *Die Freistatt*, I (1913–14), 321–324.

144 *Briefe*, I, 450.

[145] *Werdende Mensch*, p. 26. The translation is from Solomon Liptzin, *Germany's Stepchildren: An Examination of the Conflict of German and Jewish Identity in More Than Twenty Creative Figures*, 2d ed. (Cleveland and New York, 1961), pp. 231–232.

[146] For a recent comment on this phenomenon see Seymour Martin Lipset, "The Socialism of Fools': The Left, the Jews and Israel," *Encounter*, 33 (Dec. 1969).

[147] *Werdende Mensch*, pp. 122–128.

[148] GL, "Judentum und Sozialismus," *Die Arbeit: Organ der Zionistischen Volkssozialistischen Partei* (June 1920), pp. 50–51. This entire issue of *Die Arbeit* was devoted to articles by and about Gustav Landauer.

[149] GL, "Ostjuden und Deutsches Reich," *Der Jude*, I (Oct. 1916). Many German Jews feared that their poorer and more orthodox coreligionists from the east would help the anti-Semitic cause if they came to Germany. As Ismar Elbogen has pointed out (*Die Geschichte der Juden in Deutschland* [Frankfurt a. M., 1966], p. 280), many of the features of anti-Semitic action and thought were reproduced in this rejection of the *Ostjuden*.

[150] Liptzin, *Germany's Stepchildren*, p. 270.

[151] *Ibid.*, p. 238.

[152] "Gustav Landauer—Zum Gedächtnis," *Die Arbeit* (June 1920), p. 35; Martin Buber, "Der heimliche Führer," *Die Arbeit* (June 1920), p. 36.

[153] Kohn, *Martin Buber*, p. 36; Hans Kohn, *Living in a World Revolution: My Encounters with History* (New York, 1964), pp. 69–70. The name of the group was the Verein Jüdischer Hochschüler Barkochba.

[154] Mosse, *Crisis of German Ideology*, pp. 93–94.

[155] *Briefe*, I, 448. The translation is from Liptzin, *Germany's Stepchildren*, pp. 235–236.

[156] GL, "Die Lehre von Rassenkampf," *Der Sozialist*, Jan. 1, 1913.

[157] *Werdende Mensch*, p. 33.

[158] *Revolution*, p. 26.

[159] *Rechenschaft*, pp. 52–53.

[160] The failure of many historians to distinguish between antiparliamentary and antidemocratic ideas has been a frequent cause of confusion in the various attempts to trace the background of National Socialism. For a recent example of this confusion, see the work of Kurt Sontheimer, *Anti-demokratisches Denken in der Weimarer Republik* (München, 1962), and his article with

the same title in *The Path to Dictatorship,. 1918–1933*, pp. 32–49.
Although Sontheimer devotes much of his analysis to antiparliamentary views, he argues that he is tracing antidemocratic currents, neglecting the fact that there has long been a democratic
and antiauthoritarian critique of parliamentarism which, as a
result, is not protofascist, and that although most of his right-
wing examples were against parliament because they favored
monolithic control by an extraparliamentary movement, there is
no necessary connection between this and the dissatisfaction with
parliamentarism. As Landauer, Buber, Franz Oppenheimer, völkisch Zionists, and others of the communitarian Left revealed,
there is a left-wing rejection of parliaments which follows very
closely the classic analysis of Michels concerning the oligarchical
results of centralist parliamentarism. See Robert Michels, *Political Parties: A Sociological Study of the Oligarchical Tendencies
of Modern Democracy* (New York, 1962).
161 Edward Shils, "The Intellectuals and the Powers," in *On Intellectuals*, ed. Philip Rieff (New York, 1968), p. 49.
162 Berlin, "Herder and the Enlightenment," p. 77.
163 Peter Worsley's characterization of a populist Left and Right
provides a distinction that can readily be applied to the use of
the word "Volk" in Landauer's thought and that of Langbehn
and the völkisch Right: "The search for direct people-leadership
is one point along a continuum stretching from total non-
involvement of the mass of the people at one end to the ideal
anarchist self-regulating commune at the other. . . . From this
point of view, whilst we can recognize clearly mass participation
and involvement in, say, Nuremberg rallies and street-demon-
strations, it is important to distinguish serious, effective and independent popular intervention from purely illusory or symbolic
pseudo-'intervention' " (*Populism: Its Meaning and National
Characteristics*, ed. Ghitsa Ionescu and Ernest Gellner [London,
1967], p. 245).
164 Andrzej Walicki, "Russia," in *Populism*, p. 79.
165 Angus Stewart, "The Social Roots," in *Populism*, p. 192.
166 *Ibid.*, p. 183.
167 Mosse, *Crisis of German Ideology*, p. 15.
168 *Werdende Mensch*, pp. 51–52, 60–61. Recent psychological
studies, interestingly enough, have corroborated Landauer's view
of the crucial importance of prior and discriminate attachments
to family for the development of humanitarian behavior in later
life. Infants who had been brought up in public institutions and

who had not established intimate and discriminate emotional ties
with one or a few persons in early life soon exhibited both mental retardation—since memory seems to develop from the opportunity to discriminate between deeply familiar and unfamiliar
faces—and excessive aggressiveness. These findings are detailed
in an article by the child psychoanalyst Dr. Selma Fraiberg,
"The Origins of Human Bonds," *Commentary* (Dec. 1967),
pp. 47–57. Needless to say, aggressive behavior is far from precluded by such prior attachments. The point, of course, is that
they are necessary but not sufficient for precluding it.

169 *Werdende Mensch*, p. 64. See also *ibid.*, pp. 57–58, 60, and *Briefe*,
  I, 249–250.
170 *Aufruf zum Sozialismus*, p. 13.
171 *Ibid.*, pp. 6–8; "Judentum und Sozialismus," p. 50.
172 GL, *Ein Weg deutschen Geistes*, no. 2 of *Kleine Schriften*, ed.
  Wilhelm Herzog (München, 1916), pp. 4–5, 26.
173 *Rechenschaft*, p. 148.
174 *Werdende Mensch*, pp. 358–359. See also GL, "Die Neue Freie
  Volksbühne," *Die Schaubühne*, Oct. 19, 1905, p. 194.
175 *Werdende Mensch*, p. 342.
176 *Ibid.*, p. 72.
177 *Briefe*, I, 149–150.
178 GL, "Die Neue Freie Volksbühne."
179 *Ibid.*
180 *Ein Weg deutschen Geistes*, pp. 15, 31–32.
181 GL, "Walt Whitman," *Der Sozialist*, Dec. 25, 1913, reprinted
  as the introduction to Landauer's posthumously published translations of Whitman's poetry: Walt Whitman, *Gesänge und
  Inschriften* (München, 1921).
182 For a good discussion of Landauer and Hölderlin, see Wilhelm
  Michel, *Essays über Gustav Landauer, Romain Rolland, Friedrich Hölderlin: Die Metaphysik des Bürgers* (Hannover, 1920),
  pp. 6–7.
183 *Der Sozialist*, Sept. 25, 1913.
184 *Werdende Mensch*, pp. 175–187.
185 E. M. Butler, *The Tyranny of Greece over Germany* (Boston,
  1955), p. 216.
186 *Werdende Mensch*, pp. 175–178.
187 *Ein Weg deutschen Geistes*, pp. 4–5, 26, 31–32, 34.
188 Siegfried Nestriepke, *Geschichte der Volksbühne Berlin*, I
  (Berlin, 1930), 194, 308.
189 *Briefe*, II, 268–269, 290, 296; Kohn, *Martin Buber*, p. 306.

190 Maurer, *Call to Revolution*, pp. 150–151. In a letter to Jacob Hegner (GL Archiv, fol. S) dated Jan. 16, 1919, Landauer commented on the similarity of his own views with those of Dumont.

191 Blüher, *Werke und Tage*, p. 385; Arnold Zweig, "Gustav Landauers Shakespeare-Buch," in *Essays*, I (Berlin, 1959), 34; *Briefe*, II, 160, 180–187.

192 GL, *Shakespeare: Dargestellt in Vorträgen*, ed. Martin Buber, 2d ed., 2 vols. (Frankfurt a. M., 1923). The first edition of this work, published in 1920, was entitled *Vorträge über Shakespeare*. A third edition, entitled simply *Shakespeare*, was published in Hamburg in 1962 by the original publisher, Verlag Rütten & Loening.

193 For a review of the critical reception of Landauer's book see Maurer, *Call to Revolution*, pp. 155–158.

194 *Essays*, I, 35. The essay first appeared on May 7, 1950, in the Berlin paper *Sonntag*.

195 *Briefe*, II, 190.

196 *Shakespeare: Dargestellt in Vorträgen*, I, 154–155.

197 *Ibid.*, p. 215.

198 *Ibid.*, II, 394. For a different völkisch interpretation of Shakespeare see Langbehn's *Rembrandt als Erzieher*, ed. Gerhard Kruger (Berlin: T. Fritsch, 1944). Shakespeare, of course, was long a favorite of German romantics, beginning with Schlegel's famous translation of the 1790s.

199 *Shakespeare: Dargestellt in Vorträgen*, I, 240–241.

200 *Ibid.*, I, 4; II, 115.

201 *Ibid.*, II, 394.

202 *Ibid.*, p. 283. I have been guided on certain points of this analysis of Landauer's Shakespeare lectures by Maurer, *Call to Revolution*, pp. 155–164, to which the reader should turn for a more detailed description of the individual lectures. The interpretation of Landauer's Shakespeare criticism as a revelation of his völkisch romanticism and anarchist philosophy of voluntary servitude is, however, my own.

## 6. REVOLUTION IN BAVARIA

1 GL, *Sein Lebensgang in Briefen*, ed. Martin Buber, 2 vols. (Frankfurt a. M., 1929), II, 243, 255 (hereafter cited as *Briefe*).

2 *Ibid.*, p. 278.

3 *Ibid.*, pp. 275–276.

4 This view was expressed in the influential work of Arthur Rosen-

berg, *The Birth of the German Republic*, first published in 1928. See the Beacon Press edition entitled *Imperial Germany: The Birth of the German Republic* (Boston, 1964), pp. 242–278.

5 Reinhard Rürup, "Problems of the German Revolution, 1918–19," *Journal of Contemporary History*, 3 (Oct. 1968), 115–118, 134. The article is based upon the archival research contained in the important works of Eberhard Kolb, *Die Arbeiterräte in der deutschen Innenpolitik, 1918–19* (Düsseldorf, 1962), and Peter von Oertzen, *Die Betriebsräte in der Novemberrevolution* (Düsseldorf: Droste Verlag, 1965). See also Rürup's article, "Rätebewegung und Revolution in Deutschland, 1918–19," *Neue Politische Literatur*, XII (1967).

6 Alan Mitchell, *Revolution in Bavaria, 1918–19: Kurt Eisner and the Bavarian Soviet Republic* (Princeton, 1965), p. 5. This work is the clearest account I have seen of the complex events in Bavaria in 1918–19.

7 Carl Landauer, "The Bavarian Problem in the Weimar Republic, 1918–1933: Part I," *Journal of Modern History*, XVI (June 1944), 93.

8 Sterling Fishman, "Prophets, Poets and Priests: A Study of the Men and Ideas That Made the Munich Revolution of 1918–19" (Ph.D. dissertation, University of Wisconsin, 1960), p. 24.

9 Georg Franz, "Munich: Birthplace and Center of the National Socialist German Workers' Party," *Journal of Modern History*, XXIX (1957), 322–323; Fishman, "Prophets, Poets and Priests," p. 19.

10 Franz, "Munich," pp. 320–321. See also Hans Beyer, *Von der November Revolution zur Räterepublik in München* (Berlin, 1957), p. 24.

11 Franz, "Munich," pp. 320–321.

12 Koppel S. Pinson, *Modern Germany: Its History and Civilization* (New York, 1954), p. 357.

13 *Ibid.*, p. 358.

14 Fishman, "Prophets, Poets and Priests," pp. 66, 70.

15 *Ibid.*, p. 69.

16 *Briefe*, II, 289–290, 301.

17 *Ibid.*, pp. 291–292.

18 *Ibid.*, p. 300.

19 *Ibid.*, pp. 313, 318.

20 *Ibid.*, p. 292.

21 *Ibid.*, p. 322.

[22] *Ibid.*, p. 297.

[23] *Ibid.*, p. 296n. I have been unable to discover how and when Landauer and Eisner met and became friends. The first letter from Landauer to Eisner which I have seen is dated August 14, 1917, Gustav Landauer Archives, International Institute of Social History, Amsterdam, fol. R (hereafter cited as GL Archiv).

[24] *Briefe*, II, 332, 355, 359, 365.

[25] Fishman, "Prophets, Poets and Priests," pp. 63, 136–137, 145.

[26] *Ibid.*, p. 105.

[27] Erich Mühsam, *Von Eisner bis Levine: Persönlicher Rechenschaftsbericht* (Berlin, 1929), p. 14.

[28] Fishman, "Prophets, Poets and Priests," p. 53.

[29] Mühsam, *Von Eisner bis Levine*, p. 13; Beyer, *Von der November Revolution*, p. 50.

[30] Mitchell, *Revolution in Bavaria*, p. 153.

[31] *Ibid.*

[32] Franz Schade, *Kurt Eisner und die bayerische Sozialdemokratie* (Hannover, 1961), p. 154.

[33] *Briefe*, II, 366n.

[34] Oskar Maria Graf, *Prisoners All*, trans. Margaret Green (New York, 1928), p. 359.

[35] Mühsam, *Von Eisner bis Levine*, p. 16.

[36] Fishman, "Prophets, Poets and Priests," pp. 209–211.

[37] Erich Mühsam, *Unpolitische Erinnerungen* (Berlin, 1961), p. 35.

[38] Fishman, "Prophets, Poets and Priests," pp. 195–197; *Briefe*, I, 166–167.

[39] Fishman, "Prophets, Poets and Priests," pp. 209–210.

[40] *Briefe*, II, 336.

[41] *Ibid.*, p. 316.

[42] *Ibid.*, p. 308.

[43] *Ibid.*, p. 308n.

[44] *Ibid.*, p. 317.

[45] *Ibid.*, p. 311.

[46] *Ibid.*, pp. 315–316. For a recent Communist critique of Landauer's Räte conception, see Beyer, *Von der November Revolution*, pp. 84–85.

[47] This is the opinion of Helmut Rüdiger in his article, "Ein deutsche freiheitlicher Sozialist," in *Gustav Landauer: Kämpfer und Künder der Freiheit* (Darmstadt, 1951), pp. 19, 21. Landauer mentioned his reading of Frantz in his speech to the Provisional National Council, "Deutschland und seine Revolution," which was later published in *Erkenntnis und Befreiung*, I (1919), no. 9.

48 GL, "Die vereinigten Republiken Deutschlands und ihre Verfassung," in *Das Flugblatt*, ed. Norbert Einstein (Frankfurt a. M., 1918), Pt. 3, p. 5.

49 *Ibid.*, pp. 3–4.

50 See *Briefe*, II, 308–314, for other statements of Landauer's federalist dream of November 1918.

51 Fishman, "Prophets, Poets and Priests," pp. 86–88.

52 Mitchell, *Revolution in Bavaria*, p. 126.

53 Pinson, *Modern Germany*, p. 400.

54 Fishman, "Prophets, Poets and Priests," pp. 76, 79–80.

55 Pinson, *Modern Germany*, p. 368.

56 *Ibid.*, pp. 381–382.

57 *Briefe*, II, 332.

58 *Ibid.*, p. 298n.

59 *Ibid.*, p. 341.

60 *Ibid.*, p. 342.

61 *Ibid.*, p. 376.

62 *Ibid.*, p. 355. The translation is from Fishman, "Prophets, Poets and Priests," pp. 154–155.

63 Martin Buber, "Recollection of a Death," in *Pointing the Way* (New York, 1957), p. 119.

64 *Briefe*, II, 357.

65 Mitchell, *Revolution in Bavaria*, pp. 217–218.

66 Fishman, "Prophets, Poets and Priests," p. 97.

67 *Briefe*, II, 359.

68 *Ibid.*, pp. 364–365.

69 Fishman, "Prophets, Poets and Priests," p. 109.

70 *Briefe*, II, 368.

71 *Ibid.*, p. 376.

72 *Ibid.*, p. 370.

73 GL, "Überschätzung der Wahlen," *Die Republik*, Jan. 21, 1919.

74 *Ibid.*

75 Mitchell, *Revolution in Bavaria*, p. 124.

76 *Ibid.*, p. 241.

77 *Ibid.*, pp. 124–125.

78 *Briefe*, II, 360–361n.

79 *Ibid.*

80 Mitchell, *Revolution in Bavaria*, pp. 245–249.

81 *Neue Zeitung* (organ of the Bavarian USPD), Feb. 10, 1919. See also Mühsam, *Von Eisner bis Levine*, p. 20.

82 *Briefe*, II, 382–383. The rally was advocated by Landauer for the purpose of demonstrating mass support "for the Räte system and

the construction of a new, genuine democracy in opposition to the old parliamentarism" (*Neue Zeitung*, Feb. 10, 1919), but in the confused march that took place there were signs ranging from "Long Live the Council System" to "Against Bolshevism" and "For the Landtag." Estimates of attendance varied considerably: the USPD paper, *Neue Zeitung*, numbered the marchers at 150,-000 while the SPD paper, the *Münchener Post*, claimed that only 9,000 participated. The undeniable radical spirit of most of the demonstrators was rationalized by the Majority Socialists as the work of professional agitators. (Mitchell, *Revolution in Bavaria*, p. 262.)

83 *Briefe*, II, 382.

84 Fishman, "Prophets, Poets and Priests," p. 98.

85 Blüher, *Werke und Tage* (München, 1953), pp. 400-401.

86 Fritz Oerter, "Gustav Landauer," *Die Internationale*, I (Jan. 1925), 27.

87 Schade, *Kurt Eisner und die bayerische Sozialdemokratie*, pp. 85-86; Mitchell, *Revolution in Bavaria*, p. 252; Mühsam, *Von Eisner bis Levine*, p. 21.

88 *Neue Zeitung*, Feb. 14, 1919.

89 *Bayerische Staatszeitung*, Feb. 21, 1919.

90 *Münchener-Augsburger Abendzeitung*, Feb. 17, 1919.

91 *Bayerische Staatszeitung*, Feb. 18, 1919.

92 *Neue Zeitung*, Feb. 19, 1919.

93 Beyer, *Von der November Revolution*, p. 24; Fishman, "Prophets, Poets and Priests," p. 160.

94 Mitchell, *Revolution in Bavaria*, pp. 268-269.

95 *Briefe*, II, 385; Fishman, "Prophets, Poets and Priests," p.110

96 Fishman, "Prophets, Poets and Priests," p. 109.

97 See Buber, "Recollection of a Death," p. 119.

98 Mitchell, *Revolution in Bavaria*, p. 276. The entire address was printed in the journal *Arbeit und Zukunft* two days later. See GL, "Gedächtnisrede bei der Beisetzung Kurt Eisners am Februar 26, 1919, in der Halle des Ostfriedhofs," *Arbeit und Zukunft*, Feb. 28, 1919, pp. 50-54.

99 *Briefe*, II, 386.

100 Fishman, "Prophets, Poets and Priests," p. 113.

101 Kolb, *Die Arbeiterräte*, p. 335.

102 Mitchell, *Revolution in Bavaria*, p. 273.

103 Fishman, "Prophets, Poets and Priests," p. 159.

104 *Briefe*, II, 387n; see also Mühsam, *Von Eisner bis Levine*, p. 31.

105 *Briefe*, II, 387n.
106 Mühsam, *Von Eisner bis Levine*, p. 31.
107 *Ibid.*
108 Fishman, "Prophets, Poets and Priests," pp. 161–162; Mitchell, *Revolution in Bavaria*, pp. 287–289.
109 Pinson, *Modern Germany*, pp. 387–388.
110 Mitchell, *Revolution in Bavaria*, p. 286.
111 *Briefe*, II, 403.
112 *Ibid.*, pp. 403–404. This letter was reprinted in *Neue Zeitung*, March 29, 1919, and entitled "Von der Rätedemokratie und dem Weg der Revolution: Ein Brief."
113 For interesting applications of anarchist theory to the modern city, stressing the importance of decentralized local neighborhood community life, see the works of Lewis Mumford and Paul Goodman, for example, especially the latter's *Communitas* (New York: Vintage Books, 1960), and *People or Personnel* (New York: Random House, 1965).
114 *Briefe*, II, 397.
115 *Ibid.*, p. 395.
116 *Ibid.*, p. 407.
117 Fishman, "Prophets, Poets and Priests," p. 163.
118 Briefe, II, 399.
119 *Münchener-Augsburger Abendzeitung*, April 1, 1919.
120 Mühsam, *Von Eisner bis Levine*, p. 39.
121 See, for example, the account in S. William Halperin's standard political history of the Weimar Republic, *Germany Tried Democracy: A Political History of the Reich from 1918 to 1933* (New York, 1946), pp. 123–124, where the author writes: "Early in April, 1919, the Landauer-Toller group decided that the moment had come to effectuate their plans. They got the Workers' and Soldiers' Council of Augsburg to demand the establishment of a soviet republic. The Social Democrats felt powerless to resist this demand which was supported by large crowds of workers in Munich." Such a view was widely circulated in the press of the time and was based upon the statement of a certain member of the Augsburg council, named Prem, who alleged that Landauer had instructed him to have the council make this proclamation. One of the delegates who was sent to Munich to forward the decision of the Augsburg council, however, a certain Wilhelm Olschewski, was informed by Landauer that he had never spoken to Prem, that he was not

among those who were responsible for the calling of the Räterepublik, and that the calling of a council government was a machination of the Bavarian SPD. (*Briefe*, II, 412-413n, which is based upon Wilhelm Olschewski, "Die Ausrufung der Räterepublik in Augsburg am 7. April, 1919," *Neue Zeitung*, April 8, 1927.)

122 Mitchell, *Revolution in Bavaria*, p. 307. Mitchell's account includes a review of the recent literature on the proclamation of the Räterepublik.

123 Mühsam, *Von Eisner bis Levine*, pp. 45-46.

124 *Briefe*, II, 413n.

125 Mühsam, *Von Eisner bis Levine*, pp. 48-49.

126 Mitchell, *Revolution in Bavaria*, p. 309; Mühsam, *Von Eisner bis Levine*, pp. 7, 43-49; Kolb, *Die Arbeiterräte*, p. 338.

127 Mitchell, *Revolution in Bavaria*, p. 309.

128 G. L. Waite, *The Vanguard of Nazism: The Free Corps Movement in Postwar Germany, 1918-1925* (Cambridge, Mass., 1952), p. 82.

129 *Briefe*, II, 414.

130 Quoted in Fishman, "Prophets, Poets and Priests," pp. 166-167.

131 For evidence of Landauer's personality change during the last months of his life, a change marked by growing impatience and intolerance, see Stefan Grossman, "Gustav Landauer," *Das Tagebuch*, May 4, 1929, p. 736, and Julius Bab, *Gustav Landauer: Gedächtnisrede*, 2d ed. (Nürnberg, 1924), pp. 26-27.

132 Fishman, "Prophets, Poets and Priests," pp. 219, 248.

133 Mühsam, *Von Eisner bis Levine*, p. 43; Mitchell, *Revolution in Bavaria*, p. 311.

134 Mitchell, *Revolution in Bavaria*, p. 314.

135 *Ibid.*, pp. 295-297, 304-305.

136 Fishman, "Prophets. Poets and Priests," p. 249; Beyer, *Von der November Revolution*, p. 85.

137 *Münchener Neueste Nachrichten*, April 9, 1919.

138 For this and other matters connected with the University of Munich during Landauer's tenure in office in the Räterepublik, see Egon Wertheimer, "Verteidigung," *Das Tribunal*, I (Dec. 1919), 129-132, and GL Archiv, Dossier AA, pt. 2.

139 Fishman, "Prophets, Poets and Priests," p. 167.

140 Fidelis, "Gustav Landauers Kulturprogramm," *Das Forum*, 4 (May 1920), 577-599. The entire program is analyzed in detail in Fishman, "Prophets, Poets and Priests," pp. 167-170.

[141] Fields, "Gustav Landauers Kulturprogramm."

[142] Ben Hecht, *A Child of the Century* (New York, 1954), p. 306.

[143] Fidelis, "Gustav Landauers Kulturprogramm," pp. 586–588.

[144] *Ibid.*, pp. 583–586.

[145] Graf, *Prisoners All*, pp. 397–400.

[146] Max Gerstl, *Die Münchener Räterepublik* (München, 1919), p. 37.

[147] Wally Zepler, "Landauer," *Sozialistische Monatshefte*, I (1919), 646.

[148] Cf. Rudolf Rocker, "Revolution und Rückfall in die Barbarei," typescript, Rocker memoirs in Rocker Archives, International Institute of Social History, Amsterdam, III, 118; Ernst Toller, *Look through the Bars*, trans. R. Ellis Roberts (New York, 1937), pp. 51–52; Hiram K. Morderwell, "The Blood of Munich," *The Liberator* (Sept. 1919), p. 13; and Fishman, "Prophets, Poets and Priests," p. 177.

[149] Fishman, "Prophets, Poets and Priests," p. 8. Fishman relies especially on the diary of Josef Hofmiller, *Revolutionstagebuch 1918/19: Aus den Tagen der Münchener Revolution* (Leipzig: K. Rauch, 1939).

[150] Fishman, "Prophets, Poets and Priests," pp. 165, 177.

[151] *Ibid.*, p. 177.

[152] *Ibid.*, pp. 290–293.

[153] *Briefe*, II, 416.

[154] *Ibid.*, p. 418n. In the standard Communist account of the revolution, Hans Beyer's *Von der November Revolution*, Landauer is lauded for this action: "With this," Beyer writes, "he proved his great personal courage and, in spite of his rejection of Marxism, his efforts for the cause of the proletariat."

[155] *Briefe*, II, 420–421.

[156] *Ibid.*, p. 421n.

[157] On this last point see Mühsam, *Von Eisner bis Levine*, p. 60.

[158] For other assessments of Landauer's failure in 1918–19, see Blüher, *Werke und Tage*, pp. 387, 400; Edgar Hahnewald, "Landauers französische Revolutionsbriefe," *Neue Zeit*, May 16, 1919, pp. 169–170; obituary notice on Landauer written by Hans Franck in *Frankfurter Zeitung*, May 15, 1919. On the political impotency of anarchism in competition with Marxists, both Social Democrats and Communists, see Irving L. Horowitz, ed., *The Anarchists* (New York, 1964), pp. 16, 590–591, 596–597.

159 Mitchell, *Revolution in Bavaria*, p. 275.

160 Fishman, "Prophets, Poets and Priests," p. 255.

161 Ernst Toller, *I Was a German: The Autobiography of Ernst Toller*, trans. Edward Crankshaw (New York, 1934), pp. 248–249.

162 Toller, *Look through the Bars*, pp. 43–44.

163 Cf. Arthur Rosenberg, *A History of the German Republic* (London, 1936), chaps. 1, 2.

164 Fishman, "Prophets, Poets and Priests," p. 180.

165 E. J. Gumbel, "154 Bayerische Morde," *Das Forum*, VI (April 1922), 236–237, and "Gustav Landauers Ende," *Weltbühne* (1924), no. 7, p. 193.

166 *Briefe*, II, 386.

167 See Bab, *Gustav Landauer: Gedächtnisrede*, pp. 26–27; Grossman, "Gustav Landauer," p. 736.

168 Buber, *Pointing the Way*, p. 119.

169 Fritz Mauthner, "Zum Gedächtnis," *Masken*, XIV (1918–19), 304; Stefan Grossman, *Ich war begeistert: Eine Lebensgeschichte* (Berlin, 1931), p. 283.

170 B. J. Kenworthy, *Georg Kaiser* (London, 1957), p. xviii.

171 *Briefe*, II, 423–424n.

172 Arnold Zweig, "Landauer," *Arbeit* (June 1920), p. 38.

## CONCLUSION

1 Wolfgang Sauer, "National Socialism: Totalitarianism or Fascism?" *American Historical Review*, LXXIII (Dec. 1967), 423.

2 See Weber's conversation with Ludendorff in *From Max Weber: Essays in Sociology* (New York: Oxford University Press, 1958), p. 42; see also the important work by Wolfgang Mommsen, *Max Weber und die deutsche Politik* (Tübingen: Mohr, 1959).

3 Harry Pross, *Jugend-Eros-Politik: Die Geschichte der deutschen Jugendverbände* (München, 1964), pp. 220–221.

4 *Ibid.*, pp. 210–212, 216.

5 *Ibid.*, pp. 219–227.

6 Karl O. Paetel, *Jugendbewegung und Politik* (Bad Godesberg, 1961), p. 37.

7 Walter Laqueur, *Young Germany* (New York, 1962), p. 160.

8 On right-wing völkisch thought in the Weimar Republic see Kurt Sontheimer, *Anti-demokratisches Denken in der Weimarer Republik* (München, 1962). On the split between communi-

tarian and democratic currents in this period see the suggestive article by Carl E. Schorske, "Weimar and the Intellectuals," *New York Review of Books*, May 7, 21, 1970.

9 Laqueur, *Young Germany*, p. 161.

10 This tendency, for example, pervades Peter Gay, *Weimar Culture: The Outsider as Insider* (New York: Harper and Row, 1968). See the critical review by Arthur Mitzman, "Modernism and Weimar," *Dissent*, XVI (May–June 1969), 282–286.

# Bibliography

[As an aid to further research on Landauer I have included comments on the secondary works that have proved particularly helpful in my research.]

## LANDAUER'S WRITINGS

UNPUBLISHED MATERIAL

The Landauer Archives at the International Institute of Social History, Amsterdam, consist primarily of a large collection of unpublished letters written or received by Landauer from 1888 to 1919. The following is an outline of this Landauer *Nachlass.* Folio X (unpublished letters from the formative years, 1888–1900) was particularly useful for this study.

A. 1. Manuskript von Ludwig Berndl
2. GL's Briefe an LB
B. Im Memoriam GL (Originalstücke; Artikel, u.s.w.)
C. 1. Gymnasium, Universität
2–3. Processen
4. Foto
D. 1. Tagebuch 1884–85
2. Notizbücher
3–6. Notizen, u.s.w.
E–F. Briefe von GL. Familie Korrespondenz
L-Charlotte
G. L-Lachmann, Hedwig
L-Leuschner, Margaret
H. L-Neuberger, R. (mother)
I. L-Siegfried (cousin)
Clara (cousin)
J–M. Übrige Korrespondenz
N–P. Original Briefe an GL
Q–W. Briefe von GL (most of these were published in *Sein Lebensgang in Briefen*).

X. Jugendband (Briefe und Aufsätzen Landauers, 1888–1900)
Y. Manuskripte
Z. Der Kreis 1914. Briefe, Kopien, Aufsätze, u.s.w.
Dossiers:
  AA. München 1919
    1. Reden und Aufsätze von GL
    2. Die Vorgänge an der Münchener Universität unter dem Volkskommissariat GL.
  BB. 1. Studenten Kongress 1891
    2–3. Zentralstelle Völkerrecht, 1915–1918.
    4. Kleine Dossiers.

## BOOKS AND PAMPHLETS

*An den Züricher Kongress: Bericht über die deutsche Arbeiterbewegung.* Berlin: W. Werner Verlag, 1893.

*Aufruf zum Sozialismus.* 2d ed. Berlin: Paul Cassirer Verlag, 1919.

*Beginnen: Aufsätze über Sozialismus.* Ed. Martin Buber. Köln: Marean-Block Verlag, 1924.

*Ein Weg deutschen Geistes.* No. 2 of *Kleine Schriften.* Ed. Wilhelm Herzog. München: Forum Verlag, 1916.

*Ein Weg zur Befreiung der Arbeiterklasse.* Berlin: Verlag von Adolf Marreck, 1895.

*Der Fall Ziethen.* Berlin: Hugo Metscher Verlag, 1898.

*Macht und Mächte.* Berlin: Verlag Egon Fleischel, 1903.

*Rechenschaft.* 1st ed. Berlin: Paul Cassirer Verlag, 1919.

*Die Revolution.* Frankfurt a. M.: Verlag Rütten & Loening, 1908.

*Sein Lebensgang in Briefen.* Ed. Martin Buber. 2 vols. Frankfurt a. M.: Verlag Rütten & Loening, 1929.

*Shakespeare: Dargestellt in Vorträgen.* Ed. Martin Buber. 2d ed. 2 vols. Frankfurt a. M.: Verlag Rütten & Loening, 1923.

*Skepsis und Mystik: Versuche im Anschluss an Mauthners Sprachkritik.* 2d ed. Köln: F. J. Marcan Verlag, 1923.

*Social Democracy in Germany.* London, 1896.

*Der Todesprediger.* 3d ed. Köln: F. J. Marcan Verlag, 1923.

*Die vereinigten Republiken Deutschlands und ihre Verfassung.*

Heft 3 of *Das Flugblatt.* Ed. Norbert Einstein. Frankfurt
a. M.: Tiedemann und Uzielli, 1918.
*Der Werdende Mensch: Aufsätze über Leben und Schriftum.*
Ed. Martin Buber. Potsdam: G. Kiepenheuer Verlag, 1921.

TRANSLATIONS

*Briefe aus der französischen Revolution.* 2 vols. Frankfurt
a. M.: Verlag Rütten & Loening, 1918.
Kropotkin, Peter. *Die französische Revolution, 1789-1793.*
Leipzig: Theodor Thomas Verlag, 1909.
————. *Gegenseitige Hilfe in der Entwicklung.* Leipzig, 1904.
————. *Landwirtschaft, Industrie, und "Handwerk."* 2d ed.
Berlin, 1910.
*Meister Eckharts Mystische Schriften.* Berlin: Karl Schnabel
Verlag, 1903.
Shaw, Bernard. *Sozialismus für Millionäre.* Berlin: Verlag Her-
mann Ehbork, n.d.
Whitman, Walt. *Gesänge und Inschriften.* München, 1921.
Wilde, Oscar. *Der Sozialismus und die Seele des Menschen.*
Trans. Hedwig Lachmann and Gustav Landauer. Berlin:
Karl Schnabel Verlag, 1904.

ARTICLES

"Alles oder Nichts!" *Der Sozialist,* Oct. 12, 1895.
"Anarchische Gedanken über den Anarchismus," *Die Zukunft,*
Oct. 26, 1901.
"Der Anarchismus in Deutschland," *Die Zukunft,* Jan. 5, 1895.
"Arbeiter aller Länder, vereinigt euch!" *Der Sozialist,* Sept. 28,
1895.
"Aus der Zeit," *Der Sozialist,* Aug. 17, 1895.
"Aus meinem Gefängnis-Tagebuch," *Sozialistische Akade-
miker,* I (1895), nos. 13-18.
"Bayreuth," *Der Sozialist,* Aug. 15, 1912.
"Die beiden Märztage," *Der Sozialist,* March 15, 1909.
"Die Blaue Blume," *Nation: Wochenschrift für Politik, Volks-
wirtschaft und Literatur,* 17 (1900), no. 28.
"Börne und der Anarchismus," *Sozialistische Monatshefte*
(1899), pp. 353-355

"Brot," *Der Sozialist*, June 1, 1911.

"Deutschland und seine Revolution," *Erkenntnis und Befreiung*, I (1918), nos. 6, 7, 9.

"Dühringianer und Marxisten," *Der Sozialist*, Oct. 22, 1892.

"Durch Absonderung zur Gemeinschaft." In Heinrich Hart and Julius Hart, eds. *Das Reich der Erfüllung: Flugschriften zur Begründung einen neuen Weltanschauung*. Leipzig: Eugen Diedrichs Verlag, 1901.

"Der Erste Mai," *Der Sozialist*, May 1, 1909.

"Der Fall Liebknecht," *Der Sozialist*, Aug. 29, 1896.

"Fichte 1813," *Der Sozialist*, May 15, 1913.

"Die französische Syndikalisten," *Der Sozialist*, June 1, 1909.

"Der gallische Hahn und der deutsche Esel," *Der Sozialist*, Aug. 13, 1898.

"Gedächtnisrede bei der Beisetzung Kurt Eisners am Februar 26, 1919, in der Halle des Ostfriedhofs," *Arbeit und Zukunft*, Feb. 28, 1919.

"Gerhard Hauptmann," *Neue Zeit*, X (1892), 612–621.

"Die Gespenster," *Der Sozialist*, Jan. 15, 1910.

"Gewerkschaftskampf," *Der Sozialist*, June 24, 1893.

"Im Kampf um die Weltanschauung: Stimmungen zu M. von Egidy's Tod," *Der Sozialist*, IX (1899), no. 2.

"Individualismus," *Der Sozialist*, May 15, July 15, 1911.

"Judentum und Sozialismus," *Die Arbeit: Organ der Zionistischen Volkssozialistischen Partei* (June 1920).

"Die Krise in der revolutionären Bewegung," *Der Sozialist*, June 4, 1898.

"Land-Agitation," *Der Sozialist*, June 24, 1893.

"Die Lehre vom Rassenkampf," *Der Sozialist*, Jan. 1, 1913.

"Liebe Kameraden!" *Freie Arbeiter*, June 5, 1909.

"Der Londoner Kongress und die Anarchie," *Der Sozialist*, Aug. 15, 22, 1896.

"M. von Egidy und der 'Sozialistische Akademiker,'" *Sozialistische Akademiker*, II (1896), 186–187.

"MacNamara," *Der Sozialist*, March 1, 1912.

"Manchesterfreiheit-Staatshülfe-Anarchie," *Der Sozialist*, June 24, 1893.

"März 1910," *Der Sozialist*, March 15, 1910.
"Memoiren eines Revolutionäres," *Die Ziel: Wiener Wochenschrift*, Dec. 22, 1900.
"Die Neue Freie Volksbühne," *Die Schaubühne*, Oct. 19, 1905.
"Der neue Gott von Julius Hart," *Die Gesellschaft*, Oct. 2, 1899.
"Die neue Welterkenntnis," *Die Kultur*, I (1902), 607–617.
"Ostjuden und Deutsches Reich," *Der Jude*, I (Oct. 1916).
"Paracelsus," *Literarische Echo*, VII (1905), 1561.
"Parlamentskritik," *Das Blaubuch*, May 30, 1907.
"Die Partei," *Der Sozialist*, Oct. 1, 1909.
"Philister über du, Hauptmann!" *Der Sozialist*, July 1, 1913.
"Der Pionier," *Der Sozialist*, Oct. 10, 1913.
"Preussen," *Diskussion: Eine Monatschrift für aktuelle Kulturfragen* (1910), Heft 2, pp. 66–70.
"Referat über Eugen Dührings 'Kursus der National- und Sozialoekonomie,' " *Der Sozialist*, Aug. 27, 1892.
"Reiseberichte," *Der Sozialist*, Oct. 23, Nov. 27, 1897.
"Die Religiöse Jugenderziehung," *Freie Bühne für modernes Leben*, Feb. 11, 1891.
"Rückkehr in die Grossstadt," *Der Sozialist*, Sept. 15, 1912.
"Der Schlendrian," *Der Sozialist*, Sept. 15, 1910.
"Die sozialdemokratische Wahlagitation," *Der Sozialist*, June 10, 1893.
"Soziale und politische Revolution." Afterword to W. Tscherkesoff, *Die Krise in Russland*. Berlin: Verlag des Sozialistischen Bund, 1909.
"Sozialismus und Genossenschaft," *Der Sozialist*, Oct. 13, 1910.
"Tuckers Eröffnung," *Der Sozialist*, May 15, 1911.
"Über epische und dramatische Dichtung," *Deutschland*, Jan. 4, 11, 1890.
"Überschätzung der Wahlen," *Die Republik*, Jan. 21, 1919.
"Die unmoralische Weltordnung," *Der Sozialist*, Aug. 24, 1895.
"Von der tierischen Grundlage," *Weltbühne*, July 4, 1918.
"Von Micheln und Antimicheln," *Der Sozialist*, Aug. 6, 1898.
"Vortragscyklus zur Geschichte der deutsche Literatur," *Der Sozialist*, Feb. 26, 1898.

"Walt Whitman," *Der Sozialist*, Dec. 25, 1913.
"Wesen und Aussichten des Revolutionarismus," *Die Welt am Montag*, May 10, 1899.
"Die Wiedergeburt des 'Sozialist,' " *Der Sozialist*, Aug. 17, 1895.
"Wie nennen wir uns?," *Der Sozialist*, April 1, 1893.
"Zukunftsmenschen," *Die Zukunft*, June 23, 1900.
"Die Zukunft und die Kunst," *Neue Zeit*, X (1892), 532–535.
"Zur Entwicklungsgeschichte des Individuums," *Der Sozialist*, Nov. 2, 16, 30, 1895; Jan. 11, Feb. 1, 8, 1896.
"Zur frage: Wie nennen wir uns?" *Der Sozialist*, April 8, 1893.
"Zur Geschichte des Wortes 'Anarchie,' " *Der Sozialist*, June 1, 1909.
"Züricher Kongress," *Der Sozialist*, Aug. 26, 1893.
"Zur Poesie der Juden," *Freistatt*, 22 (Aug. 1913).

## OTHER PRIMARY SOURCES

NEWSPAPERS
*Bayerische Staatszeitung*
*Die Freistatt: Alljüdische Revue*
*Münchener-Augsburger Abendzeitung*
*Münchener Neueste Nachrichten*
*Neue Zeitung* (Bavarian organ of USPD)
*Der Sozialist* (Berlin)

MEMOIRS, LETTERS, AND AUTOBIOGRAPHIES
Blüher, Hans. *Werke und Tage*. München: Paul List Verlag, 1953. On Landauer, see pp. 375 ff
*Briefe an Auguste Hauschner*. Ed. Martin Beradt and Lotte Bloch-Zavkel. Berlin: Ernst Rowohlt Verlag, 1929.
Brupbacher, Fritz. *60 Jahre Ketzer: Selbstbiographie*. Zürich: B. Ruppli, 1935.
Graf, Oskar Maria. *Prisoners All*. Trans. Margaret Green. New York: Alfred A. Knopf, 1928.
Grossman, Stefan. *Ich war begeistert: Eine Lebensgeschichte*. Berlin: S. Fischer Verlag, 1931.
Hecht, Ben. *A Child of the Century*. New York: Simon & Schuster, 1954.

Hiller, Kurt. *Köpfe und Tröpfe: Profile aus einem Vierteljahr-hundert.* Hamburg: Rowohlt Verlag, 1950.

Jung, Franz. *Der Weg nach unten: Aufzeichnungen aus einer Grossen Zeit.* Berlin: Hermann Luchterhand Verlag, 1961.

Kohn, Hans. *Living in a World Revolution: My Encounters with History.* New York: Trident Press, 1964.

Leixner, Otto von. *1888 bis 1891: Soziale Briefe aus Berlin. Mit besonderer Berücksichtigung der sozialdemokratischen Strö-mungen.* Berlin: Verlag von Friedrich Pfeilstücker, 1891

Mühsam, Erich. *Unpolitische Erinnerungen.* Berlin: Verlag Volk und Welt, 1961.

——. *Von Eisner bis Levine: Persönlicher Rechenschafts-bericht.* Berlin: Fanal-Verlag, 1929.

Niekisch, Ernst. *Gewagtes Leben: Begegnungen und Begeb-nisse.* Köln and Berlin, n.d.

Oppenheimer, Franz. *Erlebtes, Erstrebtes, Erreichtes.* Berlin: Der Heine Bund, 1931.

Rocker, Rudolf. "In Sturm und Drang." Typescript. Vol. II of Rocker memoirs in Rocker Archives, International In-stitute of Social History, Amsterdam.

——. "Die Jugend eines Rebellen." Typescript. Vol. I of Rocker memoirs in Rocker Archives, International Institute of Social History, Amsterdam. See pp. 249–424 on the *Jungen* and other groups in Germany oriented toward anarchism in the early 1890s.

——. *The London Years.* London: Robert Anscombe, 1956.

——. "Revolution und Rückfall in die Barbarei." Typescript. Vol. III of Rocker memoirs in Rocker Archives, Interna-tional Institute of Social History, Amsterdam.

Toller, Ernst. *I Was a German: The Autobiography of Ernst Toller.* Trans. Edward Crankshaw. New York: W. Morrow, 1934.

——. *Look through the Bars.* Trans. R. Ellis Roberts. New York: Farrar and Rinehart, 1937.

Wertheimer, Egon. "Verteidigung," *Das Tribunal,* I (Dec. 1919), 129–132

Wille, Bruno. *Aus Traum und Kampf: Mein 60 Jähriges Leben.* Berlin: Kultur Verlag, 1920.

SECONDARY LITERATURE ON LANDAUER

Anon. "An die Genossen!" *Freie Arbeiter*, May 15, 1909.

———. "Gustav Landauer," *Encyclopaedia Judaica: Das Judentum in Geschichte und Gegenwart*. Berlin, 1928–1934. X, 609–610.

———. "Wie kann der Sozialismus kommen," *Der Anarchist* (Leipzig), nos. 8–10 (1912).

Bab, Julius. *Gustav Landauer: Gedächtnisrede*. 2d ed. Nürnberg: Verlag "Der Bund," 1924.

Bartsch, Günther. "Gustav Landauer: Der Edelanarchist," *Geist und Tat: Vierteljahrschrift für Politik und Kultur* (April–June 1969), pp. 127–128.

Bendemann, Eduard von. "Erinnerung an Gustav Landauer," *Masken*, XIV (1918–19), 306–308.

Breines, Paul. "The Jew as Revolutionary: The Case of Gustav Landauer," *Leo Baeck Yearbook*, XII (1967), 75–84.

Buber, Martin. "Gustav Landauer," *Die Zeit* (Vienna), June 11, 1904.

———. "Landauer und die Revolution," *Masken*, XIV (May 1919), 282–291.

———. *Paths in Utopia*. Trans. R. F. C. Hull. 2d ed. Boston: Beacon Press, 1960. See pp. 46–57 for a brilliant, though short, analysis of Landauer's social thought.

———. "Recollection of a Death." In *Pointing the Way*. Pp. 115–120. New York: Harper & Brothers, 1957.

C. W. "Gustav Landauer," *Anarchy*, V, no. 8 (Aug. 1965).

Esper, Thomas. "The Anarchism of Gustav Landauer." M.A. thesis, University of Chicago, 1961. The most useful part of this thesis is the author's perceptive analysis of Landauer's *Die Revolution*.

Fidelis. "Gustav Landauers Kulturprogramm," *Das Forum*, 4 (May 1920), 577–599.

Fishman, Sterling. "Prophets, Poets and Priests: A Study of the Men and Ideas That Made the Munich Revolution of 1918–19." Ph.D. dissertation, University of Wisconsin, 1960. A carefully researched study of the part played by five leading figures in the Munich Revolution: Eisner, Landauer, Mühsam, Toller, and Levine. On Landauer, see pp. 129–189.

Friedrich, Karl Josef. "Zu Gustav Landauers Tode," *Kunstwart*, III, no. 32 (May 1919), 156–157.

Giesau, Hermann. "Erinnerungen an Gustav Landauer," *Besinnung und Aufbruch* (Berlin), May 1, June 1, 1929.

Grossman, Stefan. "Gustav Landauer," *Das Tagebuch*, May 4, 1929.

Gumbel, E. J. "Gustav Landauers Ende," *Weltbühne* (1924), no. 7, pp. 191–193.

*Gustav Landauer, Gedenkheft*. Berlin: Hapoel Hazair, 1920. This June 1920 issue of *Die Arbeit: Organ der Zionistischen Volkssozialistischen Partei* contains articles on Landauer's thought by Buber, Arnold Zweig, Hans Kohn, and others.

*Gustav Landauer: Kämpfer und Künder der Freiheit*. Darmstadt: Verlag Die Freie Gesellschaft, 1951. Contains essays on Landauer by Erich Mühsam, Rudolf Rocker, Diego Santillan, and Helmut Rüdiger.

Hahnewald, Edgar. "Landauers französische Revolutionsbriefe," *Neue Zeit*, May 16, 1919, pp. 169–170.

Hauschner, Auguste. "Gustav Landauer," *Die Zukunft*, Jan. 23, 1904.

Heuss, Theodor. "Gustav Landauers politischer Nachlass," *Literarische Echo*, XXI (1919), 1095–1098.

Heydorn, Heinz-Joachim. Foreword to Gustav Landauer, *Aufruf zum Sozialismus*. Pp. 5–46. 3d ed. Frankfurt a. M.: Europäische Verlagsanstalt, 1967. A competent survey of Landauer's life and thought based only on his published works. Emphasizes Landauer's relation to Judaism.

Kalz, Wolf. *Gustav Landauer: Kultur Sozialist und Anarchist*. Meisenheim am Glau: Verlag Anton Haim, 1967. An attempt to describe systematically the political content of Landauer's published writings on socialism and anarchism. Contains (pp. 113–119) a good comparative analysis of Landauer, Proudhon, and Kropotkin. The author is not at all concerned with Landauer's intellectual development or with his historical environment; as far as Landauer's political thought is concerned, Kalz neglects the important national question.

Keller, Alfred. "Revolutionsbriefe," *Sozialistische Monatshefte*, I (1919), 52–54.

Kohn, Hans. "Gustav Landauer," *Selbstwehr: Judisches Volk-blatt*, May 16, 1924.

———. *Martin Buber: Sein Werk und seine Zeit*. 2d ed. Köln: Joseph Melzer Verlag, 1961. The best biography of Buber, this work contains some useful sections on the Neue Gemein-schaft and the social thought of Landauer. See especially pp. 28–31, 195–201.

———. *Sinn und Schicksal der Revolution*. Wien: Verlag E. P. Tal, 1923. On Landauer, see pp. 81–84.

Kranold, Albert, *Zwang und Freiheit im Sozialismus*. Jena: Thüringer Verlagsanstalt, 1925. Contains a critique of Lan-dauer's idealist and romantic form of socialism. See pp. 11–14, 82–85, 113–115.

Liptzin, Solomon. *Germany's Stepchildren: An Examination of the Conflict of German and Jewish Identity in More Than Twenty Creative Figures*. 2d ed. Cleveland and New York: Meridian Books, 1961. A sympathetic discussion of Lan-dauer's dual identity as German and Jew appears on pp. 229–238.

Loewenberg, Richard Detlev. "Gustav Landauer zum Gedächt-nis," *Der Morgen* (Dec. 1928), pp. 462–472.

Maurer, Charles. *Call to Revolution: The Mystical Anarchism of Gustav Landauer*. Detroit: Wayne State University Press, 1971. Useful on Landauer's *Skepsis und Mystik* and his literary criticism; less informed concerning his social thought and political activities, as well as the historical context in which he worked.

———. "Gustav Landauer: A Study of His Life and Work." Ph.D. dissertation, Northwestern University, 1965. The thesis upon which *Call to Revolution* is based. Although the two are very similar, there is somewhat more exclusive focus in the dissertation upon Landauer's philosophical and literary work.

Mauthner, Fritz. "Zum Gedächtnis," *Masken*, XIV (1918–19), 300–304.

Michel, Wilhelm. *Essays über Gustav Landauer, Romain Rolland, Friedrich Hölderlin: Die Metaphysik des Bürgers*. Hannover: Paul Steegemann Verlag, 1920.

Mühsam, Erich. "Gustav Landauer: Gedenkblatt zu seinem 50

Geburtstag, 7 April 1920," *Das Forum,* 4 (April 1920), 528–532.

Nettlau, Max. "Gustave Landauer," *Nervio: Critica-Artes-Letras* (Buenos Aires), II (Nov. 1932), 344–346.

——. "La Vida de Gustav Landauer segun su Correspondencia." In *Incitacion al Socialismo.* Pp. 187–325. Trans. Diego A. de Santillan. Buenos Aires: Editorial Americalee, 1947. A useful account of Landauer's career as an anarchist from 1890 to 1915, based largely on Landauer's published letters and Nettlau's personal recollections. As with Nettlau's other studies, however, this biography is more a chronicle than a historical analysis.

Oerter, Fritz. "Gustav Landauer," *Die Internationale: Organ der International Arbeiter-Assoziation* (Berlin), I (Jan. 1925).

Ramus, Pierre. "Ein Brief über den Sozialistischen Bund und gegen Landauer als Sozialist," *Jahrbuch der freien Generation: Volkskalender und Dokuments der Weltanschauung des Anarchismus-Sozialismus,* III (1912), 113–125.

Rotten, Elisabeth. " 'Durch Absonderung zur Gemeinschaft': Ein Ruf an die Jugend," *Das Werdende Zeitalter,* VIII (May–June 1929), 293–300.

Schnabel, Friedrich Gottlob. "Gustav Landauer," *Junge Menschen: Blatt der deutschen Jugend,* III (March 1922).

Simon, Ernst. "Der Werdende Mensch und der werdende Jude," *Der Jude,* VI (1921–22), 457–475. A suggestive attempt to relate Landauer's social theories to certain aspects of the Chasidic tradition studied by Buber.

Souchy, Agustin. *Landauer, el filósofo de la revolucion.* Trans. from Swedish by D. A. de Santillan. Buenos Aires: Ediciones Iman, 1934.

Susman, Margaret, *Vom Geheimnis der Freiheit: Gesammelte Aufsätze, 1914–1964.* Ed. Manfred Schlösser, Darmstadt: Agora, 1965. On Landauer, see pp. 255–270.

Toller, Ernst. "Gustav Landauer," *Weltbühne* (1924), no. 49, pp. 836–837.

Trojan, Walter. "Freie Aussprache," *Junge Menschen: Blatt der deutschen Jugend* (April 1922).

Unruh, Friedrich Franz von. "Gustav Landauer: Ein Vermächtnis," *Werdende Zeitalter,* VIII (May–June, 1929), 283–292.

Weidner, Albert. "Gustav Landauers Kampf mit Polizei, Justiz und Partei," *Die Weltbühne,* XXVI (1930), 533–536.

Zepler, Wally. "Landauer," *Sozialistische Monatshefte,* I (1919), 646.

Zweig, Arnold. "Gustav Landauers Shakespeare-Buch." In *Essays,* I, 34–39. Berlin: Aufbau Verlag, 1959.

## GENERAL WORKS

Adler, Georg. "Anarchismus," *Handwörterbuch der Staatswissenschaft.* 2d ed. 1909. I, 296–327.

Adler, H. G. *Die Juden in Deutschland: Von der Aufklärung bis zum Nationalsozialismus.* München: Kösel, 1960.

Aris, Reinhold. *History of Political Thought in Germany from 1789 to 1815.* London: G. Allen & Unwin, 1936.

Bab, Julius. *Wesen und Weg der Berliner Volksbühnenbewegung.* Berlin: Verlag Ernst Wasmuth, 1919.

———. *Wien und Berlin.* Berlin: Deutsche Buch-Gemeinschaft, 1918.

Becker, Howard. *German Youth: Bond or Free?* London: K. Paul, Trench, Trubner, 1946.

Berlin, Isaiah. "Herder and the Enlightenment." In *Aspects of the Eighteenth Century,* ed. Earl R. Wasserman. Baltimore: Johns Hopkins Press, 1965.

Bernard, Walter. *The Philosophy of Spinoza and Brunner.* New York: Spinoza Institute of America, 1934.

Bernstein, Eduard. *Die Geschichte der Berliner Arbeiterbewegung: Ein Kapitel der Geschichte der deutschen Sozialdemokratie.* Vol. III. Berlin: Buchhandlung Vorwärts, 1910.

Beyer, Hans. *Von der November Revolution zur Räterepublik in München.* Berlin: Verlag Rütten & Loening, 1957.

Bithell, Jethro. *Modern German Literature, 1880–1950.* 3d ed. London: Methuen, 1959.

Brogan, Denis. *The Development of Modern France.* London: Hamish Hamilton, 1940.

———. *Proudhon.* London: H. Hamilton, 1934.

Broszat, Martin. "Die völkische Ideologie und der Nationalsozialismus," *Rundschau,* 84 (Jan. 1958).

Brunner, Constantin. *Die Lehre von den Geistigen und vom Volke.* 3d ed. 2 vols. Stuttgart: Cotta Verlag, 1962.

Buber, Martin. *Vom Geist des Judentums.* Leipzig: Kurt Wolff Verlag, 1916. The first essay, "Die Lösung," was the source of the controversy with Landauer in May 1916.

Butler, E. M. *The Tyranny of Greece over Germany.* Boston: Beacon Press, 1955.

Carroll, E. Malcolm. *Germany and the Great Powers, 1886–1914: A Study in Public Opinion and Foreign Policy.* New York: Prentice-Hall, 1938.

Clapham, J. H. *The Economic Development of France and Germany, 1815–1914.* 4th ed. London: Cambridge University Press, 1936.

*Die Deutsche Gartenstadt Bewegung.* Berlin: Verlag der Deutschen Gartenstadt-Gesellschaft, 1911.

Dietrich, Richard. "Berlins Weg zur Industrie- und Handelstadt." In *Berlin: Neun Kapitel seiner Geschichte.* Pp. 159–198. Berlin: W. de Gruyter, 1960.

Dühring, Eugen. *Kursus der National- und Sozialökonomie.* Berlin: T. Grieben, 1873.

Elbogen, Ismar. *Die Geschichte der Juden in Deutschland.* Frankfurt a. M.: Europäische Verlags-Anstalt, 1966.

Fischer, Fritz. *Germany's Aims in the First World War.* London: Chatto and Windus, 1967.

Franz, Georg. "Munich: Birthplace and Center of the National Socialist German Workers' Party," *Journal of Modern History,* XXIX (1957), 319–334.

*"Freiland" und die Freilandbewegung.* Ed. Freiländische Actionscomite. Dresden and Leipzig: Verlag von E. Pierson, 1891.

Fried, Albert, and Ronald Sanders, eds. *Socialist Thought: A Documentary History.* New York: Doubleday, 1964.

Friedländer, Benedikt. *Der freiheitliche Sozialismus im Gegensatz zum Staatsknechtum der Marxisten.* Berlin, 1892.

Fuller, Leon W. "The War of 1914 as Interpreted by German Intellectuals," *Journal of Modern History,* XIV (June 1942), 145–160.

"The Garden City Movement," *Encyclopaedia of Social Reform* (New York and London, 1908), p. 532.

*Gartenstädte: Erste Flugblatt der Gartenstadt Gesellschaft.* Berlin, 1903.

Gay, Peter. *The Dilemma of Democratic Socialism: Eduard Bernstein's Challenge to Marx.* New York: Collier Books, 1962.

Gerstl, Max. *Die Münchener Räterepublik.* München: Verlag der Politischen Zeitfragen, 1919.

Greulich, Hermann, ed. *Protokoll des International Sozialistischen Arbeiterkongress in der Tonhalle Zürich vom 6. bis 12. August 1893.* Zürich: Buchhandlung der Schweizerischen Grutlivereine, 1894.

Gumbel, E. J. "154 Bayerische Morde," *Das Forum,* VI (April 1922), 225–240.

Halévy, Élie. *A History of the English People in the Nineteenth Century.* 2d ed. New York: Barnes & Noble, 1961.

Halperin, S. William. *Germany Tried Democracy: A Political History of the Reich from 1918 to 1933.* New York: W. W. Norton, 1946.

Hanstein, Adalbert von. *Das Jungste Deutschland: Zwei Jahrzehnte miterlebte Literaturgeschichte.* Leipzig: R. Voigtländer, 1905.

Hart, Heinrich, and Julius Hart, eds. *Die Neue Gemeinschaft: Ein Orden vom wahren Leben.* Part 2: *Das Reich der Erfüllung: Flugschriften zur Begründung einen neuen Weltanschauung.* Leipzig: Eugen Diedrichs Verlag, 1901.

Hauser, Arnold. *The Social History of Art.* Vol. IV. New York: Vintage Books, 1958.

Hoffmann, Hildegard. *Landwirtschaft und Industrie im Württemberg insbesondere im Industriegebiet der schwäbischen Alb.* Berlin: Junker und Dünnhaupt Verlag, 1935.

Holborn, Hajo. "German Idealism in the Light of Social History." In *Germany and Europe: Historical Essays by Hajo Holborn.* Pp. 1–31. New York: Doubleday, 1971.

————. *A History of Modern Germany, 1648–1840.* New York: Alfred A. Knopf, 1965.

Hook, Sidney. *From Hegel to Marx: Studies in the Intellectual Development of Karl Marx.* Ann Arbor: University of Michigan Press, 1962.

Horowitz, Irving L., ed. *The Anarchists*. New York: Dell Publishing Co., 1964. The excellent introduction to this anthology of anarchist writings is a suggestive attempt to deal with anarchism in terms of modern social developments, especially industrialization and bureaucratization.

Hughes, H. S. *Consciousness and Society: The Reconstruction of European Social Thought, 1890–1930*. New York: Vintage Books, 1961.

Hulsen, R. "Deutsche Gartenstadt Gesellschaft," *Der Genossenschafts-Pionier* (Berlin), May 16, 1903, p. 74.

Jantzen, Heinrich. *Jugendkultur und Jugendbewegung: Studie zur Stellung und Bedeutung Gustav Wynekens innerhalb der Jugendbewegung*. Frankfurt a. M.: Dipa Verlag, 1963.

Jaszi, Oscar. "Anarchism," *Encyclopedia of the Social Sciences* (New York: Macmillan, 1930), II, 46–53.

Joll, James. *The Second International, 1889–1914*. New York: Harper and Row, 1966.

Kammer, Mario. *Berlin im Wandel des Jahrhunderts: Eine Kulturgeschichte der deutsche Hauptstadt*. Berlin: Rembrandt-Verlag, 1956.

Kampffmeyer, Bernard. "Anarchisten und Sozialisten in Zürich," *Die Zukunft*, Sept. 9, 1893.

Kaufmann, Walter. *Nietzsche: Philosopher, Psychologist, Antichrist*. New York: Meridian Books, 1959.

Kenworthy, B. J. *Georg Kaiser*. London: Oxford University Press, 1957.

Klemperer, Klemens von. *Germany's New Conservatism*. Princeton: Princeton University Press, 1957.

Kluckholn, Paul. *Das Ideengut der deutschen Romantik*. 3d ed. Tübingen: Max Meineiger Verlag, 1953.

Kohn, Hans. *The Mind of Germany: The Education of a Nation*. New York: Charles Scribner's Sons, 1960.

Kolb, Eberhard. *Die Arbeiterräte in der deutschen Innenpolitik, 1918–19*. Düsseldorf: Droste Verlag, 1962.

Krieger, Leonard. *The German Idea of Freedom: History of a Political Tradition*. Boston: Beacon Press, 1957.

Krimerman, Leonard I., and Lewis Perry, eds. *Patterns of Anarchy: A Collection of Writings on the Anarchist Tradi-*

*tion.* New York: Doubleday, 1966. An excellent collection of some of the most penetrating of anarchist writings.

Kropotkin, Peter. *Fields, Factories and Workshops.* New York: G. P. Putnam's Sons, 1907.

———. *Kropotkin's Revolutionary Pamphlets.* Ed. Roger N. Baldwin. New York: Vanguard Press, 1927.

———. *Mutual Aid: A Factor in Evolution.* Boston: Extending Horizons Books, 1955.

Lamm, Hans. *Von Juden in München: Ein Gedenkbuch.* München: Ner-Tamid-Verlag, 1959.

Landauer, Carl. "The Bavarian Problem in the Weimar Republic, 1918–1933: Part I," *Journal of Modern History,* XVI (June 1944), 93–115.

———. *European Socialism: A History of Ideas and Movements from the Industrial Revolution to Hitler's Seizure of Power.* 2 vols. Berkeley and Los Angeles: University of California Press, 1959.

Lange, Annemarie. *Berlin zur Zeit Bebels und Bismarcks.* East Berlin: Verlag das Neue Berlin, 1959.

Langhard, J. *Die Anarchistische Bewegung in der Schweiz.* Bern: Stämpfli, 1909.

Laqueur, Walter. *Young Germany.* New York: Basic Books, 1962.

Lichtheim, George. *Marxism: An Historical and Critical Study.* New York: Praeger, 1961.

Lidtke, Vernon. *The Outlawed Party: German Social Democracy, 1878–1890.* Princeton: Princeton University Press, 1966.

Lorwin, Val R. *The French Labor Movement.* Cambridge, Mass.: Harvard University Press, 1954.

Lougee, Robert W. "German Romanticism and Political Thought." In *The European Past,* ed. Shepard Clough, Peter Gay, and Charles K. Warner. II, 87–98. New York: Macmillan, 1964.

Lovejoy, Arthur O. *The Great Chain of Being.* Cambridge, Mass.: Harvard University Press, 1936.

Malia, Martin. *Alexander Herzen and the Birth of Russian Socialism.* New York: Universal Library, 1965.

Mannheim, Karl. *Ideology and Utopia: An Introduction to the Sociology of Knowledge.* Trans. Louis Wirth and Edward Shils. New York: Harcourt, Brace, 1958.

Marcuse, Herbert. *Reason and Revolution: Hegel and the Rise of Social Theory.* Boston: Beacon Press, 1960.

Margalit, Elkana. "The Social and Intellectual Origins of the Hashomer Hatzair Youth Movement, 1913–1920," *Journal of Contemporary History,* 4 (April 1969), 25–46.

Marks, Harry J. "Movements of Reform and Revolution in Germany, 1890–1903." Ph.D. dissertation, Harvard University, 1937.

Marx, Karl. *The Communist Manifesto.* New York: Crofts Classics, 1955.

————. "The Economic and Philosophical Manuscripts of 1844." In *Marx's Concept of Man.* Ed. Erich Fromm. New York: Friedrich Ungar Publishing Co., 1961.

Marx, Karl, and Friedrich Engels. *Marx and Engels: Basic Writings on Politics and Philosophy.* Ed. Lewis Feuer. New York: Doubleday, 1959.

Masur, Gerhard. *Prophets of Yesterday: Studies in European Culture, 1890–1914.* New York: Macmillan, 1961.

Mauthner, Fritz. *Beiträge zu einer Kritik der Sprache.* 1st ed. 3 vols. I and II, Stuttgart: J. G. Cotta'sche, 1901; III, Stuttgart and Berlin: J. G. Cotta'sche, 1902.

Mehring, Franz. *Geschichte der deutsche Sozialdemokratie.* Vol. II. Berlin: Dietz Verlag, 1960.

Meinecke, Friedrich. *The German Catastrophe.* Boston: Beacon Press, 1963.

————. *Weltbürgertum und Nationalstaat: Studien zur Genesis der deutschen Nationalstaates.* 3d ed. München: Oldenbourg, 1915.

*Meister Eckhart: A Modern Translation.* Trans. with introduction by Raymond Bernard Blakney. New York: Harper & Brothers, 1941.

Michels, Robert. *Political Parties: A Sociological Study of the Oligarchical Tendencies of Modern Democracy.* 1st ed., 1915. New York: Collier Books, 1962.

Minogue, K. R. *Nationalism.* London: B. T. Batsford, 1967.

Mitchell, Alan. *Revolution in Bavaria, 1918–19: Kurt Eisner and the Bavarian Soviet Republic.* Princeton: Princeton University Press, 1965. The best study of the Bavarian Revolution as a whole.

Mitzman, Arthur. "Modernism and Weimar," *Dissent*, XVI (April–May, 1969), 282–286.

Morderwell, Hiram K. "The Blood of Munich," *The Liberator* (Sept. 1919), p. 13.

Mosse, George L. *The Crisis of German Ideology: The Intellectual Origins of the Third Reich.* New York: Universal Library, 1964.

———. "The Influence of the *Völkisch* Idea on German Jewry." In *Germans and Jews: The Right, the Left and the Search for a "Third Force" in Pre-Nazi Germany.* New York: Universal Library, 1970.

*Nationalism: A Report by a Study Group of Members of the Royal Institute of International Affairs.* 2d ed. London: Frank Cass, 1963.

Nestriepke, Siegfried. *Geschichte der Volksbühne Berlin.* Vol. I. Berlin: Volksbühnenen-Verlags und Vertriebes, 1930.

Nettlau, Max. *Der Anarchismus von Proudhon zu Kropotkin: Seine historische Entwicklung in den Jahren 1859–1880.* Berlin: Verlag "Der Syndikalist," 1927.

———. "Anarchisten und Sozialrevolutionäre, 1886–1914." MSS in Nettlau Archives, International Institute of Social History, Amsterdam. This manuscript, written in the years 1931 and 1932, is an invaluable source of information on the German and European anarchist movement in the years covered. For the student of Landauer the sections of particular interest are chapters 5–7, pp. 107–199, of the folio marked "1895–1914 I." Chapters 6 and 7 deal with the *Jungen* and the Independent Socialists of the early 1890s.

———. *Anarchisten und Sozialrevolutionäre: Die historische Entwicklung des Anarchismus in den Jahren 1880–1886.* Berlin: Asy Verlag, 1931.

———. *Der Vorfrühling der Anarchie: Ihre historische Entwicklung von den Anfängen bis zum Jahre 1864.* Berlin: Verlag "Der Syndikalist," 1925

Neubauer, H. *München und Moskau 1918/19: Zur Geschichte der Rätebewegung in Bayern.* München: Isar Verlag, 1958.

Nietzsche, Friedrich. *The Philosophy of Nietzsche.* New York: Modern Library, 1954.

Oppenheimer, Franz. *Freiland in Deutschland.* Berlin: F. Fontane, 1895.

Osterroth, Franz. *Biographisches Lexikon des Sozialismus.* Vol. I. Hannover: Verlag S. H. Dietz, 1960.

Paetel, Karl O. *Jugendbewegung und Politik.* Bad Godesberg: Voggenreiter Verlag, 1961.

*The Path to Dictatorship, 1918–1933: Ten Essays by German Scholars.* Trans. John Conway. New York: Doubleday, 1966.

Petersen, Cheryl Jean. "Philosophical Anarchism: A Comparative Study of American and European Theory." Ph.D. dissertation, University of California, Berkeley, 1960.

Pinson, Koppel S. *Modern Germany: Its History and Civilization.* New York: Macmillan, 1954.

*Populism: Its Meaning and National Characteristics.* Ed. Ghita Ionescu and Ernest Gettner. London: Weidenfeld and Nicolson, 1969.

Pross, Harry. *Jugend-Eros-Politik: Die Geschichte der deutschen Jugendverbände.* München: Scherz Verlag, 1964.

Proudhon, Pierre Joseph. *Proudhon's Solution to the Social Problem.* Ed. Henry Cohen. New York: Vanguard Press, 1927.

———. *What Is Property?* Trans. Benjamin Tucker. New York: Humboldt, 1890.

Pulzer, Peter G. J. *The Rise of Political Anti-Semitism in Germany and Austria.* New York: John Wiley & Sons, 1964.

Read, Herbert. "Pragmatic Anarchism," *Encounter,* 30 (Jan. 1968), 54–61.

Ritter, Gerhard A. *Der Arbeiterbewegung im Wilhelminischen Reich, 1890–1900.* Berlin: Colloquium Verlag, 1959. On the *Jungen,* see pp. 82–86.

Rosenberg, Arthur. *A History of the German Republic.* London: Methuen, 1936.

————. *Imperial Germany: The Birth of the German Republic, 1871–1918*. Boston: Beacon Press, 1964.

Rosenberg, Hans. "The Political and Social Consequences of the Great Depression in Central Europe, 1873–1896," *Economic History Review*, XIII (1943), 58–73.

Rosenthal, Berthold. *Heimatgeschichte der badischen Juden seit ihrem geschichtlichen Auftreten bis zur Gegenwart*. Bühl: Konkordia a.-g., 1927.

Rosenthal, Erich. "Trends of the Jewish Population in Germany, 1910–1939," *Jewish Social Studies*, VI (July 1944).

Rühle, Jürgen. *Literatur und Revolution: Die Schriftsteller und der Kommunismus*. Berlin: Verlag Kiepenheuer & Witsch, 1960.

Rürup, Reinhard. "Problems of the German Revolution, 1918–19," *Journal of Contemporary History*, 3 (Oct. 1968), 109–135.

Sauer, Wolfgang. "National Socialism: Totalitarianism or Fascism?" *American Historical Review*, LXXIII (Dec. 1967), 404–424.

Schade, Franz. *Kurt Eisner und die bayerische Sozialdemokratie*. Hannover: Verlag für Literatur und Zeitgeschehen, 1961.

Schnabel, Franz. *Deutsche Geschichte im neunzehnten Jahrhundert*. 4 vols. 2d ed. Freiburg im Breisgau: Herder Verlag, 1948–1951.

Schorske, Carl E. *German Social Democracy, 1905–1917: The Development of the Great Schism*. Cambridge, Mass.: Harvard University Press, 1955.

Schröder, Wilhelm. *Handbuch der Sozialdemokratischen Parteitage von 1863 bis 1909*. München: G. Birk, 1910.

Sokel, Walter H. *The Writer in Extremis: Expressionism in Twentieth-Century German Literature*. Stanford: Stanford University Press, 1959.

Stern, Fritz. *The Politics of Cultural Despair: A Study in the Rise of the Germanic Ideology*. New York: Doubleday, 1965.

Toury, Jacob. *Die politischen Orientierungen der Juden in*

*Deutschland von Jena bis Weimar.* Tübingen: J. C. B. Mohr, 1966.

Troeltsch, Ernst. "The Ideas of Natural Law and Humanity in World Politics." In Otto von Gierke, *Natural Law and the Theory of Society, 1500–1800.* Boston: Beacon Press, 1957.

Ulam, Adam. "Socialism and Utopia," *Daedalus,* 94 (Spring 1965), 382–400.

————. *The Unfinished Revolution: An Essay on the Sources of Influence of Marxism and Communism.* New York: Vintage Books, 1960.

Waite, R. G. L. *The Vanguard of Nazism: The Free Corps Movement in Postwar Germany, 1918–1925.* Cambridge, Mass.: Harvard University Press, 1952.

Weidner, Albert. *Aus den Tiefen der Berliner Arbeiterbewegung.* Berlin: Verlag von Hermann Securan Nachfolger, n.d. [1905?].

Weiler, Gershon. "Fritz Mauthner as an Historian," *History and Theory,* IV, no. 1 (1964), 57–71.

————. "On Fritz Mauthner's Critique of Language," *Mind,* LXVII (1958), 80–87.

Weise, Wilhelm. "Wie die Arbeiter-Konsumgenossenschaft 'Befreiung' entstand," *Der Genossenschafts-Pionier,* Dec. 15, 1896.

Wiese, Leopold von. "Volk," *Handwörterbuch der Sozialwissenschaften.* Vol. 11, pp. 362–365. Stuttgart and Tübingen, 1961.

Woodcock, George. *Anarchism: A History of Libertarian Ideas and Movements.* Cleveland: World Publishing Co., 1962.

————. *Pierre-Joseph Proudhon.* New York: Macmillan, 1956.

Woodcock, George, and Ivan Avakumovic. *The Anarchist Prince: A Biographical Study of Peter Kropotkin.* London: T. V. Boardman, 1950.

Zenker, E. V. *Anarchism: A Criticism and History of the Anarchist Theory.* London: Methuen, 1898.

Zweig, Arnold. *Bilanz der Deutschen Judenheit: Ein Versuch.* Amsterdam: Querido Verlag, 1934. See pp. 263–284 on German-Jewish socialists.

# Index

Adler, Max, 102, 346
Ahlborn, Kund, 347
*Aktion, Die* (periodical), 79
Anarchism, 58, 135; changing social bases of, 77–78; definition of term, 76; in Germany, 76–81, 198–200, 227; and Jewish intellectuals, 79–81; and marginal intellectuals, 78–80; and Marxism, 58, 117; at Second International Congresses, 84–86, 114–117; terrorist phase of, 87–88, 135–137. *See also* Kropotkin, Peter; Landauer, Gustav, anarchism of; Proudhon, Pierre-Joseph; Räte; Tolstoi, Leo
*Anarchist, Der* (periodical), 198
Anarcho-syndicalism, 78, 81–83, 86, 89–90, 114, 116, 207
*Anfang, Der* (periodical), 250
Anti-Semitism in Germany, 144, 166–167, 261, 267–275
Anti-Socialist Law (1878–1890), 36, 38, 52–53, 76
Arbeiter-Konsumgenossenschaft Befreiung, 96, 99–100
Arco-Valley, Count Anton von, 317
*Arme Konrad, Der* (periodical), 120
Auer, Erhard, 298, 314–315, 318
Auer, Ignaz, 52
*Aufbruch, Der* (periodical), 249–250
*Aufbruch* circle (Berlin, 1915–1916), 249–251, 346
Augustine, Saint, 131
Auschwitz, 3
Austro-Marxism, 102
*Autonomie* (periodical), 77

Bab, Julius, 11, 132, 157, 173, 229, 258, 269

Baden, 16, 24–25
Baginski, Max, 58, 66, 73
Bakunin, Mikhail, 92, 151, 223, 300
Barbarossa, Friedrich (von Hohenstaufen), 25–27, 183
Barnhardi, Friedrich von: *Germany and the Next War*, 235
Bavarian Center Party, 310
Bavarian Peoples' Party, 308, 328
Bavarian Revolution of 1918–1919, 3, 79–80, 172, 256, 362; history of, 293–296, 304–308, 310–312, 317–321, 336–337, 339–340. *See also* Räte; Munich Räterepublik
*Bayerische Kurier* (newspaper), 300, 332
Bebel, August, 52, 54, 85, 238
Beilis trial in Russia, 268
Bendemann, Eduard von, 9
Benthamism, 106
Bergson, Henri, 244
Berkeley, George, 134, 153, 164
Berlin, 17, 20, 29–30, 35, 51–52, 67; labor movement in early 1890s, 81–84, 110–112, 126; in Revolution of 1918–1919, 291–292, 305, 311–312; social and cultural situation in early 1890s, 37–41
Berliner Jungen, 17, 49–50, 63–64, 77; history of, 51–58, 72–74
Berndl, Ludwig, 173
Bernstein, Eduard, 112, 126, 204, 247
Bismarck, Otto von, 18, 35–36, 78, 233, 265, 304
Bismarck gymnasium (Karlsruhe), 21–27
Blüher, Hans, 249–250, 252, 256, 359 n. 168
Boétie, Etienne de La, 188, 225–227, 310

Böhme, Jakob, 146
Bölsche, Wilhelm, 39, 64
Bolshevik Revolution in Russia, 254, 299–301
Brahm, Otto, 39
Brecht, Bertolt, 12, 344
Brentano, Lujo, 303
Brunner, Constantin: *Die Lehre von den Geistigen und vom Volke*, 173–174, 176, 178–181, 186
Brussels Socialist Student Congress (1891), 42–44
Buber, Martin, 4–5, 145, 147, 154, 174–175, 193, 224, 240, 245–247, 251–252, 268–269, 307, 341, 345–347; humanist Zionism of, 272; Jewish Mysticism of, 4, 146, 173, 268–269
Buhr, Hermann, 68
Bund Neues Vaterland, 240, 248–249
Busch, Ernst, 96, 98

Calé, Walter, 281
Carnot, Sadi, 87
Chamberlain, Houston Stewart: *The Foundations of the Nineteenth Century*, 167, 261, 273
Cohen, Hermann, 297
Communist Party of Germany (KPD), 291, 313–319, 325–326, 333–337, 347. *See also* Spartacists
Communitarian Left in Germany, 6–8, 249–252, 346–348, 391–392. *See also* Völkisch Movement, history of concept "Volk" in, antiparliamentarism in
Cooperative movement in Germany, 95, 100

Damaschke, Adolf, 149
D'Annunzio, Gabriele, 244
Däubler, Theodor, 245
Dehmel, Richard, 244
Deutsche Gartenstadt Gesellschaft, 148–150, 347
*Deutsche Zeitung, Die* (newspaper), 24–25
Diedrichs, Eugen, 132, 249
Dilthey, Wilhelm, 102–103, 165
Dühring, Eugen, 68–69, 74; *Kursus der National- und Sozialökonomie*, 57–60, 62–63
Dumont, Louise, 286
Düsseldorfer Schauspielhaus, 286, 346

Ebert, Friedrich, 305, 311–312, 339, 341
Eckhart, Meister, 4, 130–134, 136, 138, 146, 153, 162–163, 165, 167, 174, 227, 282
Eeden, Frederik van, 9–10, 245, 262
Egidy, Moritz von, 102, 127, 139–142, 346
Einstein, Albert, 249
Eisner, Else, 335
Eisner, Kurt, 3, 294–297, 304–308, 311–314, 317–319, 327, 335–336, 338, 340, 342, 346
Engels, Friedrich, 54, 60, 203
English Garden City Association, 148
Erfurt Congress, 38, 67
Ernst, Paul, 52
Ethische Gesellschaft, 102
*Ethische Kultur* (periodical), 112
Expressionist movement in Germany, 4, 6, 65, 249–253, 344, 361. *See also* Kaiser, Georg
Ezekiel, 11, 267

Faas-Hardegger, Margarete, 192, 195
Feuerbach, Ludwig: *The Essence of Christianity*, 158
Fichte, Johann Gottlieb, 25, 134, 153, 158, 225, 244, 250, 259, 261–263
Fidelis (Communist figure in Bavarian Revolution), 330
Fidus (Völkisch painter), 149
Förster, Friedrich Wilhelm, 102, 112, 249, 294
Fourier, Charles, 223
Francis Ferdinand, archduke of Austria, 241
Freie anarchistisch-sozialistischen Vereinigung (Berlin), 140
Frantz, Konstantin, 303
Freie Arbeiter (periodical), 198

Freie Volksbühne, 39–40, 57, 64
Freikorps, 3, 327, 333, 337
French Revolution of 1789–1799, 189
French Revolution of 1848, 225
Freud, Sigmund: *Civilization and its Discontents*, 279
Friedeberg, Raphael, 89
Friedländer, Benedikt, 41, 57, 59, 62, 74, 79, 209, 359 n. 168; *Libertarian Socialism in Opposition to the State Servitude of the Marxists*, 66–69
Friedrichshagen, 41, 361

Gagern, Freiherr von, 338, 340
Gerlach, Helmuth von, 247
German Peoples' Party (Baden), 25
German Revolution of 1918–1919, 3, 9, 209, 255–256; course of, 304–306; immediate causes of, 292–293. *See also* Bavarian Revolution
Gervinus, George, 24–25
Gesell, Sylvio, 215, 328, 335
Goethe, Johann Wolfgang, 21, 248, 283, 285
Graf, Oskar Maria, 199–200
Grillenberger, Karl, 53
Groener, Wilhelm, 339
Grossman, Stefan, 79, 119, 129, 148, 340
Grün, Karl, 76
Gutkind, Erich, 245

Haase, Hugo, 247
Hague Peace Conference (1907), 234
Hammer, Walter, 347
Harden, Maximilian, 90, 135
Hardie, Keir, 115
Hart, Heinrich, 142, 145–147
Hart, Julius, 39, 142, 145, 147
Hashomer Hatzair Youth Movement, 251–252, 273
Hauptmann, Gerhard, 30, 45, 244
Hauschner, Auguste, 173
Hecht, Ben, 331
Hegel, Georg Wilhelm Friedrich, 91, 103, 205

Herder, Johann Gottfried, 7, 162, 243–244, 258–262, 265, 270, 343
Hertzka, Theodor, 69, 102
Herve, Gustav, 239
Hess, Moses, 76
Hesse, Hermann, 240, 347
Heuss, Theodor, 18
Hiller, Kurt, 249–250, 252
Hoffman, Johannes, 320–321, 323–325, 328, 333
Hölderlin, Friedrich, 4, 134, 248, 282–287, 289
Holzman, Johannes, 79
Hotman, Francois, 188
Huizinga, Johan: *The Waning of the Middle Ages*, 186
Hume, David, 156

Ibsen, Henrik, 28–30, 150
Idealism: in German thought, 102–103, 130, 153–154, 158, 201; of Jewish socialist intellectuals, 80–81. *See also* Landauer, Gustav, ethical and philosophic idealism of
Independent Labor Party of England, 115
Independent Social Democratic Party of Germany (USPD), 247, 291, 294–295, 297, 306, 308, 313, 316, 318–320, 324, 361 n. 19
Independent Socialists (1890s). *See* Berliner Jungen
International Socialist Congress in London (1896), 114–116
International Socialist Congress in Zürich (1893), 54, 84–85
Isaiah, 11, 267

Jackisch, Otto, 378
Jean Paul (Johann Paul Friedrich Richter), 262
Jesus, 9
Jews in Germany, 20–21, 79–81, 251, 268–273, 361 n. 19, 391 n. 149. *See also* Anti-Semitism in Germany
Joël, Ernst, 249–251
Joël, Karl, 264
*Jude, Der* (periodical), 246

Jung, Franz, 193
*Junge Menschen* (periodical), 347

Kahler, Erich, 272
Kaiser, Georg, 4–5, 248, 252–253, 282, 285–287, 289, 342, 347; *Die Bürger von Calais*, 285; *Gas*, 253
Kampffmeyer, Bernard, 57, 148
Kampffmeyer, Paul, 52, 57–58, 73
Kant, Immanuel, 91, 102–103, 153, 155–156, 158–161, 204; *What is Enlightenment?*, 93–94
Karlsruhe, 18, 20, 29
Kautsky, Karl, 346
Kirchner, Erwin, 281
Kohn, Hans, 137, 146, 273
Kropotkin, Peter, 4, 92, 114, 136, 150–151, 213–214, 221, 223–224, 227, 242, 347; *Fields, Factories, and Workshops*, 218–220; *Mutual Aid*, 104, 172, 176–178, 188
Krumbach (Swabia), 128, 306–307, 317
Kun, Bela, 325–326

Lachmann, Hedwig (second wife of Gustav Landauer), 128–130, 139, 143, 148, 151, 159, 174, 252, 256, 306, 317
Lagarde, Paul de, 24, 266, 275
Lamprecht, Karl, 244
Landauer, Brigitte (daughter), 174
Landauer, Clara (cousin), 40
Landauer (Leuschner), Grete (first wife), 64, 128–130
Landauer, Gudula (daughter), 174
Landauer, Gustav: anarchism of, 3–5, 17–18, 27–28, 48–51, 68–72, 75, 79–81, 90–94, 96–97, 116–117, 122, 157–159, 183–186, 188–191, 198–200, 213–233, 241–243, 266, 275–276; in Bavarian Revolution of 1918–1919, 3, 9, 11, 14, 172, 228, 290–342; and Berlin anarchist movement, 81–88, 122; and Martin Buber, 4–5, 145–146, 173–175, 193, 224, 240, 245–247, 251, 268, 272, 345–347; concept of community in thought of, 5–6, 106–107, 124–125, 132, 158, 166–168, 170–171, 174, 213, 218–220, 277–279, 321–323; death of,
3, 11, 332–333, 335–341; and Meister Eckhart, 4, 130–134, 136, 138, 146, 153, 162–163, 165, 167, 267, 283; and Moritz von Egidy, 139–142, 267; effect of Berlin on, 29, 35–41; ethical and philosophical idealism of, 11, 44, 80–81, 90–94, 100–104, 153–154, 158, 160–161, 165–166, 181–182, 201–204, 211–212, 225, 267, 274–275; on the family, 278–279, 392–393; and father, Hermann, 21–22, 64–66; federalist views of, 220–221, 295–296, 303–305; and German Expressionist movement, 4, 6, 249–253, 285–287; and German Romanticism, 5–8, 17–18, 21–23, 75, 106–110, 122, 180, 182–187, 232, 237–238, 243–244, 257–266, 273–274; against German Social Democracy, 4, 13, 17, 50–51, 66–67, 70–71, 75, 81–86, 90, 110–111, 115, 118, 195, 201, 209–211, 226, 228, 238–239, 247, 321; and German youth movement, 6, 143–146, 249–252; historical importance of, 6–8, 343–348; humanity-oriented nationalism of, 6, 232–233, 237–238, 243–244, 248, 250, 257–274, 279–280; and Ibsen, 28–30, 151; influence of Berliner Jungen on, 17–18, 49–74; and Judaism, 3, 6, 11, 15, 20–21, 79–81, 159–160, 173, 263, 267–274, 294, 361–362, 390; and Kropotkin, 4, 104, 150–151, 172, 176–178, 180, 188, 213–214, 218–221, 223–224, 242, 380–381; and Hedwig Lachmann, 128–130, 139, 143, 148, 151, 159, 174, 252, 255–256, 306, 340; as literary critic, 4, 11–12, 44–46, 121–122, 169–170, 172, 248, 252–253, 279–290; as marginal intellectual, 78–81, 196–197, 228–229, 361–362; and Marxism, 4, 17–18, 41–44, 48–51, 59–63, 71–82, 101, 117, 158, 171–172, 194, 200–213, 231, 238, 358 n. 136; and Fritz Mauthner, 15n, 153–160, 174, 176, 225, 243, 246, 365 n. 97; mysti-

cism of, 4–5, 122, 124–138, 146, 150–171, 214, 228, 278–279, 283; and needle trade strike of 1896, 110–114; and Nietzsche, 18, 30–35, 44–48, 88–89, 104, 128, 150, 159–161, 170, 201, 225, 264–265, 389 n. 121; and Old Testament prophets, 10–12, 267; pacifism of, 5, 81, 86–88, 96, 134–140, 223–230, 240, 257–258, 266, 332, 334; personality of, 8–10, 174; political isolation of, after 1897, 11, 75, 118–126, 133, 142–143, 151–153, 170–171, 244–248, 257, 291, 314; and Populism, 92, 213–217, 228, 236, 276–277, 392 n. 163; and Proudhon, 4, 18–20, 151, 213–217, 221–224; on racism, 273–275, 343; and Räte (council) movement of 1918–1919, 291, 297–298, 300–303, 310, 312–317, 321–323, 397–398; and Schopenhauer, 17–18, 22, 28, 107–108, 110, 161–164, 201, 225, 366; in Socialist Bund, 172, 190–200, 230, 234, 378 n. 98; and Stirner, 104–109, 153, 157, 225; and Swabia, 18–20, 128, 217, 256; and syndicalism, 81–83, 86, 89–90, 207, 217; and Tolstoi, 4, 134–136, 138, 213–214, 223, 227–228, 242, 283; and völkisch ideas, 5–8, 23–27, 75, 110–111, 118, 122–125, 131–133, 138–150, 166–169, 184–185, 190–191, 215–218, 232–233, 249–251, 257–267, 275–276, 280–281, 322–323, 343–348, 389 n. 123; and World War I, 174, 232–249, 253–258, 261–263; work on cooperatives, 95–101, 117, 230; and Zionist Socialists, 6, 271–272. Works: *Arnold Himmelheber*, 89; *Aufruf zum Sozialismus*, 15, 48–49, 152, 165, 171, 191, 199–213, 218, 230, 255, 292, 343; *Beginnen: Aufsätze über Sozialismus*, 224, 226, 229–230; "Dühringianer und Marxisten," 59–63; *Lebendig tot*, 129–130; *Meister Eckharts Mystische Schriften*, 130–132, 141–143, 152–153;

"The Overestimation of Voting," 309–310; *Die Revolution*, 105, 172, 175–190, 225–226, 375 n. 39; "Die Religiöse Jugenderziehung," 32–34; *Sein Lebensgang in Briefen*, 13; *Shakespeare: Dargestellt in Vorträgen*, 286–290; *Skepsis und Mystik: Versuche im Anschluss an Mauthners Sprachkritik*, 14, 15n, 105, 108, 126, 130, 138, 148, 150, 152–154, 160–171, 174–175, 178, 202–203, 214, 365 n. 97; "Social Democracy in Germany," 115; "Through Isolation to Community," 124–125, 132, 141–143, 152–153; *Der Todesprediger*, 3, 46–49, 175; "The United Republics of Germany," 303–307; "Volk und Land: Dreissig Sozialistischen Thesen," 172, 190–191, 193; *Ein Weg deutschen Geistes*, 169, 248, 253, 280, 285; *Ein Weg zur Befreiung der Arbeiterklasse*, 97–99, 214; "Zur Entwicklungsgeschichte des Individuums," 105–110, 153, 163, 166, 168

Landauer, Hermann (father), 20–21, 64–66

Landauer, Hugo (cousin), 65, 128, 301

Landauer, Siegfried (cousin), 27

Langbehn, Julius, 8, 24, 135, 265, 275–276

Languet, Hubert, 188

Lasalle, Ferdinand, 246

Lenin, Vladimir Ilyich, 254

Leonhard, Rudolf, 249, 251

Levien, Max, 300, 313

Leviné, Eugen, 314, 330, 334, 336

Liebknecht, Karl, 236, 240, 247, 302

Liebknecht, Wilhelm, 52, 54

Lietz, Hermann, 141, 249

Lindner, Alois, 318

Ludendorff, Erich, 341

Luxembourg, Rosa, 3, 73, 240

Mackay, John Henry, 41, 105

McKinley, William (American President), 135

Maistre, Joseph de, 183

Malatesta, Errico, 114, 116–117
Mann, Heinrich, 303, 344
Mann, Thomas, 344; *Betrachtungen eines Unpolitischen*, 241
Mann, Tom, 116
Mannheim, Karl, 344, 375 n. 39
Marx, Karl, 11, 44, 58, 62, 102, 126, 199, 246; analysis of capitalism in thought of, 204–206, 209–211; early utopian humanism of, 17, 59, 158, 201, 212; historical materialism of, 43, 49, 59–61, 203, 358; political tactics of, 69, 71. *See also* Marxism
Marxism, 18, 62–63, 74, 345–347; anarchist critiques of, 57–58, 66–71, 209–211, 238; of Berliner Jungen, 51–58; historical materialist views in, 201–203, 231; of Social Democratic Party of Germany (SPD), 4, 17, 38, 49–51, 59–61; of University of Berlin student circle, 41–44; urban industrial orientation of, 75, 82, 117, 171, 211. *See also* Landauer, Gustav, and Marxism; Marx, Karl; Social Democratic Party (SPD)
*Masken* (periodical), 286
Mathy, Karl, 24
Mauthner, Fritz, 15n, 108, 130, 173–174, 191, 225, 243–244, 246, 269–270, 340, 371 n. 87; *Beiträge zur einer Kritik der Sprache*, 153–160, 176, 365 n. 97
Meinecke, Friedrich, 241, 344; *Weltbürgertum und Nationalstaat*, 260
Michels, Robert, 70, 275
Mikhailovsky, N. K., 277
Moeller van den Bruck, Arthur, 24, 389 n. 123
Morris, William, 116
Möser, Justus, 258, 278
Most, Johann, 77
Mühsam, Erich, 10, 79, 145–146, 151, 173, 193, 195–196, 247, 346–347; in Bavarian Revolution of 1918–1919, 294, 297–300, 319–320, 328, 332
Mülberger, Arthur, 19, 96

Müller, Adam, 183
Müller, Hans, 52, 73
*Münchener Post* (newspaper), 195–196
Munich in Revolution of 1918–1919, 291, 294, 310–312, 328–329, 342. *See also* Bavarian Revolution; Munich Räterepublik; Räte
Munich Räterepublik (council republic) of April 1919, 319–320, 325–335, 337

Nacht, Siegfried, 79
Napoleon I (Bonaparte), 244, 254
Napoleon III, 225
Naturalist movement in Germany, 29, 38–39
Nazism, 7–8, 261, 342–345, 351 n. 4, 392 n. 163
Neue Freie Volksbühne, 64, 253, 281, 286
Neue Gemeinschaft (intellectual circle in Berlin, 1901–1902), 142–147, 153, 160, 173, 300, 346
*Neues Leben* (periodical), 120
*Neue Zeit, Die* (periodical), 45
*Neue Zeitung* (newspaper), 316
Neurath, Otto, 324
Nietzsche, Friedrich, 18, 28, 30–34, 44–49, 88–89, 104, 128, 150, 159–161, 170, 225
Nieuwenhuis, Domela, 116–117
Noske, Gustav, 335, 337, 340, 342
Novalis (Friedrich Hardenberg), 183, 185–186

Oppenheimer, Franz, 41, 149, 346
Otto, Adolf, 148, 193

Pawlowitsch, Paul, 119–120
Pfau, Ludwig, 19
Populist movement in Russia, 276–277
Potsdam circle (pacifist group of 1914), 245–246
Proudhon, Pierre-Joseph, 4, 19–20, 58, 68, 151, 213–217, 221–224, 227; *What is Property?*, 76
Prussia, 19, 52, 221, 259, 303–304
Puttkamer, Robert, 52

Quidde, Ludwig, 249

Ramus, Peter, 79, 199
Rang, Florens Christian, 245
Räte (councils) in Bavarian Revolution of 1918–1919, 291, 295, 297–298, 310–315, 336–337, 397 n. 82. *See also* Bavarian Revolution; Landauer, Gustav, and Räte; Munich Räterepublik of April 1919
Rätekongress of February–March 1919 in Bavaria, 315–318, 320–321
Reichenbach, Bernhard, 263
Reichswehr, 3, 327, 337
Revolutionäre Arbeiterrat (RAR) in Bavarian Revolution of 1918–1919, 297–299, 325
Revolutionary Internationalists of Bavaria (VRI), 299–300
Rickert, Heinrich, 102–103
Rocker, Rudolf, 9, 73, 120, 151
Rolland, Romain, 244–245
Romanticism in Germany: "community" in, 5, 106; "individuality" in, 109–110; in neo-idealist philosophy, 153–154; strength of right-wing versions of, 343; "Volk" in 258–261; and youth movement, 143–145. *See also* Landauer, Gustav, and German Romanticism; Völkisch ideas; Völkisch movement
Rosenberg, Alfred, 345
Rubiner, Ludwig, 252
Russian Revolution of 1905, 207, 234
Russian Revolution of 1917. *See* Bolshevik Revolution in Russia

Saint-Simon, Claude Henri de, 181, 223
Scheidemann, Philipp, 302, 305
Scheler, Max, 344
Schelling, Friedrich Wilhelm, 153–162
Schiller, Friedrich, 21
Schippel, Max, 52, 57, 73
Schlegel, Friedrich, 186
Schnabel Publishing House, 175
Schneppenhorst, Ernst, 325–326
Schoenberner, Franz, 10
Schöll, Ferdinand, 141

Schopenhauer, Arthur, 17–18, 22, 28, 107–108, 110, 161–165, 225, 365 n. 97
Schulze-Delitzsch, Franz Hermann, 95
Schwabing (section of Munich), 291, 294, 316, 333
Shakespeare, William, 4, 286–290, 394
Simmel, Georg, 102
*Simplicissimus* (periodical), 10
Singer, Paul, 52, 85, 115
Social Darwinism, 104, 176
Social Democratic Party of Germany (SPD), 4, 13, 38, 41, 45, 66, 77, 82, 89–90, 93, 100–101, 118, 121, 126, 195–197, 201, 275, 305–306; and anarchism, 84–86, 104–105, 114–116; antiwar left-wing in, 235–236, 247; Bavarian wing of, in 1918–1919, 295–296, 298–299, 301, 308, 312–321, 325–326, 328; and Berliner Jungen, 51–58, 73, 119, 361; bureaucratic centralism of, 17, 49–51, 69–71, 81, 209–210; effect of neoromanticism on, 144–145; Freie Volksbühne project of, 39, 64; in German Revolution of 1918–1919, 305–306, 309, 324, 328–329, 335–337, 339–340; materialist determinism of, 17, 75, 212; and needle trade strike of 1896, 110–114; response to World War I, 238–241, 254–255; tactical reformism and parliamentarism of, 50–53, 67, 83–84, 207, 208, 211. *See also* Marxism
Socialist Bund, 172, 190–200, 230, 234, 346, 378 n. 98
Sorel, Georges, 264; *Reflections on Violence*, 44
*Sozialist, Der* (periodical) of 1891–1899, 4, 61, 69–71, 77, 79, 85, 104, 110, 113, 116, 127, 135, 139–140, 216, 227, 365 n. 97; history of, 56–59, 66–67, 72–73, 83, 118–120, 124–125; Landauer as editor of, 14, 73, 95, 101, 104–105; police campaigns against, 87–88, 94
*Sozialist, Der* (periodical) of 1909–

1915, 129, 194, 196, 200, 219, 233, 237–238, 261–262, 268; history of, 192–193, 195, 213, 236, 239–240, 244, 248

Spartacists, 294, 300, 305, 308–309, 312, 339. *See also* Communist Party of Germany

Spinonza, Baruch, 22–23

Stalin, Joseph, 345

Stirner, 3, 76, 105–106, 108, 225

Swabia, 18–20, 26, 128

Swedenborg, Emmanuel, 133

Swiss Social Democratic Party, 66, 85

Teistler, Hermann, 72

Thule Society, 317, 333, 337

Timm, Johannes, 111

Toller, Ernst, 4, 252, 256, 328, 335, 338–339, 347

Tolstoi, Leo, 4, 134–136, 138, 213–214, 223, 227–228, 242, 282–283

Treaty of Brest-Litovsk (1918), 254–255

Troeltsch, Ernst, 241, 344

Türk, Julius, 39, 64

University of Berlin, 29–30, 35, 41, 49

University of Freiburg, 94

University of Heidelberg, 27–28

University of Strasbourg, 30

Vaihinger, Hans, 264

Verein Freie Bühne, 30

Verein Jüdischer Hochschüler Barkochba, 391 n. 153

Völkisch Movement in Germany: antiparliamentarism in, 266, 275, 344–345, 391 n. 160; attempted avoidance of capitalism and communism in, 215; and Aufbruch circle of 1915–1916, 249–251; authoritarian élitism of the right in, 275–276; and Garden City movement, 148–149; in gymnasiums and universities, 23–25, 147; history of the concept "Volk" in, 258–261, 265; influence of von Egidy on, 140–141; left-wing circles of, in 1900–1920 period, 6, 346–348; and mysticism, 132–133, 171; and populism, 276–277, 392 n. 163; and relation to Nazism, 343–345, 348, 351, 391 n. 160, 392 n. 163; racist and anti-Semitic ideas in, 166–167, 261, 267– 269, 273–275, 348

*Vorwärts* (newspaper), 42, 84, 105, 112, 114

Wagner, Richard, 17–18, 22, 28, 183, 286

Weber, Max, 344–345

Weidner, Albert, 73, 121

Weimar Republic, 339, 347–348

Weise, Wilhelm, 73, 96, 98

Welcker, Karl, 24

Werner, Wilhelm, 52, 57–58, 84–85

Whitman, Walt, 4, 133–134, 250, 282–283, 286–287, 289, 331

Wildberger, Karl, 39, 52–53, 57–58, 72–73

Wilhelm II, 36, 233

Wilhelmian Germany, 261; culture of, 6, 8, 346–347; political situation in, 35–36

Wille, Bruno, 39, 41, 57–58, 63, 73, 79

Wilson, Woodrow, 253–254

Windelband, Wilhelm, 102–103

Wolf, Ida, 29

Wolzogen, Ernst von, 64

World War I, 6, 9, 78, 169, 227, 232–249, 253–258; events leading up to, 233–236, 240; German domestic scene during, 240–241, 254–255

Württemburg, 18–19

Wyneken, Gustav, 249–252

Youth Movement in Germany, 6, 65, 143–146, 261, 268, 370; left-wing groups in, 249–252, 347–348

*Zeit-Echo* (periodical), 252

Ziethen trial of 1899, 127, 139

Zionist Socialists, 6, 271–272, 346

*Zukunft, Die* (periodical), 90, 93, 101, 135–136, 168, 190

Zweig, Arnold, 272